Intellectual Property Law in Africa

Examining the harmonisation of intellectual property (IP) policy, law and administration in Africa, this book evaluates the effectiveness of efforts to establish continental IP institutions and frameworks. It also considers sub-regional initiatives led by the regional economic communities and the regional IP organisations, focusing on relevant protocols and agreements that address IP as well as the implementing institutions. The book assesses the progress of such initiatives with particular reference to the current socio-economic status of African states. It argues that that harmonisation initiatives need to be crafted in a way that is supportive of the developmental goals of African states and advocates for due consideration of individual states' unique conditions and aspirations. This book will be of great relevance to scholars and policy makers with an interest in IP law and its harmonisation in Africa.

Caroline B. Ncube is Professor in the Department of Commercial Law at the University of Cape Town, South Africa, and holds a research chair in IP, Innovation and Development under the South African Research Chairs Initiative, which is funded by the South African Department of Science and Innovation and the South African National Research Foundation.

Routledge Research in Intellectual Property

Available:

Annotated Leading Trademark Cases in Major Asian Jurisdictions
Edited by Kung-Chung Liu

SEPs, SSOs and FRAND
Asian and Global Perspectives on Fostering Innovation in Interconnectivity
Edited by Kung-Chung Liu and Reto M. Hilty

Towards an Ecological Intellectual Property
Reconfiguring Relationships Between People and Plants in Ecuador
David Jefferson

The Transformation of EU Geographical Indications Law
the Present, Past and Future of the Origin Link
Andrea Zappalaglio

Copyright Law and Translation
Access to Knowledge in Developing Economies
Chamila S. Talagala

Patent Law, Green Technology and Innovation
Ankit Singh and Yogendra Kumar Srivastava

Intellectual Property and Development
Geographical Indications in Practice
Barbara Pick

Collective Management of Music Copyright
A Comparative Analysis of China, the United States and Australia
Qinqing Xu

For more information about this series, please visit: www.routledge.com/Routledge-Research-in-Intellectual-Property/book-series/INTELLPROP

Intellectual Property Law in Africa

Harmonising Administration and Policy

Second Edition

Caroline B. Ncube

Routledge
Taylor & Francis Group
LONDON AND NEW YORK

Second edition published 2023
by Routledge
4 Park Square, Milton Park, Abingdon, Oxon OX14 4RN

and by Routledge
605 Third Avenue, New York, NY 10158

Routledge is an imprint of the Taylor & Francis Group, an informa business

First edition published by Routledge 2015

British Library Cataloguing-in-Publication Data
A catalogue record for this book is available from the British Library

ISBN: 978-1-032-31532-4 (hbk)
ISBN: 978-1-032-31538-6 (pbk)
ISBN: 978-1-003-31019-8 (ebk)

DOI: 10.4324/9781003310198

Typeset in Times New Roman
by Apex CoVantage, LLC

Dedicated to my father, Alfred John Moyo (29 March 1951–18 July 2022), who shared my love of books and taught me to gaze at the stars. Thank you for leaving us a legacy of love, fortitude, dreams and peace.

Contents

Preface to the Second Edition

Since the publication of the first edition, *Intellectual Property Policy, Law and Administration in Africa: Exploring Continental and Sub-Regional Co-Operation* in 2015, much has changed in the African intellectual property (IP) landscape. Accordingly, this edition, entitled *Intellectual Property Law in Africa: Harmonising Administration and Policy*, is extensively revised to include the latest developments at sub-regional and continental levels. These include the adoption of the Statute of the Pan-African IP Organisation (PAIPO) in January 2016 and the Southern African Development Community's adoption of an IP Framework and Guidelines in 2018. By far the most wide-reaching and significant developments pertain to the negotiation, adoption and coming into force of the Agreement on the African Continental Free Trade Area (AfCFTA), which all occurred in the period 2015–2019. This led to the negotiation of the Protocol on IP Rights (IP Protocol) and its approval by the Council of Ministers responsible for trade in October 2022, followed by the necessary pre-adoption processes and its adoption by the 36th Ordinary Session of the Assembly of Heads of State and Government of the African Union in February 2023. Accordingly, the book includes a new chapter on IP in the AfCFTA which reprises the IP Protocol. The book engages with the renewed continental convergence in IP and particularly efforts to streamline administrative capacity, strengthen institutions and to secure common positions on critical issues.

Declaration

I was part of the research and drafting teams for the SADC IP Framework and the AfCFTA IP Protocol. Any account of events relating to the validation or negotiation and adoption of these instruments excludes confidential information and information that has not been made publicly available by the relevant institutions.

This book discusses the law and events, as known to the author, as of 1 March 2023.

Acknowledgements

I would like to express my deep gratitude to my family for their support and to my colleagues and students who served as a sounding board for many of my ideas. Whilst I am eschewing naming colleagues for fear of making unforgiveable omissions, I wish to name Dr McClean Sibanda and Dr Titilayo Adebola with whom I worked closely on some projects during my research for this book. I am also indebted to the teams at the Directorate of Services, Investment, Intellectual Property & Digital Trade at the AfCFTA Secretariat, the African Trade Policy Centre (ATPC) and Market Institutions Section at the Economic Commission for Africa (ECA)'s Regional Integration and Trade Division (RITD) and the New Technologies and Innovation Section, ECA Special Initiatives Division for affording me invaluable opportunities to learn about and participate in the development of a continental Intellectual Property framework in service of Africa. Similarly, the opportunity to work with teams from the SADC Secretariat, United Nations Conference on Trade and Development (UNCTAD) and various African Union divisions and task forces gave me immeasurable insights. I also thank my collaborators and partners in the Open African Innovation and Research (Open AIR) partnership.

Funding Acknowledgements

This work is based on research supported in part by the National Research Foundation (NRF) of South Africa (Grant Numbers 132090 and 115716). Any opinion, finding and conclusion or recommendation expressed in this material is that of the author and the NRF does not accept any liability in this regard.

The work was also carried out with Open African Innovation and Research (Open AIR) financial support from the International Development Research Centre, Canada, the Social Sciences and Humanities Research Council of Canada, and Queen Elizabeth Scholars. More information about Open AIR's current and previous supporters can be found at https://openair.africa/supporters. The views expressed herein do not necessarily represent those of Open AIR's funders.

Abbreviations

ABS	Access Benefit Sharing
ACTRIPS	Advisory Council on Trade-Related Innovation Policies
AEC	African Economic Community
AfCFTA	African Continental Free Trade Area
Africa CDC	Africa Centre for Disease Control and Prevention
ALI	American Law Institute
AMCOST	African Ministerial Conference on Science and Technology
AMS	ASEAN member states
AMU/UMA	Arab Maghreb Union
APEC	Asia-Pacific Economic Co-operation
ARIPO	African Regional Intellectual Property Organisation
ASEAN	Association of South East Asian Nations
ASPEC	ASEAN Patent Search and Examination Co-operation
AU	African Union
AUC	AU Commission
AUDA-NEPAD	African Union Development Agency-New Partnership for Africa's Development
AU-STRC	AU Scientific, Technical and Research Commission
AWGIPC	ASEAN Working Group on IP Co-operation
BRICS	Brazil Russia India China South Africa
CCM	MERCOSUR Council of the Common Market
CEN-SAD	Community of Sahel-Saharan States
CEPA	UN Committee of Experts in Public Administration
CFTA	Continental Free Trade Area
CDIP	WIPO Committee on Development and Intellectual Property
CDR	Community Design Regulation
COM	Council of Ministers
COMESA	Common Market for Eastern and Southern Africa
CMG	Common Market Group
COHRED	Council on Health Research for Development
CTI	Committee on Trade and Investment
CTM	Community Trademark
CU	Customs Union

DA	Development Agenda
DACD	DA Coordination Division
DAG	Development Agenda Group
DFID	UK Department for International Development
DPADM	Division for Public Administration and Development Management
DRC	Democratic Republic of the Congo
EAC	East African Community
EASTECO	East African Science and Technology Commission
ECA	UN Economic Commission for Africa
ECCAS	Economic Community of Central African States
ECJ	European Court of Justice
ECOWAS	Economic Community of West African States
ECSA-HC	East, Central and Southern African Health Community
EFTA	European Free Trade Association
EPA	Economic Partnership Agreement
EPC	Convention on the Grant of European Patents
EPO	European Patent Office
ESARIPO	Industrial Property Organisation for English-Speaking Africa
EU	European Union
FTA	Free Trade Agreement
GATS	General Agreement on Trade in Services
GATT	General Agreement on Tariffs and Trade
GI	Geographical indications
HDI	Human Development Index
HIV/AIDS	Human immunodeficiency virus/acquired immune-deficiency syndrome
HRS&T	AU Human Resources, Science and Technology
ICT	Information and communications technology
IGAD	Intergovernmental Authority on Development
IGC	Intergovernmental Committee
IGOs	Intergovernmental organisations
INPI	French National Patent Rights Institute
IPDP	Intellectual Property Development Plan
IPEG	IPR Experts Group
IP/IPRs	Intellectual property/intellectual property rights
IPR-GT	Intellectual Property Rights Get Together
LDC	Least developed country
L&E	Limitations and exceptions
MERCOSUR	Mercado Común del Sur (Common Market of the South)
MSME	Micro, Small and Medium Enterprise
MTC	MERCOSUR Trade Commission
NRF	National Research Foundation
OAMPI	L'Office Africaine et Malgache de la Propriété Industrielle
OAPI	Organisation Africaine de la Propriété Intellectuelle (African Intellectual Property Organisation)

OAU	Organisation of African Unity
OECD	Organisation for Economic Co-operation and Development
OHADA	L'Organisation pour l'Harmonisation en Afrique du Droit des Affaires (Organisation for the Harmonisation of Business Law in Africa)
OHIM	EU Office for the Harmonisation in the Internal Market
PAIPO	Pan-African Intellectual Property Organisation
PBR	Plant breeders' rights
PCT	Patent Co-operation Treaty
PMPA	AU Health Strategy and Pharmaceutical Manufacturing Plan for Africa
PRA	Property Rights Alliance
PTA	Preferential Trade Area
PVP	Plant Variety Protection
R&D	Research and Development
REC	Regional Economic Community
RIA	Regional Integration Arrangement
RISDP	Regional Indicative Strategic Development Plan
RSTI	Research, Science, Technology and Innovation
RTA	Regional Trade Agreement
SACU	Southern African Customs Union
SADC	Southern African Development Community
SADCC	Southern African Development Co-ordination Conference
SARPAM	Southern Africa Regional Programme on Access to Medicines and Diagnostics
SCCP	APEC Sub-Committee on Customs Procedures
SDGs	Sustainable development goals
SMEs	Small and medium enterprises
STI	Science, technology and innovation
STOs	Senior Trade Officials
STISA 2024	Science, Technology and Innovation Strategy for Africa 2024
TCEs	Traditional cultural expressions
TFTA	Tripartite Free Trade Area
TK	Traditional knowledge
TMD	Trademark Directive
TRIPS	Agreement on Trade-Related Aspects of Intellectual Property Rights, Including Trade in Counterfeit Goods
UNCITRAL	United Nations Commission on International Trade Law
UNCTAD	United Nations Conference on Trade and Development
UNDP	United Nations Development Programme
UNESCO	United Nations Educational, Scientific and Cultural Organisation
UNIDO	United Nations Industrial Development Organisation
UNIDROIT	International Institute for the Unification of Private Law

UPOV	International Union for the Protection of New Varieties of Plants
WAHO	West African Health Organisation
WHO	World Health Organisation
WIPO	World Intellectual Property Organisation
WTO	World Trade Organisation

1 Intellectual Property and the Public Interest in Africa

1.1 The Intellectual Property Landscape in Africa

> *Africa is not a country: it is a very heterogeneous continent comprised of . . . nations with great variations in physical, economic, political, and social dimensions.*[1]

Several years after the publication of the first edition in 2016, this revised and expanded second edition continues to consider the viability of the creation of a harmonised African continental and sub-regional intellectual property (IP) framework, keeping in sight the fact that African states[2] have different socio-economic, cultural and political contexts.[3] Their history is diverse, albeit with the widely held common experience of colonisation[4] and the legal transplants it brought with it. Unsurprisingly, they each have unique national IP environments, comprising statute and case law, policies and practices.[5] It is important to point out, at the outset, that the African IP landscape is multi-layered. In addition to relevant global and national frameworks, there are regional and sub-regional IP frameworks to consider, located either in an IP sub-regional organisation or a Regional Economic Community (REC). This terrain is further complicated by the multiplicity of RECs, which currently number about 14,[6] of which only eight are recognised by the African Union (AU) as constituent elements of the African Economic

1 Broadman (2007) p. 5.

2 In Africa 55 states are currently members of the African Union (AU). Morocco had a break in membership but rejoined the AU on 31 January 2017. See AU (n.d.) There are two disputed states – the Sahrawi Arab Democratic Republic and Somaliland – that are also not AU member states. For a history of the Sahrawi Arab Democratic Republic see Jensen (2005) and Shelley (2004).

3 Collins and Burns (2013) p. 4.

4 With the exception of Ethiopia and Liberia, all of Africa was colonised by 1914 per Boahen (1990) p. 1. Liberia had been a colony of the United States from 1820 to 1847 per Kongolo (2014) pp. 163, 168.

5 Armstrong et al. (2010) p. 5.

6 Kolbeck (2014) p. 3; African Union (AU) Study for the Quantification of RECs: Rationalization Scenarios, 2009 p. 34.

DOI: 10.4324/9781003310198-1

Community (AEC) and of the African Continental Free Trade Area (AfCFTA).[7] Many African states are members of more than one REC,[8] which compounds the situation. However, as the continent moves towards deeper integration, three of these RECs launched a Tripartite Free Trade Area, the COMESA-EAC-SADC TFTA, in 2015.[9] The second phase of the TFTA negotiations were intended to include IP. However, this has been overtaken by the Agreement on the AfCFTA which had been signed by 54 states and had been ratified by 46 states as of 1 March 2023.[10] It entered into force on 30 May 2019 and trading commenced on 1 January 2021. The second stage of its negotiations included a Protocol on IPRs (hereafter IP Protocol), which has been adopted. The latter AfCFTA IP negotiations have overtaken the former TFTA, obviating the need to conclude the former, because it makes sense to consolidate them.[11]

This edition continues with the lexicon used in the first edition – specifically, Akokpar's conceptualisation of a region as consisting of states in geographical proximity[12] – and it uses the word interchangeably with "continental," to refer to Africa. The term "sub-regional" refers to various continental sub-groupings.

Legal harmonisation is the approximation of legal standards across a defined community that permits national divergence, whilst unification is the imposition of exactly the same standards with no scope for national variances.[13] Whilst both approaches are currently in use in Africa, the AU's preferred approach is harmonisation. This preference is shared by some RECs such as the Common Market for Eastern and Southern Africa (COMESA), the East African Community (EAC), the Economic Community of West African States (ECOWAS) and the Southern African Development Community (SADC). Similarly, harmonisation is the mode of choice for the African Regional IP Organisation (ARIPO), one of the continent's two sub-regional IP organisations. In contrast, the other sub-regional IP organisation, the African Intellectual Property Organisation, or *Organisation Africaine de la Propriété Intellectuelle* in French (OAPI), and the Organisation for the Harmonisation of Business Laws in Africa (OHADA) have taken the unification approach.

7 Kolbeck (2014) p. 3, Ghathi (2011) p. 362; Assembly Decision on the Moratorium on the Recognition of Regional Economic Communities (RECs) DOC. EX.CL/278 (IX). AU Doc. Assembly/AU/Dec.111–132 (VII). The eight RECS are the Arab Maghreb Union (AMU/UMA); Community of Sahel-Saharan States (CEN-SAD); Common Market for Eastern and Southern Africa (COMESA); East African Community (EAC); Economic Community of Central African States (ECCAS/CEEAC); Economic Community of West African States (ECOWAS); the Inter-Governmental Authority of Development (IGAD); and Southern African Development Community (SADC).

8 Gathi (2011) p. 65.

9 Agreement Establishing a Tripartite Free Trade Area Among the Common Market for Eastern and Southern Africa, the East African Community and the Southern African Development Community; Sharm El Sheikh Declaration Launching the COMESA-EAC-SADC Tripartite FTA.

10 AfCFTA Secretariat (2023) p. 4.

11 Ncube (2022a)

12 Akokpari (2008) p. 88.

13 Ratchlitz (2014) p. 50.

This introductory chapter provides an overview of existing IP laws in Africa and their historical development. The chapter then introduces the concept of the public interest in IP and highlights African countries' unique challenges with an emphasis on the diversity of circumstances across the continent. This wide range of diversity necessitates an IP framework that permits sufficient flexibility to enable the appropriate calibration of national IP systems and equally malleable harmonisation models. It then turns to an overview of African states' contribution to the articulation and formulation of the Development Agenda (DA) at the World IP Organisation (WIPO), which signalled a commitment to advancing the public interest in IP. Finally, the chapter considers how African states have experienced TRIPS implementation and reprises how TRIPS flexibilities have become a central policy focus as a prelude to the discussion in subsequent chapters of ongoing efforts to nuance IP systems by states, RECs, regional IP organisations and at AU level.

1.2 Overview and History of National IP Laws

Most African states currently have separate statutes providing for the different types of IP rather than one piece of omnibus legislation catering for all types of IP. OAPI member states share the same body of IP laws as provided for in the Bangui Agreement Relating to the Creation of an African Intellectual Property Organisation of 1977. The Bangui Agreement includes a series of Annexes that regulate copyright, patent, trade marks and designs, amongst other types of IP protection. The Bangui Agreement was revised in 2015, and some of the amendments came into force in November 2020 and January 2022. OAPI's Anglophone counterpart, ARIPO's Protocols, do not have direct application in member states and must be domesticated by party states. Consequently, each ARIPO member state has its own national IP framework. A detailed overview of the content of OAPI's Bangui Agreement and its Annexures, ARIPO's Protocols and the rest of Africa's individual IP laws has been given elsewhere[14] and thus falls outside the ambit of this book. Select laws are considered, as examples, where appropriate throughout the text.

The history of IP law in Africa is inextricably linked to colonial history. Some of the first iterations of African states' IP laws were legal transplants introduced by former colonialists well before the conclusion of the Paris and Berne conventions.[15] In other cases, the first colonial IP legislation was introduced after the conclusion and entry into force of these conventions.[16] The precise method of the enactment of these laws comprised two steps. The first entailed the submission, by the colonising state, of a declaration of the application of the applicable international agreement

14 du Plessis (2012), Ncube (2021).

15 Okediji (2003) p. 323, Berne Convention for the Protection of Literary and Artistic Works (1886) 1161 U.N.T.S. 3 , Paris Convention for the Protection of Industrial Property (1883) 21 U.S.T. 1583, 828 U.N.T.S. 305 .

16 Kongolo (2013b) pp. 115–116, (2014) pp. 168–170.

to the colonised state. Declarations of the application of the Berne Convention were made in accordance with Article 19 of the original text of the convention.[17] Declarations of the applicability of the Paris Convention were made in terms of Article16*bis* (1)–(2) of the London Act of 1934 and the Lisbon Act of 1958 of the convention.[18] Secondly, the declaration of applicability of the international conventions was then followed by the extension of the colonising state's copyright or patent legislation to the colony, or the enactment of legislation applicable only to the colonised territory.[19] In either case the law was created by the colonising, rather than the colonised, state. Therefore, the goals and interests of the former, rather than the latter state, informed these IP laws.[20]

Many African states continued to adhere to these colonial laws after their independence[21] and the relevant international agreements upon which they were based. However, in some instances, after their independence some states did not immediately accede to the Berne Convention and enacted their own copyright law that repealed the colonial copyright legislation. A case in point is Ghana, which enacted its first post-independence Copyright Act in 1961 and chose to accede to the Universal Copyright Convention in 1962 instead of the Berne Convention, to which it only acceded in 1991.[22] The drafting of post-independence copyright laws was informed to a large extent by the UN Educational, Scientific and Cultural Organisation (UNESCO)–WIPO Tunis Model Copyright Law for Developing Countries, 1976.[23]

Since their independence African states have, to varying degrees, sought to revise existing IP laws[24] or to enact new IP laws.[25] However, in some ways these post-independence efforts have been constrained by the current international IP framework, primarily through the World Trade Organisation (WTO)'s Agreement on Trade-Related Aspects of Intellectual Property Rights (TRIPS).[26] The TRIPS framework has served as "a powerful mechanism for transplanting European and American law"[27] and some scholars characterise it as a "device that drives economic neo-colonialism forward."[28] Whilst African states participated in its negotiation and conclusion, they did so at a disadvantage, lacking adequate representation and resources (human and otherwise) to ensure that the agreement was truly to their benefit.[29]

17 Kongolo (2014) p. 165.
18 Kongolo (2013b) p. 107.
19 Kongolo (2013b) p. 106.
20 Kongolo (2013a) p. 1.
21 Kongolo (2013a) p. 1, Joireman (2001) p. 576.
22 Kongolo (2014) p. 173.
23 Kongolo (2014) pp. 172–173.
24 Kongolo (2013a) pp. 1, 9.
25 Okediji (2003a) p. 335.
26 Agreement on Trade-Related Aspects of Intellectual Property Rights, Including Trade in Counterfeit Goods (1994) 33 ILM 81 (TRIPS).
27 Seuba (2014) p. 3 citing Dreyfuss (2004) p. 21.
28 Rahmatian (2009) pp. 41–42.
29 Kongolo (2013a) p. 2, Watal (2011) p. 25.

Despite these disadvantages, African and other developing states successfully lobbied for the inclusion of some provisions in the agreement which seek to meet their unique circumstances. Of these, Articles 7 and 8 are discussed later in this chapter. Another important mechanism was the inclusion of a transition period for the full implementation of TRIPS by least developed countries (LDCs). This period, initially set to expire after ten years from the entry into force of TRIPS,[30] has been extended twice[31] and is currently set at 1 July 2034, or sooner if a country ceases to become an LDC before that date.[32] A similarly important transition period was granted in 2002 pursuant to paragraph 7 of the Doha Declaration on Public Health, which exempts LDCs from either granting or enforcing pharmaceutical patents and protecting test data, until 1 January 2016.[33] The pharmaceutical transition period is two-fold in the sense that it originates from two decisions, namely TRIPS Council Decision, IP/C/25, on product patent and data protections, and General Council Decision, WT/L/478, on exclusivity rights under Article 70(9). It has been extended and is current until 1 January 2033, or earlier should the LDC change its developmental status prior to that date.[34]

African states have also continued in their efforts to contribute to IP norm-setting at the WTO, as evidenced by their leadership regarding the adoption of the Doha Declaration on Public Health[35] which eventually led to the adoption of the TRIPS Amendment introducing Article 31*bis*, which as of 15 March 2022 had been accepted by more than 100 WTO member states, including 22 African states, namely Benin, Botswana, Burkina Faso, Burundi, Central African Republic, Congo, Côte d'Ivoire, Egypt, Gabon, The Gambia, Guinea, Kenya, Lesotho, Malawi, Mali, Morocco, Niger, Nigeria, Rwanda, Senegal, Sierra Leone and South Africa. It remains open for acceptance until 31 December 2023.[36]

30 Article 66(1) TRIPS.

31 Extension of the Transition Period Under Article 66.1 for Least Developed Country Members (29 November 2005) Decision of the Council for TRIPS IP/C/40. Extension of the Transition Period Under Article 66.1 for Least Developed Country Members (11 June 2013) Decision of the Council for TRIPS IP/C/64. For an overview of the genesis and extent of the original extension period as well as the extension request made in 2012, see Abbott (2013), Baker (2015).

32 Extension of the Transition Period Under Article 66.1 for Least Developed Country Members (29 June 2021) Decision of the Council for TRIPS IP/C/88.

33 Extension of the Transition Period Under Article 66.1 of the TRIPS Agreement for Least-Developed Country Members for Certain Obligations with Respect to Pharmaceutical Products (27 June 2002) Decision of the Council for TRIPS IP/C/25.

34 Extension of the Transition Period Under Article 66.1 of the TRIPS Agreement for Least Developed Country Members for Certain Obligations with Respect to Pharmaceutical Products (6 November 2015) Decision of the Council for TRIPS IP/C/73, Least-Developed Country Members – Obligations Under Article 70.8 and Article 70.9 of the TRIPS Agreement with Respect to Pharmaceutical Products (December 2015) (WT/L/971).

35 Ncube (2015b) p. 20, Loewenson, Modisenyane and Pearcey (2014) p. 9.

36 WTO General Council Decision WT/L/1122 Amendment of the TRIPS Agreement – Eighth Extension of the Period for the Acceptance by Members of the Protocol Amending the TRIPS Agreement General Council Decision, adopted on 22 November 2021.

In their revision or crafting of IP laws, African states have relied upon technical assistance from the WTO, WIPO and other United Nations specialised agencies, such as UNESCO and WHO. However, as noted by Ndulo, such assistance can become a Trojan horse that brings in detrimental ideas.[37] Therefore, the nature, scope and content of such assistance must be carefully structured and developed because it may exacerbate existing problems. Many UN agencies subscribe to progressive development theories that are informed by human rights considerations. However, concerns have been raised about whether WIPO shares this common developmental approach. These concerns culminated in the adoption of the WIPO DA that is intended to realign the organisation's approach by making it more development orientated.

In many cases the post-TRIPS IP legislation of many states is still not properly attuned to prevailing socio-economic conditions. It is only in the past few years that some African states have articulated IP policies that will be used to calibrate their IP laws to suit their national priorities, within the confines of the international, regional, sub-regional and bilateral agreements to which they are party. In addition to IP legislation and policies (where they exist), there are specific state and industry implementation practices that are yet to be comprehensively studied or reported upon. For example, an IP statute may provide for criminal sanctions for infringement, yet in practice no prosecutions ever take place. Thus, a study of the legislation only may not provide a full picture of the real situation. It is necessary to look at other constituent parts of the legal environment, which include case law (where it exists), and prevailing "perceptions of the [IP] framework, and norms, social conditions and market dynamics that affect how people access and use [IP protected works]."[38] The analysis of these other constituent elements falls beyond the scope of this book, which confines itself to a discussion of laws and policies and whether or not they serve the public interest.

1.3 IP and the Public Interest

The public interest, sometimes referred to as public welfare,[39] is distinct from public policy. Public policy is a statement of a government's chosen approach to specific matters which gives guidance to relevant persons, including government itself, on how certain goals are to be set and achieved.[40] It is crafted as part of a political process within a national legal and administrative framework. The goal of public policy should be to "further [or serve] the public interest."[41] Achieving this

37 Ndulo (2007) p. 333.
38 African Copyright and Access to Knowledge Project (ACA2K) (2008) p. 7.
39 Okediji (1999), (2003b) and (2014).
40 Belohlavek (2012) p. 118. Also see Dye (1972) p. 2, Hogwood and Gunn (1984) pp. 23–24, Wilson (2006) p. 1.
41 Ho (2012) pp. 1, 19. Also see Smith (2006) p. 730.

end is "the highest standard of governmental action, the measure of the greatest wisdom or morality in government."[42]

Despite contestations about its value and its exact meaning,[43] "public interest" is a useful concept. The general definition adopted for purposes of this text is Ho's *ex ante* analysis, which is premised on the position of the representative individual.[44] Under this approach, before selecting a policy direction, "vested interests" would be eliminated or reduced by the consideration of policy options by reference to an "imaginary person" who "could be anyone."[45] The outcome that would best cater for this individual would be in the public interest. In the IP context, I have argued elsewhere that to serve the public interest would be to "equitably balance the interests of creators and users in a manner that is beneficial to society generally."[46] However, as I have also noted elsewhere, utilising the metaphor of balance presents some conceptual difficulties.[47] These include the definition of balance, the determination of the conceptual tool or device to be used to calibrate it and the selection of appropriate means to achieve it. These difficulties with the twin concepts of the public interest and balance can be ameliorated by careful articulation of their meanings, hence their continued usage in IP discourse.

One way of carefully articulating these concepts is by differentiating normative claims according to IP rights and with reference to specific continental and national contexts. In other words, specificity will cure some of the malaise and dispel notions of a one-size-fits-all approach. Discussions of the public interest are normally held at macro level, that is, to explore what would be in the public interest generally with regard to all IP. Whilst such high-level discussions are valuable, they cannot replace the deliberate consideration of the public interest with regard to each type of IP right.[48] Examples of the articulation of carefully nuanced IP type specific public interest goals include the Adelphi Charter[49] and the Washington Declaration on IP and the Public Interest.[50] As stated, the national and continental context is also important,[51] hence this text's specific focus on Africa. However, engaging in a comprehensive discussion of the public interest in relation to all types of IP rights is beyond the scope of this work. Where appropriate, IP right specific public interest recommendations will be made, particularly in relation to patents and public health, as well as the protection of traditional knowledge (TK). The following two sub-sections speak to the geo-political context of the public interest.

42 Souraf (1957) p. 616.
43 Box (2007) p. 586, Held (1970) p. 1, Storing (1964), Friedrich (1962), Schubert (1960) p. 224, Sorauf (1957).
44 Ho (2012) p. 13.
45 Ho (2012) p. 7.
46 Ncube (2013) p. 374.
47 Ncube (2015a) pp. 54–56.
48 Okediji (2004) p. 233.
49 Royal Society of Arts (RSA) (2006).
50 Global Congress on Intellectual Property and the Public Interest (2011).
51 Okediji (2004) p. 234.

1.3.1 A Global Public Interest?

Okediji states that both global and national welfare are the aim and result of "market based efficiencies that simultaneously promote and reflect the pursuit of self-interest" on a global and national stage, respectively.[52] She also notes that the concept of global welfare or global public interest is by no means settled and that there are at least two ways of understanding this concept.[53] First, it may be conceived of as an aggregation of various states' national public interest which is reached by compromise and adherence to which is dependent on mutual co-operation. Alternatively, it may be viewed as a standard derived from international norms or doctrines to which individual states comply without regard to the position taken, or compliance thereof, by other states. The second scenario is the one which prevails, because the current international IP framework provides a public interest standard which individual states interpret and implement differently in their territories.

Whilst the concept of the global public interest is not well developed, it has been articulated to a certain extent in international IP agreements. For example, Articles 7 and 8 of TRIPS take a normative stance with regard to the welfare goals of IP standards agreed upon in the agreement.

Article 7 provides:

> The protection and enforcement of intellectual property rights should contribute to the promotion of technological innovation and to the transfer and dissemination of technology, to the mutual advantage of producers and users of technological knowledge and in a manner conducive to social and economic welfare, and to a balance of rights and obligations.

This provision takes cognisance of the competing interests of producers and users of technological knowledge and calls for an equitable balancing of these interests. However, its meaning and import is contestable, and has created a "crisis of confidence and jurisprudence in its relation to the application of the global IPR rules that developing countries have continued to grapple with."[54] For example, it has been pointed out that the transfer and dissemination of technological knowledge is upon the terms dictated by the IP right-holders, who tend to be from developed states.[55] Further, although the compulsory licensing provisions in TRIPS are supposedly "relatively generous" in theory, in practice their benefits have only been marginally realised with regard to patents.[56] They have proven to be largely

52 Okediji (1999) p. 123.

53 See for example, Okediji (2014) p. 4.

54 Adewopo (2012) p. 29. The Doha Development Agenda was established by the Doha WTO Ministerial Declaration (adopted 14 November 2001) Doc. WT/MIN(01)/DEC/1 20 November 2001.

55 Rahmatian (2009) p. 52.

56 Article 31 TRIPS and the 2003 Doha Decision on the implementation of paragraph 6 of the Doha Declaration Doc. WT/L/540 and Corr.1 (1 September 2003). For a discussion of the use of

ineffective during the COVID-19 pandemic, as illustrated by the stalled BioLyse quest to obtain a compulsory licence for the production of generic Johnson & Johnson vaccine for export to Bolivia under Canada's Access to Medicines Regime.[57] Compulsory licences have so far yielded limited results in relation to copyright and are an oft-overlooked public interest mechanism in copyright,[58] which seems to favour limitations and exceptions (L&E). The TRIPS provision for the three-step test for copyright L&E[59] is an important standard that continues to inform the enactment of L&E in the public interest. The most recent global development in this regard is the adoption of the Marrakesh Treaty to Facilitate Access to Published Works for Persons Who Are Blind, Visually Impaired, or Otherwise Print Disabled (2013)[60] whose provisions have been domesticated in a significant number of countries. Although the TRIPS Agreement provides that compulsory licences are not applicable to trade marks,[61] there has been academic commentary on the desirability of introducing them.[62]

Article 7's pro-development position is reinforced by Article 8, which in part provides:

> 1 Members may, in formulating or amending their laws and regulations, adopt measures necessary to protect public health and nutrition, and to promote the *public interest* [emphasis added] in sectors of vital importance to their socio-economic and technological development, provided that such measures are consistent with the provisions of this Agreement.
>
> 2 Appropriate measures, provided that they are consistent with the provisions of this Agreement, may be needed to prevent the abuse of intellectual property rights by right holders or the resort to practices which unreasonably restrain trade or adversely affect the international transfer of technology.

Article 8 "formulates the general guidelines to be observed by WTO members when they adopt exceptions to the exclusive rights conferred by IPRs."[63] To this

flexibilities in relation to patents for pharmaceuticals see Matthews and Correa (2011), Matthews (2005), Avafia, Berger and Hartzenberg (2006).

57 Plurinational State of Bolivia (2021a, 2021b), BioLyse (2021).

58 Victor (2020).

59 Articles 9(1) and13 TRIPS.

60 Marrakesh Treaty to Facilitate Access to Published Works for Persons Who Are Blind, Visually Impaired or Otherwise Print Disabled (2013). *International Legal Materials*, 52(6), 1309–1320.

61 Article 21 TRIPS; Rahmatian (2009) pp. 52–53.

62 Straight (2021), Kung-Chung (2012), Lane (1988), Holmes (1980), Schmalensee (1979), Dobb (1977).

63 Rodrigues (2012) p. 45.

end, it provides for the permissible "political objective" of the state and for the twin restraints of necessity and consistency that must guide the state.[64]

These two articles are particularly significant because they articulate the goal of IP law formulation, protection and enforcement as the promotion of the public interest and socio-economic welfare. They have been characterised as being "aspirational"[65] and as being the lens through which TRIPS must be viewed or interpreted.[66]

These provisions have been deployed powerfully by developing countries to achieve significant gains for the development cause. A case in point is how they have been credited as the foundation of the Doha Development Agenda[67] and its outcomes, such as the Doha Declaration on the TRIPS Agreement and Public Health.[68] A second example is how they provided pivotal support for developing countries' successful proposal for the adoption of the WIPO DA,[69] which is discussed later.

The meaning of the global public interest concept has been canvassed elsewhere at length by others who have argued that the way in which it is articulated in the TRIPS Agreement has some detrimental effects for the global south/developing world.[70] It also clearly did not serve any cohesive role nor demonstrate any meaningful solidarity in ensuring that African states were not left behind in the provision of vaccines, diagnostics and therapeutics required to meet COVID-19 needs, meaning that African solutions had to be found,[71] as attempts to achieve a timely and comprehensive TRIPS failed. African states individually and collectively lent their support to the TRIPS Waiver Proposal.[72] Therefore the global conceptualisation of the public interest is not the focus of this chapter. Instead, the next section considers how the public interest has been defined and deployed by African states, at international, continental, subregional and national levels.

64 Rodrigues (2012) p. 45.
65 Dreyfuss (2004) p. 22.
66 Gervais (2003) pp. 120, 122, Kapczynski (2009).
67 Adewopo (2012) p. 38.
68 Doha Declaration on the TRIPS Agreement and Public Health (adopted 14 November 2001), Doc. WT/MIN(01)/DEC/2 (20 November 2001). For a detailed discussion see Kongolo (2013a) pp. 199–219, 285.
69 Yu (2009).
70 Gana (1996) p. 744, Harris (2007) pp. 203–204.
71 Dos Santos, Ncube and Ouma (2022).
72 WTO Council for TRIPS. Waiver from certain provisions of the TRIPS Agreement for the prevention, containment and treatment of Covid-19 – Communication from India and South Africa IP/C/W/669. 2 October 2020, WTO Council for TRIPS. Waiver from certain provisions of the TRIPS Agreement for the prevention, containment and treatment of Covid-19 – Revised decision text communication from the African Group, The Plurinational State of Bolivia, Egypt, Eswatini, Fiji, India, Indonesia, Kenya, The LDC Group, Maldives, Mozambique, Mongolia, Namibia, Pakistan, South Africa, Vanuatu, The Bolivarian Republic of Venezuela and Zimbabwe IP/C/W/669/ Rev. 1. 25 May 2021.

1.3.2 A Continental, Sub-Regional and National Public Interest?

Internally, each state sets its own national priorities through prescribed processes such as ministerial or departmental drafting followed by necessary approvals, perhaps through parliament. For example, South Africa categorises certain economic sectors such as tourism as priority sectors. Any national regulatory scheme, including IP, would therefore have to be supportive of growth and development in these sectors. A state also has certain obligations to its citizenry to provide essential services and facilitate the attainment of their constitutional or human rights, such as the right to health[73] and a basic education.[74] Consequently, whilst IP is only one of the factors that affect the attainment of these rights, it is significant and ought to be given due weight. When IP policies and laws are being debated and crafted, the public interest is served when the concerns and rights of creators, users and society generally are all taken into account and are appropriately provided for. In some cases, constitutional rights serve as a tie-breaker of these contesting interests.[75] For instance, in discussions of patents and access to medicines or copyright and access to learning materials, the right to health and a basic education, respectively, acquire a great significance.

In its role as custodian and driver of this process, the state ought to be "a guardian of welfare for all" of its subjects. However, unfortunately, in certain cases the state's focus is captured, and driven, by the lobbying of a segment of society.[76] Sadly, examples of this are easy to find. It has been pointed out by many scholars that in the United States, copyright holders have captured copyright legislative processes through extensive and entrenched lobbying.[77] Some of these right-holders have extended their reach and influence to developing countries through local chapters or branches of international right-holder organisations.[78]

The same phenomenon is evident in the field of patents. For example, early in 2014, a strategy proposed to the Innovative Pharmaceutical Association of South Africa (IPASA) to capture the national IP policy drafting process was reported by the local and international press.[79] It was reported that IPASA members (the pharmaceutical companies) intended to work with a US lobbying group, Public Affairs Engagement, and a local "front man" to ensure that the policy protected their interests.[80] The front man was required to give the campaign a local face and veil the fact that there was foreign, US-based strategic direction being given to the campaign. The Minister of Health was livid at these revelations and went as far as to

73 For a discussion see Helfer and Austin (2011) pp. 90–170.
74 For a discussion see Helfer and Austin (2011) pp. 315–363.
75 Ncube (2013) pp. 378–381.
76 Okediji (2003b).
77 Loren (2008) p. 37, Samuelson (2013).
78 Deere-Birbkeck (2008) pp. 111, 114–115.
79 de Wet (2014a), Motsoeneng (2014).
80 See Public Affairs Engagement (PAE) (2014).

call these plans genocide.[81] Thereafter the plan was quickly disavowed[82] and some organisational changes were implemented at IPASA.[83] The relevant government departments proceeded with the national consultative processes and the National IP Policy: Phase I was eventually adopted in 2018.[84]

The capture of legislative and policy making processes by organised and well-resourced stakeholders is detrimental to the interests of other stakeholders who lack the same level of resources and organisational capacity to forcefully advance their interests. Consequently, only one voice is heard and the other is disregarded, resulting in inequitable IP regimes. Watching this scenario unfold in African states is very distressing because, as shown later, on the international plane African states have consistently called for nuanced systems which are best achieved through the prudent use of flexibility and policy space in the national sphere. Further, where existing mechanisms are inadequate, they have called for fundamental reforms or temporary waivers of the prevailing framework to meet their citizenry's needs.

1.4 African States' Diversity and the Need for Flexible and Nuanced IP Systems

An analysis of statements by African states indicates that their vision for IP laws in the public interest is for appropriately calibrated laws that are fitting for a state's current conditions. For example, at WIPO meetings and discussions, the African Group[85] and the Development Agenda Group (DAG)[86] have repeatedly said that an appropriately balanced or nuanced system is one that takes a country's socio-economic conditions and development goals into account and not one that is based on a "one size fits all" and "IP as an end in itself" perspective. These views are clearly articulated in paragraph 7 of the African proposal for the establishment of a DA for WIPO as follows:[87]

> IP is just one mechanism among many for bringing about development. It should be used to support and enhance the legitimate economic aspirations of all developing countries including LDCs, especially in the development of their productive forces, comprising of both human and natural resources. IP should therefore, be complimentary and not detrimental to individual

81 Ncube (2015b, 2022b).

82 de Wet (2014b).

83 Kahn (2014).

84 Intellectual Property Policy of the Republic of South Africa Phase I (2018), Republic of South Africa Statement on Cabinet Meeting of 23 May 2018.

85 Shabalala (2007).

86 The DAG consists of countries that subscribe to the agreed guiding principles stated in the DAG Guiding Principles Paper WIPO Doc CDIP/5/9 Rev.

87 African proposal for the establishment of a development agenda for WIPO Doc IIM/3/2 Rev, 31 July 2005.

national efforts at development, by becoming a veritable tool for economic growth.

The same perspective was expressed in paragraph 1 of the DAG's Guiding Principles where the DAG applauded the adoption of the DA as:[88]

> a milestone in achieving the historic aspiration of developing countries for a paradigm shift in the international perspective of intellectual property (IP): a shift from viewing IP as an end in itself, to viewing it as a means to serve the larger public goals of social, economic and cultural development. This vision has refuted the universal applicability of "one size fits all IP protection models" or the advisability of the harmonization of laws leading to higher protection standards in all countries irrespective of the levels of development.

Chapter six will consider the continental effort to establish the Pan-African IP Organisation (PAIPO) against the backdrop of this pro-development position taken by African states at WIPO. It will consider whether, having won a hard-fought battle with the adoption of the DA at WIPO, African states have remained true to that vision in the PAIPO Statute. Likewise, chapter seven's discussion of the AfCFTA IP Protocol will consider whether a developmental approach has been maintained.

As stated, African states exhibit extensive diversity in their national socio-economic, political and cultural profiles. The categorisation of states as either a developing country or an LDC illustrates this starkly. As of April 2021, 33 of the AU's 55 member states were classified as LDCs.[89] The rest are ranked as developing countries. However, there are disparities in their levels of development. For example, in 2013, under the more nuanced Human Development Index (HDI) calibration, Libya, Mauritius, Seychelles, Tunisia and Algeria were classified as having "high human development," making them the highest-ranking African states on the HDI for 2013.[90]

These developing-country/LDC and HDI classifications are indicators of economic development, the understanding of which has evolved over time.[91] The classic definition is that economic development is "the process by which per capita income and economic welfare of a country improve over time."[92] Working from this definition, economic development would then be measured by tracking gross domestic product (GDP) trends. There has been a definitive movement in the comprehension of how economic development happens and how it should

88 WIPO Doc CDIP/5/9 Rev, 26 April 2010.
89 UNDP (2021) p. 5.
90 UNDP (2014) pp. 160–161.
91 Adelman (1961) p. 1, Arndt (1989) pp. 1–5.
92 Jain et al. (2008) 2.

be measured.[93] The more progressive conceptualisation is that measurement of real growth in economic welfare ought to concern itself with more than just the growth of GDP.[94] Sen argues that economic development is not confined to "formal economic opportunities that are available (such as free markets, open trade, transactional facilities), but [is] ultimately about the effective freedoms and capabilities that people have . . . to have basic economic needs fulfilled."[95] Therefore we should be more concerned about "human development accounting," which "involves a systematic examination of a wealth of information about how human beings in each society live."[96] Working from this premise, the United Nations Development Programme (UNDP) has been publishing human development indices annually since 1990.

African states require flexible and nuanced or "fine tuned"[97] IP systems in view of their differing national conditions and their stated desire for appropriately nuanced solutions. The following sub-sections detail their contribution to the development of the WIPO DA and introduces TRIPS flexibilities which are a major policy focus as a preface to the in-depth discussion of these aspects in subsequent chapters.

1.4.1 African States' Contribution to the Articulation and Formulation of the Development Agenda at WIPO

> *WIPO's Development Agenda is the most significant IP matter to confront the international community since the TRIPS Agreement and perhaps ever.*[98]

As will be shown in chapter two, African states rely to a significant extent on technical assistance from WIPO to support their IP policy formulation and much of this support has been rendered under the umbrella of WIPO DA projects. Therefore, it is important to reprise how they helped shape the WIPO DA. The events and discussions leading up to the adoption of the WIPO DA have been well documented and analysed elsewhere,[99] hence this section offers only a brief synopsis. The adoption of the agenda was initiated by a proposal from Argentina and Brazil.[100] This initiative garnered the support of other developing states (collectively known as the

93 Sen (1997) pp. 1–2, 26.
94 Anand and Sen (2000) p. 2032.
95 Sen (2000a).
96 Sen (2000b) p. 18.
97 Kilic (2015) p. 209.
98 de Beer (2009) pp. 2–3.
99 See for example Sell (2011), Netanel (2009) p. 1, de Beer (2009), May (2008, 2007).
100 WIPO (n.d.a.); Proposal by Argentina and Brazil for the Establishment of a Development Agenda for WIPO, WO/GA/31/11.

Group of Friends of Development)[101] and after a series of meetings,[102] a seminar culminated in the establishment of a Provisional Committee on Proposals related to the WIPO DA (PCDA) which drafted proposals that it refined over time.[103] Ultimately in 2007, 45 recommendations were agreed upon by member states.[104] Soon thereafter, organisational changes were made at WIPO to ensure the management and implementation of the DA. The Committee on Development and Intellectual Property (CDIP) and, its secretariat, the DA Coordination Division (DACD), were created. Since then the CDIP has met annually[105] and a number of projects have been implemented,[106] some of which have been subjected to external review.[107] The CDIP reports annually to the General Assembly on its progress on its following mandate:[108]

1 develop a work program for implementing the 45 adopted DA recommendations;
2 monitor, assess, discuss and report on the implementation of all recommendations adopted, and for that purpose to co-ordinate with relevant WIPO bodies; and
3 discuss IP and development-related issues as agreed by the Committee, as well as those decided by the General Assembly.

At the adoption of the DA, its normative impact was difficult to predict due to its non-binding status in relation to both WIPO[109] and its member states.[110] However, it was clear that it could not be ignored due to its moral effect.[111] Indeed, immedi-

101 Proposal to Establish a Development Agenda for WIPO: An Elaboration of Issues Raised in Document WO/GA/31/11 WIPO Doc IIM/1/4. (Group of Friends Elaboration Document IIM/1/4). The members of the group were Argentina, Brazil, Bolivia, Cuba, Dominican Republic, Ecuador, Egypt, Iran, Kenya, Peru, Sierra Leone, South Africa, Tanzania and Venezuela; Shabalala (2007) p. 24, n18.

102 For example, see WIPO Inter-Sessional Intergovernmental Meeting on a Development Agenda for WIPO, First Session, Geneva, 11–13 April 2005 Report. (IIM/1/6).

103 WIPO Provisional Committee on Proposals Related to the WIPO Development Agenda (PCDA) First Session, 20–24 February 2006 (PCDA 1/6 Prov 2); WIPO PCDA Fourth Session, 11–15 June 2007 (PCDA/4/3) WIPO PCDA Fourth Session, 11–15 June 2007 (PCDA/4/3. Annex).

104 Assemblies of the Member States of WIPO, Forty-Third Series of Meetings, Geneva, 24 September–3 October 2007, WIPO General Assembly Report A/43/16 (12 November 2007).

105 Details of meetings and documents are available at www.wipo.int/meetings/en/topic.jsp?group_id=241

106 List of projects and progress reports are available at www.wipo.int/ip-development/en/agenda/projects.html.

107 For example the "Project on Enhancement of WIPO's Results-Based Management (RBM) Framework to Support the Monitoring and Evaluation of the Impact of the Organization's Activities on Development" which included the implementation of Development Agenda Recommendations 33, 38 and 41 was evaluated in Deere-Birkbeck and Roca (2011).

108 See annual reports at CDIP < www.wipo.int/policy/en/cdip/>.

109 de Beer (2009) p. 11.

110 de Beer (2009) p. 11.

111 de Beer (2009) p. 12.

ate organisational restructuring was carried out at WIPO, which was followed by the roll-out of projects as described earlier. Pursuant to further restructuring, the DACD now falls under the Regional and National Development Sector.[112]

Within a few years after its adoption and implementation, as initially predicted, the WIPO DA had proven to be complex and not easy to define.[113] Its distinctive features have been identified as its "malleability, complexity, opportunity and gravity."[114] It is said to be malleable because it contains ambiguities which it is hoped will be interpreted in a manner consistent with the socio-economic condition of developing states. It owes its complexity to the diverse nature of its stakeholders and the availability of other fora where it may be advanced or thwarted ("forum proliferation").[115] Despite such complexity and malleability it continues to present WIPO with an amazing opportunity to redeem itself and recreate itself as an organisation that truly advances the socio-economic development of its member states through a "calibrated" approach to IP that is country-context sensitive.[116] Sell notes that although some articulated cautionary views[117] and others were carefully optimistic[118] about the DA's ability to actually bring about real change, there have been glimmers of fulfilled promise through meaningful scrutiny of WIPO's delivery of technical assistance.[119]

In its rejection of an "IP-centric view,"[120] the WIPO DA is in essence "an attempted paradigm shift" at WIPO from the furtherance of IP-centric goals to the prioritisation of the "public policy aspects of IP rights."[121] It was clear from experience that technology transfer and foreign direct investment did not always follow from TRIPS compliance, as Dreyfuss notes; the reality was that "it had not happened."[122] It acknowledges that the impact of undifferentiated application of strong IP regimes globally is not always an increase in the various facets of creative and economic progress.[123] Instead, it is based on the premise that what is required is a calibrated approach that allows developing countries to benefit from a robust public domain and make use of flexibilities in their national policy space.[124] This exposition of the position taken by African states on the international plane will be used as a comparator for the positions these states have taken on the continent. For example, does the creation of PAIPO align with the stated African position at WIPO? An examination of the online catalogue of DA projects and outputs shows

112 WIPO (2022).
113 de Beer (2009) p. 3.
114 de Beer (2009) pp. 9, 9–17.
115 de Beer (2009) p. 13 .
116 de Beer (2009) p. 15.
117 Maksus (2009) p. 163.
118 Okediji (2009).
119 Sell (2011) p. 20.
120 Netanel (2009) p. 2.
121 de Beer (2009) pp. 2–3.
122 Dreyfuss (2004) p. 29.
123 Netanel (2009) p. 2.
124 Netanel (2009).

that a significant number of projects have been completed in Africa. Chapter two discusses the project on IP policy formulation.

1.4.2 The Dakar Declaration on IP for Africa

The Council of Ministers conference of 2015 adopted the Dakar Declaration on IP for Africa and it was then referred to the Executive Council's 28th ordinary session in 2016,[125] but it appears no decision has been taken on it since then.[126] Final formal adoption status notwithstanding, the declaration is an important articulation of how African states desire WIPO technical assistance to be conducted on the continent.

The declaration was authored by African ministers responsible for IP who participated at the African Ministerial Conference 2015: Intellectual Property for an Emerging Africa, hosted in November 2015 in Dakar by WIPO, the AU, Senegal and the Japan Patent Office.[127] Its preamble refers to the sustainable development goals (SDGs), the AU's Agenda 2063, the Science Technology and Innovation Strategy for Africa (STISA 2024), the Common African Position post-2015 development agenda and the WIPO DA as the lenses through which to consider WIPO technical assistance. It emphasised African states' priorities in relation to:[128]

> advancing innovation for sustainable agricultural technologies, for the use and transfer of environmentally sound technologies, and to help guarantee food security, improve access to health services, and combat the negative effects of climate change; and the need for a sound IP policy and institutional frameworks for the effective and balanced use of the IP system to foster innovation, creativity, entrepreneurship and development in Africa.

After articulating their commitments to various related goals, the declaration then calls on WIPO "[t]o strengthen its partnership with the African Union, Regional Economic Communities, and the African Countries in order to address the challenges mentioned above and, in particular, to enhance its technical assistance."[129] The aspects of technical assistance identified for enhancement include national IP policy making, the provision of legislative advice to create appropriately nuanced IP systems and promoting collaboration between the AU Commission, RECs, ARIPO and OAPI.[130]

The rest of this book's discussions are to be understood within this articulation of Africa's vision for development-orientated IP.

125 AU Dakar Declaration on IP for Africa, 2015.
126 Executive Council Twenty-Eighth Ordinary Session Decisions. 23–28 January 2016. Addis Ababa, Ethiopia. EX.CL/Dec. 898–918(XXVIII)Rev.1.
127 WIPO (2015) Meeting Code OMPI/PI/DAK/15.
128 Dakar Declaration on IP for Africa (2015) p. 1.
129 Dakar Declaration on IP for Africa (2015) p. 3.
130 Dakar Declaration on IP for Africa (2015) pp. 3–4.

1.4.3 TRIPS Implementation by African States: A Straitjacket or Nuancing Tool?

TRIPS implementation involves domesticating the agreement's minimum IP standards whilst making appropriate use of its flexibilities to cater for a jurisdiction's unique socio-economic conditions. Developing countries and LDCs struggle with both aspects of TRIPS implementation,[131] and those in Africa are no exception. This is largely because the TRIPS deal was not concluded in their best interests and some of the agreement's minimum standards are not tenable for them. Indeed, Deere comments that its conclusion was "a victory for those multinational companies determined to raise international IP standards and boost IP protection in developing countries."[132] She also notes that developing countries had sounded concern that the agreement would hinder the achievement of their developmental goals and would be unlikely to yield significant benefits for them.[133] Further, the very process of domestication is fraught with difficulty for developing countries and LDCs as they are hampered by their limited technical expertise.[134] Experience has shown that these misgivings were well founded, as the implementation of TRIPS has had mixed results for some African states[135] and is still nowhere near attainable for LDCs.

1.4.4 IP Policy Focus Area: TRIPS Flexibilities

"TRIPS flexibilities" are provisions in TRIPS that provide some policy space for party states to calibrate their domestic IP regimes.[136] A basic categorisation of flexibilities is the distinction between transition periods and flexibilities that pertain to the actual content of substantive provisions.

In addition to the distinction between transitional and substantive flexibilities, further distinctions can be made according to:

1 the IP right associated with the flexibilities;
2 their purpose;[137] and
3 the timing of the availability of the flexibility.

The first classification categorises flexibilities according to the type of IP they apply to, for example a copyright-related flexibility or a patent-related flexibility.

131 Kapczynski (2009).
132 Deere-Birbkeck (2009) p. 1.
133 Deere-Birbkeck (2009) p. 1.
134 Musungu, Villanueva and Blasetti (2004) p. 24.
135 For example, see the analysis of Francophone Africa's experiences of implementation from 1995 to 2007 in Deere-Birbkeck (2009) pp. 240–286.
136 For discussion of the development of the phrase see Blakeney and Mengistie (2011) pp. 243–244. Also see Patent Related Flexibilities in the Multilateral Legal Framework and Their Legislative Implementation at the National and Regional Levels (2010) CDIP/5/4 rev. para 33–34.
137 Correa (2013) p. 418.

The second categorisation addresses the reason why a state may resort to a particular flexibility. For example, it may be to meet public health goals by making pharmaceuticals more readily available at lower prices or to curb anti-competitive activities. Under the third manner of categorisation listed, a flexibility is classified according to whether it is available:[138]

(i) in the process of the acquisition of the right;
(ii) defining the scope of the right; and
(iii) in the process of enforcing the right.

Here the question being asked is at what stage in the life cycle of the IP right the flexibility is applicable. It may be when it is being created or acquired and expressed through formal or substantive requirements for application and grant. For example, it may relate to how much information is required to be disclosed by the applicant in the application.[139] In the definition of the scope of rights, flexibilities pertain to exactly what is protected by IP and which uses are permitted in the public interest. Exceptions to IPRs, compulsory licences and provisions pertaining to parallel imports are included in this category.[140] In relation to enforcement, party states have some leeway in their domestic provision for remedies for infringement. For example, they may provide for punitive damages in instances of wilful or flagrant infringement.[141]

These classifications can be used simultaneously to characterise a single flexibility. For example, one could categorise compulsory licences as patent-related flexibilities that serve public health goals and are available post–patent grant. Given the primacy of public health needs on the continent, this book will focus on patent-related flexibilities, which are outlined under the next five subheadings: Transition Periods, Definition of Invention and Other Patent Grant-Related Flexibilities, Parallel Imports, Compulsory Licences and Government Use, and Exceptions. It is important to stress that the following is not a comprehensive or exhaustive statement of flexibilities and to remind the reader that it is provided to contextualise the IP policies overview which follows.

Transition Periods

Various transition periods were provided for to enable the implementation of TRIPS by WTO member states. All WTO members were afforded a year after the

138 Patent Related Flexibilities in the Multilateral Legal Framework and their Legislative Implementation at the National and Regional Levels (2010) CDIP/5/4 rev. para 36.
139 Patent Related Flexibilities in the Multilateral Legal Framework and their Legislative Implementation at the National and Regional Levels (2010) CDIP/5/4 rev. para 37.
140 Patent Related Flexibilities in the Multilateral Legal Framework and their Legislative Implementation at the National and Regional Levels (2010) CDIP/5/4 rev. para 38.
141 Patent Related Flexibilities in the Multilateral Legal Framework and their Legislative Implementation at the National and Regional Levels (2010) CDIP/5/4 rev. para 39.

coming into force of TRIPS before they became obliged to comply with it.[142] In addition, developing countries were afforded an additional four years' transition period in recognition of their disadvantaged position.[143] However, they were required to comply with Articles 3, 4 and 5, which pertain to non-discrimination. This meant that they did not have to apply TRIPS in full until 1 January 2000. Further, they could postpone pharmaceutical and agricultural chemicals patent protection until 1 January 2005.[144] If they did so, they were required to permit the filing of patent applications from 1 January 1995, which would be examined when that country began to issue these patents.[145] If the product was marketed during the transition period, exclusive marketing rights were to be granted to the patent applicant.[146] As indicated in section 1.2, there is also an LDC transition period has been extended to 1 July 2034 or sooner if a country ceases to be an LDC before that date[147] and the LDC pharmaceutical products transition period which has been extended to 1 January 2033.[148]

Definition of Invention and Other Patent Grant–Related Flexibilities

Article 27.1 of TRIPS provides

> Subject to the provisions of paragraphs 2 and 3, patents shall be available for any inventions, whether products or processes, in all fields of technology, provided that they are new, involve an inventive step and are capable of industrial application. Subject to paragraph 4 of Article 65, paragraph 8 of Article 70 and paragraph 3 of this Article, patents shall be available and patent rights enjoyable without discrimination as to the place of invention, the field of technology and whether products are imported or locally produced.

Whilst party states are obliged to extend patent protection to inventions in all fields of technology, they have leeway when it comes to defining what constitutes an invention. This flexibility can be used to prohibit the patenting of second or new uses of pharmaceuticals,[149] a practice commonly known as

142 Article 65(1) TRIPS.
143 Article 65(2) TRIPS.
144 Article 65(4) TRIPS.
145 Article 70(8) TRIPS.
146 Article 70(9) TRIPS.
147 WTO Decision of the Council for Trade-Related Aspects of Intellectual Property Rights Extension of the Transition Period Under Article 66.1 for Least-Developed Country Members (29 June 2021) IP/C/88.
148 WTO Decision of the Council for Trade-Related Aspects of Intellectual Property Rights Extension of the Transition Period Under Article 66.1 of the TRIPS Agreement for Least-Developed Country Members for Certain Obligations with Respect to Pharmaceutical Products (6 November 2015) IP/C/73.
149 Musungu, Villanueva and Blasetti (2004) p. 15.

"ever-greening." Typically, it plays itself out as follows: a patent subsists in a pharmaceutical compound that is used for the treatment of a certain condition, perhaps in particular dosage and in combination with another compound. A few years before the expiry of the patent, the patent holder discloses that that use of the compound is no longer effective and it now has to be used in combination with another compound or in a different dosage or changes its pharmaceutical composition slightly. Alternatively, a new use could be found for the medication (second medical indication). A patent is then registered over the "new" compound, combination or use, thus further extending the patent holder's economic exclusivity or "ever-greening" the patent. In order to avert or curb this practice, national legislation could provide that new uses of compounds are excluded from patentability.[150]

In addition to policy space pertaining to the definition of an invention, states may also regulate the following in a flexible way:[151]

- the determination of what constitutes an inventive step;
- the disclosure that is required to sustain a successful patent application;
- the examination of patent applications; and
- whether or not substances existing in nature are patentable.

It has been suggested that a strict test for inventive step that references a "person highly skilled in the art" instead of the commonly used ordinary skill standard ought to be introduced in order to ensure that stronger patents are registered.[152] It has also been suggested that states should require the disclosure of "all modes" of implementing an invention, an "express indication of the best mode for carrying out an invention by experts skilled in the art, who reside in the respective" jurisdiction and information pertaining to related foreign patent applications and the grant thereof.[153] The substantive examination of patents would also weed out sub-patentable inventions. Finally, it has been recommended that natural substances should be excluded from patentability.[154]

Parallel Imports

Parallel importation occurs when goods that are lawfully available in one market (A) are purchased there and imported into another jurisdiction (B) without the authorisation of the holder of IP rights in the goods and are thereafter traded on the open market in B, in competition with the IP right-holder or his licensees.[155]

150 Musungu, Villanueava and Blasetti (2004) p. 15.
151 Correa (2013) pp. 419–423, Sibanda (2013).
152 EAC TRIPS Policy p. 13, Park, Prabhala and Berger (2013).
153 EAC TRIPS Policy p. 17.
154 EAC TRIPS Policy p. 13.
155 Musungu, Villanueva and Blasetti (2004) p. 13.

The TRIPS provision that grants party states policy space to provide for parallel importation in their domestic laws is Article 6, which provides:[156]

> For the purposes of dispute settlement under this Agreement, subject to the provisions of Articles 3 and 4 nothing in this Agreement shall be used to address the issue of the exhaustion of intellectual property rights.

An IP right-holder's rights are exhausted when the protected goods have been lawfully sold or distributed. If a jurisdiction subscribes to the principle of national exhaustion then the rights are exhausted when the product is first distributed on the national market. Where international exhaustion applies, then its distribution anywhere in the world exhausts the right-holders' rights.

As is clear from Article 6, each WTO member state is at liberty to select either the national or international regime of exhaustion. Where international exhaustion applies, a citizen or resident of that country is able to purchase the product from another market and then import it into their country of residence for further trade or distribution. This is a very useful way of accessing products from another market when they are not available or are unaffordable in a person's country of residence and has been used in various contexts, for example by South African activists to procure generic medication for HIV/AIDS.[157]

Compulsory Licences and Government Use

"A compulsory license is a license granted by an administrative or judicial body to a third party to exploit an invention without the authorisation of the patent holder."[158] Such licences may be issued to permit the production and distribution of generic medications,[159] which are often cheaper than patented and branded medications. Article 31 of TRIPS provides a series of conditions under which such licences may be issued. Examples of these conditions include the following: Article 31(h) provides that satisfactory remuneration must be paid to the patent-holder paying consideration to the "economic value of the license." Article 31(f) provides that use of the medicines manufactured under compulsory licence shall be "predominantly for the supply of the domestic market." This limitation prevents countries with the capacity to make generics under compulsory licences from exporting a significant

156 Also see para. 5(d) of the Doha Declaration on the TRIPS Agreement and Public Health WT/MIN (01)/DEC/W/2, 14 November 2001.

157 For example see Heywood (2001) for an account of how activists brought HIV/AIDS medication into South Africa.

158 Musungu, Villanueva and Blasetti (2004) p. 12.

159 Ncube (2009) p. 681 defines generics as "medication that consists of the same active medicinal substance as an originator pharmaceutical product and because they act in the same way in the human body, they are interchangeable with the originator product." It is important to note that there are many practical and capacity problems that attach to the local manufacture of generics. For example, see Owoeye (2014), UNCTAD (2011).

amount of those generics to other countries, which is to the detriment of countries who would seek to import generics from them. It has since been "softened" by the "paragraph 6 solution" of the 2003 Waiver Decision, which was then incorporated into TRIPS as Article 31*bis* by the 2005 amendment of the agreement. The amendment will come into force after its acceptance by two-thirds of WTO members and in the interim the Waiver Decision applies.[160] This solution is a rule-based waiver of the Article 31(f) requirement. It removed the limits on exports under compulsory licence to WTO member states with limited pharmaceutical products manufacturing capacity, provided that the relevant member states met certain conditions. For example, both the exporting and importing countries have to issue compulsory licences and advise the TRIPS Council of the import and export. However, this solution is complex and impracticable[161] and has only been used once, by Rwanda and Canada.[162]

Exceptions

Article 30 of TRIPS provides:

> Members may provide limited exceptions to the exclusive rights conferred by a patent, provided that such exceptions do not unreasonably conflict with a normal exploitation of the patent and do not unreasonably prejudice the legitimate interests of the patent owner, taking account of the legitimate interests of third parties.

This provision contains the so-called Three Step Test, which made its first appearance in the Berne Convention. Examples of exceptions under this provision include the research and experimentation exception and the early working exception, which is also known as the Bolar provision.[163] The research and experimentation exception allows creators and manufacturers scope to use patented technology (e.g., a product or pharmaceutical) experimentally to create alternatives.[164] The Bolar provision enables competitors to use or otherwise exploit patented pharmaceuticals to make a generic version, then to obtain "the regulatory approval and registration of a generic product before the expiry of the patent term."[165]

160 WTO (n.d.); WTO General Council Decision WT/L/1122 Amendment of the TRIPS Agreement – Eighth Extension of the Period for the Acceptance by Members of the Protocol Amending the TRIPS Agreement General Council Decision, adopted on 22 November 2021.

161 For a detailed statement of its working see WHO, WIPO and WIPO (2012) pp. 224–228.

162 For commentary, see Owoeye (2014), Nkomo (2013), Outterson (2010), Ncube (2009) pp. 686–687, Andemariam (2007), Abbott and Reichman (2007).

163 Musungu, Villanueva and Blasetti (2004) p. 17.

164 Musungu, Villanueva and Blasetti (2004) p. 17. *Canada: Patent Protection of Pharmaceutical Products*, Report of the Panel adopted on 7 April 2000 (WT/DS114/R, 17 March 2000).

165 Musungu, Villanueva and Blasetti (2004) p. 17.

1.4.5 Ongoing Work on Nuancing African IP Systems

Generally, many African LDCs have benefitted from using transition periods and recent research has identified its use by 28 LDCs, some show multiple instances of such use,[166] which is more than 50% of the total of African states. However, pharmaceutical patents are granted by many LDCs despite existence of the LDC transition period for granting these patents until January 2033. For example, LDC SADC member states grant such patents.[167] African states are yet to make full use of substantive patent-related TRIPS flexibilities.[168] Continuing efforts are being made, with technical assistance from UNDP and other UN agencies, to achieve this, some of which have resulted in the adoption of national IP policies that expressly reference flexibilities.[169] There are several significant international and continental developments that are relevant to these endeavours. These include the WHO's Global Strategy and Plan of Action on Public Health, Innovation and IP, the African Union Health Strategy and Pharmaceutical Manufacturing Plan for Africa (PMPA), 2007 and the initiative on Strengthening Pharmaceutical Innovation Africa.[170] In 2012 the AU Heads of State endorsed the PMPA Business Plan (PMPA BP) which was jointly developed by the AU Commission (AUC) and UNIDO. The PMPA BP reiterated the reasons for African states' failure to utilise flexibilities noted previously and made this stark call:

> Africa therefore faces a simple choice in the next four years – to fully exploit the TRIPS flexibilities and accelerate the ongoing negotiations for an extension to the 2016 transition period or face the prospect of paying more for drugs in the future.[171]

It then detailed options for implementation at various levels. Notably, it stresses that RECs and ARIPO have a role to play in leading and supporting their member states' efforts to domesticate and implement flexibilities.[172] Several other related developments have followed, specifically in the wake of the COVID-19 pandemic. For instance, the African Development Bank embarked on the establishment of the African Pharmaceutical Technology Foundation in 2022 with the goal of boosting the continental pharmaceutical industry, vaccine manufacturing capacity, and healthcare infrastructure.[173]

RECs have responded to the call to provide support and have initiated subregional initiatives to realise the meaningful use of patent-related flexibilities in

166 Vadwa and Shozi (2020) p. 14.
167 Musungu (2012) p. 9.
168 Baker (2019), Kameni (2015), Adusei (2012), Avafia, Berger and Hartzenberg (2006).
169 For example, see Republic of Botswana (2013) and Botswana Intellectual Property Policy BIPP (2022) p. 25 para 5.4.3(c).
170 Berger et al. (2010) p. 7.
171 AU PMPA BP (2012) p. 50.
172 AU PMPA BP (2012) pp. 77, 79–80.
173 African Development Bank (2022).

tandem with pharmaceutical business plans – for example, the EAC Regional Pharmaceutical Manufacturing Plans of Action (2012–2016 and 2017–2027), its Regional Health Sector Policy (2016) and SADC's Pharmaceutical Business Plans (2007–2013 and 2015–2019). The EAC and ECOWAS have developed policies and protocols on the incorporation of patent-related TRIPS flexibilities into national laws,[174] whilst COMESA has an IP policy,[175] and SADC has adopted an IP framework and guidelines,[176] building on the foundation laid in its Protocol on Trade (1996) and Protocol on Science, Technology and Innovation (2008).

These policy instruments are discussed in chapter three. African intergovernmental organisations (IGOs) are also involved in efforts to implement these flexibilities. A case in point is the East, Central and Southern Africa Health Community (ECSA-HC).[177] The current membership of this community comprises Eswatini, Kenya, Lesotho, Malawi, Mauritius, Tanzania, Uganda, Zambia and Zimbabwe.[178] More recently, along with the AU, the RECs have cooperated to mount a continental response to the COVID-19 pandemic, coalesced around the Africa Centre for Disease Control (Africa CDC).[179] These efforts have inevitably required engagement with IP frameworks, and as indicated previously, African states lent their support to the TRIPS Waiver Proposal.

1.5 Book Overview

Against this background, the book proceeds as follows.

Chapter two discusses national IP policies and evaluates to what extent, if any, they serve the public interest. Chapter three discusses IP harmonisation efforts by RECs, including their IP policies, with a view to evaluating their public interest goals and achievements, specifically the extent to which they have been translated to and implemented on the domestic plane by their member/partner states. Chapter four considers the harmonisation and unification of IP frameworks by ARIPO and OAPI, respectively, through a similar lens. Chapter five discusses the key considerations in the development of a continental IP system, including the various legal harmonisation models in play in Africa and beyond, as a backdrop to chapters six and seven's discussions of recent continental developments. Chapter six outlines the historical development of plans to establish PAIPO and

174 EAC Regional Intellectual Property Policy on the Utilisation of Public Health–Related WTO-TRIPS Flexibilities and the Approximation of National Intellectual Property Legislation (2013) and Health Protocol on Public Health–Related WTO-TRIPS Flexibilities (2013), ECOWAS Development of a Harmonized TRIPS Policy for Adoption by ECOWAS Member States That Employ TRIPS Flexibilities to Improve Access to Medicines in the Region (2012) and Guidelines for Implementation of TRIPS Flexibilities in National Legislation to Improve Access to Medicines in the West African Region (2012).

175 COMESA Regional Policy on IP Rights and Cultural Industries (COMESA IP Policy) (2011).

176 SADC Ministerial Meeting Statement (2019).

177 See for example EQUINET and ECSA HC (2011).

178 See https://ecsahc.org/partners/

179 Medinilla, Byiers and Apiko (2020) p. 11.

canvasses some public interest concerns that are raised by such development. Chapter seven discusses the AfCFTA IP Protocol and chapter eight concludes the text by discussing the viability of current and future IP harmonisation initiatives with reference to the current socio-economic status of African states. It asks whether such harmonisation efforts would be in the public interest and urges due consideration of individual states' unique conditions and aspirations in any harmonisation venture.

Reference List

Primary Sources: Agreements, Decisions and Official Documents

National Instruments

Republic of Botswana, 2022. *Botswana Intellectual Property Policy*, BIPP IP Policy (BIPP).

Republic of South Africa, 2018. *Statement on the Cabinet Meeting of 23 May 2018*. Available at www.gov.za/speeches/statement-cabinet-meeting-23-may-2018-24-may-2018-0000 [accessed 5 January 2023].

Republic of South Africa, 2018, August 31. *Intellectual Property Policy of the Republic of South Africa Phase I, GN 518 of GG 41870*. Available at www.gov.za/sites/default/files/gcis_document/201808/ippolicy2018-phasei.pdf [accessed 5 January 2023].

AU

Agreement Establishing the African Continental Free Trade Area (AfCFTA Agreement), 2018.

Assembly Decision on the Moratorium on the Recognition of Regional Economic Communities (RECs) DOC. EX.CL/278 (IX). AU Doc. Assembly/AU/Dec.111–132 (VII). Assembly of the African Union. Seventh Ordinary Session, 1–2 July 2006. Banjul, The Gambia.

AU Commission and UNIDO Pharmaceutical Manufacturing Plan for Africa Business Plan, 2012.

Dakar Declaration on IP for Africa, 2015. EX.CL/945(XXVIII) Add.7 Executive Council Twenty-Eighth Ordinary Session, 23–28 January 2016. Addis Ababa, Ethiopia. Available at https://archives.au.int/handle/123456789/4931?show=full [accessed 9 January 2023].

Executive Council Twenty-Eighth Ordinary Session Decisions. EX.CL/Dec.898–918(XXVIII) Rev.1, 23–28 January 2016. Addis Ababa, Ethiopia. Available at https://au.int/en/decisions-4 [accessed 9 January 2023].

Health Strategy and Pharmaceutical Manufacturing Plan for Africa, 2007. Study for the Quantification of Regional Economic Communities (RECs): Rationalisation Scenarios (Provisional Report), 2009. Available at https://au.int/sites/default/files/newsevents/workingdocuments/12553-wd-rationalisation_study_english.2.pdf [accessed 15 March 2023].

COMESA

COMESA Regional Policy on IP Rights and Cultural Industries (COMESA IP Policy), 2011. Available at www.ip-watch.org/weblog/wp-content/uploads/2013/05/Comesa-IP-policy-May-2013.pdf [accessed 15 March 2023].

COMESA-EAC-SADC Tripartite Free Trade Area

Agreement Establishing a Tripartite Free Trade Area Among the Common Market for Eastern and Southern Africa, the East African Community and the Southern African Development Community.

Sharm El Sheikh Declaration Launching the COMESA-EAC-SADC Tripartite FTA.

EAC

EAC Regional Health Sector Policy (2016). Available at https://health.eac.int/publications/eac-regional-health-sector-policy-2016#gsc.tab=0 [accessed 2 January 2023].

Health Protocol on Public Health Related WTO-TRIPS Flexibilities (2013).

Regional Intellectual Property Policy on the Utilisation of Public Health-Related WTO-TRIPS Flexibilities and the Approximation of National Intellectual Property Legislation (2013).

Regional Pharmaceutical Action Plan (2017–2027). Available at http://repository.eac.int/handle/11671/24343 [accessed 3 January 2023].

Regional Pharmaceutical Manufacturing Plan of Action (2012–2016).

Regional Pharmaceutical Manufacturing Plan of Action (2017–2027).

ECOWAS

Development of a Harmonized TRIPS Policy for Adoption by ECOWAS Member States That Employ TRIPS Flexibilities to Improve Access to Medicines in the Region (2012).

Guidelines for Implementation of TRIPS Flexibilities in National Legislation to Improve Access to Medicines in the West African Region (2012).

OAPI

Bangui Agreement Relating to the Creation of an African Intellectual Property Organisation, 1977, as revised. Available at www.oapi.int/Ressources/accord_bangui/2020/anglais.pdf [accessed 17 March 2022].

SADC

Pharmaceutical Business Plan (2007–2013).

Pharmaceutical Business Plans (2015–2019).

Protocol on Science, Technology and Innovation (2008).

Protocol on Trade (1996).

SADC IP Framework and Guidelines (2018).

SADC Ministerial Meeting Statement: The Joint Meeting of the SADC Ministers Responsible for Education and Training; and Science, Technology and Innovation, 20–21 June 2019 Safari Hotel Windhoek, Namibia. Available at www.sadc.int/files/6315/6115/1098/Statement_ET-STI__21_June_2019_final.pdf [accessed 28 April 2022].

WHO

Global Strategy and Plan of Action on Public Health, Innovation and Intellectual Property (2008).

WIPO

African Ministerial Conference 2015: Intellectual Property (IP) for an Emerging Africa, 3–5 November 2015. Meeting Code OMPI/PI/DAK/15. Available at www.wipo.int/meetings/en/details.jsp?meeting_id=37206 [accessed 9 January 2023].
African Proposal for the Establishment of a Development Agenda for WIPO Doc IIM/3/2 Rev, 31 July 2005.
Assemblies of the Member States of WIPO, Forty-Third Series of Meetings, Geneva, September 24 to October 3, 2007, WIPO General Assembly Report A/43/16 (November 12, 2007).
Berne Convention for the Protection of Literary and Artistic Works (1886) 1161 U.N.T.S. 3.
Information on the Development Agenda Group Guiding Principles WIPO Doc CDIP/5/9 Rev, 26 April 2010.
Marrakesh Treaty to Facilitate Access to Published Works for Persons Who are Blind, Visually Impaired, or Otherwise Print Disabled (2013). *International Legal Materials (ILM)*, 52(6), 1309–1320.
Paris Convention for the Protection of Industrial Property (1883) 21 U.S.T. 1583, 828 U.N.T.S. 305.
Patent Related Flexibilities in the Multilateral Legal Framework and Their Legislative Implementation at the National and Regional Levels (2010) CDIP/5/4 rev para 33–34.
Proposal of Argentina and Brazil, for the Establishment of a Development Agenda for WIPO, 27 August 2004, document WO/GA/31/11.
Proposal to Establish a Development Agenda for WIPO: An Elaboration of Issues Raised in Document WO/GA/31/11 WIPO Doc IIM/1/4 (Group of Friends Elaboration Document IIM/1/4).
Universal Copyright Convention (Paris Act/Text, 1971) 25 U.S.T. 1341, 943 U.N.T.S. 178.
WIPO (2015) *CDIP Annual Reports*. Available at www.wipo.int/policy/en/cdip/.
WIPO Inter-Sessional Intergovernmental Meeting on a Development Agenda for WIPO, First Session, Geneva, 11–13 April 2005 Report (IIM/1/6).
WIPO PCDA Fourth Session, 11–15 June 2007 (PCDA/4/3).
WIPO PCDA Fourth Session, 11–15 June 2007 (PCDA/4/3. Annex).
WIPO Provisional Committee on Proposals Related to the WIPO Development Agenda (PCDA) First Session, 20–24 February 2006 (PCDA 1/6 Prov 2).

WTO

Agreement on Trade-Related Aspects of Intellectual Property Rights, Including Trade in Counterfeit Goods (1994) 33 ILM 81 (TRIPS).
Doha Decision on the Implementation of par 6 of the Doha Declaration/ (2003). Doc. WT/L/540 and Corr.1.
Doha Declaration on the TRIPS Agreement and Public Health (adopted 14 November 2001), Doc. WT/MIN(01)/DEC/2 (20 November 2001).
Doha WTO Ministerial Declaration (adopted 14 November 2001) Doc. WT/MIN(01)/DEC/1 (20 November 2001).
Extension of the Transition Period Under Article 66.1 for Least-Developed Country Members (29 November 2005) Decision of the Council for TRIPS (IP/C/40).
Extension of the Transition Period Under Article 66.1 for Least Developed Country Members (11 June 2013) Decision of the Council for TRIPS (IP/C/64).

Extension of the Transition Period under Article 66.1 for Least-developed Country Members (29 June 2021) Decision of the Council for TRIPS (IP/C/88).
Extension of the Transition Period under Article 66.1 of the TRIPS Agreement for Least-Developed Country Members for Certain Obligations with Respect to Pharmaceutical Products (27 June 2002) Decision of the Council for TRIPS (IP/C/25).
Extension of the Transition Period Under Article 66.1 of the TRIPS Agreement for Least-Developed Country Members for Certain Obligations with Respect to Pharmaceutical Products (06 November 2015) Decision of the Council for TRIPS (IP/C/73).
LDC Members – Obligations Under Article 70.9 of TRIPS Agreement with Respect to Pharmaceutical Products (8 July 2002) (WT/L/478).
Least-Developed Country Members – Obligations Under Article 70.8 and Article 70.9 of the TRIPS Agreement with Respect to Pharmaceutical Products (December 2015) (WT/L/971).
Panel Report, Canada Patent Protection of Pharmaceutical Products, f 7.23, WT/DS114/R (17 March 2000).
WTO Council for TRIPS. Waiver from Certain Provisions of the TRIPS Agreement for the Prevention, Containment and Treatment of Covid-19 – Communication from India and South Africa IP/C/W/669, 2 October 2020.
WTO Council for TRIPS. Waiver from Certain Provisions of the TRIPS Agreement for the Prevention, Containment and Treatment of Covid-19 – Revised Decision Text Communication from the African Group, The Plurinational State of Bolivia, Egypt, Eswatini, Fiji, India, Indonesia, Kenya, The LDC Group, Maldives, Mozambique, Mongolia, Namibia, Pakistan, South Africa, Vanuatu, The Bolivarian Republic of Venezuela and Zimbabwe IP/C/W/669/Rev.1, 25 May 2021.
WTO General Council Decision WT/L/1122 Amendment of the TRIPS Agreement – Eighth Extension of the Period for the Acceptance by Members of the Protocol Amending the TRIPS Agreement General Council Decision, adopted on 22 November 2021.

WTO Notifications

Plurinational State of Bolivia, 2021a. Notification of Intention to Use the Special Compulsory Licensing System as An Importing Member, Council for Trade-Related Aspects of Intellectual Property Rights, IP/N/8/BOL/1 (19 February 2021).
Plurinational State of Bolivia, 2021b. Notification of Intention to Use the Special Compulsory Licensing System as An Importing Member, Council for Trade-Related Aspects of Intellectual Property Rights, IP/N/9/BOL/1 (11 May 2021).

Secondary Sources

Abbott, F.M., 2013. *Technical Note: The LDC TRIPS Transition Extension and the Question of Rollback.* Policy Brief No 15. Geneva, Switzerland: International Centre for Trade and Sustainable Development.
Abbott, F.M. and Reichman, J.H., 2007. The Doha Round's Public Health Legacy: Strategies for the Production and Diffusion of Patented Medicines under the Amended TRIPS Provisions. *Journal of International Economic Law*, 10, 921–987.
Adelman, I., 1961. *Theories of Economic Growth and Development.* Stanford, CA: Stanford University Press.
Adewopo, A., 2012. *According to Intellectual Property: A Pro-Development Vision of the Law and the Nigerian Intellectual Property Law and Policy Reform in the Knowledge Era.* Lagos: Nigerian Institute of Advanced Legal Studies.

Adusei, P., 2012. *Patenting of Pharmaceuticals and Development in Sub-Saharan Africa: Laws, Institutions, Practices, and Politics*. Heidelberg: Springer.

AfCFTA Secretariat, 2023. *AfCFTA Fact Sheet*. Accra, Ghana: AfCFTA Secretariat. Available at https://au-afcfta.org/about/ [accessed 1 April 2023].

African Copyright and Access to Knowledge Project (ACA2K), 2008. *Methodology Guide*. International Development Research Centre (IDRC), Shuttleworth Foundation and LINK Centre, University of the Witwatersrand.

African Development Bank, 2022. *African Development Bank's Board Approves Landmark Institution: Establishment of African Pharmaceutical Technology Foundation to Transform Africa's Pharmaceutical Industry*. Available at www.afdb.org/en/news-and-events/press-releases/african-development-banks-board-approves-landmark-institution-establishment-african-pharmaceutical-technology-foundation-transform-africas-pharmaceutical-industry-52727 [accessed 1 December 2022].

Akokpari, J., 2008. Dilemmas of Regional Integration and Development. In Akokpari et al (ed.) *The African Union and Its Institutions*. Auckland Park: Fanele, 85–110.

Anand, S. and Sen, A., 2000. Human Development and Economic Sustainability. *World Development*, 28(12), 2029–2049.

Andemariam, S.W., 2007. The Cleft-Stick Between Anti Retroviral Drug Patents and HIV/AIDS Victims: An In-Depth Analysis of the WTO's TRIPS Article 31 *bis* Amendment Proposal of 6 December 2005. *Intellectual Property Quarterly*, 4, 414–466.

Armstrong, C., de Beer, J., Kawooya, D., Prabhala, A. and Schonwetter, T., 2010. Introduction. In Armstrong, C., de Beer, J., Kawooya, D., Prabhala, A. and Schonwetter, T. (eds.) *Access to Knowledge in Africa: The Role of Copyright*. Cape Town: UCT Press.

Arndt, H.W., 1989. *Economic Development: The History of an Idea*. Chicago: University of Chicago Press.

AU, n.d. *Member States' Country Profiles*. Available at https://au.int/en/member_states/countryprofiles2 [accessed 4 January 2024].

Avafia, T., Berger, J. and Hartzenberg, T., 2006. *The Ability of Select Sub-Saharan African Countries to Utilize TRIPs Flexibilities and Competition Law to Ensure a Sustainable Supply of Essential Medicines: A Study of Producing and Importing Countries*. Stellenbosch: ICTSD, UNCTAD and Tralac.

Baker, B., 2015. *LDC Members' Entitlement to and Need for a Further Extension of Their Pharmaceutical Transition Period*. Available at http://infojustice.org/archives/33969 [accessed 1 March 2015].

Baker, B., 2019. *A Full Description of WTO TRIPS Flexibilities Available to ARIPO Member States and a Critique of ARIPO's Comparative Study Analyzing and Making Recommendations Concerning Those Flexibilities*. Available at www.bu.edu/gdp/files/2020/05/ARIPO-Member-States-obligations-and-flexibilities-under-the-WTO-TRIPS-Agreement-March-2019.pdf [accessed 2 January 2023].

Belohlavek, A.J., 2012. Public Policy and Public Interest in International Law and EU Law. In Belohlavek, A. and Rozehnalova, N. (eds.) *Cyil – Czech Yearbook of International Law: Public Policy and Ordre Public* (Vol. III). New York: Huntington Inc., 117–147.

Berger, M., Murugi, J., Buch, E., Ijsselmuiden, C., Moran, M., Guzman, J., Devlin, M. and Kubata, B., 2010. *Strengthening Pharmaceutical Innovation in Africa*. Council on Health Research for Development (COHRED); New Partnership for Africa's Development (NEPAD). Available at https://www.unido.org/sites/default/files/2016-01/COHRED-NEPAD_Strengthening_Pharmaceutical_Innovation_Africa__Report_May_2010_FINALweb_0.pdf [accessed 2 January 2023].

BioLyse, 2021. *Letter to Canadian Minister of Innovation, Science and Industry*. Available at https://www.keionline.org/35587 [accessed 10 April 2023].

Blakeney, M. and Mengistie, G., 2011. Intellectual Property and Economic Development in Sub-Saharan Africa. *Journal of World Intellectual Property*, 14(3/4), 238–264.

Boahen, A.A. (ed.), 1990. *General History of Africa VII: Africa Under Colonial Domination. 1880–1935*. London: James Currey Publishers.

Box, R.C., 2007. Redescribing the Public Interest. *The Social Science Journal*, 44(4), 585–598.

Broadman, H.G. and Isik, G., 2007. *Africa's Silk Road: China and India's New Economic Frontier*. Washington, DC: World Bank.

Collins, R.O. and Burns, J.M., 2013. *A History of Sub-Saharan Africa* (2nd ed.). Cambridge: Cambridge University Press.

Correa, C.M., 2013. Multilateral Agreements and Policy Opportunities. In Cimoli, M., Dosi, G., Maskus, K.E., Okediji, R.L. and Reichman, J.H. (eds.) *Intellectual Property Rights: Legal and Economic Challenges for Development*. Oxford: Oxford University Press, 417–438.

de Beer, J., 2009. Defining WIPO's Development Agenda. In de Beer, J. (ed.) *Implementing the World Intellectual Property Organisation's Development Agenda*. Waterloo, Ontario: International Development Research Centre and Wilfrid Laurier University Press.

Deere-Birbkeck, C., 2008. The Politics of Intellectual Property Reform in Developing Countries: The Relevance of the World Intellectual Property Organisation. In Netanel, N.W. (ed.) *The Development Agenda: Global Intellectual Property and Developing Countries*. Oxford: Oxford University Press, 111–131.

Deere-Birbkeck, C., 2009. *The Implementation Game: The TRIPS Agreement and the Global Politics of Intellectual Property Reform in Developing Countries*. New York: Oxford University Press.

Deere-Birkbeck, C. and Roca, S., 2011. *An External Review of WIPO Technical Assistance in the Area of Cooperation for Development*. Geneva, Switzerland: WIPO. Available at www.wipo.int/edocs/mdocs/mdocs/en/cdip_8/cdip_8_inf_1-annex1.pdf [accessed 6 January 2023].

de Wet, P., 2014a. Motsoaledi: Big Pharma's 'Satanic' Plot Is Genocide. *Mail & Guardian*, 17 January 2014.

de Wet, P., 2014b. How the Big 'Pharma' Plot Died an Early Death. *Mail & Guardian*, 18 January 2014.

Dobb, S.V., 1977. Compulsory Trademark Licensure as a Remedy for Monopolization. *Catholic University Law Review*, 26, 589–605.

dos Santos, F., Ncube, C.B. and Ouma, M., 2022. Intellectual Property Framework Responses to Health Emergencies – Options for Africa. *South African Journal of Science*, 118(5/6). https://doi.org/10.17159/sajs.2022/12775

Dreyfuss, R.C., 2004. TRIPS-Round II: Should Users Strike Back? *University of Chicago Law Review*, 71(1), 21–35.

du Plessis, E. (ed.), 2012. *Adams & Adams Practical Guide to Intellectual Property in Africa*. Pretoria: Pretoria University Law Press.

Dye, T., 1972. *Understanding Public Policy*. Englewood Cliffs, NJ: Prentice Hall.

EQUINET and ECSA-HC, 2011. Preventing Substandard, Falsified Medicines and Protecting Access to Generic Medicines in Africa. *Supporting Global Health Diplomacy in East*, Central and Southern Africa Policy Series No. 24.

Friedrich, C.J. (ed.), 1962. *Nomos V: The Public Interest. Yearbook of the American Society for Political and Legal Philosophy*. New York: Atherton Press.

Gana, R.L., 1996. Prospects for Developing Countries Under the TRIPs Agreement. *Vanderbilt Journal of Transnational Law*, 29, 735–755.

Gervais, D., 2003. *The TRIPS Agreement: Drafting History and Analysis* (2nd ed.). London: Sweet and Maxwell.

Ghathi, J.T., 2011. *African Regional Trade Agreements as Legal Regimes*. Cambridge: Cambridge University Press.

Global Congress on Intellectual Property and the Public Interest, 2011. The Washington Declaration on Intellectual Property and the Public Interest. Available at http://infojustice.org/washington-declaration [accessed 1 March 2015].

Harris, D.P., 2007. TRIPS and Treaties of Adhesion Part II: Back to the Past or a Small Step Forward? *Michigan State Law Review*, 185–214.

Held, V., 1970. *The Public Interest and Individual Interests*. New York: Basic Books.

Helfer, L. and Austin, G.W., 2011. *Human Rights and Intellectual Property Mapping the Global Interface*. New York: Cambridge University Press.

Heywood, M., 2001. Debunking "Conglomo-talk": A Case Study of the Amicus Curiae as an Instrument for Advocacy, Investigation and Mobilization. *Law, Democracy & Development*, 5(2), 133–162.

Ho, L.S., 2012. *Public Policy and the Public Interest*. Abingdon: Routledge.

Hogwood, B.W. and Gunn, L., 1984. *Policy Analysis for the Real World*. Oxford: Oxford University Press.

Holmes, W.C., 1980. Compulsory Patent and Trademark Licensing: A Framework for Analysis. *Loyola University of Chicago Law Journal*, 12, 43–77.

Jain, T.R., Bajaj, B.K., Gupta, A. and Sandhu, A.S., 2008. *Development Economics*. New Delhi: VK Publications.

Jensen, E., 2005. *Western Sahara: Anatomy of a Stalemate*. London: Lynne Rienner Publishers.

Joireman, S.F., 2001. Inherited Legal Systems and Effective Rule of Law: Africa and the Colonial Legacy. *Journal of Modern African Studies*, 39(4), 571–596.

Kahn, T., 2014. IPASA Axes Committee in Wake of Patents Row. *Business Day*, 7 February 2014.

Kameni, I.E., 2015. Implementation of TRIPS Public Health Flexibilities in the African Intellectual Property Organisation (OAPI) Region: Problems and Prospects, Unpublished LLD Thesis, University of Pretoria. Available at http://hdl.handle.net/2263/52384 [accessed 17 October 2020].

Kapczynski, A., 2009. Harmonization and Its Discontents: A Case Study of TRIPS Implementation in India's Pharmaceutical Sector. *California Law Review*, 97(6), 1571–1649.

Kilic, B., 2015. *Boosting Pharmaceutical Innovation in the Post-TRIPS Era*. Cheltenham and Northampton: Edward Elgar.

Kolbeck, B., 2014. Legal Analysis on the Relationship between the AU/AEC and RECs: Africa Lost in a "Spaghetti Bowl" of Legal Relations? Thesis (LLM), University of Cape Town.

Kongolo, T., 2013a. *African Contributions in Shaping the Worldwide Intellectual Property System Farnham*. Surrey: Ashgate.

Kongolo, T., 2013b. Historical Developments of Industrial Property Laws in Africa. *WIPO Journal*, 5(1), 105–117.

Kongolo, T., 2014. Historical Evolution of Copyright Legislation in Africa. *WIPO Journal*, 5(2), 163–175.

Kung-Chung, L., 2012. The Need and Justification for a General Competition-Oriented Compulsory Licensing Regime. *IIC International Review of Intellectual Property and Competition Law*, 43(6), 679–699.

Lane, W.J., 1988. Compulsory Trademark Licensing. *Southern Economic Journal*, 54(3), 643–655.

Loewenson, R., Modisenyane, M. and Pearcey, M., 2014. African Perspectives in Global Health Diplomacy. *Journal of Health Diplomacy*, 1(2), 1–20.

Loren, L.P., 2008. The Pope's Copyright? Aligning Incentives with Reality by Using Creative Motivation to Shape Copyright Protection. *Louisiana Law Review*, 69, 1–41.

Maksus, K.K., 2009. The WIPO Development Agenda: A Cautionary Note. In Netanel, N.W. (ed.) *The Development Agenda: Global Intellectual Property and Developing Countries*. Oxford: Oxford University Press.

Matthews, D., 2005. TRIPS Flexibilities and Access to Medicines in Developing Countries: The Problem with Technical Assistance and Free Trade Agreements. *European Intellectual Property Review*, 27(11), 420–427.

Matthews, D. and Correa, C., 2011. *The Doha Declaration Ten Years on and Its Impact on Access to Medicines and the Right to Health*. New York: United Nations Development Programme.

May, C., 2007. *The World Intellectual Property Organisation: Resurgence and the Development Agenda*. Abingdon, Oxford: Routledge.

May, C., 2008. The World Intellectual Property Organisation and the Development Agenda. *Global Society*, 22(1), 97–113.

Medinilla, A., Byiers, B. and Apiko, P., 2020. *African Regional Responses to COVID-19*. ECDPM Discussion Paper No. 272. Available at https://ecdpm.org/work/african-regional-responses-to-covid-19 [accessed 5 January 2023].

Motsoeneng, T., 2014. Big Pharma May Threaten to Cut South Africa Investment in Generics Row. *Reuters*, 17 January 2014.

Musungu, S.F., 2012. *Pharmaceutical Patents, TRIPS Flexibilities and Access to Medicines in SADC'*. Gaborone: SADC.

Musungu, S.F., Villanueva, S. and Blasetti, R., 2004. *Utilizing Trips Flexibilities for Public Health Protection Through South-South Regional Frameworks*. Geneva, Switzerland: South Centre.

Ncube, C.B., 2009. Enforcing Patent Rights against Goods in Transit: A New Threat to Trans-Border Trade in Generic Medicines. *SA Mercantile Law Journal*, 21, 680–694.

Ncube, C.B., 2013. Harnessing Intellectual Property for Development: Some Thoughts on an Appropriate Theoretical Framework. *PER/PELJ*, 16(4), 369–487.

Ncube, C.B., 2015a. Fair is as Fair Does: Contractual Normative Regulation of Copyright User Contracts in South Africa. In Dinwoodie, G.B. (ed.) *Intellectual Property and General Legal Principles: Is IP a Lex Specialis*? Cheltenham: Edward Elgar, 49–68.

Ncube, C.B., 2015b. The Politics of National Intellectual Property Policy Design and the Provision of Health Services in South Africa. *South African Intellectual Property Law Journal*, 3, 15–39.

Ncube, C.B., 2022a. Intellectual Property and the African Continental Free Trade Area: Lessons and Recommendations for the IP Protocol. *Journal of International Trade Law and Policy*, 21(2), 105–121. https://doi.org/10.1108/JITLP-09-2021-0051

Ncube, C.B., 2022b. Limiting Access to Life-Saving Medications: Three South African Case Studies. In Bonadio, E. and O'Connell, A. (eds.) *Intellectual Property Excesses: Exploring the Boundaries of IP Protection*. Oxford: Hart, 163–177.

Ndulo, B.J., 2007. The Evolution of Global Development Paradigms and Their Influence on African Economic Growth. In Ndulu, B.J., O'Connell, S.A., Bates, R.H., Collier, P. and Soludo, C.C. (eds.) *The Political Economy of Economic Growth in Africa, 1960–2000*. Cambridge: Cambridge University Press.

Netanel, N.W., 2009. The WIPO Development Agenda and Its Development Policy Context. In Netanel, N.W. (ed.) *The Development Agenda: Global Intellectual Property and Developing Countries*. Oxford: Oxford University Press.

Nkomo, M., 2013. Rwanda's New Intellectual Property Law and Compulsory Licensing for Export Under the WTO: Not Quite a Panacea. *African Journal of International and Comparative Law*, 21(2), 279–294.

Okediji, R.L., 1999. Copyright and Public Welfare in Global Perspective. *Indiana Journal of Global Legal Studies*, 7(1), 117–189.

Okediji, R.L., 2003a. The International Relations of Intellectual Property: Narratives of Developing Country Participation in the Global Intellectual Property System. *Singapore Journal of International & Comparative Law*, 7, 315–385.

Okediji, R.L., 2003b. Public Welfare and the Role of the WTO: Reconsidering the TRIPs Agreement. *Emory International Law Review*, 17, 819–918.

Okediji, R.L., 2004. Africa and the Global Intellectual Property System: Beyond the Agency Model. *African Yearbook of International Law*, 12, 207–251.

Okediji, R.L., 2009. History Lessons for the WIPO Development Agenda. In Netanel, N.W. (ed.) *The Development Agenda: Global Intellectual Property and Developing Countries*. Oxford: Oxford University Press, 137–162.

Okediji, R.L., 2014. Public Welfare and the International Patent System. In Okediji, R.L. and Bagley, M.A. (eds.) *Patent Law in Global Perspective*. Oxford: Oxford University Press, 1–50.

Outterson, K., 2010. Disease-Based Limitations on Compulsory Licenses Under Articles 31 and 31*bis*. In Correa, C. (ed.) *Research Handbook on the Protection of Intellectual Property under WTO Rules*. Cheltenham: Edward Elgar, 673–697.

Owoeye, O.A., 2014. Compulsory Patent Licensing and Local Drug Manufacturing Capacity in Africa. *Bull World Health Organ*, 92, 214–219.

Park, C., Prabhala, A. and Berger, J., 2013. *Using Law to Accelerate Treatment Access in South Africa: An Analysis of Patent, Competition and Medicines Law*. New York: UNDP.

Public Affairs Engagement, 2014. Campaign to Prevent Damage to Innovation from the Proposed Draft National IP Policy in South Africa. *Proposal Prepared for PhRMA and IPASA*. Available at https://serve.mg.co.za/content/documents/2014/01/16/skmbt363140 11511040.pdf [accessed 19 March 2023].

Rahmatian, A., 2009. Neo-Colonial Aspects of Global Intellectual Property Protection. *The Journal of World Intellectual Property*, 12(1), 40–74.

Ratchlitz, R., 2014. Effective Private Law Harmonization: A Comparative Analysis of the EU Draft Regulation on Common European Sales Law and the OHADA Uniform Acts. *Journal of Comparative Law in Africa*, 47–65.

Republic of Botswana, 2013. *Implementation of TRIPS Flexibilities in National IP Legislation for Strengthening Access to Medicines in Botswana*. Gaborone: UNDP-SARPAM-Botswana Government Workshop Report.

Rodrigues, E.B., Jr. 2012. *The General Exception Clauses of the TRIPS Agreement: Promoting Sustainable Development*. New York: Cambridge University Press.

Royal Society for the Encouragement of Arts, Manufacturers and Commerce (RSA) 2006. Adelphi Charter on Creativity, Innovation and Intellectual Property. In *Promoting Innovation and Rewarding Creativity: A Balanced Intellectual Property Framework for the Digital Age 4–5*. London: RSA.

Samuelson, P., 2013. Is Copyright Reform Possible? *Harvard Law Review*, 126, 740–779.

Schmalensee, R., 1979. On the Use of Economic Models in Antitrust: The ReaLemon Case. *University of Pennsylvania Law Review*, 127(4), 994–1050.

Schubert, G., 1960. *The Public Interest: A Critique of the Theory of a Political Concept*. Glencoe: The Free Press.

Sell, S.K., 2011. Everything Old is New Again: The Development Agenda then and Now. *The WIPO Journal*, 3(1), 17–23.

Sen, A., 1997. *Development Thinking at the Beginning of the 21st Century*. LSE STICERD Research Paper No. DEDPS 02. DEDPS, 2. Suntory and Toyota International Centres for Economics and Related Disciplines. London: London School of Economics and Political Science.

Sen, A., 2000a. What is the Role of Legal and Judicial Reform in the Development Process? The Role of Legal and Judicial Reform in Development. *World Bank Legal Conference*, Washington, DC, 5 June 2000.

Sen, A., 2000b. A Decade of Human Development. *Journal of Human Development*, 1(1), 17–23.

Seuba, X., 2014. *International Regulation of Pharmaceuticals, Codification by Means of Legal Transplantation*, Information Note, Programme on Innovation, Technology and Intellectual Property, International Centre for Trade and Sustainable Development, Geneva, Switzerland, 3.

Shabalala, D., 2007. *A Citizen's Guide to WIPO*. Geneva: CIEL.

Shelley, T., 2004. *Endgame in the Western Sahara: What Future for Africa's Last Colony*? London: Zed Books.

Sibanda, M., 2013. Patent-related Flexibilities in Multilateral Treaties and Their Importance for Developing countries and LDCs. *2nd WIPO Inter-Regional Meeting on South-South Cooperation on Patents*, Trademarks, Geographical Indications, Industrial Designs and Enforcement, May 2013.

Smith, K.B., 2006. Economic Techniques. In Moran, M., Rein, M. and Goodin, R.E. (eds.) *The Oxford Handbook of Public Policy*. New York: Oxford University Press, 729–745.

Sorauf, F., 1957. The Public Interest Reconsidered. *Journal of Politics*, 19, 616–639.

Storing, H.J., 1964. Review: The Crucial Link: Public Administration, Responsibility, and the Public Interest. *Public Administration Review*, 24(1), 39–46.

Straight, L., 2021. A Case for Compulsory Licensing in Instances of Reverse Trademark Confusion. *Connecticut Law Review*, 464.

UNCTAD, 2011. *Using Intellectual Property Rights to Stimulate Pharmaceutical Production in Developing Countries: A Reference Guide*. Geneva: UNCTAD.

UNDP, 2014. *Human Development Report 2014 Sustaining Human Progress: Reducing Vulnerabilities and Building Resilience*. New York: UNDP.

UNDP, 2021. *Graduation of African Least Developed Countries (LDCs): Emerging Issues in a New Development Landscape*. New York: UNDP.

Vadwa, Y. and Shozi, B., 2020. Eighteen Years After Doha: An Analysis of the Use of Public Health TRIPS Flexibilities in Africa. *South Centre Research Papers*, 103.

Victor, J., 2020. Reconceptualizing Compulsory Copyright Licenses. *Stanford Law Review*, 72, 915–994.

Watal, J., 2011. From Punta Del Este to Doha and Beyond: Lessons from the TRIPs Negotiating Processes. *WIPO Journal*, 3(1), 24–35.

WHO, WIPO and WTO, 2012. *Promoting Access to Medical Technologies and Innovation: Intersections between Public Health, Intellectual Property and Trade*. Geneva: WHO, WIPO & WTO.

Wilson, R., 2006. Policy Analysis as Policy Advice. In Moran, M., Rein, M. and Goodin, R.E. (eds.) *The Oxford Handbook of Public Policy*. New York: Oxford University Press, 152–168.

WIPO, n.d.a. Activities by Unit. Available at www.wipo.int/about-wipo/en/activities_by_unit/ [accessed 26 April 2022].

WTO, n.d. Members Accepting Amendment of the TRIPS Agreement. Available at www.wto.org/english/tratop_e/trips_e/amendment_e.htm [accessed 5 January 2023].

Yu, P.K., 2009. A Tale of Two Development Agendas. *Ohio National University Law Review*, 35, 465–573.

2 National IP Policy Frameworks in Africa

2.1 Introduction

This chapter reprises national IP policies on the continent. Attention is given to IP policies because of their significant influence on IP legislation and the national IP institutional infrastructure. The chapter seeks to identify the stated national IP policy goals to gauge the appropriateness of national approaches to IP. For instance, a policy foundation that does not centre developmental priorities as found in the continental blueprint Agenda 2063 and national development plans, human rights considerations nor acknowledge prevailing national socio-economic realities is unlikely to be fit for purpose.

This chapter defines key terms used in the IP policy lexicon. Then it considers the significance of IP policies in Africa and the factors affecting policy design, including the role and impact of technical assistance. Next, it provides country profiles of some IP policies in Africa. These profiles are non-exhaustive because of the paucity of publicly available accurate information on national IP policies which is not remedied by the existing repositories such as WIPOLex or regional IP organisation websites. This is because a search of such repositories and websites shows that member states do not timeously lodge their policies there and neither do they publish them on their government websites. The chapter then evaluates these IP policies before concluding.

2.2 Definitions

It is apt to begin this chapter on IP policies with a clarification of terminology. In the discourse on IP policy, the phrases one encounters most frequently are "IP strategy," "IP policy" and "IP plan." An external evaluation of WIPO technical assistance pointed out that WIPO and some of its member states appear to use these terms interchangeably, even though there was a clear divergence in what the users of each term meant by it.[1] It is therefore necessary to define these terms before embarking on a substantive discussion to avoid replicating the shortcoming identified in WIPO documents and to ensure that the discussion proceeds from a point of clarity.

1 Deere-Birkbeck and Roca (2011) p. 80.

DOI: 10.4324/9781003310198-2

2.2.1 IP Policy

The definition of public policy is nebulous and several formulations have been suggested over the years.[2] This work adopts the UN's Committee of Experts in Public Administration (CEPA) and the Division for Public Administration and Development Management (DPADM) conceptualisation of public policy as:

1 The organising framework of purposes and rationales for government programs that deal with specified societal problems; and
2 The complex of programs enacted and implemented by the government.[3]

From this, one can deduce that an IP policy is the over-arching framework, consisting of aims and objectives for government programs that are directed at issues affected by, and affecting, IP. Such a policy would be cross-cutting, implicating issues of culture, education, health, scientific innovation and trade.

2.2.2 IP Strategy

In ordinary parlance a strategy is simply "a planned series of actions for achieving something."[4] In policy discourse, a strategy is defined as a "high-level plan or course of action that will be taken to bring change"[5] or to implement a policy. An IP strategy would therefore be a government's processes and procedures set to accomplish its IP policy objectives. WIPO advances the following two definitions of IP strategy:[6]

> A set of measures formulated and implemented by a government to encourage and facilitate the effective creation, development, management and protection of IP at national level . . .
>
> A comprehensive national document which outlines how all policy developments related to IP, and the implementation of these developments, should take place in a coordinated manner within a national framework.

As will be seen, several African states have joint policies and strategies, aptly named National IP Policy and Strategy (NIPPS). These are The Gambia, Ghana, Namibia and Nigeria.

2 Dye (1972) p. 2, Anderson (1984) p. 3, Hogwood and Gunn (1984) pp. 23–24, Wilson (2006) p. 154. Simon (2007) p. 1.
3 UN (n.d.).
4 Longman Dictionary of Contemporary English (2003).
5 Sykes (2011) p. 4.
6 WIPO Methodology for the Development of National Intellectual Property Strategies: Tool 1: The Process.

2.2.3 IP Plan

An IP plan is one level below a strategy. It arises out of the strategy and is one of its constituent parts, as is clear from its definition as "a set of actions for achieving something in the future, especially a set of actions that has been considered carefully and in detail."[7] Plans are more "strategic or directive" than policies.[8] A series of plans constitutes a strategy. Based on these definitions, to speak about IP plans is to take a very detailed approach that focuses on implementation. This book focuses on a higher level and discusses IP policies at the greatest level of abstraction when compared to strategies and plans.

2.2.4 IP Development Plan

Another term that is also frequently encountered in WIPO and national literature is "IP Development Plan" (IPDP). The earlier IPDPs are not publicly available, but descriptions of them are. For example, a 2008 WIPO Press Release stated the following with regard to Ghana's IPDP:

> The World Intellectual Property Organisation (WIPO) reinforced its cooperation with the Republic of Ghana with the signing on May 7, 2008 of an intellectual property (IP) development plan which aims to build the country's capacity to create, protect and utilise IP as a power tool for economic growth and development. . . . The IP Development Plan covers a range of activities including legislative advice and workshops on strategic use of different aspects of the IP system targeting various stakeholders including small and medium-sized enterprises, research and development institutes, and the judiciary. It also includes support and advice to promote the development of creative industries, electronic commerce, copyright collective management, traditional knowledge, agricultural development and plant varieties. The plan further seeks to enhance the country's IP infrastructure through modernising and automating national IP administration to ensure high quality service delivery, extensive training and public awareness programs and the development of a national IP strategy to support economic growth and development.[9]

An examination of publicly available IPDPs shows that they are IP–policy related strategic documents which usually also include detailed implementation steps or an IP Plan. Therefore, an IPDP is a comprehensive document made up of a state's IP policy direction, strategy and plans. This is seen in the case of Liberia which,

7 Longman Dictionary of Contemporary English (2003).
8 Howlett and Lejano (2013) p. 359.
9 WIPO (2008).

following a needs evaluation,[10] had an IPDP formulated in 2009, which was updated with WIPO technical assistance in 2017.[11] The 2017 IPDP contains the usual constituent elements of a national IP policy, strategy and plans, including sections on vision and mission, objectives, purpose, priority sectors and context. Whilst IPDPs are structured like IP policies they are not IP policies. Three examples illustrate this point: first, Ghana adopted its National IP Policy and Strategy (NIPPS) in 2016. Second, Botswana had an IPDP and also adopted an IP policy in 2022. Third, Mauritius' 2017 IPDP expressly acknowledges that the state has no IP policy and recommends that one be developed.[12]

2.2.5 *Policy Design, Governance and Public Administration*

The process of crafting or formulating policy is known as policy design, which is defined as

> the effort to more or less systematically develop efficient and effective policies through the application of knowledge about policy means gained from experience, and reason, to the development and adoption of courses of action that are likely to succeed in attaining their desired goals or aims.[13]

The policy design process unfolds in the context of governance and public administration, a field that has been the subject of sustained scholarship for a long time.[14] Oluwu notes that there are several definitions of governance and the concept is contested.[15] However, there are broadly two main core definitions. The first is used by the UN and conceives of governance as an intra-governmental leadership matter or "the manner in which (state) political leaders manage or use (or misuse) power – whether it promotes social and economic development or pursues agendas that undermine such goals."[16] The second category of definitions conceives of governance as "multi-organisational" and broader than governmental leadership because it "focuses on the sharing of authority for public management between state and non-state organisations."[17] The second definition has more currency and is more

10 Technical Assistance Database: Needs Evaluation and Technical Support Relating to the IP Development Plan Formulation for the Republic of Liberia 9 March – 8 April 2009.

11 Republic of Liberia Intellectual Property Development Plan (IPDP) for the Government of Liberia (2017), Republic of Liberia. Country Report on the Intellectual Property System, Republic of Liberia (2017).

12 Republic of Mauritius. National IP Development Plan for the Republic of Mauritius: Needs Evaluation Report and Implementation Matrix (2017) p. 12 and p. 14.

13 Howlett and Lejano (2013) p. 359.

14 Olowu (2002) p. 345

15 Olowu (2002) p. 345.

16 Olowu (2002) p. 346.

17 Olowu (2002) p. 346.

broadly accepted by scholars in the field.[18] For instance, it is clearly expressed in Howlett and Lejano's following definition of governance as:[19]

> the broadening of the notion of "government" away from a state-centered concept toward more diffuse, often boundary-spanning, networks of governmental and nongovernmental actors. . . . In its broadest sense, "governance" is a term used to describe the mode of coordination exercised by state actors in their interactions with societal actors and organisations.

The scope of this chapter does not extend to a detailed discussion of governance and public administration. Rather, having stated these working definitions as shown, it proceeds to consider the significance of IP policies in Africa and the factors affecting policy design, including the role and impact of technical assistance. Thereafter, it turns to an overview of some IP policies in Africa. As indicated in the introduction, this exercise is at best an approximation because there is as yet no complete database of IP policies and repositories such as WIPOLex and the regional IP organisations' websites do not contain all their member states' policies nor do all states publish their IP policies.

2.3 The Importance of IP Policies in Africa

As briefly shown in chapter one, in the 21st century African states have become more involved in the global IP law system, with one of their most auspicious moments being the adoption of the WIPO DA in 2007.[20] Since the adoption of the WIPO DA, several projects have been initiated in Africa with a view to enhancing development through appropriately calibrated IP systems. These systems are crafted through legislation thus making IP policies that inform the legislation a focal area for analysis of IP systems.

In an ideal world, legislation is informed by a thoroughly researched policy that has been comprehensively consulted upon. Many African states' reality is far from this ideal, as they have IP legislation that they inherited from their colonisers and have had to review to comply with TRIPS without the benefit of meaningful national policy formulation.[21] Many African states embarked on policy formulation only in the post-TRIPS era, some with the assistance of WIPO under the rubric of WIPO DA Recommendation 10, which mandates WIPO:

> To assist Member States to develop and improve national intellectual property institutional capacity through further development of infrastructure and other facilities with a view to making national intellectual property institutions more efficient and promot[ing] fair balance between intellectual

18 Olowu (2002) p. 346.
19 Howlett and Lejano (2013) pp. 365–366.
20 de Beer (2009) p. 15, Musungu (2010), May (2007).
21 Ncube (2018) p. 419.

property protection and the public interest. This technical assistance should also be extended to sub-regional and regional organisations dealing with intellectual property.

This, then, is an important undertaking which should enable African states to reset the course of their IP strategies, policies, law, institutions and practices in alignment with their developmental goals. Therefore, technical assistance must be carefully conceptualised and delivered to ensure that this opportunity is well used. In particular, the way African states are leveraging technical assistance from WIPO and other developmental agencies in the furtherance of their socio-economic goals is of great significance. An external review and an evaluation of WIPO's technical assistance with respect to IP policy were conducted at the organisation's behest.[22] It is not possible for this chapter to undertake a similar evaluation because the documents detailing the legislative and policy advice provided by WIPO and other relevant information are held in confidence. Therefore, the following sections discuss WIPO technical assistance in relatively abstract terms, without reference to the minutiae of the agreements between it and its member states, nor the full detail of the activities carried out thereunder.

2.4 Factors Affecting IP Policy Design

Deere-Birkbeck states that national IP policy formulation and law reform processes are significantly shaped by a trio of factors, namely "(i) the degree of public engagement; (ii) the internal capacity of governments on IP matters; and (iii) the degree of government coordination."[23] Pugatch identifies the same three factors although he merges (ii) and (iii) and creates a new third factor of "global influences on decision-making regarding IP policies."[24] The next few paragraphs of this chapter discuss Deere-Birkbeck's three factors and Pugatch's fourth factor. The fifth factor it discusses is the role and impact of technical assistance.

Where these five factors are in deficit, the resultant IP policy and consequent legislative reforms are sub-optimal. To put it differently, IP policy or reform that has been hampered by limited public consultation, low levels of governmental capacity on IP and co-ordination, and policy space that has not been meaningfully leveraged invariably fails to deliver outcomes that are in the national public interest. Consequently, these policies or reforms fail to advance the relevant state's national socio-economic and developmental goals.

22 Deere-Birkbeck and Roca (2011), WIPO CDIP: Tenth Session. Geneva, 12–16 November 2012. Evaluation Report on the Project on Improvement of National, Sub-Regional and Regional IP Institutional and User Capacity. CDIP/10/7.

23 Deere-Birbkeck (2009) p. 113.

24 Pugatch (2011) p. 72.

2.4.1 Public Engagement and Interest Representation

Stakeholders or policy actors involved in public engagement have been clustered into three categories at primary, secondary and tertiary levels.[25] The primary level consists of the executive arm of government which, in the case of South Africa, Booysen describes as being constituted of the ruling party, cabinet, the presidency and policy bureaucrats. The last-named are defined as "top officials in government departments, including the Directors-General and their immediate circles of policy advisers and policy consultants."[26] The secondary level comprises "policy partners of government," which will vary from state to state, but are most likely to include business, labour, the legislature, the judiciary to the extent that it makes rulings that affect policy formulation and implementation, and other spheres of government, such as provincial and local government.[27] The tertiary level includes those in civil society and other actors who participate in policy making when the issues at stake intersect with their mandate or the interests of the constituencies they serve or represent. Stakeholder participation and public engagement are critically important aspects of policy making and legislative processes which contribute to efforts to make policies and laws context sensitive and aligned to national priorities. Consequently, national laws and constitutions include provisions for stakeholder participation and public engagement. For example, the Constitution of South Africa, 1996, at sections 56(d) and 69 (d) provides that the bicameral parliament, namely the National Assembly and the National Council of Provinces, "may receive petitions, representations or submissions from any interested persons or institutions." In addition, there are national guidelines on the conduct of public participation,[28] as well as relevant case law.[29]

Amongst the many factors that negatively affect public consultation, perhaps the key factor is the tendency to frame IP matters as technical issues upon which only appropriately trained individuals can comment. Such perceptions are bolstered by the use of jargon in consultative documents that then places the debate beyond those not schooled in the jargon and legalese. In addition, the failure to properly contextualise these IP matters as having a wider societal significance also discourages the public from engaging with them. In some cases this approach may be intentional and adopted with a view to avoiding public engagement and in others it may be an unintended consequence of the adoption of an overly technical approach. Public engagement may be encouraged by the involvement of civil society.

Another detrimental feature of public engagement and stakeholder consultation is the opportunity for the processes to be overrun by the views of the better resourced and highly organised stakeholders, who then advance an unbalanced approach that best serves their interests to the disadvantage of other interests. This

25 Booysen (2001) p. 132.
26 Booysen (2001) p. 134.
27 Booysen (2001) pp. 136–139.
28 Republic of South Africa, Department of Provincial and Local Government (2007).
29 Nyati (2008).

is most pronounced in states where corporate or business lobbying is entrenched as a part of IP policy making and legislative processes, as is the case in the United States.[30] The phenomenon and its impact on multi-lateral norm setting has been discussed by several scholars.[31] On the African continent, such lobbying has not yet reached the same extent, although there have been instances where concerns have been raised about the manner of corporate interest representation. Whilst lobbying has its place and may have a positive impact on policy making,[32] it is important to comment, as has been done previously, on its potential negative impacts.

South Africa presents a case study of an instance where lobbying almost upended a national policy making process. It was in the early stages of South Africa's policy design process when media coverage detailed the involvement of a US-based lobbying firm in the process, to which the Minister of Health had a very robust response, likening the leaked plan to genocide and an attempt to bulldoze South Africa.[33] He emphasised that the national approach was human rights based and intended to preserve lives and health. This episode became known as Pharmagate 2 and led to leadership changes in the national association of pharmaceutical companies. The first Pharmagate related to the legislative amendments to the Medicines and Related Substances Control Act of 1965 and involved litigation[34] which was settled following a strong civil society campaign and a political resolution between South Africa and the US which included an executive order from the Clinton administration.[35] As I and others have argued, the discourse and strategies employed by stakeholders in the public engagement process and related legislative or policy design processes have a huge impact on how a state develops its IP instruments.[36] From this instance, it can be seen that in South Africa three main types of interventions have been deployed, namely lobbying, litigation and civil society activism, including demonstrations.

2.4.2 Governmental Capacity and Co-ordination

In relation to governmental capacity, the most important determinant factors are "the level of technical IP capacity in governments, the strength and efficiency of government institutions, and the relative autonomy of IP offices responsible for TRIPS implementation."[37] Unfortunately, in most governmental institutions, technical capacity is weak and capacity resides in a few technocrat IP office staffers

30 Liu (1994) pp. 87–88, Litman (2009).
31 Gad (2003).
32 Hall and Deardorff (2006) p. 69.
33 Ncube (2015) pp. 34–35.
34 *The Pharmaceutical Manufacturers Association & Others v the President of the Republic of South Africa & Others* Case no 4183/98, High Court.
35 Executive Order 13155 of 10 May 2000 Access to HIV/AIDS Pharmaceuticals and Medical Technologies para 10(a).
36 Ncube (2022), Ncube (2021), Ncube (2015), Darch (2014), Heywood (2001).
37 Deere-Birbkeck (2009) p. 115.

who receive significant levels of technical training from WIPO. The manner in which technical assistance is rolled out, in such contexts, is significant primarily because the sometimes IP-centric message of WIPO[38] gets fed without nuance to developing country officials who imbibe the message and translate it into national positions, without the necessary further calibration.[39] One of the reasons for this failure to factor in public interest considerations is that some of these technocrat national IP office personnel often have no training in public policy.[40] Consequently, their focus remains on national compliance with international obligations rather than the appropriate nuancing of policy and law.[41] Due to their expertise, they tend to be autonomous and are often tasked with policy design through to legislative drafting with little input from outside a closed circle of IP attorneys and right-holder groups. Legislatures rely heavily on the expertise of IP offices and the responsible ministries and, feeling out of their depth, frequently simply pass these laws without any input of their own nor of others outside the circle. This type of IP regulation has been aptly labelled "insider governance."[42]

This unfortunate state of affairs can be remedied in at least three ways. One is to revise the WIPO message so that it is not primarily IP-centric and generic but includes context-specific advice that is development orientated. Indeed, this is one of the aims of the WIPO DA. The second way is to capacitate IP office and government department personnel so that they are more appreciative of the developmental and public interest relevance of IP and are skilled in aligning IP laws and policies to these wider goals. The third way is to open up the insider governance model so that other players who may be more public interest orientated are included in deliberations on policy formulation and/or reforms. Progress is being made on all three fronts and although the policy making space remains heavily contested, the centring of developmental perspectives and the involvement of more voices in policy formulation are welcome developments.

The third factor affecting IP reforms and policies, government coordination, is affected by the relationship between government departments, those departments with the relevant country's Geneva representatives and between third parties such as international organisations and donor agencies.[43] Here, national departments may have different positions on certain aspects. For example, a department of trade and industry may be more IP-centric and right-holder focused in its approach, whilst a department of arts and culture or health may be more user-, patient- or author/creator-friendly and thus less IP-centric in its views. If one of these departments is seized with IP policy making, it may do so in a manner that sidelines the approach of the other departments. A country's Geneva-based representatives

38 For example, WIPO technical assistance has been faulted for not incorporating flexibilities; see Abdel Latif (2011) p. 37, Netanel (2009) p. 7.

39 Deere-Birbkeck (2009) pp. 114–115.

40 Deere-Birbkeck (2009) p. 115.

41 Deere-Birbkeck (2009) p. 116.

42 Deere-Birbkeck (2009) p. 116.

43 Deere-Birbkeck (2009) p. 117.

may be more in tune with public interest views due to their proximity to, and interaction with, international civil society groups. Therefore, they may advance more pro-development positions on behalf of a country at international fora that do not seem to be taken up at national level. At national level, right-holders may have more influence over IP offices and government departments due to funding models that see IP offices deriving most of their income from right-holder fees. IP offices and government departments are also heavily influenced by WIPO in a way that has been characterised as "a combination of material enticements and socialization."[44]

2.4.3 Global Influences

The fourth factor, that of global influences, is in turn a coalescence of three other considerations.[45] First, states are obliged to comply with binding international IP agreements to which they are party. As noted in chapter one, this will invariably include TRIPS. Secondly, they may also be bound to regional, sub-regional and bi-lateral trade agreements which limit their policy choices. Policy space is often whittled down by concessions made in trade agreements.[46] Finally, as a result of globalisation, they may have to factor in the interests of non-citizen parties. This is mostly seen when industry lobbies get involved in domestic policy formulation and legislative processes as seen in South Africa's two "pharmagates," discussed previously.

2.4.4 Technical Assistance

IP-specific technical assistance may be rendered to developing countries and LDCs directly by developed states, the WTO and WIPO, other UN specialised organisations, civic society or any other interested parties. The provision of legal-technical assistance to its member states is one of WIPO's core functions.[47] Following the entry into force of TRIPS, WIPO and WTO entered into a co-operation agreement regarding their mutual provision of legal-technical assistance and technical co-operation to each other's developing-country member states.[48] More recently, WIPO, WTO and WHO have hosted trilateral symposia and published studies on public health, intellectual property and trade.[49] In recent years the symposia have focussed on new technologies,[50] and in the wake of the COVID-19 pandemic, the 2022 trilateral symposium held on 16 December 2022 was convened

44 Deere-Birbkeck (2009) p. 125.
45 Pugatch (2011).
46 Correa (2006), Sell (2007), Frankel (2008).
47 Article 4(v) Convention Establishing the WIPO (1967).
48 Article 4 Agreement between the WIPO and the WTO (1995). For commentary, see Salmon (2003).
49 WTO, WHO and WIPO (2020), WIPO (n.d.).
50 WIPO (2019).

under the theme "COVID-19 Pandemic: Response, Preparedness, Resilience."[51] The three organisations have also launched a technical assistance platform specific COVID-19 to support member states.[52]

Developed countries are required to provide technical assistance to developing and LDC WTO members to aid their efforts to implement TRIPS standards by Article 67 of TRIPS, which provides:

> In order to facilitate the implementation of this Agreement, developed country Members shall provide, on request and on mutually agreed terms and conditions, technical and financial cooperation in favour of developing and least-developed country Members. Such cooperation shall include assistance in the preparation of laws and regulations on the protection and enforcement of intellectual property rights as well as on the prevention of their abuse, and shall include support regarding the establishment or reinforcement of domestic offices and agencies relevant to these matters, including the training of personnel.

This requirement is amplified by the annex to the protocol amending TRIPS of 8 December 2005 (WT/L/641), which provides:

> 5. With a view to harnessing economies of scale for the purposes of enhancing purchasing power for, and facilitating the local production of, pharmaceutical products, it is recognized that the development of systems providing for the grant of regional patents to be applicable in the Members described in paragraph 3 of Article 31*bis* should be promoted. To this end, developed country Members undertake to provide technical cooperation in accordance with Article 67 of this Agreement, including in conjunction with other relevant intergovernmental organisations.

The process which has been followed to meet this obligation has included the submission of status updates and detailed requests for assistance by LDCs to the TRIPS Council, technical assistance fora and the implementation of some projects.[53] Technical assistance has been rendered to developing states and LDCs pursuant to this process. There are numerous instances of the provision of such technical assistance which are curated in a catalogue of DA projects and outputs.

51 WIPO (2022a).

52 The WHO-WIPO-WTO COVID-19 Technical Assistance Platform: www.who-wipo-wto-trilateral.org/

53 Blakeney and Mengistie (2011) p. 250, referring to an IP Technical Assistance Forum sponsored by the UK Department for International Development (DFID) in 2006 and a pilot project flighted by the ICTSD Program on IPRs and Sustainable Development in collaboration with Saana Consulting in 2007.

However, for purposes of this discussion, the following two initiatives are of immediate interest:

1 Improvement of National, Sub Regional and Regional IP Institutional and User Capacity (Development Agenda Project DA_10_05)
2 The WIPO Director General–Led Framework on Designing National IP Strategies[54] under which WIPO rolled out an IP Policy Toolkit.

These initiatives are outlined in the following sections.

Improvement of National, Sub-Regional and Regional IP Institutional and User Capacity

This three-year project (WIPO DA Project DA_10_05) was initiated in April 2009 and completed in April 2012 under Recommendation 10 of the WIPO DA. It was initially intended to be completed in two years with five pilot countries, namely the Dominican Republic, Mali, Moldova, Mongolia and Tanzania.[55] Its objective was the creation of tools to be used in the policy making cycle[56] by providing an integrated set of policies and strategies, institutional and enterprise-level interventions, including tools and mechanisms, directed at IP administrations, at the national, sub-regional and regional levels, and to enterprise support institutions, the aim being to enhance both the efficiency and utilisation of the IP system in developing LDCs, as well as countries in transition, by fulfilling their development objectives.[57]

For purposes of implementation, the project was divided into the following three distinct rungs:[58]

a) to develop and pilot a standard methodology for IP policy/strategy development and institutional reform;
b) to promote work sharing or other cooperation mechanisms, with a focus on the Caribbean region; and

54 www.wipo.int/ipstrategies/en/.
55 WIPO CDIP: Eighth Session. Geneva, 14–18 November 2011. Progress Reports on Development Agenda Projects. CDIP/8/2 Annex VIII pp. 2–3.
56 WIPO Methodology and Tools for the Development of National IP Strategies (2014). Also see WIPO; CDIP. Project Documents for Implementation of Recommendations 2, 5, 8, 9 and 10. CDIP/3/INF/2. (2009), CDIP Progress Report on Projects for Implementation of Recommendations 2, 5, 8, 9 and 10. CDIP/4/2 Annex VIII (2009).
57 WIPO CDIP: Sixth Session. Geneva, 22–26 November 2010. Progress Reports on Development Agenda Projects. CDIP/6/2 Annex IX p. 1.
58 WIPO CDIP: Tenth Session. Geneva, 12–16 November 2012. Evaluation Report on the Project on Improvement of National, Sub-Regional and Regional IP Institutional and User Capacity. CDIP/10/7 p. 8.

c) to develop and/or improve IPR support services for SMEs, through developing and piloting standardised methodology for surveys/studies on IP and SMEs, training of trainers and further developing IP panorama.

Of these items, rung (a) is of relevance to this section. A sixth pilot country, Algeria, was included in the project in May 2011.[59] This project was externally reviewed along with other WIPO technical assistance projects in the 2008–2010 biennium and a final review report was issued in August 2011.[60] This report found that the project implementation process was iterative and responsive but that the audit and benchmarking tools which had been developed were "imperfect."[61] It pointed out specific inadequacies in the benchmarking questionnaire and lamented the fact that the toolkit did not provide countries with implementation, monitoring and evaluation support after their adoption of IP policies.[62] In May 2012 the DAG group and the Africa Group proposed that the Secretariat should publish the "tools, methodologies and other relevant documentation" that were developed under this project.[63] Consequently, the toolkit was published on the WIPO website and may be used by any country. It consists of the following four tools:

Tool 1: The Process[64]
Tool 2: Baseline Questionnaire[65]
Tool 3: Benchmarking Indicators[66]
Tool 4: National IP Strategies (NIPS) Online Survey[67]

Following the completion of the project and the publication of the toolkit, WIPO undertook its own review of the project, under the leadership of an external expert. This review found that its implementation process was sufficiently consultative and responsive to the needs of member states.[68] The review also found that the

59 WIPO CDIP: Eighth Session. Geneva, 14–18 November 2011. Progress Reports on Development Agenda Projects. CDIP/8/2 Annex VIII p. 3.
60 WIPO (2012), Deere-Birkbeck and Roca (2011).
61 Deere-Birbkeck and Roca (2011) p. 82.
62 Deere-Birkbeck and Roca (2011) pp. 83–84.
63 WIPO CDIP: Ninth Session. Geneva, 7–11 May 2012. Joint Proposal by the Development Agenda Group and the Africa Group on WIPO's Technical Assistance in the Area of Cooperation for Development. CDIP 9/16.
64 WIPO Methodology for the Development of National Intellectual Property Strategies: Tool 1: The Process WIPO Pub_958_1 (2014).
65 WIPO Methodology for the Development of National Intellectual Property Strategies Tool 2: Baseline Questionnaire WIPO Pub 958 2 (2014).
66 WIPO Methodology for the Development of National Intellectual Property Strategies Tool 3: Benchmarking Indicators WIPO Pub 958_3 (2014).
67 WIPO Methodology for the Development of National Intellectual Property Strategies Tool 4: National IP Strategies (NIPS) Online Survey (2014).
68 WIPO CDIP: Tenth Session. Geneva, 12–16 November 2012. Evaluation Report on the Project on Improvement of National, Sub-Regional and Regional IP Institutional and User Capacity.

toolkit is both "replicable and adaptable," as evidenced by its use by at least 10 other countries.[69] However, it found that a "baseline analysis" ought to have been conducted in Tanzania prior to the commencement of work on a single IP policy for the country's bifurcated legal regime.[70] The evaluation report noted that whilst the project had been "fairly well designed," significant "political risks associated with both the IP strategies and the subregional/regional component of the project" had been overlooked.[71] These risks were the national contexts and the political processes which were the ultimate determinants of whether policies were adopted. Consequently, although draft policies had been prepared, not all of the pilot states adopted them. The evaluation team made the related point that the abrupt end of the project meant that beneficiary states were uncertain as to the next steps and who had responsibility for them, citing Tanzania as an example of this, which resulted in stagnation.[72]

After the conclusion of the project in 2012, work seemed to be continuing on Tanzania's IP policy, in 2022, a decade later. In a report at the end of 2014, WIPO reported that it was still in consultation with Tanzania in relation to the formulation of its IP Strategy and IP Policy.[73] A bifurcated national IP policy has been developed, heeding the 2012 review report's comments on the need for separate policies for Tanzania-Mainland and Zanzibar. The Business Registrations and Licensing Agency, which administers IP for Tanzania-Mainland, published an action plan for the development of IP policies for the mainland and Tanzania-Zanzibar on its website.[74] However, as of January 2023 the policies had not yet been formally adopted by Tanzania. Likewise, for Algeria, another project pilot state, beyond a series of entries in the Technical Assistance Database on the formulation of a national IP strategy for Algeria in 2011–2012,[75] there is no public information on the adoption of an IP policy. These two examples demonstrate very slow progress towards the conclusion of a policy making process, even with technical assistance.

CDIP/10/7 p. 16.

69 WIPO CDIP: Tenth Session. Geneva, 12–16 November 2012. Evaluation Report on the Project on Improvement of National, Sub-Regional and Regional IP Institutional and User Capacity. CDIP/10/7 p. 17.

70 WIPO CDIP: Tenth Session. Geneva, 12–16 November 2012. Evaluation Report on the Project on Improvement of National, Sub-Regional and Regional IP Institutional and User Capacity. CDIP/10/7 p. 17.

71 para 34 and 35.

72 para. 38.

73 WIPO Committee on Development and Intellectual Property (CDIP): Thirteenth Session. Geneva, 19–23 May 2014. Director General's Reports on Implementation of the Development Agenda. CDIP 13/2.

74 Action Plan for Realising the IP Potentials of Tanzania.

75 WIPO Technical Assistance Database Beneficiary Country: Algeria www.wipo.int/tad/en/activitysearchresult.jsp?bcntry=DZ

WIPO Framework for Developing National IP Strategies for Innovation

In 2011 WIPO also initiated a second project, the Framework for Developing National IP Strategies for Innovation (the IP Strategies Framework), which it describes as having been established

> to create a framework to assist all countries in developing national IP strategies for innovation which directly reference and support their development needs and priorities and take into account their specific economic circumstances and aspirations. The framework, which will provide a conceptual basis for the design of IP strategies, has strong links with project DA_10_05, which aims to develop a practical methodology, validated by a piloting process in selected countries, using a series of practical tools.[76]

The framework was to be developed by "expert working groups comprised of eminent development economists from around the world, IP experts and advisors from UN organisations, in the fields of trade, environment, culture and education, industry, health, agriculture, and science and technology."[77] This project approached IP policy making from a different vantage point than that taken by the WIPO DA project. The former project was conceptualised as a "high-level," expert-driven initiative aimed at ministerial level, whilst the latter was "a bottom or ground up approach" aimed at giving voice to "national stakeholders."[78] The 2011 External Review Report noted that a clear articulation of the synergy between the two projects was required.[79] It was not possible at that stage for the external reviewers to undertake an in-depth evaluation of the IP Strategies Framework project as it was in very early stages of implementation.

The DAG and Africa Group echoed the external reviewers' call for clarification of the relationship between the two projects and requested that regular updates be provided to the CDIP on the IP Strategies Framework project's objective, purpose, methodology and outcomes.[80]

76 WIPO CDIP: Eighth Session. Geneva, 14–18 November 2011. Progress Reports on Development Agenda Projects. CDIP/8/2 Annex VIII p. 3.

77 WIPO CDIP: Eighth Session. Geneva, 14–18 November 2011. Progress Reports on Development Agenda Projects. CDIP/8/2 Annex VIII p. 3. Also see WIPO General Assembly Forty-First (21st Extraordinary) Session. Geneva, 1–9 October 2012. Report of the CDIP. WO/GA/41/12 Appendix III pp. 4–5.

78 Deere-Birkbeck and Roca (2011) p. 84.

79 Deere-Birkbeck and Roca (2011) p. 85.

80 WIPO CDIP: Ninth Session. Geneva, 7–11 May 2012. Joint Proposal by the Development Agenda Group and the Africa Group on WIPO's Technical Assistance in the Area of Cooperation for Development. CDIP 9/16 p. 10.

Following this, the management response to the External Review, tabled at the CDIP's ninth session in 2012, indicated that the two projects were[81]

> being mainstreamed into the Organisation's work, in collaboration with the Regional Bureaus, and will be further developed and implemented through the Regional Bureaus' work. The ensuing national IP strategies will provide the comprehensive framework for WIPO's IP-related technical assistance to countries to ensure alignment with national development goals and accountability, as recommended in the Report.

Having thus been mainstreamed, the two projects were then not reported upon in the Director General's Reports on Implementation of the Development Agenda and Progress Reports submitted to the CDIP at its 11th session (May 2013),[82] 12th session (November 2013),[83] 13th session (May 2014)[84] and 14th session (November 2014),[85] nor in any subsequent reports since then.

The Dakar Declaration on IP for Africa

As outlined in chapter one, the Dakar Declaration on IP for Africa of 2015 was a pointed articulation of Africa's expectations regarding technical assistance provided in the process of mainstreaming the WIPO DA. Chronologically, it followed the conclusion of the two projects outlined earlier and therefore can be taken to be informed by their experience of technical assistance up to that point. In brief, it emphasised the need for the provision of technical assistance that is development orientated, centres stated priorities and is coordinated with the relevant AU structures, RECs, ARIPO and OAPI. In other words, it should be context specific and grounded in local realities and informed by the expertise and experience of local institutions. Technical assistance rendered by WIPO since 2015 would therefore be expected to be guided by these expectations.

81 WIPO CDIP: Ninth Session. Geneva, 7–11 May 2012. Management response to the external review of WIPO technical assistance in the area of co-operation for development (CDIP/8/inf/1). CDIP9/14.

82 WIPO CDIP: Eleventh Session. Geneva, 13–17 May 2013. Director General's Report on Implementation of the Development Agenda. CDIP/11/2.

83 WIPO CDIP: Twelfth Session. Geneva, 18–21 November 2013: Progress reports. CDIP 12/2.

84 WIPO Committee on Development and Intellectual Property (CDIP): Thirteenth Session. Geneva, 19–23 May 2014. Director General's Reports on Implementation of the Development Agenda. CDIP 13/2.

85 WIPO CDIP: Fourteenth Session. Geneva, 10–14 November 2014. Revised Report on the Measurement of the Millennium Development Goals (MDGs) in other United Nations Agencies and Specialized Agencies, and on the Contribution to WIPO to the Implementation of the MDGs (November 2014) CDIP/14/12 Rev. Annex II, 8; and CDIP: Fourteenth Session. Geneva, 10–14 November 2014. Progress Reports. CDIP/14/2.

2.5 State Profiles: National IP Policies

This section summarises the findings of a survey of African states' IP policies conducted primarily online through searching WIPO's online repository of national IP laws and related literature, WIPOLex,[86] WIPO's Technical Assistance Database,[87] the relevant states' government websites and a general internet search for news and other reports.[88] The aim of the survey was to

1 determine if a country has an IP policy in place;
2 if there is a policy in place, to summarise the policy; and
3 if there is no policy, to establish if there is any publicly available information on the preparation of such a policy.[89] In some states, there is an IPDP in place and where this is the case it is indicated.

Where an IP policy or IPDP is both in place and publicly available, a brief commentary on its contents is given. However, in many cases these were not publicly available. There are separate sections dealing with policies and IPDPs as these are different instruments.

A major limitation of the survey was the lack of publicly available official information about national IP policies. States seem to prefer maintaining their policies in confidence and WIPOLex and other repositories publish only what is submitted to them for publication. The WIPO Technical Assistance Database is useful since it provides details of activities and even though it does not disclose the substantive content of technical legal advice given. The details pertaining to those activities that are listed are also scant. All that is usually provided is a meeting title, without an agenda or related documents.[90] The picture that emerged from the survey is thus limited. However, it is useful to the extent that it maps IP policy development in Africa.

The findings of the first survey were tabulated in the first edition and reflected 10 states with an IP policy or IPDP in place, 19 states with IP policies under formulation and 25 states for which no IP policy formulation information was available.[91] Since then, there have been several changes as follows:

(1) Some previously unavailable documents are now available, making it possible to assess them and categorise them properly. For instance, whilst reliance was placed on references reporting that IP policies or strategies were in place for Liberia, Mauritius, Senegal and Seychelles, it is now clear that the instruments are actually IPDPs.

86 www.wipo.int/wipolex/en/main/home
87 www.wipo.int/tad/en/
88 See Ncube (2013–2015) for early survey results.
89 Ncube (2013).
90 For a similar finding see Deere-Birkbeck and Roca (2011) p. 95.
91 Ncube (2016) p. 54.

(2) Policy making has been completed and new IP policies were adopted by several states, namely Botswana, Egypt, The Gambia, Madagascar, Malawi, Namibia, Nigeria, South Africa, Uganda and Zimbabwe.
(3) Existing policies were revised and issued for a new term in Rwanda and Zambia.
(4) IPDPs have been revised and issued for a new term in Liberia and Mauritius.
(5) IP policies have run their term and are yet to be renewed in Mozambique (IP Strategy 2008–2018) and Zimbabwe (IP Policy 2018–2022); and
(6) Several states are continuing or have stalled in their policy making processes.

A revised table (Table 2.1) is presented that reflects these updates. The table also reflects the existence of REC IP policies, some of which were developed with WIPO technical assistance[92] (discussed in chapter three) because although some states do not have national IP policies, they draw guidance from the REC policies. The table is followed by a narrative summary which provides further information on those states that have IP policies and IPDPs as well those states that are currently engaged in policy formulation. The summaries note only the main or overarching objectives of each policy and do not itemise specific objectives. Each policy references relevant development-orientated national instruments such as national development plans (NDPs), related national policies and legislation. Some also refer to constitutional provisions. Many states have IP-adjacent policies which include policies on IP, TK and TCEs.[93] These aspects are not detailed in the summaries, which focus exclusively on IP policies.

2.5.1 States With National IP Policies

Botswana

Botswana's National Competition Policy (2005) expressly excludes IP from its ambit. The country's Research, Science, Technology and Innovation (RSTI) policy (Republic of Botswana. Ministry of Infrastructure Science and Technology 2011) states at clause 5.9.3 that a national IP policy "needs to be developed." Consequently, the IPDP for the Republic of Botswana (2012) included a report on an IP Audit and a strategy road map for the development of a national IP policy. At the end of 2014, WIPO reported that it was in consultation with Botswana in relation

92 COMESA IP Policy (2011) supra, EAC Regional Policy on the Utilisation of Public Health WTO-TRIPS Flexibilities (2013) supra, ECOWAS Guidelines for Implementation of TRIPS Flexibilities in National Legislation to Improve Access to Medicines in the West African Region (2012) supra, SADC IP Framework and Guidelines (2018) supra, Technical Assistance Database: Visit to WIPO Headquarters by Three Senior Officials from COMESA, October 2011.

93 For example, South Africa: Policy Framework for the Protection of Indigenous Traditional Knowledge Through the Intellectual Property System and the Intellectual Property Laws Amendment Bill (2008) and Kenya: National Policy on Traditional Knowledge, Genetic Resources and Traditional Cultural Expressions (2009).

Table 2.1 IP Policies in Africa

REC IP POLICY COVERAGE	
COMESA Burundi, Comoros, Democratic Republic of Congo, Djibouti, Egypt, Eritrea, Eswatini, Ethiopia, Kenya, Libya, Madagascar, Malawi, Mauritius, Rwanda, Seychelles, Sudan, Uganda, Zambia, Zimbabwe	**EAC TRIPS Policy** Burundi Kenya Rwanda Tanzania Uganda
ECOWAS TRIPS Policy Benin, Burkina Faso, Cape Verde, Côte d'Ivoire, The Gambia, Ghana, Guinea, Guinea-Bissau, Liberia, Mali, Niger, Nigeria, Senegal, Sierra Leone, Togo	**SADC IP Framework and Guidelines** Angola, Botswana, Comoros, Democratic Republic of Congo, Eswatini, Lesotho, Madagascar, Malawi, Mauritius, Mozambique, Namibia, Seychelles, South Africa, United Republic of Tanzania, Zambia, Zimbabwe
States With National IP Policies (14)	
1. Botswana (2022)*	8. Namibia (2019–2024)
2. The Gambia (2018)	9. Nigeria (2022)
3. Ghana (2016)*	10. Rwanda (2018)**
4. Egypt	11. South Africa (2018)
5. Madagascar (2016)	12. Uganda (2019)
6. Malawi (2019)	13. Zambia (2020)**
7. Mozambique (2008–2018)	14. Zimbabwe (2018–2022)
States With IPDPs (6)	
15. Eswatini	18. São Tomé and Principe
16. Liberia***	19. Senegal
17. Mauritius***	20. Seychelles
States With IP Policies Under Formulation (11)	
21. Algeria	27. Mali
22. Burundi	28. São Tomé and Principe
23. Central African Republic	29. Sierra Leone
24. Chad	30. Tanzania
25. Kenya	31. Togo
26. Lesotho	

* Where a state has both and IPDP and an IP policy, only the IP policy is reflected in the table.
** Second policy
*** Second IPDP

to the formulation of its IP strategy.[94] Following the completion of a mapping exercise in 2011 and 2012, an IP Field Study report in 2017[95] and the necessary policy formulation processes, the Botswana IP Policy (BIPP) was launched in November 2022. The policy consists of seven chapters, titled as follows: (1) Introduction,

94 WIPO Committee on Development and IP (CDIP) Revised Report on the Measurement of the Millennium Development Goals (MDGs) in Other United Nations Agencies and Specialized Agencies, and on the Contribution to WIPO to the Implementation of the MDGs (November 2014) CDIP/14/12 Rev. Annex II, 8.

95 Republic ofBotswana IP Policy (BIPP) (2022) p. 17.

(2) Background, (3) Botswana's IP Landscape, (4) IP Framework, (5) Policy Focus Areas, (6) IP Policy Institutional Structure and (7) Policy Review, Monitoring and Evaluation. The BIPP lists the following five policy priority areas: (1) Enabling IP Governance Framework, (2) Financing for IP Generation and Commercialisation, (3) Development of IP Awareness, Education and Training Capacities, (4) IP Entrepreneurship and Enterprise Development and (5) strengthening IP negotiant structures.[96] The priority industries addressed under (4) are agri-business and agro-industries, the creative sector, healthcare, tourism, and information communications technologies.[97] The main policy objective is "to ensure that the entire IP governance framework contributes towards the harnessing of the country's IP potential for economic transformation as well as inclusive and sustainable economic growth and development."[98]

Egypt

Egypt's National IP Strategy (NIPS) was launched on 21 September 2022.[99] As of January 2023, the NIPS was not publicly available, so reliance as to its contents is placed on others. Loufti notes that these four goals drive it: "(1) Governance of the IP institutional Structure, (2) Configuring the legislative environment for IP, (3) Optimising the economic return of IP in achieving the sustainable development goals and (4) Raising awareness in the Egyptian society about IP."[100] The duration of the policy is reportedly five years (2022–2027), but without examining it, it is neither possible to confirm that nor to comment on it.

The Gambia

The Gambia's NIPPS 2018 was adopted by the cabinet in 2019.[101] Its contents comprise the following: (1) Introduction, (2) Vision, (3) Mission, (4) Objectives, (5) Policy Guiding Principles, (6) Key Policy and Strategic Issues, (7) Implementation, (8) Monitoring, Evaluation and Review and (10) Five-Year Implementation Plan. In the discussion of the Policy Guiding Principles, the NIPPS states that its main objective is "to provide a framework for effective utilisation of IP as an instrument for meeting national and sectoral development policy goals and enhancing social and economic development."[102] It recommends that "existing intellectual property laws [be] revised and new laws [be] enacted considering the goals and objectives of national and sectoral development policies, the need for balance between the interest of the right holders and the public as well as exploiting flexibilities available in international IP treaties to which the country

96 BIPP (2022) pp. 22–26.
97 BIPP (2022) pp. 24–26.
98 BIPP (2022) p. 22.
99 WIPO (2022b), Republic of Egypt (2022).
100 Loutfi (2022).
101 Ceesay 2020.
102 Republic ofThe Gambia NIPPS (2018–2023) p. 8.

belongs."[103] Worth noting is that it prioritises "empowerment of the youth and women, meeting the needs of persons with disabilities, addressing environment concerns and promotion of green technologies."[104] The implementation section outlines a timeframe, institutional arrangements, popularisation and resource mobilisation.

Ghana

Ghana's NIPPS was formulated under the auspices of the Swiss Ghana IP Project, which was a partnership between Ghana's Ministry of Trade and Investment, Ministry of Justice and the Swiss Federal Institute of IP.[105] The policy was developed with assistance from the US Commercial Law Development Program[106] and WIPO under an IPDP concluded in 2008.[107] The NIPPS was adopted[108] and launched in 2016.[109] I was unable to locate a copy of the NIPPS so it is not possible to outline its contents.

Madagascar

Madagascar was working on its national IP policy by 2013,[110] with financial assistance from the WTO and technical assistance from WIPO.[111] The IP Policy was launched in 2016,[112] however it has only been published in French.

Malawi

Malawi launched its National IP Policy in 2019 after a lengthy formulation process that was in motion by 2011, when it was reported that the country had a draft IP Policy.[113] The policy has the following sections: (1) Introduction, which includes the policy's purpose and how it aligns with other national policies and international instruments, (2) Broad Policy Direction, consisting of goal, outcomes and objectives, (3) Policy Priority Areas and (4) Policy Implementation Arrangements. Two

103 Republic of The Gambia NIPPS (2018–2023) p. 7.
104 Republic of The Gambia NIPPS (2018–2023) p. 7.
105 Hopeson (2013), Swiss Federal Institute of Intellectual Property (2011).
106 US Commercial Law Development Program (n.d.).
107 Mould Iddrisu (2010), WIPO (2008).
108 Swiss State Secretariat for Economic Affairs (SECO) (2013) p. 14.
109 Ntrakwah-Mensah (2016).
110 WIPO support to NEPAD in collaboration with other United Nations Agencies (2012–2013) p. 1.
111 Technical Assistance Database: Reconnaissance Mission as Part of the Formulation of Innovation and Intellectual Property Policy and Strategy in Madagascar and Planning and Training Mission as Part of the Technology Support Centers Program, 26–30 August 2013.
112 Republic of Madagascar, National Policy and Strategy of Innovation in the Field of Intellectual Property for Madagascar (2016).
113 Chatema (2011).

annexes are appended to the policy, namely an Implementation Plan for 2019–2023 and a Monitoring and Evaluation Plan. The priority areas listed under (3) are an "effective institutional framework for modernising administration of IPRs, generation and protection of IP Assets, Effective and Balanced Legal Regime for IPRs and IP Awareness Creation and Capacity Building."[114] The main policy objective is to "leverage IP as a tool for promoting and stimulating creativity and innovation for economic growth and development."[115]

Mozambique

Mozambique's ten-year IP Strategy (2008–2018) articulates the following vision:

> "The Mozambican government regards intellectual property as an instrument for stimulating and protecting creativity and innovation to promote the country's economic, scientific, technological and cultural development."[116] Its overall goal is "to create the basic preconditions for promoting creativity, the results of scientific and technological research and local innovative capacity, thereby furthering the use of the intellectual property system for the benefit of the scientific, technological, economic, cultural and social development of the country."[117]

The strategy cross-references several relevant national policies. It canvasses the current IP laws of the country, discusses the significance of IP and presents a strategic framework. This framework targets the following seven areas: (1) Dissemination of IP; (2) Education and IP; (3) Scientific and Technological Research; (4) Innovation and Competitiveness in Industry; (5) Traditional Knowledge and Biodiversity; (6) Creativity and Development of the Cultural Industry; and (7) Administration of the IP System. Annex II of the strategy presents an IP Action Plan which outlines 25 strategic goals to which short-term and medium-term actions are assigned. The mid-term achievement target was set as 2012. The policy was implemented and has lapsed, but has not yet been renewed, although plans are reportedly being made to do so.

Namibia

Namibia's NIPPS 2019–2024 developed with support from WIPO and was founded partially on an IP needs assessment which was also supported by WIPO.[118] The NIPPS is structured into four parts, namely (1) introduction, background, rationale, alignment and policy guiding principles, (2) policy direction consisting of vision,

114 Republic of Malawi, National IP Policy (2019) pp. 7–12.
115 Republic of Malawi, National IP Policy (2019) p. 6.
116 Republic of Mozambique, IP Strategy (2007) p. 17.
117 Republic of Mozambique, IP Strategy (2007) p. 18.
118 Republic of Namibia, National IP Policy and Strategy (NIPPS) (2019–2024) p. 2.

mission and goals and policy objectives and strategies, (3) implementation framework consisting of institutional arrangement, legal and regulatory arrangements, resource mobilisation, monitoring and evaluation framework and reporting and advocacy and dissemination (communication strategy) and (4) conclusion.[119] It has two annexes, one being an implementation five-year plan and the other a bibliography. The objectives of the NIPPS are:[120]

> using the intellectual property system as a tool for meeting development policy goals, encouraging the generation, protection and exploitation of intellectual property assets; providing guidance in the strengthening of the intellectual property legal and institutional framework; linking the national IP system with the international IP system and maximizing from opportunities offered by its membership to regional and international IP treaties and organisation s that administer such treaties.

Nigeria

Nigeria had commenced an IP policy formulation process, with technical assistance from WIPO, by 2013.[121] By June 2022, this process had generated a final draft of the NIPPS. It is expected that it will be validated, which may lead to some changes in the text, then it would be launched soon thereafter. The June 2022 version consists of six chapters: (1) Introduction, (2) Situational Analysis, (3) Strategic Direction, which includes vision, mission and strategic objectives, (4) Policy Objectives and Strategies, which itemises nine aspects, (5) Programs and Projects, which lists nine focal aspects and (6) Implementation Structure, which covers the necessary framework, communication, resource mobilisation, and monitoring, evaluation and reporting. The main policy objective is "to contribute towards the realization of Nigeria's current development plan (2021–2025) and long-term development agenda (Vision 2050)."[122]

Rwanda

Rwanda's first IP policy (2009)[123] ran its course and was revised in 2018. The revised policy consists of nine main topics as follows: (1) The Issue, (2) Context and Background, (3) Vision, Mission and Objectives, (4) Analysis, which covers IPRs, TK and TCEs, IP administration, enforcement and awareness, (5) Stakeholder Views, (6) Implementation Plan, (7) Financial Implications, (8) Legal Implications and (9) Handling Plan. Annexed to the policy is an implementation road map covering the periods from March 2018 onwards and March 2019

119 Republic of Namibia, NIPPS (2019–2024) p. 4.
120 Republic of Namibia, NIPPS (2019–2024) p. 12.
121 WIPO support to NEPAD in collaboration with other United Nations agencies (2012–2013) p. 3.
122 Republic of Nigeria, NIPPS (June 2022) p. 27.
123 WIPO support to NEPAD in collaboration with other United Nations agencies (2013) p. 3.

onwards without identifying any further dates. Under heading 4 are several legislative reform proposals with regard to each of the IPRs covered. The policy also expressly refers to TRIPS flexibilities and to the EAC TRIPS Flexibilities Policy in relation to patents.[124] The policy's main objective is as stated at paragraph 3.3 as being to provide "guidance and a road map to ensure that the IP laws, practices and strategies in Rwanda support and facilitate the achievement of the country's high-level vision and targets."

South Africa

After a long, drawn-out process, during which the draft national IP policy was released for public comment in September 2013, South Africa's IP policy Phase I was adopted by the cabinet in May 2018, as noted in chapter one. It consists of these substantive parts: (1) Introduction, (2) Problem Statement, (3) Purpose, (4) Strategy, (5) Inter-Ministerial Committee on IP, (6) Phase I, which focuses on IP and public health and international co-operation, (7) In-Built Agenda and (8) Conclusion.

The section on IP and public health covers these areas: (1) local manufacture and export, (2) substantive search and examination in the health sector, (3) patent opposition, (4) patentability criteria, (5) disclosure requirements, (6) parallel importation, (7) exceptions, (8) voluntary licences, (9) compulsory licences, (10) IP and competition law and (11) rule of law, legal certainty and security of investments.[125]

The policy states that its

> overarching objective is to ensure that this comprehensive IP Policy becomes a just, balanced, and integral part of the broader development strategy for South Africa by assisting in transforming the South African economy, and thereby leveraging human resources for the broader economic benefit, increasing local manufacturing, and generating more employment.[126]

It recommends several key reforms, including the introduction of substantive patent application examination "in the health sphere" and to leverage TRIPS health-related flexibilities to ensure that the protection of IPRs is coupled with "promoting public health, local manufacture, research and development, innovation, food security, environmental considerations, transfer of technology and broad socio-economic development."[127] The In-Built Agenda section indicates areas to be addressed in Phase II of the policy, which include "IPRs and the informal sector" and "IPRs and the environment/climate change/green technologies."[128] It also contains the monitoring and evaluation aspects of the policy.

124 Republic of Rwanda Revised IP Policy (2018) pp. 15–16.
125 The Intellectual Property Policy of the Republic of South Africa Phase I (2018) pp. 15–31.
126 The Intellectual Property Policy of the Republic of South Africa Phase I (2018) p. 2.
127 The Intellectual Property Policy of the Republic of South Africa Phase I (2018) p. 5.
128 The Intellectual Property Policy of the Republic of South Africa Phase I (2018) pp. 43–44.

Uganda

Uganda formulated its national IP policy with technical assistance from WIPO[129] and adopted it in 2019.[130] The policy consists of two chapters. The first chapter has the following subheadings: (1) Introduction, (2) Background and Context, (3) Situation Analysis, (4) Problem Statement and (5) Policy Development Process. The second chapter has the following headings: (1) Vision, (2) Mission, (3) National IP Policy Issues, (4) Policy Goals, (5) Policy Objectives, Statements, Strategies and Key Actions and (6) Policy Implementation. An IP policy monitoring and evaluation matrix is annexed to the policy. The main objectives or goals of the policy are: "a) To establish appropriate IP infrastructure that supports innovation and creativity; b) To develop human capital for the IP value chain; and c) To enhance utilisation of the IP system."[131]

Zambia

Zambia's first IP policy (2009) was finalised and adopted in 2010.[132] The 2009 policy contained an overview of then current law, a statement of the country's vision and goals for IP, a synopsis of related national policies, a discussion of guiding principles and a ten-year implementation framework. It also discussed the country's aspirations with regard to the protection of traditional knowledge and new plant varieties. The revised policy was adopted in 2020. It consists of the following chapters: (1) Introduction, (2) Situation Analysis, (3) Vision, (4) Rationale, (5) Guiding Principles, (6) Policy Objectives, (7) Measures and (8) Implementation Framework. The overall objective of the revised policy is "to facilitate the creation of an environment that stimulates and fosters the generation, protection, enforcement, management and increased exploitation of IPRs."[133]

Zimbabwe

Zimbabwe formulated a draft national IP policy, with technical assistance from WIPO,[134] which ultimately became the National IP Policy and Implementation Strategy (2018–2022). It consists of these four parts: (1) Introduction, (2) IP Policy, (3) Implementation Strategy and (4) Conclusion. The second part, which details the policy direction, proceeds under these sub-headings: (1) Vision Statement, (2)

129 WIPO Technical Assistance Database: Consultative Meeting and High-Level National IP Policy Meeting: The Role of Innovation and Creativity Policies and Strategies for Technological Capacity Building, Economic Growth and Development. Kampala, Uganda. 22–24 April 2013.

130 Republic of Uganda National Intellectual Property Policy (2019).

131 Republic of Uganda National Intellectual Property Policy (2019) p. 23.

132 WIPO support to NEPAD in collaboration with other United Nations Agencies (2012–2013). p. 3.

133 Republic of Zambia Revised National IP Policy (2020) p. 7.

134 WIPO Technical Assistance Database: Finalisation of the IP Policy and IP Strategy for the Republic of Zimbabwe. Harare, Zimbabwe. 4–5 November 2014.

Mission Statement, (3) Objectives, (4) Sectoral Focus. The overall objective is to "ensure that the entire IP governance framework . . . leverages the country's IP potential for inclusive and sustainable economic growth and development."[135] The nine priority sectors are agriculture; industry; health; education, training and professional development; environment; culture; trade; tourism; and small- and medium-scale enterprises. The implementation strategy in part 3 does not contain any timelines. The policy has lapsed and by January 2023 had not been revised and reissued for a further term.

2.5.2 States With IPDPs

Botswana and Ghana also had IPDPs but these are not summarised here because they now have IP policies.

Eswatini

In 2014 Eswatini commenced IP policy formulation with technical assistance from WIPO,[136] which it committed to finalising by 2020.[137] It seems this process was replaced with an IPDP which was validated in 2015.[138] However, it is not publicly available, so it is not possible to outline or comment on it.

Liberia

Liberia obtained technical assistance from WIPO with regard to the formulation of its IPDP, the terms of which are partially captured in an IPDP-needs evaluation report prepared in 2009.[139] The IPDP was revised and a new version was issued in 2017 (IP Development Plan (IPDP) for the Government of Liberia, 2017). It consists of these six sections: (1) Liberia IPDP, which covers the background, objectives of the assignment, process of developing the IPDP and linking the IPDP to existing NDPs, (2) Components of the IPDP, which are vision and mission, objectives, purpose, design and framework, priority sectors and context, (3) Strategic Objective 1: Building an IP conscious nation, (4) Strategic Objective 2: Developing Liberia as an IP power house, (5) Strategic Objective 3: Building a business friendly IP enforcement system and (6) Action Plan. An implementation matrix is annexed to the IPDP.

135 Republic of Zimbabwe National IP Policy and Implemental Strategy (2018–2022) p. 7.

136 WIPO Technical Assistance Database: National IP Policy Workshop: The Strategic Use of IP for Technological Capacity Building, Economic Growth and Development. Mbabane, Swaziland. 19–20 May 2014.

137 Dlamini (2014).

138 WIPO Technical Assistance Database: Validation of the IPDP Swaziland – Second Experts Field Mission, Mbabane, Swaziland 27–30 July 2015.

139 WIPO Intellectual Property Development Plan for the Republic of Liberia: Final Report on the Needs Evaluation (2009).

Mauritius

As indicated, Mauritius does not have an IP policy[140] but has an IPDP which was formulated with technical assistance from WIPO in 2009.[141] The IPDP was adopted and under implementation by the end of 2011.[142] In March 2014, it was reported that an IP Council would be set up to co-ordinate and lead national IP initiatives and that a new IPDP would be formulated "to mainstream IP into . . . economic and social development and to further promote innovation and creativity through a more holistic approach to IP matters."[143] Ultimately, this led to a review of the IPDP in 2016[144] which was published in January 2017, with the following objectives, to:[145]

> (a) contribute to enriching the new IP Bill prior to its enactment; (b) Identify strengths and weakness of the current IP system; and (c) Make recommendations on the measures that should be taken in addressing challenges and weaknesses as well as enhancing Mauritius' capacity to make strategic use of the IP system as an effective tool in attaining national development goals.

The revised IPDP recommended that Mauritius formulate a national IP policy through a process "involving key stakeholders both from the public and private sectors, taking into account existing and draft national and sectoral development policies as well as international commitments based on international best practices."[146]

São Tomé and Principe

São Tomé and Principe has an IPDP developed with technical assistance from WIPO for which a validation meeting was held in September 2014.[147] However, it is not publicly available, so it is not possible to outline or comment on it.

140 National IP Development Plan for the Republic of Mauritius: Needs Evaluation Report and Implementation Matrix (2017) p. 12.
141 WIPO support to NEPAD in collaboration with other United Nations agencies (2013) p. 3.
142 WIPO support to NEPAD in collaboration with other United Nations agencies (2013) p. 3.
143 Boolell (2014).
144 Technical Assistance Database: National IP Policy/Strategy: Validation Workshop for review of IPDP + Experts Field Mission 20 October – 10 November 2016.
145 National IP Development Plan for the Republic of Mauritius: Needs Evaluation Report and Implementation Matrix (2017) p. 8.
146 National IP Development Plan for the Republic of Mauritius: Needs Evaluation Report and Implementation Matrix (2017) p. 14.
147 WIPO Technical Assistance Database: Réunion de validation et d'appropriation du Plan national de développement de la propriété intellectuelle de la République de Sao Tomé-et-Principe. 2–9 September 2014.

Senegal

Senegal's IPDP was developed with technical assistance from WIPO[148] and it is reported to have been under implementation for several years.[149] However, it is not publicly available, so it is not possible to outline or comment on it.

Seychelles

Seychelles' IPDP (2010) has been under implementation for several years.[150] The IPDP is not publicly available but a needs assessment report for the IPDP is. This report consists of the following five chapters: (1) Introduction, (2) IP Policy, Legal and Institutional Framework, (3) Use of the IP System, IP Awareness and IPR Enforcement, (4) Membership of International IP Treaties and Existing and Potential Partners and (5) Identified Sector for Pilot Project. The report recommends the preparation of a national IP policy.[151]

2.5.3 States With National IP Policies Under Formulation

There are 11 states reportedly involved in IP policy making. These developments are described here. As indicated previously, Algeria is in the process of formulating an IP policy and received technical assistance from WIPO under Development Agenda Project DA_10_05: Development of National IP Strategies.[152] Further, in 2009 Algeria finalised a National Strategy and Action Plan on Copyright and Related Rights in 2009, with technical assistance from WIPO.[153] Information on the adoption and implementation of the strategy is not publicly available. Burundi's IP Policy has reportedly been under formulation for a protracted period[154] and a draft was formulated several years ago.[155] The Central African Republic has

148 Technical Assistance Database: Activity Details: Formulation of the National Intellectual Property Development Plan in Senegal. Dakar, Senegal. 1 July–31 December 2009.

149 WIPO support to NEPAD in collaboration with other United Nations agencies (2013) p. 3.

150 WIPO support to NEPAD in collaboration with other United Nations agencies (2013) p. 3.

151 IPDP for Seychelles (2010) p. 8.

152 WIPO Technical Assistance Database: Development of a National IP Strategy for Algeria. Assessment Mission: 1 January–31 May 2012.

153 WIPO Technical Assistance Database: Development of a National IP Strategy for Algeria. Assessment Mission: 1 January–31 May 2012, Technical Assistance Database: Elaboration of National Strategies and Action Plans on Copyright and Related Rights, and a Road Map for Their Finalisation and Formal Adoption for Algeria, Jordan, Lebanon and Tunisia. Tunis, Tunisia, 17–21 November 2009.

154 WIPO Technical Assistance Database: Expert Mission to Review the Draft National Intellectual Property Policy, and Stakeholders Workshop to Validate the Draft National Intellectual Property Policy of Burundi. 29 November 2012–28 February 2013.

155 SAANA Consulting (2013).

been working on an IP policy since 2010.[156] Chad also commenced work on an IP policy with WIPO technical assistance several years ago.[157] Kenya has a policy on traditional knowledge[158] and started work on an IP policy several years ago,[159] and by 2012 had a third draft of the IP policy prepared with technical assistance from WIPO.[160]

Lesotho is also working on a national IP policy with technical assistance from WIPO.[161] Mali's national IP Policy has been under discussion and formulation since 2011.[162] Sierra Leone's IP policy formulation process was commenced in 2012, with an IP audit undertaken with technical assistance from WIPO.[163] As indicated previously, Tanzania is currently working on the formulation of a national IP policy with technical assistance from WIPO.[164] Togo commenced the IP policy formulation process in 2010, with technical assistance from WIPO.[165] Without exception, there is virtually no further publicly available information about progress on policy formulation, hence the brevity of this section. What is most striking about these processes is how long they have taken.

2.5.4 Evaluation of National IP Policies and IPDPs

The IP policies considered in section 2.5.1 cover similar aspects, such as objectives, vision, mission, institutional arrangements, IPRs (general and specific aspects and recommendations), related regulatory instruments at global, continental, sub-regional and national level, awareness raising and dissemination as well as monitoring, reporting and evaluation mechanisms. The IPDPs that are publicly available are comprehensive and cover much the same ground as IP policies, even though they themselves are not IP policies and some expressly recommend the formulation of IP policies. In some cases, countries that have IPDPs have successfully developed and adopted IP policies.

156 WIPO Technical Assistance Database: Consolidation of Intellectual Property Development Plan of Central African Republic, 20–26 May 2010. Bangui, CAR.

157 WIPO Technical Assistance Database: Projet de plan de développement de la pI et de l'innovation technologique (PNDPI). N'Djaména, Chad. 10–13 September 2013.

158 Republic of Kenya. *The National Policy on Traditional Knowledge, Genetic Resources and Traditional Cultural Expressions* (2009).

159 Nzomo and Rutenberg (2017).

160 Republic of Kenya Draft IP Policy and Strategy (version 3) (2012).

161 WIPO support to NEPAD in collaboration with other United Nations agencies (2012–2013) p. 1.

162 WIPO support to NEPAD in collaboration with other United Nations agencies (May 2011–April 2012) p. 2 and WIPO support to NEPAD in collaboration with other United Nations Agencies (2012–2013) p. 2.

163 WIPO support to NEPAD in collaboration with other United Nations Agencies (2012–2013) p. 1, Kanu (2012); WIPO. CDIP: Fourteenth Session. Geneva, 10–14 November 2014. Revised Report on the Measurement of the Millennium Development Goals (MDGs) in Other United Nations Agencies and Specialised Agencies, and on the Contribution to WIPO to the Implementation of the MDGs (November 2014) CDIP/14/12 Rev. Annex II, 8 p. 31.

164 WIPO support to NEPAD in collaboration with other United Nations agencies (2012–2013). p. 3.

165 WIPO support to NEPAD in collaboration with other United Nations agencies (2012–2013) p. 3.

The elements covered by both IPDPs and IP policies are those required of any sound policy and which have been identified as such in the WIPO-developed toolkits referred to previously. Those supported by WIPO and WTO were developed by IP experts appointed as consultants by WIPO, who either provided or enhanced national technical expertise where it was lacking or limited. Several of the policies were drafted by the same expert, so there is a level of congruency even though they differ significantly because they are customised to national contexts and are based on needs analyses.

The situational analyses and discussions of national contexts acknowledge prevailing national socio-economic realities. Flowing from this, all the policies seek to prioritise developmental goals as found in NDPs. Some policies, such as South Africa's, refer to constitutions, which indirectly brings in human rights considerations. Some, like South Africa's and Rwanda's, prioritise public health and expressly refer to the effective use of TRIPS flexibilities. References to REC IP policies, such as Rwanda's reference to the EAC TRIPS, are also significant in that they show alignment to regional positions. The policy intentions are good and the ultimate test will be implementation, so implementation plans are important. Here the performance of the policies is uneven, with some being clear, detailed and with specific timelines whilst others are vague and cover unrealistically short timelines or have no timelines at all. Another gauge of performance is the evaluation of national action pursuant to the policy. For instance, four years since the passage of the South African IP policy, substantive patent application examination has not been implemented, nor have draft bills introducing the changes it recommended been published as of January 2023.

Another area that needs attention is the review, revision and re-issuance of lapsed policies. Mozambique's policy lapsed in 2018 and Zimbabwe's lapsed in 2022. Ideally a new policy must be ready at least a year before the lapse of the current policy to ensure sufficient time for validation processes so that there is seamless continuity. However, it is only fair to note that some states have timeously revised their IP policies and IPDPs so they are in the second iteration of these policies or IPDPs.

The fact that some IP policies and IPDPs are not publicly available is of concern because one of the key objectives of these policy instruments is public awareness, so it is counterproductive if the relevant policy document is itself unavailable.

2.6 Conclusion

This chapter shows that African states are coming to grips with the importance of establishing a well-articulated written policy stance as the foundation of IP legislative frameworks. Fourteen states have adopted national IP policies, two of which also had IPDPs, whilst six states have only IPDPs and there are public records of 11 states being involved in policy formulation. This brings the total to 31 states which are active in the IP policy sphere. As noted, this an approximation founded on publicly available information, so there may be other states which fall into these categories. In addition, a larger number of states are covered by REC IP policies, which are the subject of the next chapter.

Most states undertake policy formulation with technical assistance. The discussion of the factors affecting policy formulation highlighted challenges relating to public consultation processes, governmental capacity and co-ordination, undue global influence and technical assistance. However, some states have shown resilience in meeting these challenges. Since the adoption of the WIPO DA, WIPO and the adoption of the Dakar Declaration on IP for Africa in 2015, technical assistance has become much more context sensitive and incorporates advice on the use of TRIPS flexibilities, which is important for developing countries and LDCs. Of the 20 IP policies and IPDPs, some are not publicly available, making their evaluation unachievable. The evaluation shows that these policies are generally comprehensive in their coverage, are context specific, centre developmental priorities and make sound linkages with other relevant regulatory instruments. Shortcomings are identified with respect to implementation and timeous revision.

Reference List

Primary Sources: National and REC Policies/Strategies, Agreements, Decisions and Official Documents

Republic of Botswana, 2022. *Botswana IP Policy BIPP*. IP Policy (BIPP).

Republic of Botswana. Ministry of Infrastructure Science and Technology, 2011. *Research, Science, Technology and Innovation (RSTI) Policy*. Gaborone: Botswana Government Printing and Publishing Services.

Republic of Botswana. Ministry of Trade and Industry, 2005. *National Competition Policy*. Gaborone: Botswana Government Printing and Publishing Services.

Republic of Egypt, 2022. *National IP Strategy*.

Republic of The Gambia, 2018–2023. *Gambia's National IP Policy and Strategy (NIPPS)*. Available at www.aripo.org/wp-content/uploads/2020/04/THE-GAMBIA-IP-POLICY-2018-2023.doc [accessed 4 January 2023].

Republic of Ghana, 2016. *National IP Policy and Strategy (NIPPS)*.

Republic of Kenya, 2009. *The National Policy on Traditional Knowledge, Genetic Resources and Traditional Cultural Expressions*. Available at www.wipo.int/wipolex/en/text.jsp?file_id=246993 [accessed 6 January 2023].

Republic of Kenya, 2012 November. *National Intellectual Property Policy and Strategy – Draft Three*.

Republic of Liberia, 2017. *Country Report on the Intellectual Property System, Republic of Liberia*. 57th Series of Assemblies of WIPO Member States October 2–11, 2017, Geneva, Switzerland. Available at www.wipo.int/edocs/mdocs/govbody/en/a_57/a_57_105.pdf [accessed 2 April 2022].

Republic of Liberia, 2017. *IP Development Plan (IPDP) for the Government of Liberia*. Available at www.aripo.org/wp-content/uploads/2020/04/FINAL-IPDP-2017-FOR-LIBERIA-REVISED.pdf [accessed 2 April 2022].

Republic of Madagascar, 2016. *National Policy and Strategy of Innovation in the Field of IP for Madagascar*. Available at www.wipo.int/wipolex/en/legislation/details/16417 [accessed 4 January 2023].

Republic of Malawi, 2019. *National IP Policy*. Available at www.registrargeneral.gov.mw/acts_regulations/National_IP_Policy_.pdf [accessed 5 January 2023].

Republic of Mauritius, 2017. *National IP Development Plan for the Republic of Mauritius: Needs Evaluation Report and Implementation Matrix*. Available at www.mauritiustrade.mu/ressources/pdf/IPDP-FINAL-REPORT-2.pdf [accessed 4 January 2023].

Republic of Mozambique, 2007. *Intellectual Property Strategy 2008–2018*. Available at www.wipo.int/wipolex/en/text.jsp?file_id=202233 [accessed 1 March 2023].

Republic of Namibia, *National IP Policy and Strategy (NIPPS) 2019–2024*. Available at https://wipolex-res.wipo.int/edocs/lexdocs/laws/en/na/na031en.pdf [accessed 4 January 2023].

Republic of Nigeria, 2022 June. *National IP Policy and Strategy*.

Republic of Rwanda, Ministry of Trade and Industry, 2009. *Rwanda IP Policy*. Available at https://www.wipo.int/wipolex/en/legislation/details/8960 [accessed 1 April 2023].

Republic of Rwanda, Ministry of Trade and Industry, 2018. *Rwanda Revised IP Policy*. Available at https://org.rdb.rw/wp-content/uploads/2020/09/Rwanda_Revised_Policy_on_Intellectual_Property_2018.pdf [accessed 6 June 2023].

Republic of Seychelles, 2010. IPDP.

Republic of South Africa, 2018 August 31. *Intellectual Property Policy of the Republic of South Africa Phase I*, GN 518 of GG 41870.

Republic of South Africa, Department of Trade and Industry, 2008. *Policy Framework for the Protection of Indigenous Traditional Knowledge through the Intellectual Property System and the Intellectual Property Laws Amendment Bill*. Pretoria, South Africa: Department of Trade and Industry.

Republic of South Africa, Department of Provincial and Local Government, 2007. *National Policy Framework for Public Participation*. Pretoria, South Africa: Department of Provincial and Local Government.

Republic of Tanzania, *Action Plan for Realising the IP Potentials of Tanzania*.

Republic of Uganda, 2019. *National Intellectual Property Policy*. Available at www.wipo.int/wipolex/en/legislation/details/20192 [accessed 4 January 2023].

Republic of Zambia, 2009. *National IP Policy*. Available at www.aripo.org/wp-content/uploads/2020/04/Zambia-National-IP-Policy-2009.pdf [accessed 4 January 2023].

Republic of Zambia, 2020. *Revised National IP Policy*. Available at www.aripo.org/wp-content/uploads/2020/04/Zambia-National-IP-Policy-2009.pdf [accessed 4 January 2023].

Republic of Zimbabwe, 2014. *Draft National Intellectual Property Policy for Zimbabwe*.

Republic of Zimbabwe, 2018–2022. *National Intellectual Property Policy for Zimbabwe*.

AU

Dakar Declaration on IP for Africa, 2015. EX.CL/945(XXVIII) Add.7 Executive Council Twenty-Eighth Ordinary Session, 23–28 January 2016. Addis Ababa, Ethiopia.

United States

Executive Order 13155 of May 10, 2000 Access to HIV/AIDS Pharmaceuticals and Medical Technologies para 10(a). Available at www.govinfo.gov/content/pkg/FR-2000-05-12/pdf/00-12177.pdf [accessed 15 December 2022].

WIPO (Chronological Order)

Agreement between the World Intellectual Property Organisation and the World Trade Organisation (1995). Available at https://www.wto.org/english/tratop_e/trips_e/wtowip_e.htm [accessed 12 April 2023].

CDIP: Eighth Session. Geneva, 14–18 November 2011. Progress Reports on Development Agenda Projects. CDIP/8/2 Annex VIII.

CDIP: Eleventh Session. Geneva, 13–17 May 2013. Director General's Report on Implementation of the Development Agenda. CDIP/11/2.

CDIP: Fourteenth Session. Geneva, 10–14 November 2014. Progress Reports. CDIP/14/2.

CDIP: Fourteenth Session. Geneva, 10–14 November 2014. Revised Report on the Measurement of the Millennium Development Goals (MDGs) in Other United Nations Agencies and Specialised Agencies, and on the Contribution to WIPO to the Implementation of the MDGs (November 2014) CDIP/14/12 Rev. Annex II, 8.

CDIP: Ninth Session. Geneva, 7–11 May 2012. Joint Proposal by the Development Agenda Group and the Africa Group on WIPO's Technical Assistance in the Area of Cooperation for Development. CDIP 9/16.

CDIP: Progress Report on Projects for Implementation of Recommendations 2, 5, 8, 9 and 10. CDIP/4/2 Annex VIII (2009).

CDIP: Project Documents for Implementation of Recommendations 2, 5, 8, 9 and 10. CDIP/3/INF/2 (2009).

CDIP: Seventh Session. Geneva, 2–6 May 2011. Director General's Report on Implementation of the Development Agenda. CIDP7/2 Annex 1.

CDIP: Sixth Session. Geneva, 22–26 November 2010. Progress Reports on Development Agenda Projects. CDIP/6/2 Annex IX.

CDIP: Tenth Session. Geneva, 12–16 November 2012. Evaluation Report on the Project on Improvement of National, Sub-Regional and Regional IP Institutional and User Capacity. CDIP/10/7.

CDIP: Thirteenth Session. Geneva, 19–23 May 2014. Director General's Reports on Implementation of the Development Agenda. CDIP 13/2.

CDIP: Twelfth Session. Geneva, 18–21 November 2013: Progress Reports. CDIP 12/2.

Convention Establishing the World Intellectual Property Organisation (1967).

General Assembly Forty-First (21ST Extraordinary) Session. Geneva, 1–9 October 2012. Report of the CDIP. WO/GA/41/12 Appendix III.

Intellectual Property Development Plan for the Republic of Liberia: Final Report on the Needs Evaluation (2009). Available at www.moci.gov.lr/doc/LiberiaFinalConsolidatedIPDP.pdf [accessed 6 January 2023].

Methodology and Tools for the Development of National IP Strategies. Available at www.wipo.int/ipstrategies/en/methodology/ [accessed 6 January 2023].

Methodology for the Development of National Intellectual Property Strategies: Tool 1: The Process WIPO Pub_958_1 (2014).

Methodology for the Development of National Intellectual Property Strategies Tool 2: Baseline Questionnaire WIPO Pub 958 2 (2014).

Methodology for the Development of National Intellectual Property Strategies Tool 3: Benchmarking Indicators WIPO Pub 958_3 (2014).

Methodology for the Development of National Intellectual Property Strategies Tool 4 – National IP Strategies (NIPS) Online Survey (2014) . Available at www.wipo.int/ipstrategies/en/methodology/nips_survey.html [accessed 16 January 2023].

Technical Assistance Database: Activity Details: Formulation of the National Intellectual Property Development Plan in Senegal. Dakar, Senegal, 1 July–31 December 2009. Available at www.wipo.int/tad/en/activitydetails.jsp?id=1092 [accessed 6 January 2023].

Technical Assistance Database: Needs Evaluation and Technical Support Relating to the IP Development Plan Formulation for the Republic of Liberia 9 March – 8 April 2009. Available at https://www.wipo.int/tad/en/activitydetails.jsp?id=973 [accessed 6 January 2023].

Technical Assistance Database: Elaboration of National Strategies and Action Plans on Copyright and Related Rights, and a Road Map for Their Finalization and Formal Adoption for Algeria, Jordan, Lebanon and Tunisia. Tunis, Tunisia, 17–21 November 2009. Available at www.wipo.int/tad/en/activitydetails.jsp?id=1167 [accessed 6 January 2023].

Technical Assistance Database: Consolidation of Intellectual Property Development Plan of Central African Republic, 20–26 May 2010. Bangui, CAR. Available at www.wipo.int/tad/en/activitydetails.jsp?id=1138 [accessed 6 January 2023].

Technical Assistance Database: Development of a National IP Strategy for Algeria. Assessment Mission: 1 January–31 May 2012. Available at www.wipo.int/tad/en/activitydetails.jsp?id=2722 [accessed 6 January 2023].

Technical Assistance Database: Expert Mission to Review the Draft National Intellectual Property Policy, + Stakeholders Workshop to Validate the Draft National Intellectual Property Policy of Burundi, 29 November 2012 – 28 February 2013.

Technical Assistance Database: Consultative Meeting and High-Level National IP Policy Meeting: The Role of Innovation and Creativity Policies and Strategies for Technological Capacity Building, Economic Growth and Development. Kampala, Uganda, 22–24 April 2013. Available at www.wipo.int/tad/en/activitydetails.jsp?id=4934 [accessed 6 January 2023].

Technical Assistance Database: Reconnaissance Mission as Part of the Formulation of Innovation and Intellectual Property Policy and Strategy in Madagascar and Planning and Training Mission as Part of the Technology Support Centers Program, 26–30 August 2013. Available at https://www.wipo.int/tad/en/activitydetails.jsp?id=6354 [accessed 6 January 2023].

Technical Assistance Database: Projet de plan de développement de la pI et de l'innovation technologique (PNDPI). N'Djaména, Chad, 10–13 September 2013. Available at www.wipo.int/tad/en/activitydetails.jsp?id=5637 [accessed 6 January 2023].

Technical Assistance Database: Finalisation of the IP Policy and IP Strategy for the Republic of Zimbabwe. Harare, Zimbabwe, 4–5 November 2014. Available at www.wipo.int/tad/en/activitydetails.jsp?id=7294 [accessed 6 January 2023].

Technical Assistance Database: National IP Policy/Strategy: Validation Workshop for review of IPDP + Experts Field Mission 20 October – 10 November 2016. Available at https://www.wipo.int/tad/en/activitydetails.jsp?id=11364 [accessed 6 January 2023].

Technical Assistance Database: National IP Policy Workshop: The Strategic Use of IP for Technological Capacity Building, Economic Growth and Development. Mbabane, Swaziland, 19–20 May 2014. Available at www.wipo.int/tad/en/activitydetails.jsp?id=6763 [accessed 6 January 2023].

Technical Assistance Database: Réunion de validation et d'appropriation du Plan national de développement de la propriété intellectuelle de la République de Sao Tomé-et-Principe, 2–9 September 2014. Available at www.wipo.int/tad/en/activitydetails.jsp?id=7519 [accessed 6 January 2023].

Technical Assistance Database: Validation of the IPDP Swaziland – Second Experts Field Mission Mbabane, Swaziland, 27–30 July 2015. Available at www.wipo.int/tad/en/activitydetails.jsp?id=16584 [accessed 6 January 2023].

Technical Assistance Database: Visit to WIPO Headquarters by Three Senior Officials from COMESA, October 2011. Available at www.wipo.int/tad/en/activitydetails.jsp?id=2283 [accessed 6 January 2023].

WIPO CDIP: Ninth Session. Geneva, May 7 to 11, 2012. Management Response to the External Review of WIPO Technical Assistance in the Area of Cooperation for Development (CDIP/8/inf/1). CDIP9/14.

WIPO Support to NEPAD in Collaboration with other United Nations Agencies (May 2011 until April 2012).

WIPO Support to NEPAD in Collaboration with other United Nations Agencies (2012–2013).

Secondary Sources

Abdel Latif, A., 2011. Change and Continuity in the International Intellectual Property System: A Turbulent Decade in Perspective. *WIPO Journal*, 3(2), 36–55.

Anderson, J.E., 1984. *Public-Policy Making: An Introduction* (3rd ed.). Boston, MA: Houghton Mifflin.

Blakeney, M. and Mengistie, G., 2011. Intellectual Property and Economic Development in Sub-Saharan Africa. *Journal of World Intellectual Property*, 14(3/4), 238–264.

Boolell, A., 2014. *Statement at the Opening of the Workshop on Intellectual Property Rights at the Intercontinental Hotel*, Balaclava, Mauritius 5 March 2014.

Booysen, S., 2001. Transitions and Trends in Policy Making in Democratic South Africa' 2001. *Journal of Public Administration*, 36(2), 125–144.

Ceesay, H., 2020. *IP Policy Implementation Process Underway* [online], 27 July 2020. Available at www.moj.gm/news/92b81f01-d00a-11ea-837b-025103a708b7 [accessed 4 January 2023].

Chatema, Z., 2011. Presentation on Country Experiences in Implementation of Intellectual Property Rights – Malawi. *WTO Symposium on LDC Priority Needs for Technical and Financial Cooperation*, Geneva Switzerland, 19–21 October 2011. Available at www.wto.org/english/tratop_e/trips_e/zakeyo_chatima_malawi_presentation_e.pdf [accessed 6 January 2023].

Correa, C.M., 2006. Implications of Bilateral Free Trade Agreements on Access to Medicines. *Bull World Health Organ*, 84(5), 399–404.

Darch, C., 2014. Politics, Law and Discourse: Patents and Innovation in Post-Apartheid South Africa. In David, M. and Halbert, D. (eds.) *The Sage Handbook on Intellectual Property*. London: Sage Publishers.

de Beer, J., 2009. Defining WIPO's Development Agenda. In de Beer, J. (ed.) *Implementing the World Intellectual Property Organisation's Development Agenda*. Waterloo, Ontario: International Development Research Centre and Wilfrid Laurier University Press.

Deere-Birbkeck, C., 2009. *The Implementation Game: The TRIPS Agreement and the Global Politics of Intellectual Property Reform in Developing Countries*. New York: Oxford University Press.

Deere-Birkbeck, C. and Roca, S., 2011. *An External Review of WIPO Technical Assistance in the Area of Cooperation for Development*. Geneva, Switzerland: WIPO. Available at www.wipo.int/edocs/mdocs/mdocs/en/cdip_8/cdip_8_inf_1-annex1.pdf [accessed 6 January 2023].

Dlamini, T., 2014. Intellectual Property Laws, Strategy Operational by 2020. *The Swazi Observer*, 20 May 2014.

Dye, T., 1972. *Understanding Public Policy*. Englewood Cliffs, NJ: Prentice Hall.

Frankel, S., 2008. The Legitimacy and Purpose of Intellectual Property Chapters in FTAs. In Buckley, R.P., Lo, V.I. and Boulle, L. (eds.) *Challenges to Multilateral Trade: The Impact of Bilateral, Preferential and Regional Agreements*. The Netherlands: Kluwer Law International, 185–200.

Gad, M.O., 2003. Impact of Multinational Enterprises on Multilateral Rule Making: The Pharmaceutical Industry and the TRIPS Uruguay Round Negotiations. *Law and Business Review of the Americas*, 9, 667–698.

Hall, R. and Deardorff, A., 2006. Lobbying as Legislative Subsidy. *American Political Science Review*, 100(1), 69–84.

Heywood, M., 2001. Debunking "Conglomo-talk": A Case Study of the Amicus Curiae as an Instrument for Advocacy, Investigation and Mobilisation. *Law, Democracy & Development*, 5(2), 133.

Hogwood, B.W. and Gunn, L., 1984. *Policy Analysis for the Real World*. Oxford: Oxford University Press.

Hopeson, D., 2013. Cooperative Approaches to IPR Protection in Ghana. *Workshop on the Practical Approaches to IP Utilization and Protection in Africa*, Dar es Salaam, Tanzania, 19–21 March, 2013.

Howlett, M. and Lejano, R.P., 2013. Tales From the Crypt: The Rise and Fall (and Rebirth?) of Policy Design. *Administration & Society*, 45(3), 357–381.

Kanu, O., 2012. Sierra Leone Presentation on Challenges in Formulation and Implementation of National Intellectual Property Policies and Strategies. *WIPO Conference on The Role of Intellectual Property Offices (IPOs) in Promoting Innovation, Business Competitiveness and Economic Growth*. Tokyo, Japan. 2–3 February 2012. WIPO/INN/TYO/12/REF/T3SIERRA-LEONE. Available at www.wipo.int/edocs/mdocs/aspac/en/wipo_inn_tyo_12/wipo_inn_tyo_12_ref_t3sierra_leone.pdf [accessed 6 January 2023].

Litman, J.D., 2009. The Politics of Intellectual Property. *Cardozo Arts & Entertainment Law Journal*, 27(2), 313–320.

Liu, P.C.B., 1994. U.S. Industry's Influence on Intellectual Property Negotiations and Special 301 Actions. *Pacific Basin Law Journal*, 13(1), 87–117.

Longman Dictionary of Contemporary English, 2003, 4th ed. Harlow: Pearson Education.

Loutfi, Z., 2022. *Egypt's National Strategy for Intellectual Property – What Impact on Copyright*? 20 October 2022 Kluwer Copyright Blog. Available at http://copyrightblog.kluweriplaw.com/2022/10/20/egypts-national-strategy-for-intellectual-property-what-impact-on-copyright/ [accessed 6 January 2023].

May, C., 2007. The World Intellectual Property Organisation and the Development Agenda. *Global Governance*, 13, 161–170.

Mould Iddrisu, B., 2010. *Attorney General Launches Ghana's Intellectual Property Development Plan*, 23 July 2010. Available at https://bettymould.wordpress.com/2010/07/23/attorney-general-launches-ghana%E2%80%99s-intellectual-property-development-plan/ [accessed 6 January 2023].

Musungu, S.F., 2010. The Development Agenda and the Changing Face of the World Intellectual Property Organisation (WIPO). *Iqsensato Studies* 2 (Working Draft).

Ncube, C.B., 2013. New A–Z Series: IP Policies in Africa – No. 1 Algeria, 23 August 2013. Available at http://afro-ip.blogspot.com/2013/08/new-z-series-ip-policies-in-africa-no-1.html [accessed 6 January 2023].

Ncube, C.B., 2013–2015. A–Z Series: IP Policies in Africa. In *Afro-IP*. Available at http://afro-ip.blogspot.com/ [accessed 6 January 2023].

Ncube, C.B., 2015. The Politics of National Intellectual Property Policy Design and the Provision of Health Services in South Africa. *South African Intellectual Property Law Journal*, 3, 15–39.

Ncube, C.B., 2016. *Intellectual Property Policy, Law and Administration in Africa: Exploring Continental and Sub-Regional Co-Operation*. Abingdon: Routledge.

Ncube, C.B., 2018. Three Centuries and Counting: The Emergence and Development of Intellectual Property Law in Africa. In Rochelle, C., Dreyfuss, R.C. and Pila, J. (eds.) *The Oxford Handbook of Intellectual Property Law*. Oxford: Oxford University Press, 409–443.

Ncube, C.B., 2021. South Africa's Three Decades of Access to Medicine Discourse: Blight or Benefit. In Ragavan, S. and Vanni, A. (eds.) *Intellectual Property Law and Access to Medicines TRIPS Agreement, Health, and Pharmaceuticals*. Abingdon: Routledge, 235–251.

Ncube, C.B., 2022. Limiting Access to Life-Saving Medications: Three South African Case Studies. In Bonadio, E. and O'Connell, A. (eds.) *Intellectual Property Excesses: Exploring the Boundaries of IP Protection*. Oxford: Hart, 163–177.

Netanel, N.W., 2009. Introduction: The WIPO Development and Its Development Policy Context. In Netanel, N.W. (ed.) *The Development Agenda: Global Intellectual Property and Developing Countries*. Oxford: Oxford University Press, 1–29.

Ntrakwah-Mensah, A., 2016. *Ghana launches a National Intellectual Property Policy* [online], 25 January 2016. Available at www.lexology.com/library/detail.aspx?g=89862cf5-4fb1-4d5e-88b6-34112cbc9fb4#:~:text=The%20mission%20is%20to%20contribute,and%20industrial%20development%20in%20Ghana [accessed 4 January 2023].

Nyati, L., 2008. Public Participation: What Has the Constitutional Court Given the Public? *Law, Democracy & Development*, 12(2), 102–110.

Nzomo, V. and Rutenberg, I., 2017. Towards an Intellectual Property Policy in Kenya. *Jahazi*, 6(1), 27–31.

Olowu, D., 2002. Introduction-Governance and Public Administration in the 21st Century: A Research and Training Prospectus. *International Review of Administrative Sciences*, 68, 345–353.

Pugatch, M.P., 2011. Intellectual Property Policy Making in the 21st Century. *WIPO Journal*, 3(1), 71–80.

SAANA Consulting, 2013. *Factual Overview on Technical & Financial Cooperation for LDCs Related to TRIPS*. Available at www.wto.org/english/tratop_e/trips_e/ldc_overview_08.05.2013_ch3.pdf [accessed 6 January 2023].

Salmon, P., 2003. Cooperation Between the World Intellectual Property Organisation (WIPO) and the World Trade Organisation (WTO). *Journal of Civil Rights and Economic Development*, 17(3), 429–441.

Sell, S., 2007. TRIPS-Plus Free Trade Agreements and Access to Medicines. *Liverpool Law Review*, 28(1), 41–75.

Simon, C.A., 2007. *Public Policy: Preferences and Outcomes*. New York: Pearson Longman.

Swiss Federal Institute of IP, 2011. *Swiss Ghana Intellectual Property Project*. Available at www.ige.ch/fileadmin/user_upload/recht/entwicklungszusammenarbeit/factsheet_ghana_phase_1.pdf [accessed 6 January 2023].

Swiss State Secretariat for Economic Affairs (SECO), 2013. *Swiss Economic Cooperation and Development Ghana Country Strategy Report 2013–2016*. Berne, Switzerland: SECO

Sykes, S., 2011. Policy: What is It? How is it Made? In Porter, E. and Coles, L. (eds.) *Policy and Strategy for Improving Health and Wellbeing*. Exeter: Learning Materials, 1–21.

UN, n.d. *UN On-Line Glossary on Governance and Public Administration*. Available at www.unpog.org/page/sub5_3.asp [accessed 6 January 2023].

US Commercial Law Development Program, n.d. *Developing Regional IP Task Force Co-ordination Action Plans for Ghana, Liberia, Nigeria and Kenya, August 1, 2011–August 5, 2011*. Washington, DC: US CLDP.

Wilson, R., 2006. Policy Analysis as Policy Advice. In Moran, M., Rein, M. and Goodin, R.E. (eds.) *The Oxford Handbook of Public Policy*. New York: Oxford University Press, 152–168.

WIPO, 2008. *WIPO Signs Intellectual Property Development Plan with the Republic of Ghana*. Geneva, May 8, 2008. PR/2008/551. Available at www.wipo.int/pressroom/en/articles/2008/article_0024.html [accessed 2 April 2022].

WIPO, 2019. *Cutting-Edge Health Technologies: Opportunities and Challenges, a Joint Technical Symposium by WHO, WIPO and WTO*. Available at www.wipo.int/meetings/en/details.jsp?meeting_id=54128 [accessed 20 December 2022].

WIPO, 2022a. *WHO, WIPO & WTO Trilateral Symposium 2022: COVID-19 Pandemic: Response, Preparedness, Resilience*. Available at www.wipo.int/meetings/en/details.jsp?meeting_id=72248 [accessed 20 December 2022].

WIPO, 2022b. *Director General Visits Egypt; Meets with the President and Other Officials, Participates in the Launching of Egypt's First National Intellectual Property Strategy*, 22 September 2022. Available at www.wipo.int/about-wipo/en/dg_tang/news/2022/news_0052.html

WIPO, n.d. *WHO, WIPO, WTO Trilateral Cooperation on Public Health, IP and Trade*. Available at www.wipo.int/policy/en/global_health/trilateral_cooperation.html [accessed 6 January 2023].

WTO, WHO and WIPO, 2020. *Promoting Access to Medical Technologies and Innovation: Intersections between Public Health, Intellectual Property and Trade* (2nd ed.). Geneva: WTO, WHO and WIPO. Available at www.wipo.int/edocs/pubdocs/en/wipo_pub_628_2020.pdf [accessed 20 December 2022].

3 Regional Economic Communities, Trade and IP

3.1 Introduction

This chapter outlines existing sub-regional trade co-operation and integration in Africa and considers to what extent, if any, IP has been included in these schemes. There is a wealth of sound scholarship on regional economic integration generally[1] and in Africa, in particular,[2] which this chapter does not replicate. Instead, it focuses on the place of IP in the legal frameworks of these structures. (Chapter four will discuss the harmonisation and unification efforts of ARIPO and OAPI in relation to the IP frameworks of their member states.) This chapter considers the same efforts by RECs, specifically COMESA, EAC, ECOWAS and SADC. This raises the question of duplication and how to effectively coordinate REC initiatives and involvement in this arena. Another pertinent enquiry is the relationship between community and national laws.

The inclusion of IP in the regulatory frameworks of RECs is motivated by a number of factors. These include the entrenchment of IP matters within the trade context to which they indisputably belong. IP is an important aspect of trade and excluding its detailed treatment from binding REC instruments would be disadvantageous.[3] This is because when trade in goods and services occurs across the borders of REC member states, the affected trade partners would have to seek relevant IP protection in the different countries across which trade is occurring. This task is very onerous where the IP laws of those countries are different. For OAPI member states this problem does not arise because their IP laws are unified. However, for ARIPO member states, this is a very real problem because their IP systems are diverse and fragmented because subscription to, and domestication of, ARIPO Protocols is uneven across the membership.[4]

Another important reason is that REC harmonisation of IP would be more inclusive than those of the regional IP organisations because not all AU member

1 For example see Perdikis (2007), Matthias and Bhagwati (2002).

2 For example see Osiemo (2014), Matambalya (2014) pp. 131–162, Gottschalk (2012), Oppong (2011), Ghathi (2011), Ghathi (2010), Kouassi (2007), Lee (2002), Asante (1997), Oyejide, Elbadawi and Collier (1997).

3 Nkomo (2014) p. 324.

4 Nkomo (2014) p. 321.

DOI: 10.4324/9781003310198-3

states are members of either of these organisations. Most notably, South Africa and Nigeria belong to neither.[5] This reason has been cited as the justification for the establishment of PAIPO. However, if it is also being cited as the reason for REC engagement with IP, as it is, the next question that would arise is whether continental institutions, such as PAIPO and the IP Protocol's institutional infrastructure would then duplicate REC initiatives. As will be shown in subsequent chapters, the PAIPO Statute and IP Protocol have been worded to exclude or minimise such duplication. However, as noted in chapter one, the RECs are building blocks of the AEC, so it is reasonable to expect that there will be meaningful efforts to coordinate initiatives.

A further justification for IP harmonisation by RECs is that some RECs have dispute resolution fora such as tribunals which the regional IP organisations may lack.[6] As will be shown in chapter four, ARIPO only has an appellate body to deal with appeals against registration decisions, whilst OAPI has broader enforcement and dispute resolution arrangements. The REC dispute resolution fora are thus considerably stronger than those which pertain at the regional IP organisations and therefore more desirable to states, particularly when they wish to have the might of trade-related sanctions. Indeed, at the global level, this was one of the primary reasons for the negotiation and adoption of the TRIPS Agreement at the WTO.

The cogency of these reasons may be questioned, but the reality is that most RECs already include IP in their mandates and have some regulatory instruments that engage with IP. Article 5(b) of the AfCFTA Agreement provides that eight RECs are the constitutive elements of the AfCFTA, therefore their IP mandates will be consolidated.[7] In the light of the operationalisation of the AfCFTA and the IP Protocol under the AfCFTA Agreement, there are further prospects for better alignment of IP systems across the continent. As stated in chapter one, some RECs, such as SADC, have articulated their intent to deepen their harmonisation of IP amongst their member states. Several have also formulated IP policies which are discussed later.

Further, as stated in chapter one, COMESA, EAC and SADC launched their Tripartite Free Trade Area (COMESA-EAC-SADC TFTA) in 2015. As will be shown, a detailed IP Agenda was included in the 2009 draft agreement text[8] and IP negotiations were intended to form part of Phase II negotiations. However, this trajectory has been superseded by the operationalisation of the AfCFTA, the conclusion of negotiations on the IP Protocol and its adoption, leaving no doubt that IP matters will soon be firmly located in a continental trade context. It is thus important to grapple with the IP aspects of regionalism in this chapter.

5 Nkomo (2014) p. 333.

6 Nkomo (2014) p. 333.

7 Also see AU Decision on the protocol on relations between the African Union and the Regional Economic Communities (RECs) DOC. EX.CL/348 (XI); Gerout, MacLeod and Desta (2019) p. 24.

8 Annex 9: Annex on Intellectual Property Rights under Article 27(1) of the Agreement Establishing the Tripartite Free Trade Area (2009).

This chapter proceeds as follows: It gives a general overview of regionalism as it has unfolded in Africa. Then it considers the relationship between community and national laws. This is followed by a consideration of selected RECs' regulation of IP. In particular, this consideration canvasses the IP frameworks of COMESA, EAC, ECOWAS and SADC. These RECs have been selected because they are "indisputably, Africa's four leading RECs today"[9] and because they are the core of the AfCFTA, which is a critical formative phase of the AEC. The IP Agenda of the COMESA-EAC-SADC TFTA is then canvassed, prior to the conclusion of the chapter.

3.2 Regionalism

There is much intellectual debate about the precise definition of the core concepts in trade-related discourse and a tendency to conflate them.[10] It is thus necessary to present the definitions used in this work. Regionalisation is a wide concept that includes the actions of state and non-state actors in the pursuit of their political, economic and social goals with regard to both formal and informal sectors.[11] Regionalism is narrower in that it excludes non-state actors. It is "the adoption of a regional project by a formal regional economic organisation designed to enhance the political, economic, social, cultural, and security integration and/or co-operation of member states."[12] This definition encompasses both regional co-operation and regional integration.[13] Some authors use the two terms interchangeably, whilst others treat them as distinct.[14] This work falls in the latter camp and sets out disparate definitions of the two terms, together with definitions of market integration, development integration and neo-functional integration.

3.2.1 Regional Co-operation

Regional co-operation is project centred in the sense that countries collaborate on specific issues to achieve agreed social, economic and political ends, usually based on trade agreements.[15] It is popularly viewed as the preliminary stage towards, and the means to, integration.[16] However, it is important to note that this is not always the case and states may co-operate with no intention to pursue ultimate integration.[17]

An example of regional co-operation is the formation of the Southern African Development Co-ordination Conference (SADCC) to reduce the economic

9 Gottschalk (2012) p. 23.
10 Akokpari (2008) p. 86, Olivier and Olivier (2004) p. 353.
11 Afadameh-Adeyemi (2013) pp. 15–6, Akokpari (2008) p. 88.
12 Lee (2003) p. 8.
13 Mutai (2007) p. 31.
14 Afadameh-Adeyemi (2013) p. 12, Mutai (2007) p. 32, Asante (1997) p. 20.
15 UNCTAD (2007) p. 88.
16 Akokpari (2008) p. 86, Haas (1970) p. 610.
17 Mutai (2007) p. 32.

vulnerability to which its members were exposed by their dependence on trade with apartheid South Africa.[18] Once that vulnerability was reduced by the democratisation of South Africa, SADCC morphed into SADC, which is discussed further in the following section. Some scholars have argued that SADCC fits into the regional integration, development integration or neo-functional integration models, but the more persuasive view is that it does not fit into any of these models,[19] and is more aptly classified as regional co-operation.

3.2.2 Regional Integration

Regional integration is the end-game towards which some regional co-operation strives.[20] Lee defines it as

> a process by which a group of nation states voluntarily and in various degrees have access to each other's markets and establish mechanisms and techniques that minimize conflicts and maximise internal and external economic, political, social and cultural benefits of their interaction.[21]

Coining a precise definition of this term has proven elusive and it has often been concretised by aligning it to economic integration.[22] Indeed, the first part of Lee's definition incorporates Asante's following classic definition of economic integration as

> a process whereby two or more countries in a particular area voluntarily join together to pursue common policies and objectives in matters of general economic development . . . to the mutual advantage of all the participating states.[23]

From a theoretical point of view, regional integration may take the form of market integration, development integration or neo-functional integration.

3.2.3 Market Integration

Market integration is the sequential or linear development by a group of states to an economic union that progresses through "integration of goods, labour and capital markets, and eventually monetary and fiscal integration."[24] Despite its

18 Khadiagala (2012) pp. 27–30.
19 Ostergaard (1993) p. 45.
20 Asante (1997) p. 21.
21 Lee (2002) p. 4.
22 Afadameh-Adeyemi (2013) p. 15, Akokpari (2008) p. 87, Mutai (2007) p. 31.
23 Asante (1997) p. 19, citing Mutharika (1972) p. 15.
24 Hartzenberg (2011) p. 2. Also see Hartzenberg and Malungisa (2011) p. 62, Lee (2002) p. 1.

significant challenges, it is Africa's mode of choice.[25] It is achieved through RTAs or Regional Integration Arrangements (RIAs). The classic economic typology of RTAs identifies four kinds of RTAs, namely free trade areas (FTAs), customs unions (CUs), common markets and economic unions.[26] Some scholars add "total economic integration"[27] or "political union"[28] to this list. These terms are defined in the following paragraphs. FTAs and CUs are defined with reference to the WTO's General Agreement on Tariffs and Trade (GATT) and General Agreement on Trade in Services (GATS).[29]

An FTA is a "group of two or more customs territories in which the duties and other restrictive regulations of commerce . . . are eliminated on substantially all the trade between the constituent territories in products originating in such territories."[30] Rules of origin are put into place to prevent non-members of the FTA from seeking to circumvent the trade barriers that apply to them by routing their wares through a member of the FTA.[31]

A CU is

> the substitution of a single customs territory for two or more customs territories, so that
>
> (i) duties and other restrictive regulations of commerce . . . [barring some permissible necessary exceptions] are eliminated with respect to substantially all the trade between the constituent territories of the union or at least with respect to substantially all the trade in products originating in such territories, and
> (ii) subject to the provisions of paragraph 9, substantially the same duties and other regulations of commerce are applied by each of the members of the union to the trade of territories not included in the union.[32]

In other words, a CU is one step beyond a FTA because it maintains the FTA and adds to it a common external tariff that is applicable to trading partners outside the CU.[33]

A common market proceeds beyond a CU by adding the unrestrained exchange of capital and labour between its members.[34] An economic union is the endgame;

25 Lee (2002) p. 1, Ostergaard (1993) p. 27.
26 Perdikis (2007) pp. 82–83, Fiorentino, Verdeja and Toqueboeuf (2006) p. 23, Crawford and Fiorentino (2005) pp. 3–4.
27 Lee (2002) p. 3, Balassa (1961) p. 2.
28 Ostergaard (1993) p. 30.
29 See WTO n.d.
30 Paragraph 8(b) of Article XXIV of the General Agreement on Tariffs and Trade (GATT) 1994.
31 Perdikis (2007) p. 83.
32 Paragraph 8(a) of Article XXIV of GATT 1994. For discussion see Viner (1950) and Oslington (2013).
33 Lee (2002) p. 3, Perdikis (2007) p. 83.
34 Lee (2002) p. 3, Perdikis (2007) p. 83.

it entails fiscal and monetary policy harmonisation.[35] The distinction between an economic union and total economic integration is that the latter encompasses unification, rather than harmonisation, of fiscal and monetary policy.[36]

The laws on the multilateral trading system regulate RTAs. A full purview of these laws is beyond the scope of this work.[37] Suffice it to state that this regulation is necessary because RTAs are inherently discriminatory, which runs contrary to the non-discriminatory fundamental principle of the multilateral trading system.[38] The market integration model has been faulted on various grounds, the primary of which is the fallibility of its underlying assumptions, which envisage perfect market conditions –sadly not the reality of many developed countries and more so in developing countries.[39] Another oft-cited flaw is the model's failure to factor in the reality that due to the different industrial capacities of participating countries, some countries would benefit from integration whilst others would not.[40]

3.2.4 Development Integration

Development integration does not focus only on trade, like market integration, through maximising production capacity but serves as a catalyst for production capacity, via state intervention fuelled by heightened political co-operation amongst the members of the REC.[41] The uneven distribution of trade profits is rectified through the use of compensatory measures such as transfer tax or budgetary transfers, and corrective measures which afford favourable treatment to the economically weaker countries.[42]

Whilst it is clearly more nuanced and better suited to developing states, development integration has been criticised because it does not always succeed in its goal of equitably distributing trade gains.[43] Examples cited in this regard include the failed first iteration of the EAC and the SACU.[44]

3.2.5 Neo-Functional Integration

Neo-functional integration is a progressive sectoral approach that extends integration to other sectors due to "political spillover" inspired by preceding successful

35 Lee (2002) p. 3, Perdikis (2007) p. 83.
36 Lee (2002) p. 3, Balassa (1961) p. 2.
37 Article XXIV: 5 GATT. For in-depth discussion, see Perdikis (2007) pp. 85–87. Also see WTO Understanding on the Interpretation of Article XXIV of the General Agreement on Tariffs and Trade (1994).
38 Perdikis (2007) pp. 84–85.
39 Mutai (2007) p. 36, Ostergaard (1993) p. 31.
40 Mutai (2007) p. 37, Ostergaard (1993) p. 33.
41 Mutai (2007) p. 38, Ostergaard (1993) p. 34.
42 Ostergaard (1993) p. 35.
43 Ostergaard (1993) pp. 35–39.
44 Mutai (2007) p. 38.

integration.[45] This spillover may be explained as the development of new political goals motivated by the pressure created by integrated sectors.[46] Such pressure would be generated by affected interest groups and political actors. Like the other theories of integration, neo-functionalism is also criticised on a number of grounds. Chief of these, for present purposes, is its reliance on the agency of economic and political actors, which is often lacking in Africa.[47]

As stated earlier, the predominant mode of regional integration in Africa and the core Pan-African approach is market integration. Some historical foregrounding of the Pan-African project is essential, as an introduction to the discussion of the IP regulatory frameworks of some African RECs. Accordingly, the following section sets out the Pan-African plan for the establishment of the AEC.

3.3 The AU and the AEC

It is beyond the scope of this chapter to fully detail the genesis of Pan-Africanism and the history of its institutionalism through the Organisation of African Unity (OAU) which later became the AU.[48] For present purposes, a brief excursus follows.

The OAU was created in 1963 and soon thereafter began to consider means of strengthening Africa's economic status through regionalism, ultimately culminating in the establishment of the AEC. A series of decisions and declarations progressively crystallised this vision, the key of which will be mentioned here. The first of these was the Addis Ababa Declaration of 1973, which strongly asserted the necessity for Africa to take charge of its destiny by crafting its own regional solutions.[49] The Kinshasa Declaration of 1976 articulated the plan to create the AEC within a maximum of 20 years.[50] The OAU Summit adopted this declaration and its accompanying Revised Master Plan in 1977.[51] The commitment to the AEC was confirmed by the Monrovia Declaration of Commitment of the Heads of State and Government of the OAU on Guidelines and Measures for National and Collective Self-Reliance in Social and Economic Development for the Establishment of a New International Economic Order (1979).[52] Consequently an extraordinary assembly was held in 1980 to pursue this vision and resulted in the adoption of the Lagos Plan of Action and its annexure, the Final Act of Lagos, which committed the OAU to the creation of the AEC by 2000.[53] A major step towards the achievement of that goal was the adoption of the Abuja Treaty Establishing the AEC in

45 Ostergaard (1993) p. 39.
46 Jensen (2013) pp. 62–64.
47 Ostergaard (1993) p. 41.
48 For an overview of this history see Gottschalk (2012) pp. 9–10, Kouassi (2007), Murithi (2005).
49 Kouassi (2007) p. 2.
50 Kouassi (2007) pp. 2–3.
51 Kouassi (2007) p. 3.
52 Kouassi (2007) p. 3.
53 Kouassi (2007) p. 3.

1991, which came into force in 1994.[54] There has been significant commentary on this treaty,[55] which will not be rehashed here as the purpose of this section is to merely present the long-term vision, rather than to interrogate the merits of that vision.

It soon became evident that it would not be possible to realise the AEC by 2000, as originally intended. The OAU then adopted the Sirte Declaration in 1999, which resolved to form the AU to accelerate the implementation of the Abuja Treaty.[56] The AU was formed in July 2001 at Lusaka, Zambia, with the adoption of the Constitutive Act of the AU, which came into force on 26 May 2001.[57] Its mandate includes the promotion of sustainable socio-economic and cultural development and the integration of African economies.[58] It also extends to "co-ordinat[ing] and harmonis[ing] the policies between the existing and future RECs" and promoting research in science and technology, amongst other fields.[59] A large part of this mandate is being pursued through a strategic programme, the New Partnership for Africa's Development then called NEPAD, which was established by the AU in 2001 (converted to African Union Development Agency-New Partnership for Africa's Development [AUDA-NEPAD] in 2018)[60] and is implemented mostly at REC level.[61] In addition, some AU and AUDA-NEPAD matters are discussed at regional level to better facilitate final AU collective decisions that are reached at the Assembly of Heads of State and Government, the highest organ of the AU. To this end, AU member states are organised into five geographic regions, namely central, eastern, northern, southern and western.[62]

The Abuja Treaty sets out an implementation plan for the establishment of the AEC by 2028 through a progressive six-stage process to be achieved within 34 years,[63] with the possibility of an extension to a maximum of 40 years.[64] As stated in chapter one, AMU/UMA, CEN-SAD, COMESA, EAC, ECCAS/CEEAC, ECOWAS, IGAD and SADC are intended to merge into the AEC. UMA is currently dormant,[65] and ECCAS was dormant for a significant period before being

54 Kouassi (2007) p. 5.
55 Mutai (2007), Thompson (1993), Mukisa and Thompson (1995).
56 Kouassi (2007) pp. 8–9.
57 Kouassi (2007) p. 9, Mugabe (2006) p. 9.
58 Article 3(j) Constitutive Act of the African Union (2000).
59 Article 3(l)–(m) Constitutive Act of the African Union (2000).
60 It was officially adopted in 2002 by the African Union Summit through the Declaration on the Implementation of NEPAD (Assembly/AU/Decl. 1 (I)), Assembly Decision on the Transformation of the NEPAD Planning and Coordinating Agency (NPCA) into the African Union Development Agency (AUDA) – Doc. Assembly/AU/2(XXXI).
61 AU Commission, New Zealand Ministry of Foreign Affairs and Trade/Manat Aorere (2014) p. 98.
62 Article 1(d) Abuja Treaty; AU Commission, New Zealand Ministry of Foreign Affairs and Trade/Manat Aorere (2014) p. 14.
63 Article 6(1) Abuja Treaty.
64 Article 6(6) Abuja Treaty; Kouassi (2007) p. 7.
65 Gottschalk (2012) p. 16.

operationalised in 1999.[66] The total number of RECs in Africa hovers around 14. This multiplicity poses problems of conflicting obligations for states that have multiple REC memberships. Such conflicts arise from the nuances in REC approaches and the differences in the nature of the RECs themselves. Further, if the ultimate goal is the creation of the AEC through merging eight RECs, the creation of further RECs is difficult to justify. Consequently, in 2006 the AU placed a moratorium on the recognition of new RECs.[67]

The eight RECs that are listed above have agreed through a protocol on how to co-operate with each other and the AU in their progress towards the creation of the AEC.[68] One of the major steps towards this is the creation of inter-REC FTAs that are expected to then merge into the AEC.[69] As noted previously, COMESA, EAC and SADC agreed to the creation of a TFTA, which is discussed later. Preceding that discussion, this chapter first provides an overview of individual RECs. In particular, the following sections focus on ECOWAS, SADC, COMESA and EAC for the reasons stated previously.

Relational issues between the AU, AEC and RECs, surprisingly, remain largely unaddressed.[70] The Protocol on the Relations Between the African Union and the RECs fails to provide for the legal status of RECs within this configuration.[71] The RECs are not members of the AU nor party to the AEC Treaty, therefore they are not obliged to attain the AU's vision of their merging into the AEC.[72] The legal status of the AEC is that it "form[s] an integral part" of the AU.[73] It has been argued that this means that the AEC will not have separate legal personality but will be subsumed into the AU, which has such personality. Embedding the AEC in the AU in this way has been critiqued as being "unrealistic in expecting organisations like the [AU] which are primarily concerned with matters of a political nature, to take on the additional technical responsibilities required by the AEC . . .".[74] Oppong argues that scholarly discourse ought to extend beyond discussions of the legal status of the AEC to a conceptualisation of it as a legal system.[75] His main concern pertaining to this system is that whilst its observance is required,[76] there is no express mention of the establishment of such a legal system in the AEC's constitutive treaty.

66 AU (n.d.).
67 Mutai (2007) p. 106; AU, Decisions and Declarations – Assembly Decision on the Moratorium on the Recognition of Regional Economic Communities (RECs) DOC. EX.CL/278 (IX). AU Doc. Assembly/AU/Dec.111–132 (VII). Assembly of the African Union, Seventh Ordinary Session, 1–2 July 2006, Banjul, The Gambia.
68 Protocol on Relations Between the AU and the RECs, 2007.
69 ECA (2011) p. 6.
70 Oppong (2010) pp. 92–93.
71 Kolbeck (2014) p. 23.
72 Oppong (2010) p. 94.
73 Article 98(1) Treaty establishing the AEC.
74 Mutai (2007) p. 107.
75 Oppong (2006).
76 Article 3(e) AEC Treaty.

3.4 The Relationship Between Community Laws and National Laws

It is important to preface the discussion of the IP regulatory framework of RECs with an overview of the import of these frameworks for REC member states. The core question is whether community laws are both binding and enforceable through national courts. This section distinguishes between direct applicability and direct effect. The former refers to when community laws automatically acquire force of law in a party state's jurisdiction upon ratification or accession.[77] The latter refers to instances when community law may be raised by individuals before national courts, typically in pursuit of the enforcement of their rights.[78]

The answer to this question of whether community law is directly applicable or has direct effect depends on the nature of the relevant community law and national approaches to the reception of community laws that encompass constitutional or legislative provisions, "public awareness," "legal culture" and "judicial philosophy."[79] Some community laws are directly applicable, in which case no positive action is required at national level to receive or translate the law into a particular jurisdiction.[80] The constitutive treaties of the four RECs considered in this chapter do not provide for the direct applicability of their community laws.[81] The treaties provide that member states have to take appropriative affirmative action to domesticate community laws.[82] In contrast, some African states' legislation provides for direct applicability of community laws in their jurisdictions. These are Uganda,[83] Kenya,[84] Rwanda[85] and Tanzania.[86] In addition, in EAC member states, community laws are afforded supremacy.[87]

Where laws are not directly applicable, they have to be received or translated into domestic law. The translation of community laws into domestic legal systems is generally regulated by the constitution of the relevant country.[88] The relevant

77 Oppong (2008) p. 151, Winter (1972) p. 425.
78 Oppong (2008) p. 158, Winter (1972) pp. 425–426.
79 Oppong (2008) p. 149.
80 Oppong (2008) p. 151.
81 Oppong (2008) p. 152.
82 Oppong (2008) pp. 152–154; Articles 5(2) (b), 10 and 12(1) COMESA Treaty; Articles 8(2) and 14(5) EAC Treaty; Articles 9(6) and 12(4) ECOWAS Treaty; Article 6(5) SADC Treaty.
83 East African Community Act, 2002.
Act 13 of 2002 (date of entry into force 15 January 2005 per East African Community Act [Commencement] Instrument, 2005); Onoria (2011) p. 600, Oppong (2008) p. 153.
84 Section 8 Treaty for the Establishment of the East African Community Act 2 of 2000 (Cap 4C); Oppong (2008) p. 153.
85 Article 190 of Rwanda Constitution, 2003.
86 Tanzania: Treaty for the Establishment of East African Community Act 2001; Oppong (2008) p. 153.
87 Oppong (2008) p. 155.
88 Oppong (2008) p. 157.

provisions refer broadly to international law, of which community law is a species. African constitutions usually provide for one or more of the following:[89]

a) express acknowledgement of the RECs to which the country belongs together with an intention to align the state to the community vision and mission;
b) an articulation of the national goal of promoting and abiding by community objectives;
c) the mechanism or process by which international law is to be domesticated or otherwise acquires force of law;
d) the supremacy of the constitution; and
e) how conflicts between international law and national legislation are to be resolved.

In relation to (c) to (e), it is important to note that African states tend to fall into either one of two camps depending on their colonial history and post-colonial legal and cultural legacy. Countries formerly colonised by the French are monist; their constitutions usually provide that international law is automatically received into national law upon ratification or accession and also "has precedence over national laws."[90] Countries formerly colonised by the British are dualist; their constitutions require affirmative national action to receive international law into national law and in many cases there are no provisions on whether it has precedence over domestic law.[91]

The four RECs considered in this chapter also do not provide for the direct effect of community laws that would enable their enforcement through national courts.[92] However, COMESA, EAC and ECOWAS envisage that community laws would be placed before national courts and consequently provide a procedure through which national courts can refer related issues to community courts.[93] Articles 14 and 15 of the SADC Protocol on the Tribunal and Rules of Procedure Thereof provide that domestic remedies must be exhausted before recourse is made to the tribunal. It is not clear whether national courts can refer matters to it, as Article 18 provides that a "competent institution or organ of the Community" may refer matters to the tribunal. In ordinary parlance, one would not consider a national court to be an institution of the tribunal. Oppong notes that national courts of the member states of COMESA, EAC and ECOWAS have applied community laws that were neither directly applicable nor domesticated in the relevant jurisdiction to matters placed before them.[94] It is thus difficult to make general statements about the import of community laws in Africa in general. To make an accurate statement about the position in a country, one would have to assess the

89 Oppong (2008) pp. 158–161.
90 Oppong (2008) p. 159.
91 Oppong (2008) p. 160.
92 Oppong (2008) p. 155.
93 Oppong (2008) p. 155; Article 30 COMESA Treaty, Article 34 EAC Treaty; Article 10(f) Protocol of the ECOWAS Community Court of Justice, Article 16 Protocol to the SADC Tribunal and Rules.
94 Oppong (2008) pp. 166–17.

relevant constitutional provisions as well as any relevant legislation and judicial precedents. It is with this background in mind that the chapter now turns to a discussion of individual RECs.

3.5 COMESA

COMESA was founded in 1994[95] and its member states are Burundi, Comoros, DR Congo, Djibouti, Egypt, Eritrea, Eswatini, Ethiopia, Kenya, Libya, Madagascar, Malawi, Mauritius, Rwanda, Seychelles, Somalia, Sudan, Tunisia, Uganda, Zambia and Zimbabwe.[96] COMESA was the planned outcome of a predecessor Preferential Trade Area (PTA) which had been formed in 1981.[97] COMESA's ultimate goal, like SADC's, is the formation of a single-currency Monetary Union by 2025.[98] This is preceded by a FTA[99] and a CU[100] which were formed in 2000 and 2009, respectively.

3.5.1 IP Regulatory Framework

The Treaty Establishing COMESA (COMESA Treaty) provides for co-operation in respect of the regulation of IP. First, Article 104(1)(d) provides for information sharing on "legislation on patents, trademarks and designs." Further, Article 128(e) provides:

> In order to promote co-operation in science and technology development, the Member States agree to jointly develop and implement suitable patent laws and industrial licensing systems for the protection of industrial property rights and encourage the effective use of technological information contained in patents.

These clauses focus on industrial property and exclude copyright. Since the conclusion of the COMESA Treaty in 1994, COMESA has not passed any binding regulatory instruments dealing with IP.

3.5.2 IP Policy

In 2011 COMESA's Council of Ministers adopted the COMESA IP Policy together with guidelines for preparing a national IP Policy in accordance with this policy.[101]

95 The Treaty Establishing the Common Market for Eastern and Southern Africa was signed on 5 November 1993 and came into force on 8 December 1994.
96 COMESA (n.d.).
97 Gathii (2011) p. 165.
98 COMESA Treaty Article (4)(4)(a).
99 COMESA Treaty Article 45.
100 COMESA Treaty Article 45.
101 COMESA Council of Ministers Decision 90 (f) (2011), COMESA Report of the Thirtieth Meeting of the Council of Ministers. (October 2011) CS/CM/XXX/2 para 249(c) p. 61.

The policy was formulated with some technical assistance from WIPO.[102] It is structured as in Table 3.1.

The policy is a detailed statement of the COMESA member states' commitments to regulating and implementing IP in a particular manner. Key amongst these are their undertakings to fully exploit available flexibilities "to facilitate access to medicines for all people particularly the marginalised of society"[103] and the promotion of a harmonised IP legislative framework.[104] In relation to copyright the main policy objective is to "encourage and promote copyright protection for socio-economic development within the COMESA member States, recognising that copyright is a major component of intellectual property."[105] There is no express commitment to using available flexibilities to achieve other public interest goals like education or access to knowledge, which would have been an important policy signal. The guidelines for preparing a national IP Policy are not publicly available, so it is not possible to discuss them substantively. However, one can anticipate that they would be close to the WIPO guidance given in the projects described in chapter two.

Table 3.1 COMESA IP Policy

Part A: COMESA Policy on Intellectual Property Rights	*Part B: COMESA Policy on Copyright and Copyright-Related Industries*
Introduction (paras 1–3) Overview of IP (paras 4–8) Opportunities Created by IP (paras 9–10) IP and Economic Development (paras 11–14) IP and Trade (paras 15–20) IP and Cultural Industries (paras 21–26) IP and TK and Expressions of Folklore (paras 27–30) IP and ICT (paras 31–32) IP Audit and Valuation (paras 33–34) Copyright and Related Rights (paras 35–37) Industrial Property (paras 38–39)	Introduction (paras 1–4) Situation Analysis (paras 5–7) Policy Objectives (paras 8–9) Applicability (para 10) Benefits (para 11) Role of the COMESA Secretariat (para 12) Copyright (paras 13–14) Publishing (paras 15–16) Media and Advertising (paras 17–19) Computer Software (paras 20–22) Music (paras 23–25) Film (paras 26–28) Theatre and Performing Arts (paras 29–31) Collective Management Organisations (paras 32–33) Traditional Cultural Expressions (paras 34–35) Valuation of Copyright (paras 36–37) Legal Framework (para 39) Commercialisation of Copyright Works (para 40)

102 WIPO Technical Assistance Database: COMESA – Comments on draft model law on IP policy and draft model law on IP, October 2011.

103 Para 39(d) Part A.

104 Para 39(e) Part A.

105 Para 8 Part B.

COMESA commissioned a study on IP entitled "Intellectual Property Rights, Innovation and Trade in Developing Countries: Evidence From COMESA Countries" which advised that its member states' IP frameworks should be crafted to meet their developmental status and needs.[106] It published a series of a policy briefs on IP, innovation and trade in 2020, based on this study and other research.[107] It concluded a co-operation agreement with WIPO in 2020 for "collaboration in capacity building programmes" to be rolled out for personnel at the COMESA Secretariat personnel office and COMESA member states' IP offices.[108]

The COMESA IP Policy does not give as detailed guidance on TRIPS flexibilities as the other REC IP policies described here, because it is a general policy and is not specifically directed to flexibilities like the EAC and ECOWAS policy instruments discussed later. Consequently, no assessment is made here of COMESA member states' translation and implementation of the guidance on flexibilities. Fortunately, because of overlapping REC memberships, some COMESA member states also benefit from the more detailed guidance of the EAC, ECOWAS and SADC on health-related patent flexibilities, described in the next sections.

3.6 EAC

The EAC was established in 2000[109] and its current members are Burundi, Kenya, Rwanda, Tanzania and Uganda. Kenya, Tanzania and Uganda were its founding members, and Rwanda and Burundi joined in 2007.[110] This small group exhibits diversity and complexity in its legal landscape. For example, Burundi and Rwanda are Francophone civil jurisdictions whilst the other EAC member states are common-law jurisdictions. Tanzania comprises the former states of Tanganyika and Zanzibar, which merged politically in 1964. However, legally two systems continue to co-exist in Mainland Tanzania and the former Zanzibar. This means that, in effect, whilst there are five EAC member states, there are six legal systems in play. Economically, of the five member states, only Kenya is not an LDC. The EAC's ultimate goal is the creation of a political federation preceded by a monetary union, a common market, and a CU, in reverse order.[111] So far, the CU has been attained[112] and the common market has been established.[113]

106 Gakunga (2019).

107 Chikabwi (2020), Makochekanwa and Mashura (2020), Masunda (2020).

108 Gakunga (2020).

109 The Treaty for Establishment of the East African Community (Treaty establishing the EAC) was signed on 30 November 1999 and entered into force on 7 July 2000.

110 Gathii (2011) p. 181.

111 Gathii (2011) p. 181.

112 Protocol for the Establishment of the EAC CU, 2004 which came into force on 1 January 2005.

113 Protocol on the Establishment of the EAC Common Market, which came into force on 1 July 2010.

3.6.1 IP Regulatory Framework

The EAC's regulatory instruments comprise protocols, regulations, directives and decisions of the council that are binding on member states.[114] Of these, the Protocol on the Establishment of the EAC Common Market provides for the co-operation between party states in the area of IP.[115] The details of the nature of this co-operation are spelt out in Article 43 of the protocol, which encompasses all areas of IP[116] and re-affirms a commitment to abide by international IP obligations.[117] The two-fold objective of co-operation between the party states is to:[118]

(a) promote and protect creativity and innovation for economic, technological, social and cultural development in the Community; and
(b) enhance the protection of intellectual property rights.

To this end the party states are required to:[119]

(a) put in place measures to prevent infringement, misuse and abuse of intellectual property rights;
(b) cooperate in fighting piracy and counterfeit activities;
(c) exchange information on matters relating to intellectual property rights;
(d) promote public awareness on intellectual property rights issues;
(e) enhance capacity in intellectual property;
(f) increase dissemination and use of patent documentation as a source of technological information;
(g) adopt common positions in regional and international norm setting in the field of intellectual property; and
(h) put in place intellectual property policies that promote creativity, innovation and development of intellectual capital.

In particular, the party states are obliged to create regulatory frameworks for:[120]

(a) legal protection of the traditional cultural expressions, traditional knowledge, genetic resources and national heritage;
(b) protection and promotion of cultural industries;
(c) use of protected works for the benefits of the communities in the partner states; and

114 Article 16 Treaty establishing the EAC.
115 Article 5(3)(k) which provides: "For the purposes of facilitating the implementation of the Common Market, the Partner States further agree to co-operate in the promotion and protection of intellectual property rights."
116 Article 43(2).
117 Article 43(6).
118 Article 43(1).
119 Article 43(3).
120 Article 43(4).

(d) cooperation in public health, food security, research and technological development.

Whilst there is provision for the enactment of directives on co-operation with regard to IP,[121] none have been issued as yet. In the interim some research has been carried out on existing levels of harmonisation of IP laws.[122]

In 2009 the EAC member states agreed to aspire to the creation and implementation of a new commonly held IP regime by January 2014 in anticipation of a bilateral agreement with the EU.[123] The EAC-EU Economic Partnership Agreement (EPA) was finally signed on 16 October 2014.[124]

Motivated by this ambition and by information they received on the "harmful impacts of counterfeiting and piracy in East Africa" together with the imminent establishment of the Common Market, the EAC commissioned a report in 2008 on an appropriate policy approach.[125] Following this, the EAC issued a draft policy on Anti-Counterfeiting, Anti-Piracy and Other Intellectual Property Rights Violations in 2009[126] and the EAC Anti-Counterfeit Bill in 2010, which has since been revised.[127] The draft policy has not been finalised nor has the bill been enacted. These drafts were heavily criticised because they espoused a TRIPS-plus position that was, and continues to be, inappropriate for developing countries, and more so in the EAC's case because four of its member states are LDCs. In particular, both the policy and bill "fail to distinguish between various IPR infringements, contain overbroad and imprecise definitions and do not consider the impact of the foreseen measures on access to knowledge, agriculture and public health."[128] The approach of these two draft instruments "would have led to incoherence with the TRIPS Flexibilities Policy due to their impact on the production and distribution of generic medication in the region."[129]

The EAC Bill (Draft 251011) defined counterfeiting as follows:

(a) the possessing, manufacturing, producing or making, packaging, re-packaging or labeling whether in the Community or elsewhere, of any goods whereby those protected goods are imitated in such manner and to such a degree that those other goods are substantially identical copies of the protected goods without the authority of the Owner of any Intellectual Property Right subsisting in the relevant Partner State of Protected Goods;

121 Article 43(5).
122 For example Magogo (2013).
123 Blakeney and Mengistie (2011) p. 245.
124 Mwanza (2014).
125 Blakeney and Mengistie (2011) p. 258.
126 Draft 260609, prepared by Iseme Kamau & Maema Advocates and Mohammed Muigai Advocates.
127 Draft EAC Anti-Counterfeit Bill, 2011 Draft 251011.
128 Health Action International Africa (HAIA) (2010). Also see Musungu (2010), CEHRUD (2010).
129 Ncube (2021) p. 84.

(b) the possessing, manufacturing, producing or making or applying to goods, whether in the Community or elsewhere, the subject matter of that Intellectual Property Right, or a colourable imitation thereof so that other goods are calculated to be confused with or to be taken as being the Protected Goods of the said Owner or any goods manufactured, produced or made under his license without the authority of the Owner of any Intellectual Property Right subsisting in the relevant Partner State in respect of the Protected Goods.

This definition was then incorporated into EAC partner states' anti-counterfeit legislation.[130] For example, section 2 of Kenya's Anti-Counterfeit Act, Act No. 13 of 2008, provided for a similar definition, which read in part:

> counterfeiting means taking the following actions without the authority of the owner of intellectual property right subsisting in Kenya or elsewhere in respect of protected goods –
>
> (d) in relation to medicine, the deliberate and fraudulent mislabeling of medicine with respect to identity or source, *whether or not such products have correct ingredients, wrong ingredients, have sufficient active ingredients or have fake packaging* (emphasis added).

A Kenyan High Court held that this definition

> would encompass generic medicines produced in Kenya and elsewhere and thus is likely to adversely affect the manufacture, sale, and distribution of generic equivalents of patented drugs. This would affect the availability of the generic drugs and thus pose a real threat to the petitioners' right to life, dignity and health under the Constitution.[131]

This decision has had a chilling effect and, with the exception of Tanzania, none of the EAC partner states have enacted anti-counterfeiting legislation. The decision was not appealed, so it stands, but this definition was not amended either, even though other sections of the act have been amended since.[132] Should the act be implemented in a manner that restricts access to generics in the manner described by the judge in the previous extract, then such action would be unconstitutional. Further, enforcement provisions in both Tanzania's and Kenya's laws are beyond what is required by TRIPS minimum standards.[133]

130 The Anti-Counterfeit Act, (2008) Kenya; The Counterfeit Goods Bill (Uganda); 2008 Merchandise Marks Regulations in Tanzania [made under Section 18A of the Merchandise Marks Act, Chapter 85 Laws of Tanzania].

131 *Patricia Asero Ochieng, Maurine Atieno and Joseph Munyi v The Attorney General* HCCC Petition No. 409 of 2009 Para 78. For discussion, see Nyachae and Ogendi (2012).

132 Ogendi (2018) pp. 198–199.

133 Olatunji (2021), Olatunji (2022) p. 403, Ogendi (2018) p. 200.

3.6.2 IP Policy

EAC is approaching IP policy from several angles. First, it adopted a TRIPS flexibilities-focused policy in 2013, the Regional IP Policy on the Utilisation of Public Health-Related WTO-TRIPS Flexibilities and the Approximation of National IP Legislation. Second, the intent was that it would consider IP in the second phase of TFTA negotiations; this is briefly discussed later in a separate paragraph. Third, a general and broader IP policy which is not restricted to health-related flexibilities was developed under the auspices of the East African Science and Technology Commission (EASTECO) in terms of its Annual Operational Plan for 2017–2018.[134] The stated goal of the policy is "to encourage technical innovation, and to promote the industrial and commercial use of technical inventions and innovations so as to contribute to the social, economic, industrial and technological development of the Community."[135] A validation workshop for the IP policy was held in 2018,[136] followed by adoption by the EASTECO Governing Board in 2019 and a referral to the EAC Council of Ministers.[137] However, that policy is not publicly available nor is there further information on its adoption since then.

The Regional IP Policy on the Utilisation of Public Health-Related WTO-TRIPS Flexibilities and the Approximation of National IP Legislation is based on the analysis of the EAC partner states' national legislation and it aims to assist these states to meaningfully domesticate and implement TRIPS flexibilities. To this end, it makes the 11 policy statements summarised in the following list. Member states ought to:

1 "Take advantage of the 2016 transition period" and abolish any mailbox provisions in their laws.[138]
2 "Strictly define" patentability criteria specifically with regard to novelty, inventive step and industrial application. These aims are to be achieved in the following ways:

   a considering a wide concept of prior art consisting of everything disclosed to the public whether by use, in written or oral form, including patent applications, information implied in any publication or derivable from a combination of publications, which are published anywhere in the world and which can be actually or theoretically accessed by the general public;
   b Clearly define the inventive step standard by referring to a "highly" skilled person;

134 East African Science and Technology Commission (EASTECO) (n.d.)
135 East African Science and Technology Commission (EASTECO) (n.d.).
136 EASTECO (2018).
137 East Africa Entrepreneurs Association (EAEA) (2018), EASTECO (n.d.).
138 EAC TRIPS Policy p. 12.

c Strictly apply the industrial application requirement and limit the patentability of research tools to only those for which a specific use has been identified.[139]

3 Exclude the following from patentability:

i Natural substances including micro-organisms, even if purified or otherwise isolated from nature;
ii New medical uses of known substances including micro-organisms; EAC Partner States seeking to consider new medical uses principally patentable as processes under the patentability criteria, shall strictly apply the patentability requirements on a case-by-case basis;
iii Derivatives of medical products that do not show significantly enhanced therapeutic efficacy/significant superior properties.

b EAC Partner States, in order to protect small-scale innovations, e.g. in the areas of traditional medicines or genetic resources, shall reward such inventors with a right to compensation from third parties who use the inventions for follow-on improvements (use-and-pay/compensatory liability).[140]

4 Provide for research exceptions that:

a Explicitly authorise research for scientific, non-commercial and commercial purposes. The preponderant purpose of commercial research must be the generation of new knowledge of the patented substance.
b Provide a right to claim a non-exclusive licence for the use of patented research tools against payment of compensation.[141]

5 Provide for a Bolar exception that permits the "use [of] patented substances for acts 'reasonably related' to the development and submission of information required for marketing approvals."[142]
6 Upon the expiry of relevant transition periods, protect "test and other data" in a way that enables the continued reliance on original test data by medicines regulatory authorities in their evaluation of generics. Further, patents and marketing authorisation should not be connected in a manner that inhibits or prevents the grant of marketing approvals for generics during the validity of the relevant patent.[143]
7 Require the disclosure of all modes, including the best mode, of implementing an invention by "experts skilled in the art who reside in EAC partner states" in patent applications. In addition, the applicant must disclose "the International

139 EAC TRIPS Policy pp. 12–13.
140 EAC TRIPS Policy p. 14.
141 EAC TRIPS Policy p. 15.
142 EAC TRIPS Policy p. 16.
143 EAC TRIPS Policy p. 16.

Non-proprietary Name (INN) of a pharmaceutical substance or an active pharmaceutical ingredient as soon as it is available."[144]

8 Provide for "effective pre- and post-grant administrative patent opposition procedures." ARIPO member states are required to discuss the amendment of the Harare Protocol to provide for opposition procedures and a possible extension of the six-month period within which national patent offices have to approve ARIPO patents.[145]

9 Provide for international exhaustion in relation to patent, copyright and trademark laws.[146]

10 Provide for compulsory licences that enable "the export of up to 100% of pharmaceuticals" to countries without adequate manufacturing capacity; adopt relevant guidelines or regulations to enable such import and export of pharmaceuticals and "waive remuneration for import compulsory licenses" in specified circumstances.[147] They are also required to enact legislative provisions that

- cap remuneration at 4% and consider anti-competitive behaviour in setting such remuneration;
- limit the licence negotiation period to 90 days, after which the potential licensee may apply for a compulsory licence
- permit the waiver of prior negotiation periods "in case of national emergency, other situations of extreme urgency, public non-commercial use [or] government use, and to remedy anti-competitive behaviour of the patent right-holder." In addition, an "institutional monitoring mechanism" must be operationalised in order to monitor the implementation of this provision.
- preclude the use of interdicts as a remedy where government use licences are in issue.[148]

  - Finally, the grant of compulsory licences is to be an administrative, rather than a judicial, function.[149]

11 Enumerate licensing terms "that may be considered unjustified restrictions of competition and authorise the patent registrar to refuse the registration of such licensing contracts." Such terms are to be based on exiting statutory provisions under Kenyan, Rwandese, Tanzanian-Mainland and Ugandan laws.[150]

As far as these recommendations go, the first has been overtaken by events and a revision of the policy would be in order. Its specific reference to the LDC transition

144 EAC TRIPS Policy p. 17.
145 EAC TRIPS Policy p. 18.
146 EAC TRIPS Policy p. 18.
147 EAC TRIPS Policy p. 20.
148 EAC TRIPS Policy p. 20.
149 EAC TRIPS Policy p. 20.
150 EAC TRIPS Policy p. 21.

period in relation to pharmaceutical products that was current until 2016 is now outdated as the current LDC pharmaceutical products transition period is in place until 1 January 2033, as noted in chapter one.

In addition, the EAC has developed the Regional Protocol on Health-Related WTO-TRIPS Flexibilities, extracts of which are included as Annex 1 to the Health-Related WTO-TRIPS Flexibilities Policy. Once adopted and in force, the protocol will give the policy's recommendations force of law. However, the protocol must go through a signature and ratification process before it becomes effective.[151]

The EAC's two-pronged focus of beginning with the Health-Related WTO-TRIPS Flexibilities Policy and then progressing to a general IP Policy can be understood as starting with the pressing public health issue first, then moving on to a more general policy. The health-related flexibilities policy is rightfully contextualised within the EAC's other public health–related instruments. For instance, it is cross-referenced in the EAC Regional Health Sector Policy (2016)[152] and the EAC Regional Pharmaceutical Action Plan (2017–2027).[153]

Despite this detailed guidance on how to best utilise TRIPS flexibilities, EAC partner states have not made the best use of flexibilities. For example, they have voluntarily foregone the benefit of the general LDC transition period, as discussed in chapter one, and, of the LDC states, only Rwanda excludes pharmaceutical products from patent protection.[154] The other three have prematurely provided patent protection for pharmaceuticals.[155]

3.7 ECOWAS

ECOWAS was formed in 1975 and its members are Benin, Burkina Faso, Cape Verde, Cote d'Ivoire, The Gambia, Ghana, Guinea, Guinea Bissau, Liberia, Mali, Niger, Nigeria, Senegal, Sierra Leone and Togolese Republic. It is currently "a fully-fledged Customs Union with a Common External Tariff and common trade policy."[156]

3.7.1 IP Regulatory Framework

Article 27(10) (c) of the ECOWAS Treaty provides that:

> In their cooperation in this field, Member States shall harmonize their national technological development plans by placing special emphasis on

151 Article 151(3) EAC Treaty.
152 EAC Regional Health Sector Policy (2016) p. 5.
153 EAC Regional Pharmaceutical Action Plan (2017–2027) para. 3.1.5 p. 30.
154 EAC Regional Intellectual Property Policy on the Utilization of Public Health-Related WTO-TRIPS Flexibilities and the Approximation of National Intellectual Property Legislation, 2013 (EAC TRIPS Policy) p. 29.
155 EAC TRIPS Policy p. 29.
156 Ngwenya (2015).

indigenous and adapted technologies as well as their regulations on industrial property and transfer of technology.

ECOWAS law is contained in Protocols, Regulations and Decisions. It also provides policy guidance through policies. In relation to IP harmonisation, ECOWAS states have adopted a TRIPS Policy and Guidelines (discussed in the following sections) and they have not adopted any other IP regulatory instruments.

3.7.2 ***IP Policy***

ECOWAS's health-related initiatives are led by the West African Health Organisation (WAHO), an ECOWAS specialised institution which was created in 1987. Its constitutive protocol merged the West African Health Community and the *Organisation de Co-ordination et de Co-operation pour la Lutte contre les Grandes Endemies* to create it.[157] WAHO was operationalised in 2000 following a decision made by the heads of state to select the seat of the institution and appoint a director and deputy director of the organisation.[158] A supplementary protocol[159] amending its constitutive protocol is yet to come into force.

WAHO prepared a TRIPS Policy[160] and Guidelines[161] for ECOWAS, which were adopted in October 2012. The policy's primary objectives are to enhance access to essential medicines through the provision of "legal and technical guidance for the development and marketing of medicines" and "for implementing TRIPS compliant national legislations or regulations."[162] To this end, a review of member states' relevant legislation was undertaken. The findings of this review then informed the following patent legislation–specific recommendations made by the policy:

1 Dishonest and unfair commercial use of test data must be prohibited, taking care to ensure that "protection of test data should not unreasonably prevent or hamper the development of generic medicines."[163]
2 Experimental (research) and Bolar exceptions ought to be provided for.[164]
3 The disclosure of the "best mode" of implementation of inventions must be required from applicants for patents.[165]

157 Article II Protocol A/P.2/7/87 on the Establishment of a West African Health Organisation.
158 ECOWAS Heads of State Decision A/Dec.9/10/98.
159 Supplementary Protocol A/SP.1/01/06 amending Articles VI-C, VI-L, IX-8, XI-2 and XII of Protocol A/P2/7/87 on the Establishment of the WAHO.
160 ECOWAS TRIPS Policy supra.
161 Guidelines for Implementation of TRIPS Flexibilities in National Legislation to Improve Access to Medicines in the West African Region (2012) supra.
162 ECOWAS TRIPS Policy pp. 11–12.
163 ECOWAS TRIPS Policy pp. 25–26.
164 ECOWAS TRIPS Policy p. 28.
165 ECOWAS TRIPS Policy p. 28.

4 Ever-greening ought to be curbed by "preventing the extension of existing patents and patenting of trivial and/or non-efficacious variants of existing chemical substances. Product derivatives of a known chemical substance should be patentable only if, when compared to the original substance, they show significant improvements in therapeutic efficacy."[166]
5 International exhaustion should be provided for.[167]
6 TRIPS Articles 31(b) and (k) should be domesticated.[168]

These recommendations are reiterated in the accompanying guidelines which give direction to ECOWAS member states on how to incorporate them into national legislation and provide an implementation action plan for the sub-region for the period 2012–2015. In 2021 ECOWAS and WTO, in collaboration with WHO and WIPO, hosted a joint workshop for ECOWAS member states and the ECOWAS Commission on "health, intellectual property (IP) and trade policy-making" intended, in part, "to build capacity for an integrated and coordinated response to the COVID-19 pandemic."[169]

The impact of ECOWAS policy guidance has been sub-optimal because ECOWAS member states do not abide by all of it. For example Benin, Burkina Faso, Guinea, Guinea Bissau, Mali, Niger, Senegal and Togo grant pharmaceutical patents, despite the currency of the LDC pharmaceutical patents transition period.

3.8 SADC

The current member states of SADC are Angola, Botswana, Comoros, Democratic Republic of Congo, Eswatini, Lesotho, Madagascar, Malawi, Mauritius, Mozambique, Namibia, Seychelles, South Africa, Tanzania, Zambia and Zimbabwe. SADC is the successor to SADCC, which was formed in 1980.[170] Comoros is the newest member, having been admitted in 2017 and becoming a full member in 2018.[171] SADC's predecessor SADCC's member states were Angola, Botswana, Lesotho, Malawi, Mozambique, Swaziland, Tanzania, Zambia and Zimbabwe. Its key aim was to "reduce economic dependence on apartheid South Africa."[172] It neither have formal legal status nor did it own assets and sought to achieve its aims through collaborative projects.[173] As the liberation of South Africa was on the cusp, it became necessary to reconfigure SADCC. In view of this, and to strengthen its capacity, it was decided in 1992 to upgrade SADCC into SADC,

166 ECOWAS TRIPS Policy p. 30.
167 ECOWAS TRIPS Policy p. 32.
168 ECOWAS TRIPS Policy p. 37.
169 WTO (2021).
170 See SADC (n.d.a, n.d.b), Gathii (2011) p. 211.
171 SADC (2019) p. 1.
172 Hartzenberg (2011) p. 5.
173 SADCC Memorandum of Understanding (1981).

which had legal status.[174] After the dawn of democracy in South Africa in 1994, South Africa joined SADC.

Unlike SADCC, SADC's key aims include economic integration, the implementation of which is spelt out in its Regional Indicative Strategic Development Plan (RISDP). The first RISDP was approved in 2003 and planned development over a period of 15 years (2005–2020).[175] It was revised for the period 2015–2020,[176] and the current RISDP, 2020–2030, was approved in 2020,[177] together with SADC Vision 2050. The core components of the first RISDP were the creation of a FTA, CU, Common Market, Monetary Union and ultimately the adoption of a single currency.[178] Of these, the FTA was established, within the planned timeframe, in August 2008 and continues to progress meaningfully.[179] The CU was initially intended for launch in 2010 but this was not achieved.[180] A later implementation date of 2013[181] was then set, but it also was not achieved. In its 2019 integration status report the SADC Secretariat reported that SADC member states were in discussion over establishing Common External Tariff as part of the progression towards establishing the CU.[182] These discussions appear to be continuing as there has been no further decision taken on the CU. The main reasons for the delay in launching the CU include the complexities brought about by the concurrent membership of numerous RECs (COMESA, EAC and SADC) as well as the Southern Africa CU (SACU)[183] and the COMESA CU by some SADC member states.[184] Each of these CUs has different common external tariffs and tariff schedules. It is hoped that these challenges will be overcome by the creation of the TFTA which, in turn, will create a CU.[185] As stated previously, it is envisaged that these three RECs would then merge with five others to form the AEC and they are the constitutive elements of the AfCFTA.

SADC's performance and its underpinning neo-liberal perspective have been evaluated elsewhere by other scholars;[186] therefore, this chapter will not replicate such evaluation, which falls beyond its remit. Instead, it turns to an overview of SADC regulatory instruments in the following section, with an emphasis on IP-related instruments.

174 Article 3, Declaration and Treaty of the Southern African Development Community, (SADC) 1992 (as amended). For a full historical discussion of this upgrade see Ng'ong'ola (2000) pp. 485–506, Ng'ong'ola (2008).
175 RISDP (2005–2020), SADC RISDP Summary (2011).
176 Revised RISDP (2015–2020).
177 RISDP (2020–2030).
178 Hartzenberg (2011) pp. 5–6.
179 Sandrey (2013) p. 2, Gathii (2011) p. 212.
180 Gathii (2011) p. 221.
181 SADC (n.d.a)
182 SADC (2019) p. 10.
183 The SACU member states are Botswana, Lesotho, Namibia, South Africa, and Swaziland. All five are SADC member states.
184 Gathii (2011) p. 213, Draper, Halleson and Alves (2007).
185 SADC (2019) p. 11.
186 Pallotti (2004), Lee (1999), Tsie (1996) pp. 85–86.

3.8.1 Regulatory Instruments

SADC's legal instruments include protocols that become binding after ratification by two-thirds of SADC member states.[187] Two of its protocols expressly reference IP. The first of these is the Protocol on Trade of 1996, which entered into force on 25 January 2001. The objectives of this protocol are the following:[188]

1 To further liberalise intra-regional trade in goods and services on the basis of fair, mutually equitable and beneficial trade arrangements, complemented by protocols in other areas.
2 To ensure efficient production within SADC reflecting the current and dynamic comparative advantages of its members.
3 To contribute towards the climate for domestic, cross-border and foreign investment.
4 To enhance the economic development, diversification and industrialization of the region.

The protocol therefore establishes a framework within which these objectives may be achieved. In particular, it regulates trade in goods,[189] customs procedures,[190] trade laws,[191] trade-related investment matters,[192] trade in services,[193] IP[194] and competition policy[195] *inter alia.* In the context of its regulation of trade in goods, it prohibits the use of any quantitative import[196] and export[197] restrictions by party states. However, there are wide-ranging general exceptions to these prohibitions, which include IP enforcement. Article 9(d) provides that:

> Subject to the requirement that such measures are not applied in a manner which would constitute a means of arbitrary or unjustifiable discrimination between Member States, or a disguised restriction on intra-SADC trade, nothing in Articles 7 and 8 of this protocol shall be construed as to prevent the adopting or enforcement of any measures by a Member State necessary to protect intellectual property rights, or to prevent deceptive trade practices.

Border control IP enforcement measures are thus permissible. These are to be structured within the TRIPS framework as all SADC member states (with the

187 Article 22 Declaration and Treaty of the SADC; see for example Article 16 Protocol on Trade.
188 Article 2.
189 Articles 3–11.
190 Articles 12–15.
191 Articles 16–21.
192 Article 22.
193 Article 23.
194 Article 24.
195 Article 25.
196 Article 7(1).
197 Article 8(1).

exception of Comoros, which is due to complete its WTO accession processes in early 2024)[198] are also WTO members and, as such, are obliged to be TRIPS compliant. Indeed, the protocol expressly reminds party states of this obligation in Article 24, which provides:

> Member states shall adopt policies and implement measures within the community for the protection of intellectual property rights, in accordance with [the] WTO Agreement on Trade-Related Aspects of Intellectual Property Rights.

Consequently, one of the key harmonisation goals of SADC has been articulated as the pursuit of TRIPS compliance by member states in a report commissioned by the ECA in its provision of assistance to SADC.[199]

The second SADC Protocol that refers to IP is the Protocol on Science, Technology and Innovation (STI) of 2008.[200] Following 12 years after the Protocol on Trade, the Protocol on STI's main purpose is to "foster co-operation and promote, the development, transfer and mastery of science, technology and innovation in member states" so as to achieve a wide range of related goals.[201] Amongst these is "the development and harmonisation of STI policies in the region"[202] and "the enhance[ment] and strengthen[ing] of the protection of intellectual property rights."[203]

3.8.2 IP Framework and Guidelines

As noted in chapter one, the SADC Council of Ministers in August 2018 approved the IP Framework and Guidelines, which were partially based on several studies.[204] These instruments do not have binding force and serve as normative blueprints and policy guidelines. The framework consists of these substantive parts: (1) Introduction, (2) State of IP in the SADC Region, (3) TRIPS Agreement and Regional Best Practices and (4) SADC Regional IP Framework. The framework has the following two annexures:

1 National IP Strategy and/or Policy Outline which is informed, in part, by the WIPO IP policies toolkit discussed in chapter two and has an outline of Zimbabwe's National IP Policy and Implementation Strategy appended to it as a sample.

198 WTO (2023).
199 ECA (2014).
200 Signed 17 August 2008.
201 Article 2 Protocol on STI.
202 Article 2(c).
203 Article 2(m).
204 Economic Commission for Africa (ECA) (2018), SADC (2017), ECA Subregional Office South Africa (SRO-SA) (2015).

2 A Model Framework IP Policy for universities and public research institutions.

These are intended to assist member states in their IP policy formulation.

The framework expressly refers to COMESA, EAC and ECOWAS IP policies as well as the COMESA-EAC-SADC TFTA's IP agenda[205] which is important because of cross-memberships of member states. Specifically, nine SADC member states are also COMESA member states and one is also an EAC partner state. This means that alignment is required between REC IP policies.

Noting that SADC member states are at different levels of development, the framework as outlined in part 4 focuses on

> mutual cooperation on the basis of agreed areas of mutual interest in using IP as an instrument for socio-economic development and to drive industrialisation within the region, with harmonisation being a desired long-term objective, thereby enabling countries to use IP to transition their economies to innovation driven knowledge economies at their own pace and in mutual cooperation and with the assistance of other SADC Member States.[206]

The framework enumerates 11 "key considerations," which include TRIPS minimum standards and other relevant "international and continental instruments,"[207] such as the Marrakesh Treaty, and it notes access to copyright-protected works should be enabled for persons with disabilities.[208] It also emphasises the importance of meaningful use of TRIPS flexibilities, among other aspects.[209] The specific recommendations it makes in relation to TRIPS flexibilities are the following:[210]

> [1] Member States make use of the full extent of the flexibilities provided under the TRIPS Agreement . . .
> [2] . . . that LDCs take full advantage of the TRIPS transition periods . . .
> [3] Flexibilities should not be limited to health-related considerations;
> [4] Research flexibilities should be used to support STI objectives in accordance with the SADC STI Protocol;
> [5] Early working (Bolar) or regulatory exception provisions should be enacted to support the development of a pharmaceutical industry within the SADC region, with particular emphasis on development of a manufacturing industry for generic drugs, in support of the SADC Business Plan on Pharmaceuticals.
> [6] In order to stimulate local manufacturing, and support bulk imports into one country and re-exportation into the rest of the region, SADC

205 SADC IP Framework and Guidelines (2018) supra p. 16.
206 SADC IP Framework and Guidelines (2018) p. 19.
207 SADC IP Framework and Guidelines (2018).
208 SADC IP Framework and Guidelines (2018) p. 20.
209 SADC IP Framework and Guidelines (2018) p. 21.
210 SADC IP Framework and Guidelines (2018) pp. 20–21.

Member States should domesticate the waiver decision (Article 31*bis* of TRIPS). Domesticating the waiver has the potential to stimulate local or regional generic manufacturing capacity and provide the means to implement any compulsory licences that may be issued by Member States.

[7] Compulsory licences are an effective tool for curbing abuse of the exclusive rights granted by a patent, as well as ensuring a balance between the public interest and the rights of the IP owner.

Its main goal is "to foster mutual cooperation on IP issues within the context of industrialisation, trade, and addressing socio-economic development and competitiveness of the SADC Region in its transition to innovation driven knowledge economies."[211] The framework is then elucidated on these six pillars: (1) Policy and Legislative, (2) Human and Administrative Infrastructure, (3) Use of IPRs, (4) Governance, (5) Communication and Advocacy and (6) Monitoring and Evaluation.[212]

It proposes the development of a SADC IP protocol in the medium to long term and suggests aspects to be covered by said protocol.[213] Plans for this protocol have been overtaken by the AfCFTA IP Protocol and it would not be prudent to seek to develop another IP protocol at sub-regional level.

SADC member states' usage of TRIPS flexibilities has been mixed, with eight of the 15 using flexibilities, specifically compulsory licences or government use and "non-enforcement of patents using the LDC transition provision."[214]

3.9 TFTA

The COMESA-EAC-SADC TFTA is a significant building block of the AfCFTA.[215] As noted previously, the TFTA was launched in June 2015, pursuant to an agreement reached between the RECs. Article 39(3) of the agreement provides that it will enter into force 30 days after the 14th instrument of ratification is lodged. However, that threshold had not been met by March 2023.[216] Under Article 45 of the agreement, the tripartite parties should commence negotiations on trade in services and other trade-related areas such as competition policy and intellectual property rights within 24 months of the entry into force of the agreement. Protocols on each of these aspects would be negotiated and adopted. As indicated in chapter one, the ratification rate and subsequent entry into force of the AfCFTA Agreement has overtaken the TFTA.

The 2009 draft agreement contained a detailed IP agenda based on its Article 27 and Annex 9 on IPRs, which did not ultimately form part of the final agreement. The aspects covered included traditional knowledge (TK), genetic resources

211 SADC IP Framework and Guidelines (2018) p. 22.
212 SADC IP Framework and Guidelines (2018).
213 SADC IP Framework and Guidelines (2018) pp. 32–33.
214 't Hoen, Kujinga and Boulet (2018).
215 ECA (2012) p. 21.
216 COMESA (2023).

and folklore[217] for which "IP or sui generis systems" of protection were recommended.[218] Such systems would include "the creation of databases, development of guidelines for access benefit sharing (ABS) and prior informed consent."[219] Articles 6 and 7 dealt with copyright and industrial property, respectively, and set out five similar undertakings in relation to each.

All the aspects identified in this TFTA IP agenda can, and should, be subsumed under the AfCFTA IP Protocol negotiations. This would be the most efficient approach, rather than to replicate the AfCFTA-level negotiations amongst the TFTA parties which would be incorporated into the AfCFTA anyway, as these three RECs are amongst the eight that will constitute the AfCFTA.

3.10 Conclusion

The overview given here has shown the extent to which RECs are involved in IP harmonisation and integration. It is clear that the four RECs under discussion have made significant progress on this front. This work has to be incorporated into any continental IP integration efforts, especially since the COMESA-EAC-SADC TFTA has been overtaken by the AfCFTA. Similarly, it has to be framed within the context of the work that has been done by the sub-regional IP organisations that are the subject of chapter four. Therefore, the nature of the relationship between the regional IP organisations and the RECs becomes significant because their membership consists of the same countries. Co-operation and co-ordination between them is managed, in part, through memoranda of understanding through which the RECs draw upon the expertise of the regional IP organisations' secretariats. Cultivating such relationships avoids duplication of efforts and allows effective use of expertise across the organisations and RECs. REC IP policies, whether they be general or specific to patent-related flexibilities, are a welcome development as they provide a policy model for individual states to follow. As they are collective in their conceptualisation, they also contribute to a harmonised regional approach which aids regional cohesiveness and facilitates collaborative approaches to public interest problems such as securing access to pharmaceuticals. However, as shown here, their detailed guidance has not comprehensively been translated into domestic legislation nor implemented.

Reference List

Primary Sources

Case Law

Patricia Asero Ochieng, Maurine Atieno and Joseph Munyi v The Attorney General HCCC. Petition No. 409 of 2009 Para 78.

217 Annex 9,2009 Draft Agreement, Article 4.
218 Annex 9, 2009 Draft Agreement, Articles 4(b) and 4(d).
219 Annex 9, 2009 Draft Agreement, Article 4(c).

Legal Instruments

AU

AU Commission, New Zealand Ministry of Foreign Affairs and Trade/Manat Aorere, 2014. *AU Handbook*. Wellington: Ministry of Foreign Affairs and Trade/Manat Aorere.

Assembly Decision on the Moratorium on the Recognition of Regional Economic Communities (RECs) DOC. EX.CL/278 (IX). AU Doc. Assembly/AU/Dec.111–132 (VII). Assembly of the African Union, Seventh Ordinary Session, 1–2 July 2006. Banjul, The Gambia.

Assembly Decision on the Transformation of the NEPAD Planning and Coordinating Agency (NPCA) into the African Union Development Agency (AUDA) – Doc. Assembly/AU/2(XXXI). Thirty-First Ordinary Session, 1–2 July 2018. Nouakchott, Mauritania. Assembly/AU/Dec.691(XXXI).

Constitutive Act of the African Union (2000).

Monrovia Declaration of Commitment of the Heads of State and Government, of the OAU on Guidelines and Measures for National and Collective Self-Reliance in Social and Economic Development for the Establishment of a New International Economic Order (1979).

Protocol on Relations Between the AU and the RECs (2007).

Treaty Establishing the African Economic Community (Abuja Treaty) (1991).

COMESA

COMESA Report of the Thirtieth Meeting of the Council of Ministers CS/CM/XXX/2 (2011).

Council of Ministers Decision 90(f). Official Gazette Volume 16 (15 October 2011).

Treaty Establishing the Common Market for Eastern and Southern Africa (1993).

EAC

Draft Anti-Counterfeit Bill 2011 (Draft 251011).

Draft Policy on Anti-Counterfeiting, Anti-Piracy and other Intellectual Property Rights Violations (2009) (Draft 260609).

EAC Regional Health Sector Policy (2016).

Protocol on the Establishment of the EAC Common Market (2009).

Protocol for the Establishment of the EAC Customs Union (2004).

Treaty for Establishment of the EAC (1999).

ECOWAS

Economic Community of West African States, Revised Treaty (1993).

Heads of State Decision A/Dec.9/10/98 (1998).

Protocol A/P.2/7/87 on the Establishment of a West African Health Organisation (1987).

Supplementary Protocol A/SP.1/01/06 Amending Articles VI-C, VI-L, IX-8, XI-2 and XII of Protocol A/P2/7/87 on the Establishment of the WAHO (2006).

SADC

Declaration and Treaty of the SADC (1992).
Protocol on Trade (1996).
Regional Indicative Strategic Development Plan (RISDP) (2020–2030).
Revised RISDP (2015–2020).
RISDP Summary (2011).
RISDP (2005–2020)
RISDP (2003).
SADC IP Framework and Guidelines (2018).
SADCC Memorandum of Understanding (1981).
SADC Protocol on the Tribunal and Rules of Procedure Thereof (2000).
SADC Vision 2050.

COMESA-EAC-SADC Tripartite FTA

Agreement Establishing the Tripartite Free Trade Area among the COMESA, EAC and SADC (2015).
Annex 9: Annex on Intellectual Property Rights under Article 27(1) of the Draft Agreement Establishing the Tripartite Free Trade Area (2009).

WIPO

Technical Assistance Database: COMESA – Comments on Draft Model Law on IP Policy and Draft Model Law on IP, October 2011. Available at www.wipo.int/tad/en/activitydetails.jsp?id=2246 [accessed 6 January 2023].

WTO

General Agreement on Tariffs and Trade (GATT) (1994) 33 I.L.M. 1125, 1154.
General Agreement on Trade in Services (GATS) (1994) 33 I.L.M. 1125, 1167.
WTO Understanding on the Interpretation of Article XXIV of the General Agreement on Tariffs and Trade (1994). Available at https://www.wto.org/english/docs_e/legal_e/10-24.pdf [accessed 6 January 2023].

National Legislation

Kenya: The Anti-Counterfeit Act (2008).
Kenya: Treaty for the Establishment of the East African Community Act 2 of 2000 (Cap 4C).
Rwanada: Constitution (2003).
Tanzania: Merchandise Marks Regulations in Tanzania [made under Section 18A of the Merchandise Marks Act, Chapter 85 Laws of Tanzania].
Uganda: The Counterfeit Goods Bill (2008).

Secondary Sources

Afadameh-Adeyemi, A., 2013. Securing Compliance with African Economic Integration Treaties. Thesis (PhD). University of Cape Town.

Akokpari, J., 2008. Dilemmas of Regional Integration and Development in Africa. In Akokpari, J. et al. (eds.) *The African Union and its Institutions*. Auckland Park, South Africa: Fanele, 85–110.

Asante, S.K.B., 1997. *Regionalism and Africa's Development: Expectations, Reality and Challenges*. London: Palgrave Macmillan.

AU, n.d. *Economic Community of Central African States (ECCAS)*. Available at www.au.int/en/recs/eccas [accessed 6 November 2022].

Balassa, B.A., 1961. *The Theory of Economic Integration*. Homewood, IL: Richard Dale, Inc.

Blakeney, M. and Mengistie, G., 2011. Intellectual Property and Economic Development in Sub-Saharan Africa. *Journal of World Intellectual Property*, 14(3/4), 238–264.

CEHRUD, 2010. Anti-Counterfeiting Laws and Access to Essential Medicines in East and Southern Africa EQUINET, CEHRUD. *TARSC Policy Brief 22*, Harare: EQUINET.

Chikabwi, D., 2020. Do Stronger Intellectual Property Rights Stimulate Intra-COMESA Exports? In *Promoting Intra-COMESA Trade Through Innovation, COMESA Policy Brief on Key Issues in Regional Integration* (Vol. 8) [online], October 2020, 19–21. Available at www.comesa.int/wp-content/uploads/2021/02/210218_Policy-Brief-on-Key-Issues-Volume-8.pdf [accessed 2 January 2023].

COMESA, 2023. Tripartite Council of Ministers Adopt Legal Instruments to Implement the Tripartite Free Trade Area, 29 March 2023. Available at https://www.comesa.int/tripartite-council-of-ministers-adopt-legal-instruments-to-implement-the-tripartite-free-trade-area/ [accessed 12 April 2023].

COMESA, n.d. *COMESA Member States*. Available at www.comesa.int/comesa-members-states/ [accessed 7 January 2023].

Crawford, J. and Fiorentino, R., 2005. *The Changing Landscape of Regional Trade Agreements*. Discussion Paper No. 8. Geneva, Switzerland: WTO.

Draper, P., Halleson, D. and Alves, P., 2007. *SACU, Regional Integration and the Overlap Issue in Southern Africa: From Spaghetti to Cannelloni*? Johannesburg: The South African Institute of International Affairs.

East Africa Entrepreneurs Association (EAEA), 2018. *Regional Stakeholder Workshop to Validate the Draft Report for the EAC Regional Policy for Science Technology and Innovation and Intellectual Property on 24th–25th September 2018 at Kenya School of Monetary Studies*, Nairobi, Kenya [online]. Available at https://eaentrepreneurs.org/regional-stakeholder-workshop-to-validate-the-draft-report-for-the-eac-regional-policy-for-science-technology-and-innovation-and-intellectual-property-on-24th-25th-september-2018-at-kenya-school-of-mo/ [accessed 2 January 2023].

East African Science and Technology Commission (EASTECO), 2018. *Regional Stakeholder Workshop on EAC Regional Policy for Intellectual Property (IP)*, set for 25th September 2018 in Nairobi, Kenya [online], 24 September 2018. Available at www.eac.int/press-releases/1222-regional-stakeholder-workshop-on-eac-regional-policy-for-intellectual-property-ip-set-for-25th-september-2018-in-nairobi,-kenya [accessed 2 January 2023].

EASTECO, n.d. *Development of the East African Regional Policy for Intellectual Property* [online]. Available at https://easteco.org/development-of-the-east-african-regional-policy-for-intellectual-property/#:~:text=The%20EAC%20Intellectual%20Property%20Policy,technological%20development%20of%20the%20Community [accessed 2 January 2023].

ECA, 2011. *Final Report: Study on the Establishment of Inter-RECs' Free Trade Areas in Africa Drawing on Lessons From the COMESA-SADC-EAC FTA Experience*. Addis Ababa: ECA.

ECA, 2012. *Assessing Regional Integration in Africa (ARIA V): Towards an African Continental Free Trade Area*. Addis Ababa: ECA. Available at https://repository.uneca.org/handle/10855/22110 [accessed 7 January 2023].

ECA (Ncube, C.B.), 2018. *Developing an Intellectual Property Rights (IPR) Framework in the Southern African Development Community (SADC)*. Addis Ababa: ECA. Available at https://archive.uneca.org/sites/default/files/PublicationFiles/e1700855_developing_an_intellectual_property_rights_framework_in_the_southern_african_development_community.pdf [accessed 7 January 2023].

ECA Southern Africa Office, 2014. *Opportunities and Challenges in Using Intellectual Property Systems to Strengthen Regional Cooperation through Policy Harmonization in the SADC Region*. ECA-SA/TP.IPR/2014.

ECA Subregional Office South Africa (SRO-SA), (Sibanda, G.), 2015. *Opportunities and Challenges in Using Intellectual Property Systems to Strengthen Regional Cooperation Through Policy Harmonization in the Southern African Development Community*. Addis Ababa: ECA. Available at https://hdl.handle.net/10855/22686 [accessed 7 January 2023].

Fiorentino, R.V., Verdeja, L. and Toqueboeuf, C., 2006. *The Changing Landscape of Regional Trade Agreements: 2006 Update*. Discussion Paper No. 12, Geneva, Switzerland: WTO.

Gakunga, M., 2019. *Go Easy on Stringent Intellectual Property Rights – Research* [online], 4 September 2019. Available at www.comesa.int/stringent-intellectual-property-rights-impede-innovations-in-trade-research/ [accessed 2 January 2023].

Gakunga, M., 2020. COMESA, WIPO Sign Pact to Boost Intellectual Property Rights [online], 21 February 2020. Available at www.comesa.int/comesa-wipo-sign-pact-to-boost-intellectual-property-rights-2/ [accessed 2 January 2023].

Gathii, J.T., 2011. *African Regional Trade Agreements as Legal Regimes*. Cambridge: Cambridge University Press.

Gerout, G., MacLeod, J. and Desta, M, 2019. The AfCFTA as Yet Another Experiment Towards Continental Integration. In Luke, D. and MacLeod, J. (eds.) *Inclusive Trade in Africa: The African Continental Free Trade Area in Comparative Perspective*. Abingdon: Routledge, 15–34.

Ghathii, J.T., 2010. African Regional Trade Agreements as Flexible Legal Regimes. *North Carolina Journal of International Law and Commercial Regulation*, 35(3), 572–668.

Gottschalk, K., 2012. The African Union and its Sub-Regional Structures. *Journal of African Union Studies*, 1(1), 9–39.

Haas, E., 1970. The Study of Regional Integration: Reflections on the Joy and Anguish of Pre Theorizing. *International Organisation*, 24(4), 607–646.

HAIA, 2010. *Report of the International Meeting on the Proliferation of Anti-counterfeiting Legislation in the East African Community: Addressing Public Health, Copyright and Developmental Concerns*. Arusha, Tanzania: HAIA.

Hartzenberg, T., 2011. *Regional Integration in Africa*. WTO Economic Research and Statistics Division Working Paper ERSD-2011–14. Geneva, Switzerland: WTO.

Hartzenberg, T. and Malungisa, D., 2011. Regional Integration in Southern Africa: Key Issues and Challenges. In Volz, U. (ed.) *Regional Integrations, Economic Development and Global Governance*. Cheltenham, UK: Edward Elgar.

Jensen, C.S., 2013. Neo-Functionalism. In Cini, M. and Borragan, N.P.-S. (eds.) *European Union Politics* (4th ed.). Oxford: Oxford University Press, 59–70.

Khadiagala, G., 2012. The SADCC and Its Approaches to African Regionalism. In Dzinesa, G.A., Nagar, D. and Saunders, C. (eds.) *Region-Building in Southern Africa: Progress, Problems and Prospects*. London and New York: Zed Books, 25–38.

Kolbeck, B., 2014. Legal Analysis on the Relationship Between the AU/AEC and RECs: Africa Lost in a "Spaghetti Bowl" of Legal Relations? Thesis (LLM). University of Cape Town.

Kouassi, R.N., 2007. The Itinerary of the African Integration Process: An Overview of the Historical Landmarks. *African Integration Review*, 1(2), 1–23.

Lee, M.C., 1999. Development, Cooperation and Integration in the SADC Region. *University of Mauritius Research Journal*, 2, 29–61.

Lee, M.C., 2002. Regionalism in Africa: A Part of the Problem or a Part of the Solution. *Polis/RCSP/CPSR*, 9, 1–24.

Lee, M.C., 2003. *The Political Economy of Regionalism in Southern Africa*. Cape Town and Boulder: UCT Press and Lynne Rienner Publishers.

Magogo, T.D.B., 2013. Harmonization of Copyright Within the East African Community: An Analysis of the Kenyan and Tanzanian Copyright Legislation. Mini-thesis LLM. University of the Western Cape.

Makochekanwa, A. and Mashura, S., 2020. Innovation and the Architecture of IPR Regimes: Evidence from COMESA Countries. In *Promoting Intra-COMESA Trade Through Innovation, COMESA Policy Brief on Key Issues in Regional Integration* (Vol. 8) [online], October 2020, 10–14. Available at www.comesa.int/wp-content/uploads/2021/02/210218_Policy-Brief-on-Key-Issues-Volume-8.pdf [accessed 2 January 2023].

Masunda, S., 2020. The Role of Intellectual Property Rights Protection on Intra-COMESA Trade: The Case of Trademarks. In *Promoting Intra-COMESA Trade Through Innovation, COMESA Policy Brief on Key Issues in Regional Integration* (Vol. 8) [online], October 2020, 26–28. Available at www.comesa.int/wp-content/uploads/2021/02/210218_Policy-Brief-on-Key-Issues-Volume-8.pdf [accessed 2 January 2023].

Matambalya, F.A.S.T., 2014. Integration of Industrialisation in Sub-Regional Development Agendas: Overviews of African Regional Economic Communities. In Matambalya, F.A.S.T. (ed.) *African Industrial Development and EU Cooperation: Prospects for a Reengineered Partnership*. Abingdon, Oxfordshire: Routledge.

Matthias, J.H. and Bhagwati, J., 2002. *Regional Trade Agreements in the GATT/WTO: Article XX1V and the Internal Trade Requirement*. The Hague: TMC Asser Press.

Mugabe, J., 2006. *Africa's Science and Technology: Consolidated Plan of Action*. Pretoria: New Partnership for Africa's Development (NEPAD). Available at: https://library.au.int/africas-science-and-technology-consolidated-plan-action-3 [accessed 2 January 2023].

Mukisa, R. and Thompson, B., 1995. Prerequisites for Economic Integration in Africa: An Analysis of the Abuja Treaty. *Africa Today*, 42(4), 56–80.

Murithi, T., 2005. *The African Union: Pan-Africanism, Peacebuilding and Development*. Aldershot, Hampshire: Ashgate.

Musungu, S.F., 2010. *The Potential Impact of the Proposed East African Community (EAC) Anti-Counterfeiting Policy and Bill on Access to Essential Medicines*. UNDP BDP HIV Practice/March 2010 Discussion Paper.

Mutai, H.K., 2007. *Compliance with International Trade Obligations: The Common Market for Eastern and Southern Africa*. Netherlands: Kluwer Law International.

Mutharika, B., 1972. *Towards Multinational Economic Cooperation in Africa*. New York: Praeger.

Mwanza, W., 2014. *Review of Trade Related Developments in 2014* [online]. Stellenbosch: TRALAC. Available at http://www.tralac.org/discussions/article/6803reviewoftraderelateddevelopmentsin2014.html [accessed 4 February 2023].

Ncube, C.B., 2021. *Science, Technology & Innovation and Intellectual Property: Leveraging Openness for Sustainable Development in Africa*. Cape Town: Juta.

Ng'ong'ola, C., 2000. Regional Integration and Trade Liberalization in the Southern African Development Community. *Journal of International Economic Law*, 3, 485–506.

Ng'ong'ola, C., 2008. The Legal Framework for Regional Integration in the Southern African Development Community. *University of Botswana Law Journal*, 8, 3–46.

Nkomo, M., 2014. Regional Integration in the Area of Intellectual Property: The Case for Southern African Development Community Involvement. *Law Democracy & Development*, 18, 317–333.

Nyachae, J. and Ogendi, P., 2012. Anti-Counterfeiting and Access to Generic Medicines in Kenya: Reviewing Patricia Osero Ochieng & 2 Others v Attorney General. *ESR Review: Economic and Social Rights in South Africa*, 13(3), 12–15.

Ogendi, P.O., 2018. Pharmaceutical Trade Policies and Access to Medicines in Kenya, LLD Thesis, University of Pretoria, Pretoria. Available at http://hdl.handle.net/2263/68334 [accessed 8 January 2023].

Olatunji, O.A., 2021. How Much Is Too Much? Anti-Counterfeit Measures and Access to Medicines in the East African Community. *European Intellectual Property Review*, 9, 594–608.

Olatunji, O.A., 2022. Historical Account of Dwindling National Flexibilities from the Paris Convention to Post-TRIPS Era: What Implications for Access-to-medicines in Low-and-middle-income-countries? *The Journal of World Intellectual Property*, 25, 391–411. https://doi.org/10.1111/jwip.12228

Olivier, G. and Olivier, M., 2004. Models of Regional Integration: The European Union and the African Union. *SA Public Law (SAPR/PL)*, 19, 351–364.

Onoria, H., 2011. Uganda. In Shelton, D. (ed.) *International Law and Domestic Legal Systems: Incorporation, Transformation, and Persuasion*. Oxford: Oxford University Press, 594–619.

Oppong, R.F., 2006. Observing the Legal System of the Community: The Relationship Between Community and National Legal Systems Under the African Economic Community Treaty. *Tulane Journal of International and Comparative Law*, 15, 41–87.

Oppong, R.F., 2008. Making Regional Economic Community Laws Enforceable in National Legal Systems – Constitutional and Judicial Challenges. In Bosl, A., Breytenbach, W., Hartzenberg, T., McCarthy, C. and Schade, K. (eds.) *Monitoring Regional Integration in Southern Africa Yearbook Volume 8*. Stellenbosch: Trade Law Centre for Southern Africa, the Konrad Adenaur Stiftung and the Namibian Economic Unit, 149–178.

Oppong, R.F., 2010. The African Union, the African Economic Community and Africa's Regional Economic Communities: Untangling a Complex Web. *African Journal of International and Comparative Law*, 18, 92–103.

Oppong, R.F., 2011. *Legal Aspects of Economic Integration in Africa*. Cambridge: Cambridge University Press.

Osiemo, O., 2014. Lost in Translation: The Role of African Regional Courts in Regional Integration in Africa. *Legal Issues of Economic Integration*, 41(1), 87–122.

Oslington, P., 2013. Contextual History, Practitioner History, and Classic Status: Reading Jacob Viner's the Customs Union Issue. *Journal of the History of Economic Thought*, 3(4), 491–515.

Ostergaard, T., 1993. Classical Models of Regional Integration-What Relevance for Southern Africa? In Oden, B. (ed.) *Southern Africa After Apartheid, Regional Integration and External resources*. Uppsala: Nordic Africa Institute, 27–47.

Oyejide, A., Elbadawi, I. and Collier, P. (eds.), 1997. *Regional Integration and Trade Liberalization in Sub-Saharan Africa: Framework, Issues and Methodological Perspectives*. Basingstoke: Palgrave Macmillan.

Pallotti, A., 2004. SADC: A Development Community Without a Development Policy? *Review of African Political Economy*, 31(101), 513–531. http://doi.org/10.1080/0305624042000295576

Perdikis, N., 2007. Overview of Trade Agreements: Regional Trade Agreements. In Kerr, W.A. and Gaisford, J.D. (eds.) *Handbook on International Trade Policy*. Cheltenham: Edward Elgar.

SADC (Sibanda, M.), 2017. *Study on Developing an Intellectual Property Rights (IPR) Framework in the Southern African Development Community (SADC)*. Gaborone, Botswana: SADC.

SADC, 2019. *Status of Integration in the Southern African Development Community (SADC)*. Gaborone, Botswana: SADC.

SADC, n.d.a. *Customs Union*. Available at https://www.sadc.int/integration-milestones/customs-union [accessed 12 April 2023].

SADC, n.d.b. *History*. Available at https://www.sadc.int/pages/history-and-treaty [accessed 12 April 2023].

Sandrey, R., 2013. *An Analysis of the SADC FTA*. Tralac Trade Brief D13TB01/2013.

't Hoen, E.F.M., Kujinga, T. and Boulet, P., 2018. Patent Challenges in the Procurement and Supply of Generic New Essential Medicines and Lessons from HIV in the Southern African Development Community (SADC) Region. *Journal of Pharmaceutical Policy and Practice*, 11, 31. http://doi.org/10.1186/s40545-018-0157-7

Thompson, B., 1993. Economic Integration Efforts in Africa: A Milestone – the Abuja Treaty. *African Journal of International and Comparative Law*, 5, 743–767.

Tsie, B., 1996. States and Markets in the Southern African Development Community (SADC): Beyond the Neo-Liberal Paradigm. *Journal of Southern African Studies*, 22(1), 75–98. http://doi.org/10.1080/03057079608708479

UNCTAD, 2007. *Trade and Development Report: Regional Cooperation for Development*. UNCTAD/TDR/2007. Geneva: UNCTAD. Available at https://unctad.org/system/files/official-document/tdr2007_en.pdf [accessed 12 April 2023].

Viner, J., 1950. *The Customs Union Issue*. New York: Carnegie Endowment for International Peace.

Winter, J.A., 1972. Direct Applicability and Direct Effect Two Distinct and Different Concepts in Community Law. *Common Market Law Review*, 9(4), 425–438.

WTO, 2021. *WTO-ECOWAS Workshop Addresses Health, Intellectual Property and Trade Policy-Making* [online], 29 March 2021. Available at www.wto.org/english/news_e/news21_e/heal_29mar21_e.htm [accessed 4 January 2023].

WTO, 2023. *Members Commend Comoros' Efforts to Clear Final Hurdles on Path to WTO Accession by MC13*, 9 January 2023. Available at https://www.wto.org/english/news_e/news23_e/acc_19jan23_e.htm [accessed 12 April 2023].

WTO, n.d. *Regional Trade Agreements Information System (RTA-IS) User Guide*. Available at http://rtais.wto.org/UserGuide/RTAIS_USER_GUIDE_EN.html#_Toc201649637 [accessed 15 March 2023].

4 Sub-Regional IP Organisations

4.1 Introduction

This chapter considers co-operation with respect to IP in specific sub-regional organisations where IP is the sole focus, namely in ARIPO and OAPI. Chapter three focused on African states' collaboration with respect to trade through RECs that include IP, amongst other aspects of trade. Many states are involved in both types of collaboration, and also have multiple REC memberships. This chapter details each sub-regional IP organisation's organs and regulatory frameworks in turn. It does not give a detailed overview of all of the substantive content of these frameworks. To enable comparative analysis of the two organisations, it outlines only those areas where both organisations have legal instruments in place, namely patents, utility models, industrial designs, trade marks and plant variety protection to enable some comparative commentary.

At the outset, it is important make the following comments about the two regional IP organisations' frameworks. OAPI's legal framework is much broader in coverage than ARIPO and it includes annexes on literary and artistic property, geographical indications, trade names, layout designs of integrated circuits and unfair competition which ARIPO does not have protocols on. In relation to copyright, covered by the Bangui Agreement Annex on literary and artistic property, ARIPO has a counterpart in its recently adopted Kampala Protocol on Voluntary Registration of Copyright and Related Rights of 2021. The difference between the two is that the Bangui Agreement covers substantive elements such as eligibility for protection, rights and duration whilst the Kampala Protocol is only about the registration of said rights. Where both organisations have regulatory instruments covering the same subject matter, there are also differences in approach that are noted later. Finally, there are areas covered by ARIPO and not OAPI, namely ARIPO's Swakopmund Protocol, which covers traditional knowledge, whilst OAPI does not yet have an equivalent legal instrument.

Whilst the ARIPO and OAPI IP frameworks have significant substantive and procedural differences, which will soon become apparent, they cooperate with each other in various ways. For instance, they entered into a quadripartite co-operation agreement in 1985 (with WIPO and the African Regional Centre for Technology)

DOI: 10.4324/9781003310198-4

and into a dual co-operation agreement in 1996.[1] Another instance of their co-operation is the joint response of the ARIPO and OAPI Secretariats to the creation of PAIPO, announced in April 2014, which is discussed in chapter five. In that communiqué they referred to the possibility of an amalgamation between them to create a single African IP Office.[2] The chapter concludes with a consideration of the viability of such amalgamation. They have a long-standing bilateral co-operation through their Joint Commission, under which they meet often.[3] Continuing their co-operation with other entities, in 2018 they created the further tripartite co-operation framework of WIPO-ARIPO-OAPI (WAO), pursuant to a memorandum of understanding signed on 1 October 2018.[4]

4.2 ARIPO

As of 31 May 2022, ARIPO had 21 member states, namely Botswana, Eswatini, The Gambia, Ghana, Kenya, Lesotho, Liberia, Malawi, Mauritius, Mozambique, Namibia, Rwanda, São Tomé and Principe, Seychelles, Sierra Leone, Somalia, Sudan, Tanzania, Uganda, Zambia and Zimbabwe. ARIPO cooperates with the following 12 non-member states which have observer status in the meetings of its main organs: Algeria, Angola, Burundi, Egypt, Eritrea, Ethiopia, Libya, Mauritius, Nigeria, Seychelles, South Africa and Tunisia.[5]

ARIPO was initially known as the Industrial Property Organisation for English-speaking Africa (ESARIPO).[6] It was established on 9 December 1976 through the adoption of the Agreement on the Creation of the Industrial Property Organisation for English-speaking Africa at a diplomatic conference held in Lusaka, Zambia (the Lusaka Agreement). The Lusaka Agreement came into force on 15 February 1978, thereby bringing ESAPIRO into operation. It was created with technical and administrative assistance from the UN Economic Commission for Africa (ECA) and WIPO.[7] Consequently, in Article 5 the Lusaka Agreement mandates that ARIPO "shall establish and maintain close and continuous working relationships" with these two organisations and the African Union.

Upon its establishment, membership of the organisation was limited to Anglophone African countries, but in December 1985, Article 4 of the Lusaka Agreement was amended in order to expand the pool of states eligible for membership to include all members of ECA or the OAU (now the AU).[8] The organisation's name

1 Chirambo (2002) paras 29–30.
2 ARIPO and OAPI (2014).
3 ARIPO (2022).
4 WIPO Coordination Committee (2018) WO/CC/75/1 Annex I.
5 In terms of Article VI of the Lusaka Agreement on the Creation of the African Regional Intellectual Property Organisation (ARIPO) (1978) as amended (Lusaka Agreement).
6 Kongolo (2013) p. 75, Adewopo (2005) p. 2, Nwauche (2003) p. 123.
7 Chirambo (2002) para 6.
8 Chirambo (2002) para 7, Adewopo (2005) p. 2.

was then changed to the African Industrial Property Organisation (ARIPO) in order to reflect its new membership profile.[9] Whilst the acronym remained constant, ARIPO again changed its full name to the African Regional IP organisation in 2004.[10] The original reference to industrial property in the organisation's name was a reflection of its initial exclusive focus on industrial property. As will be shown, its first two protocols dealt with marks, patents and industrial designs. With the passage of time the organisation's focus expanded to include other types of IP, necessitating the replacement of industrial property with IP in its name. More recently it has consolidated its activities in the field of copyright, and in 2021 it adopted the Kampala Protocol on the Voluntary Registration of Copyright.

The main motivating factor behind the establishment of ARIPO was to more effectively leverage member states' resources and obtain various advantages through collaboration. The preamble to the Lusaka Agreement states that member states are "aware of the advantage to be derived by them from the effective and continuous exchange of information and harmonization and co-ordination of their laws and activities in industrial property matters." ARIPO's objectives are then spelt out in full in Article 3 of the Lusaka Agreement. In summary, they pertain to the harmonisation of IP frameworks and the sharing of related resources with the intention of achieving technological advancement for economic and industrial development of the member states.

4.2.1 Organs

ARIPO has three primary organs, namely the Council of Ministers, the Administrative Council and the Secretariat.[11] ECA and WIPO acted as a joint Secretariat of ARIPO, in its first iteration as ESARIPO from its inception until 1 June 1981 when it established its own Secretariat.[12] Thereafter, the Administrative Council established more subsidiary organs, namely the Finance Committee and the Board of Appeal in 1993 and 1997, respectively,[13] followed by an Audit Committee, a Staff Affairs Committee (renamed the Human Capital Committee)[14] and several technical committees. Each of these organs' composition and principal duties are summarised in the following sections.

Council of Ministers

The Council of Ministers is ARIPO's "supreme body" and, as such, bears ultimate responsibility for its policy direction and has oversight of its activities.[15] The membership

9 Chirambo (2002) para 7, Adewopo (2005) p. 2, Nwauche (2003) p. 128.
10 Kongolo (2013) p. 75, Amendment to the Lusaka Agreement adopted by the Council of Ministers on 13 August 2004.
11 Article II of the Lusaka Agreement.
12 Chirambo (2002) para 6.
13 Chirambo (2002) para 15.
14 ARIPO (2018).
15 Articles VI*bis* (2) and (3)(e) Lusaka Agreement.

of the Council of Ministers consists of the government ministers responsible for the administration of IP in each member state.[16] Its functions include the receipt of various annual reports, budgets and accounts;[17] resolving disputes and problems that are beyond the Administrative Council;[18] determining any special contributions to be paid by members[19] and determining the location of ARIPO headquarters.[20] Any of these powers may be delegated by the Council of Ministers to the Administrative Council.[21] Ordinary meetings of the Council of Ministers are convened at least once every two years and may be attended by accredited observer states.[22]

Administrative Council

The Administrative Council is composed of the Heads of Offices dealing with the administration of IP in the member states.[23] However, a person who does not hold such a position but who has the requisite IP knowledge may be nominated to represent a member state.[24] The functions of the Administrative Council include the formulation and execution of ARIPO policy;[25] the approval of ARIPO's program of activities, annual reports, accounts and budgets;[26] the determination of annual and special member contributions;[27] the establishment of the Secretariat and the appointment of the Director General;[28] and creating any necessary subsidiary organs.[29] Any of these powers may be delegated to the chair and/or vice-chair of the Administrative Council, the Director General or any subsidiary organ.[30]

The Administrative Council's function in setting special contributions overlaps directly with the council's exercise of the same function. To avoid a duplication of roles, it might have been better to exclusively reserve the power of setting special contributions for the Council of Ministers. This would leave the setting of annual contributions to the Administrative Council.

Ordinary sessions of the Administrative Council are convened at least once every year and extraordinary sessions may be convened as necessary in accordance with internal procedural rules.[31]

16 Article VI*bis* (1) Lusaka Agreement.
17 Article VI*bis* (3)(a) Lusaka Agreement.
18 Article VI*bis* (3)(b) Lusaka Agreement.
19 Article VI*bis* (3)(c) Lusaka Agreement.
20 Article VI*bis* (3)(d) Lusaka Agreement.
21 Article VI*bis* (6) Lusaka Agreement.
22 Article VI*bis* (4)–(5) Lusaka Agreement.
23 Article VII (1) Lusaka Agreement.
24 Article VII (1) Lusaka Agreement.
25 Article VII (5)(a) Lusaka Agreement.
26 Article VII (5)(b) Lusaka Agreement.
27 Article VII (5)(c) Lusaka Agreement.
28 Article VII (5)(d) Lusaka Agreement.
29 Article VII (5)(e) Lusaka Agreement.
30 Article VII (6) Lusaka Agreement.
31 Article VII (3) Lusaka Agreement.

Secretariat

The Secretariat is under the management of the Director General, who is the "principal executive officer" of ARIPO and may serve for a maximum of two fixed terms of four years each.[32] The Secretariat's functions include the exploration of possible means to achieve ARIPO's objectives, and where appropriate, reporting its findings to the Administrative Council;[33] carrying out any work, studies or services as directed by the Administrative Council;[34] and drafting annual reports and programmes of activities, accounts and budgets.[35] In summary, the Secretariat takes charge of the day-to-day running of the organisation, with the co-operation of ARIPO member states that are enjoined to cooperate with it and assist it in the fulfilment of its functions.[36] It operates from the seat of the organisation in Harare, Zimbabwe.

Board of Appeal

The Board of Appeal was established by Administrative Council through an amendment to the Harare Protocol.[37] Its functions are to hear appeals against the decisions of the ARIPO Office pertaining to patent applications,[38] the review of final administrative decisions of the office pertaining to the implementation of ARIPO Protocols[39] and to make decisions on related or incidental matters.[40] Its membership comprises five persons experienced in IP matters, two of whom are required to be patent examiners.[41] The quorum for a board sitting is three members,[42] including at least one patent examiner.[43] It commenced its activities in 2000[44] and its decisions are available on the ARIPO website.

Committees

Article 2 of the Lusaka Agreement provides that the Administrative Council may establish any subsidiary organs it deems fit. As noted previously, it has established

32 Article VIII (1) Lusaka Agreement.
33 Article VIII (2) Lusaka Agreement.
34 Article VIII (3) Lusaka Agreement.
35 Article VIII (4) Lusaka Agreement.
36 Articles VIII (5)–(6) Lusaka Agreement.
37 Section 4*bis* (1) Protocol on Patents and Industrial Designs Within the Framework of the African Regional Intellectual Property Organisation (ARIPO) (adopted by the Administrative Council of ARIPO at Harare, Zimbabwe, on 10 December 1982) as amended (Harare Protocol).
38 Section 4*bis* (5)(a) Harare Protocol.
39 Section 4*bis* (5)(b) Harare Protocol.
40 Section 4*bis* (5)(b) Harare Protocol.
41 Section 4*bis* (2) Harare Protocol.
42 Section 4*bis* (6) Harare Protocol.
43 Section 4*bis* (3) Harare Protocol.
44 ARIPO (2016a) p. 26.

several committees, namely the Finance Committee, the Audit Committee, the Human Capital Committee and Technical committees. The Finance and Audit Committees advise the Director General on financial matters and the Human Capital Committee deals with matters related to the welfare of ARIPO personnel. Previously ARIPO had only one technical committee that considered all technical issues, a task which is likely to have been overwhelming considering the number of issues that could potentially emerge in the different areas of IP. To ease this burden, the Administrative Council established technical committees on industrial property, copyright and related rights and the protection of new varieties of plants.[45] Each of these technical committees has a manageable scope and comprises experts in the relevant area. Accordingly, they should find it easier to fulfil their mandates.

4.2.2 Regulatory Instruments

In addition to its constitutive act, the Lusaka Agreement, ARIPO has five protocols with binding effect on contracting states. These are the

1 Harare Protocol on Patents and Industrial Designs of 1982,[46] its Administrative Instructions[47] and Guidelines for Examination at ARIPO
2 Banjul Protocol on Marks of 1993,[48] and its Administrative Instructions
3 Swakopmund Protocol on the Protection of Traditional Knowledge and Expressions of Folklore of 2010,[49] Regulations[50] and Administrative Instructions. There is also an explanatory guide for party states[51] and a Policy Framework on Access and Benefit Sharing arising from the Use of Genetic Resources in ARIPO Member States of 2016.[52]

45 ARIPO (2016b) p. 32.
46 Harare Protocol on Patents and Industrial Designs of 1982, as amended.
47 Administrative Instructions Under the Regulations for Implementing the Protocol on Patents and Industrial Designs Within the Framework of the African Regional Intellectual Property Organisation (ARIPO).
48 Banjul Protocol on Marks Within the Framework of the ARIPO, adopted by the Administrative Council of ARIPO at Banjul, The Gambia, on 19 November 1993 as amended.
49 Swakopmund Protocol on the Protection of Traditional Knowledge and Expressions of Folklore Within the Framework of the ARIPO, adopted by the Diplomatic Conference of ARIPO at Swakopmund, Namibia, on 9 August 2010, entered into force 11 May 2015, ARIPO (2015).
50 Regulations for Implementing the Swakopmund Protocol on Traditional Knowledge and Expressions of Folklore Within the Framework of the African Regional Intellectual Property Organisation (ARIPO) [text entered into force on 11 May 2015 and amended on 6 December 2016].
51 Explanatory Guide to the Swakopmund Protocol on the Protection of Traditional Knowledge and Expressions of Folklore, 2012.
52 Policy Framework on Access and Benefit Sharing Arising from the Use of Genetic Resources in ARIPO Member States, 2016.

4 Arusha Protocol for the Protection of New Varieties of Plants, 2015,[53] and its Regulations.[54] The protocol is not yet in force as the requisite ratifications have not yet been achieved. Article 40(3) of the Arusha Protocol provides that it will come into force 12 months after four states have deposited their instruments of ratification or accession.
5 Kampala Protocol on Voluntary Registration of Copyright and Related Rights, 2021,[55] which will enter into force three months after five states have deposited their instruments of ratification or accession.

The current subscription (as of 1 January 2023) to the protocols is as follows:

Table 4.1 ARIPO Protocols – State Parties

Protocol	*State parties*
Harare Protocol	Botswana, Cape Verde, Eswatini, The Gambia, Ghana, Kenya, Lesotho, Liberia, Malawi, Mozambique, Namibia, Rwanda, São Tomé and Principe, Seychelles, Sierra Leone, Sudan, Uganda, Tanzania, Zambia, Zimbabwe (20)
Banjul Protocol	Botswana, Cape Verde, Eswatini, The Gambia, Lesotho, Liberia, Malawi, Mozambique, Namibia, São Tomé and Principe, Uganda, Tanzania, Zimbabwe (13)
Swakopmund Protocol	Botswana, The Gambia, Liberia, Malawi, Namibia, Rwanda, Zambia, Zimbabwe (8)
Arusha Protocol	Rwanda, São Tomé and Principe, Tanzania (3)
Kampala Protocol	Signed by Ghana, Liberia, Malawi, Mozambique, São Tomé and Principe, Sierra Leone, Sudan, Tanzania and Uganda. No ratifications yet. The protocol will come into force three months after five states have deposited their instruments of ratification or accession.

In addition to the Protocols, ARIPO has the following Model Law and guidelines:

1 Model Law on Copyright and Related Rights[56]
2 Guidelines for Ratification or Accession and Domestication of International Instruments on Copyrights and Related Rights[57]

53 Arusha Protocol for the Protection of New Varieties of Plants Within the Framework of the ARIPO, approved by the Council of Ministers at Uganda, November 2013.
54 Regulations for Implementing the Arusha Protocol for the Protection of New Varieties of Plants Within the Framework of the African Regional Intellectual Property Organisation (ARIPO) [adopted by the Administrative Council of ARIPO at Lilongwe, Malawi, on 22 November 2017]
55 Kampala Protocol on Voluntary Registration of Copyright and Related Rights Within the Framework of the African Regional Intellectual Property Organisation (ARIPO) (Adopted on 28 August 2021 at Kampala, Uganda).
56 ARIPO Model Law on Copyright and Related Rights (2019).
57 ARIPO Guidelines for Ratification or Accession and Domestication of International Instruments on Copyrights and Related Rights (2019).

3 Guideline for Ratification or Accession and Domestication of the Marrakesh Treaty[58]
4 ARIPO Guidelines to Contracts: Literary Works (2018)[59]
5 ARIPO Contract Guidelines: Music Genre (2017)[60]
6 Guidelines for the Development of a Business Plan for CMOs in ARIPO Member States (2021)[61]
7 ARIPO Guidelines to Audiovisual Contracts (2020)[62]

The following section sets out some of the key aspects of the protocols.

Harare Protocol

The Harare Protocol was adopted by the Administrative Council of ARIPO in Harare, Zimbabwe, in December 1982 and entered into force in 1984. It has been amended several times since then, most recently in 2021, with the amendments coming into force on 1 January 2022 (referred to as the 2022 amendments) and on 1 January 2023 (referred to as the 2023 amendments).[63] Some of these amendments are highlighted in the following paragraphs, but procedural steps and timelines are not detailed. The Harare Protocol empowers ARIPO, through its Secretariat (the ARIPO Office), to receive and process patent, utility models and industrial design applications on behalf of state parties to the protocol.[64] The duration of protection granted under the protocol is 20 years for patents[65] 10 years for utility models[66] and 15 years for industrial designs.[67] The duration of protection for industrial designs was increased from 10 years to 15 years by the 2022 amendments.

The Harare Protocol requires the filing of the application to be made at a contracting state's industrial property office or at the ARIPO Office.[68] National offices which receive such applications are required to transmit them to the ARIPO Office within one month.[69] An applicant for the grant of a patent or the registration of an industrial design or utility model can, by filing only one application, designate any of the contracting states in which he wishes his invention or industrial design or utility model to be accorded protection.[70] The Harare Protocol and its Implementing

58 ARIPO Guideline for Ratification or Accession and Domestication of the Marrakesh Treaty (2018).
59 ARIPO Guidelines to Contracts: Literary Works (2018)
60 ARIPO Contract Guidelines: Music Genre (2017).
61 Guidelines for the Development of a Business Plan for CMOs in ARIPO Member States (2021).
62 Guidelines to Audiovisual Contracts (2020).
63 ARIPO (2021b), ARIPO (2023).
64 Section 1(1) Harare Protocol.
65 Section 3.1(11) Harare Protocol.
66 Section 3*ter* (10) Harare Protocol.
67 Section 4 (6) Harare Protocol.
68 Section 2(1) Harare Protocol.
69 Section 2(5) Harare Protocol.
70 Section 1*bis* Harare Protocol.

Regulations were amended by the insertion of section 3*bis* to create a link between the protocol and the Patent Co-operation Treaty (PCT) in 1994.[71] In terms of this amendment, any applicant filing a PCT application may designate ARIPO, which in turn means a designation of all states party to both the Harare Protocol and the PCT. The ARIPO office acts as a receiving office under the PCT for such states.

After their grant, these rights are designated as ARIPO patents, ARIPO utility models and ARIPO industrial designs, respectively.[72] Once granted, these ARIPO industrial property rights are equivalent to national rights granted by the relevant designated contracting state.[73] Therefore, they are subject to the applicable national law's provisions pertaining to compulsory licences, forfeiture or use in the public interest.[74] Similarly, infringements are dealt with under national laws.[75] The following sections briefly outline the protocol's provisions in relation to patents, industrial designs and utility models.

Patents

SUBSTANTIVE REQUIREMENTS

Patentability requirements are provided for in section 3(10)(a), which reads

> ARIPO patents shall be granted for any inventions, in all fields of technology, provided that they are new, involve an inventive step and are susceptible of industrial application.

Sections 3(10)(b)–(j) then elaborate on each of the criteria, mirroring TRIPS minimum standards and in most cases using the verbatim provisions. Absolute novelty is required, and an invention will have novelty only if it has not been anticipated anywhere in the world.[76] Inventiveness is evaluated using the standard test of obviousness to a person skilled in the art.[77] Similarly, industrial applicability of an invention is assessed per the usual standard of the capability to manufacture or use it in industry and agriculture.[78] Exclusions from patentability follow TRIPS and are set out in section 3(10)(h)–(j), which list the following:

1 The qualified exclusion of "discoveries, scientific theories and mathematical methods; aesthetic creations; schemes, rules and methods for performing mental acts, playing games or doing business, and programs for computers; and

71 By the Administrative Council at its second extraordinary session in April 1994. For commentary, see Kongolo (2013) pp. 81–82.
72 Section 1(2) Harare Protocol.
73 Section 1(3) Harare Protocol.
74 Sections 3(12), 3*ter* (13) and 4(7) Harare Protocol.
75 Section 3(14)(d) Harare Protocol.
76 Section 3(10)(b)–(d) Harare Protocol.
77 Section 3(10)(e) Harare Protocol.
78 Section 3(10)(f) Harare Protocol.

presentations of information." Such inventions are excluded to the extent that they related to the listed subject matter or activities "as such." This qualification is the same as that found in the European Patent Convention Articles 52(2)–(3).

2 Inventions which, if they were to be commercially exploited, would be contrary to "ordre public" or morality.
3 "Plant or animal varieties or essentially biological processes for the production of plants or animals." Microbiological processes and products are patentable, as noted later.
4 "Methods for treatment of the human or animal body by surgery or therapy and diagnostic methods practised on the human or animal body."

The 2023 amendments introduced a new provision to Rule 7*bis* 3 which reads "(2) Under Section 3(10)(j)(ii), ARIPO patents shall not be granted in respect of plants or animals exclusively obtained by means of an essentially biological process." As is evident, this reinforces an existing Harare Protocol provision.

PROCESS

The formal requirements that must be met by a patent application are set out in sections 2*bis* and 3(1). An application relates to one invention or a group of inventions that constitute an inventive concept.[79] The application is required to make clear and complete disclosure,[80] have clear and concise claims supported by the description, have an abstract and be accompanied by drawings and sequence listing, where necessary.[81] The abstract is not considered as an interpretative aid but simply as a "source of technical information."[82]

As noted, applicants may submit their patent applications via the PCT system, a national patent office or directly to the ARIPO office. The ARIPO office, on receipt of the patent application, first establishes whether the application meets formal or procedural requirements and if so, allocates it a filing date[83] and notifies the designated states of the application.[84] If the application does not meet formal requirements, the applicant is given a time period within which to rectify it, failing which the application will be refused.[85] The ARIPO office then carries out a substantive examination of applications that meet formal requirements to ensure that the invention which is the subject of the application is patentable[86] – in other words, that it is new, involves an inventive step and is capable of being applied in industry.[87] If

79 Section 2*bis*(1)(a) Harare Protocol.
80 Section 2*bis*(1)(b)–(c) Harare Protocol.
81 Sections 2*bis*(2) and 3(1)(a)(ii) Harare Protocol.
82 Section 2*bis*(3) Harare Protocol.
83 Section 3(2)(a) Harare Protocol.
84 Section 3(2)(c) Harare Protocol.
85 Section 3(2)(b) Harare Protocol.
86 Section 3(3) Harare Protocol.
87 Section 3(10) Harare Protocol.

the invention does not meet these requirements, it will be rejected and an applicant may request the office to reconsider it.[88] If the rejection is upheld, an applicant may then appeal the office's decision to the Board of Appeal.[89] Alternatively, an applicant may, within three months of the notification of the upholding of the rejection by the ARIPO office, request that any designated state treat the application as an application according to its national law.[90]

When the application complies with the substantive requirements (see the following subsection), copies thereof plus search and examination reports (where applicable) are sent to each designated state which may, within six months, notify the ARIPO office if the ARIPO patent would not be valid in their territory.[91] The 2022 amendments of section 3(6) provide the opportunity for an applicant to amend the application in response to a designated state's rejection of the application,[92] which is to be followed by a response from the designated state.[93] Should the designated state refuse the application despite the amendments or representations of the applicant, the applicant "may request that the application be treated in the designated States, as [an] application according to the national laws of that State."[94] After the expiry of this six-month period, the ARIPO office will grant the application and publish it in accordance with the regulations.[95] A patent application can be converted into an application for a utility model at any time before a decision to reject or grant the patent.[96]

The 2022 amendments introduced section 2*quater* which provides for observation by third parties during the application process, enabling them to make representations regarding the patentability of the invention. Rule 19*ter* of the regulations sets out the procedural aspects of filing the observations. Filing observations does not make the person who submits them a party to the proceedings; the office will acknowledge receipt of the observations but will not advise the person of "any further action it takes in response to them."[97] However, the observations shall be considered by the office in proceedings before it[98] and they must be communicated to the patent applicant if the office considers them to be substantiated.[99] Observations filed after a decision has been rendered by the office on the patent application will simply be included in the patent file, without consideration of their content.[100]

88 Section 3(4) Harare Protocol.
89 Section 3(5) Harare Protocol.
90 Section 3(8) Harare Protocol.
91 Section 3(6)(a)–(b) Harare Protocol.
92 Section 3(6)(c) Harare Protocol.
93 Section 3(6)(d) Harare Protocol.
94 Section 3(6)(e) Harare Protocol.
95 Section 3(7) Harare Protocol.
96 Section 3(9) Harare Protocol.
97 Rule 19*ter* (7) Regulations.
98 Rule 19*ter* (9) Regulations.
99 Rule 19*ter* (8) Regulations.
100 Rule 19*ter* (10) Regulations.

In 1999, the Harare Protocol was amended to make provision for patent applications involving micro-organisms.[101] Where a patent application that describes or claims a micro-biological process or a related product is filed and its performance requires the use of a micro-organism which is not available to the public on the filing date of the application and which cannot be made or obtained on the basis of the description in the application,[102] the micro-organism-made cultures of the micro-organisms have to be deposited.[103]

Utility Models

In the absence of a universally accepted definition of utility models and working with very broad policy space,[104] the Harare Protocol defines a utility model as

> any form, configuration or disposition of elements of some appliance, working tools and implements as articles of everyday use, electrical and electronic circuitry, instrument, handicraft, mechanism or other object or any part thereof in so far as they are capable of contributing some benefit or new effect or saving in time, energy and labour or allowing a better or different functioning, use, processing or manufacture of the subject matter or that gives utility advantages, environmental benefit, and includes micro-organism or other self-replicable material, products of genetic resources, herbal as well as nutritional formulations which give new effects.[105]

It was necessary to provide such a broad definition to cater for the varying national laws of member states.

A patent application can be converted at any time prior to its acceptance or rejection by the ARIPO office into an application for a utility model.[106] Likewise, an application for a utility model may be converted into a patent application prior to the pronouncement of a decision on the application by the ARIPO office.[107] Utility models are registered if they are new and industrially applicable.[108] The 2022 amendments revised section 3*ter* (2) to provide definitions for novelty and industrial applicability. Section 3*ter* (2)(ii) provides that a utility model will be novel "if it is not anticipated by prior art within the jurisdiction of the contracting states of

101 In accordance with the Budapest Treaty on the International Recognition of the Deposit of Micro-Organisms for the Purposes of Patent Procedures.
102 Section 3 (1)(b) Harare Protocol.
103 Rule 6*bis* Regulations for Implementing the Protocol on Patents and Industrial Designs within the Framework of the ARIPO.
104 Grosse Ruse-Khan (2012) pp. 1–2,Aleman (2012).
105 Section 3*ter* (1) Harare Protocol.
106 Section 3(9) Harare Protocol.
107 Section 3*ter* (11) Harare Protocol.
108 Section 3*ter* (2)(i) Harare Protocol.

the Protocol." Section 3*ter* (2)(iii) defines industrial applicability as the capacity to "be made or utilized in any kind of industry including agriculture."

Applications for utility models are dealt with in the same way as those for patents. They must comprise a request for registration, a description of the utility model, a claim or claims, a drawing or drawings and an abstract.[109] The first step is a formal examination. If an application does not meet the formal requirements, the applicant will be afforded an opportunity to rectify the shortcomings, failing which the application will be denied.[110] If the formal requirements are met, the office sends a notification to that effect to each designated state.[111] Thereafter the office is required to undertake or arrange for a substantive examination.[112] If the application does not meet the substantive requirements of novelty and industrial applicability, it will be refused.[113]

As with the position with respect to patents, an unsuccessful applicant for the registration of a utility model may ask the office to reconsider a rejected application.[114] If the rejection is upheld, then the applicant can lodge an appeal with the Board of Appeal[115] or ask designated states to consider the application under national laws.[116]

If the office finds that substantive requirements are met and decides to grant an application, it is required to notify both the applicant and the designated state(s), affording the state(s) a six-month period to respond to the notification.[117] During the six-month period after the notification, a designated state may notify the office in writing of the reasons why the utility model would not be valid in its territory.[118] After the expiry of the six-month period, the office will register the utility model and it will be valid in the designated state(s) which did not give notice of invalidity in their territories.[119]

The office will publish the ARIPO utility model applications "as soon as possible" after 18 months from the date of filing or priority, and before the expiry of such 18-month period where the applicant requests it.[120] If the decision to register the utility model becomes effective before the expiry of the 18-month period, the application must be published simultaneously with the specification.[121]

109 Section 3*ter* (3) Harare Protocol.
110 Section 3*ter* (4)(a) Harare Protocol.
111 Section 3*ter* (4)(b) Harare Protocol.
112 Section 3*ter* (4)–(5) Harare Protocol.
113 Section 3*ter* (5) Harare Protocol.
114 Section 3*ter* (6) Harare Protocol.
115 Section 3*ter* (7) Harare Protocol.
116 Section 3*ter* (10) Harare Protocol.
117 Section 3*ter* (8) (b) Harare Protocol.
118 Section 3*ter* (8)(a) Harare Protocol.
119 Section 3*ter* (9) Harare Protocol.
120 Section 3*quater* (1) Harare Protocol.
121 Section 3*quater* (2) Harare Protocol.

Industrial Designs

For industrial design applications, only a formality examination is performed.[122] Applications must consist of a request for registration and a reproduction of the industrial design concerned.[123] Where the application does not meet the formality requirements and the applicant fails to rectify it, it will be rejected.[124]

If the application fulfils the formal requirements, the ARIPO office notifies designated states of the application[125] and affords them a six-month period within which to respond to the notification.[126] Under s 4(3)(a), the grounds upon which states may reject designs are:

(i) that the industrial design is not new;
(ii) that, because of the nature of the industrial design, it cannot be registered or a registration has no effect under the national law of that state; or
(iii) that, in the case of a textile design, it is the subject of a special register.

The most recent amendments introduced an opportunity for the applicant to submit amendments in response to a rejection of the application,[127] which is to be followed by a response from the designated state.[128] Should the designated state refuse the application despite the amendments or representations of the applicant, the applicant "may request that the application be treated in the designated States, as [an] application according to the national laws of that State."[129]

After the expiry of this six-month response period, the ARIPO office will grant the design and it will be effective in all non-rejecting designated states. If the office refuses the application, as with patents and utility models, within three months of such rejection, an unsuccessful industrial design applicant may request any designated state to consider the application under national law.[130]

INFRINGEMENT AND ENFORCEMENT OF PATENTS, UTILITY MODELS AND INDUSTRIAL DESIGNS

Infringement is dealt with under national laws.[131] Some ARIPO member states' domestic legislation expressly refers to ARIPO patents and trade marks, making

122 Section 4(2)(a) Harare Protocol.
123 Section 4 Harare Protocol.
124 Section 4(2)(b) Harare Protocol.
125 Section 4(2)(c) Harare Protocol.
126 Section 4(3) Harare Protocol.
127 Section 4(3)(b) Harare Protocol.
128 Section 4(3)(c) Harare Protocol.
129 Section 4(3)(d) Harare Protocol.
130 Section 4(5) Harare Protocol.
131 Sections 14(d) Harare Protocol for patents.

it clear that they are enforceable domestically.[132] However, they have also been enforced in member states with domestic legislation that does not refer to ARIPO-registered IPRs.[133] The ARIPO website maintains a database of IP case law from its member states,[134] but this contains case law from only a few states, which may indicate that there is limited case law or simply be a result of the database not being actively maintained.

Banjul Protocol on Marks

The Banjul Protocol was adopted by the Administrative Council of ARIPO in December 1993, in Banjul, The Gambia, and entered into force in 1997. Like the Harare Protocol, it was most recently amended in December 2021 and the amendments came into force in January 2022 and January 2023.[135] The protocol empowers the ARIPO office to receive and process trademark applications on behalf of states party to the protocol.[136]

The Banjul Protocol and its implementing regulations[137] do not provide for substantive trademark law. The protocol merely provides for the duration of trade marks and the possibility of renewal.[138] Marks are registered for an initial period of ten years,[139] which is renewable.[140] It provides that trademark applications will be examined in accordance with national laws,[141] which will also govern the cancellation of trade marks,[142] since registered marks have the "same effect in each designated State" as marks filed and registered under national law.

As under the Harare Protocol, applications under the Banjul Protocol may be filed in a party state or at the ARIPO office[143] and must designate the states in which protection is sought.[144] Where the application is filed in a contracting state, such state is required to transmit the application to the ARIPO office within one month.[145] The applicant is required to identify the goods or service for which protection is

132 Schneider and Ferguson (2020) pp. 42–43.
133 Schneider and Ferguson (2020) p. 43.
134 www.aripo.org/ip-case-laws/ [accessed 23 September 2022].
135 ARIPO (2021a), ARIPO (2023).
136 Section 1.1 Banjul Protocol.
137 Regulations for Implementing the Banjul Protocol on Marks Within the Framework of the ARIPO, adopted by the Administrative Council of ARIPO at Kariba, Zimbabwe on 24 November 1995, as amended.
138 Sections 7.1–7.2 Banjul Protocol.
139 Section 7.1 Banjul Protocol.
140 Section 7.2 Banjul Protocol.
141 Section 6.1 Banjul Protocol.
142 Section 8.2 Banjul Protocol.
143 Section 2.1 Banjul Protocol.
144 Section 3.1 Banjul Protocol.
145 Section 2.4 Banjul Protocol.

being sought, as well as the relevant Nice classification.[146] The ARIPO office will then verify the correctness of the applicant's classification, and effect amendments where required, subject to the payment of a classification fee.[147] Certain declarations are required when colour[148] and three-dimensional[149] marks are applied for. The applicant is also required to declare actual use of the mark or an intention to use the mark or apply to register another person as the user of the mark.[150] The ARIPO office checks for compliance with these formal requirements[151] and affords non-compliant applicants an opportunity to rectify applications, failing which the application will be rejected.[152] An unsuccessful applicant may ask the office to reconsider an application.[153] Where the reconsideration upholds the rejection, the applicant may then lodge an appeal with the Board of Appeal[154] or request designated states to consider the application under their national law.[155]

Where an application passes the formality examination, the ARIPO office notifies designated states,[156] which then have a nine-month response period within which to indicate whether they will afford protection to the mark in their jurisdictions.[157] Designated states undertake substantive examination of the application in order to determine whether they will afford protection to the mark.[158] Where a designated state decides to reject an application, it is required to advise the ARIPO office of the grounds under its national laws on which the application has been rejected, within one month of making the decision.[159] The ARIPO office must, without delay, convey these grounds to the applicant,[160] who has the right of reply as well as of appeal or review under the relevant national law.[161] The request for review or appeal is filed via the ARIPO office, which conveys it to the designated state which must, in turn, convey its decision to the office within one month of such decision.

This procedure is different from that under the Harare Protocol in two important respects. First, the length of the response period extends to designated states longer than that extended to designated states under the Banjul Protocol. Second,

146 Section 3.2 Banjul Protocol.
147 Section 3.2 Banjul Protocol.
148 Section 3.3 Banjul Protocol.
149 Section 3.4 Banjul Protocol.
150 Section 3.5 Banjul Protocol.
151 Section 5.1 Banjul Protocol.
152 Section 5.2 Banjul Protocol.
153 Section 5*bis*.1 Banjul Protocol.
154 Section 5*bis*.2 Banjul Protocol.
155 Section 5.4 Banjul Protocol.
156 Section 5.3 Banjul Protocol.
157 Section 6.2 Banjul Protocol.
158 Section 6.1 Banjul Protocol.
159 Section 6.3 Banjul Protocol.
160 Section 6.3 Banjul Protocol.
161 Section 6.4 Banjul Protocol.

the substantive examination for the protection of marks is undertaken by national offices, whereas under the Harare Protocol the substantive examination in relation to patents is undertaken by the ARIPO office. Therefore the Banjul Protocol affords designated states a longer time for response.

Applications which have been rejected by the ARIPO Office for non-compliance with the formal requirements or by a designated state for not meeting substantive requirements under its national law will be published in the *Marks Journal* as having been conditionally refused or refused respectively.[162] If there has been no written communication to ARIPO from a state to the effect that it will not afford protection to the mark, the mark will be granted protection in designated states after the completion of a further two-stage process. First, the acceptance of the mark will be announced through publication in the *Marks Journal* as a provisionally accepted mark.[163] Secondly, after a three-month period, during which opposition proceedings may be commenced, the mark will be registered upon payment of the application fee and a registration certificate will be issued.[164] Where a designated state accepts the registration of a mark, it will be published in the *Marks Journal* as such[165] and will be registered after the lapse of a three-month period.[166] If an opposition is filed during this three-month period, it will be determined in accordance with the relevant national laws.[167] If the opposition fails, the mark will be registered. The registration of the mark, pursuant to any of the described scenarios, must be published in the *Marks Journal*.[168]

Infringement is litigated in national courts, which also enforce ARIPO marks. For instance, a Ugandan court enforced an ARIPO trademark, holding that Mekako, the mark in question, "had been registered under the relevant Protocol [and] that Uganda was a designated member state for purposes of the trademark."[169]

Arusha Protocol

The history of the Arusha Protocol dates to 2009 when the Council of Ministers approved the initiation of work on a PVP protocol and policy.[170] The draft protocol was prepared with technical assistance from the International Union for the Protection of New Varieties of Plant (UPOV).[171] It was approved by the Council of

162 Section 6*bis*:1(c) Banjul Protocol.
163 Section 6*bis*:1(a) Banjul Protocol.
164 Sections 6*bis*:2.
165 Section 6*bis*:1(a) Banjul Protocol.
166 Sections 6*bis*:2 Banjul Protocol.
167 Section 6*bis*:4 Banjul Protocol.
168 Section 6*bis*:3 Banjul Protocol
169 *Anglo Fabrics (Bolton) Ltd and Anor v African Queen Ltd and Anor* (HCT-00-CC-CS-0632–2006) ((Bolton)) [2008] UGCOMMC 67 (27 January 2008) at para. 4.
170 Kongolo (2013) p. 104.
171 Kongolo (2013) p. 104.

Ministers at its 14th session in Uganda, November 2013, and by the UPOV Council in April 2014.[172] The protocol was adopted at a diplomatic conference in Arusha, Tanzania, 6 on July 2015. Its implementing regulations were adopted by the Administrative Council at Lilongwe, Malawi, on 22 November 2017. The protocol has not yet come into force and will do so 12 months after four states have acceded or ratified.[173]

The Arusha Protocol is a *sui generis* framework for the protection of new plant varieties[174] which is based primarily on the UPOV 1991 Act (UPOV 1991).[175] A plant variety is defined:

> as a plant grouping within a single botanical taxon of the lowest known rank, which grouping, irrespective of whether the conditions for the grant of a breeder's right are fully met, can be:
>
> (a) defined by the expression of the characteristics resulting from a given genotype
> or combination of genotypes;
> (b) distinguished from any other plant grouping by the expression of at least one of
> the said characteristics; and
> (c) considered as a unit with regard to its suitability for being propagated unchanged.

The protocol affords plant breeders' rights (PBR) to plant varieties that are "new, distinct, uniform and stable,"[176] as does UPOV 1991.[177] The variety must fall within a denomination as provided for by Article 27 of the protocol, the application must meet all formality requirements and the necessary fees must be paid. Each of the substantive eligibility criteria are elucidated in the protocol. A variety will have novelty if, at the time the application is filed,

> propagating or harvested material of the variety has not been sold or otherwise disposed of to others, by or with the consent of the breeder of the variety, for purposes of exploitation of the variety:
>
> (a) in the territories of the Contracting States earlier than one yearbefore the date of filing of an application; and

172 De Jonge (2014) p. 102.
173 Article 40(3) Arusha Protocol.
174 Preamble, Arusha Protocol.
175 International Convention for the Protection of New Varieties of Plants of 2 December 1961, as Revised at Geneva on 10 November 1972, on 23 October 1978, and on 19 March 19, 1991 (UPOV 1991).
176 Article 6(1) Arusha Protocol.
177 Article 5(1) UPOV 1991.

(b) in a territory other than that of the territories of the Contracting States earlier than four years or, in the case of trees or of vines, earlier than six years before the date of filing of an application.[178]

Where the protocol's application is extended to a genus or species to which it did not previously apply, Article 7(2) provides that the novelty periods will be extended to four years before the date of filing or, for trees or vines, within six years before the date of filing, even where the variety has been sold or otherwise disposed of in the contracting states' territories. However, these extensions are applicable only to applications that are filed within two years of the protocol becoming applicable to the relevant genera or species.[179]

Distinctiveness is determined by reference to varieties that are commonly known, and to be distinct a variety must be "clearly distinguishable from any other variety whose existence is a matter of common knowledge at the time of the filing of the application."[180] To meet the uniformity requirement, a variety must be "sufficiently uniform in its relevant characteristics," bearing in mind the expected variation within that variety.[181] A variety has the requisite stability "if its relevant characteristics remain unchanged: (a) after repeated propagation; or (b) in the case of a particular cycle of propagation, at the end of each such cycle."[182] Existing varieties developed by farmers which may be based on their traditional knowledge do not meet these criteria, especially the novelty requirement.

The holder of a PBR has the exclusive right to authorise the following acts in respect of the protected plant variety:[183]

(a) production or reproduction (multiplication);
(b) conditioning for the purpose of propagation;
(c) offering for sale;
(d) selling or other marketing;
(e) exporting;
(f) importing;
(g) stocking for any of the purposes mentioned in (a) through (f).

The duration of a PBR is 20 years generally and 25 years for trees and vines.[184] There are exceptions to the PBR, which include acts done privately, for non-commercial purposes and/or for experimental purposes.[185] PBRs will be exhausted

178 Article 7(1) Arusha Protocol.
179 Article 7(3) Arusha Protocol.
180 Article 8 Arusha Protocol.
181 Article 9 Arusha Protocol.
182 Article 10 Arusha Protocol.
183 Article 21(1)(a) Arusha Protocol.
184 Article 26 Arusha Protocol.
185 Article 22(1) Arusha Protocol.

by the sale or other marketing of material or of its derivatives by the breeder or with his consent in the territories of the contracting states.[186] However, exhaustion does apply where there is "further propagation of the variety in question" or "an export of material of the variety, which enables the propagation of the variety, into a country which does not protect varieties of the plant genus or species to which the variety belongs, except where the exported material is for final consumption purposes."[187] Compulsory licences may be granted, upon application, in the public interest by a national authority in contracting states.[188] Such licences should indicate the acts to which they relate and "specify the reasonable conditions which shall include the payment of equitable remuneration to the breeder."[189] Contracting states are at liberty to "regulate the production, certification and marketing of material of varieties or the importing or exporting of such material."[190] A farmers' exception is provided for in Article 22.

The administrative arrangements provided for by the Arusha Protocol are similar to those in other ARIPO Protocols with the ARIPO office playing a pivotal role,[191] which includes maintaining a register of PBRs.[192] Once the protocol comes into force, it will be possible to file a single application, which, if successful, will secure PBRs in all contracting states.[193] Such application can be filed directly with the ARIPO office or through a National Authority of a Contracting State,[194] which would check whether the application provides the information required by the regulations and, if so, then transmit it to the ARIPO office within one month.[195] Applications will be published in the *ARIPO Journal*.[196] There will then be an opportunity for interested parties to lodge a written objection to the grant of PBRs.[197] The window for filing such objects is three months from publication in the *ARIPO Journal*. The ARIPO office is required to undertake formal and substantive examinations of applications[198] or to make arrangements for examination of the distinctness, uniformity and stability of plant varieties by competent institutions.[199]

There was opposition from civil society organisations to ARIPO's adoption of the UPOV 1991 model.[200] De Jonge crisply summarises the grounds of such opposition as "1) the fear that biopiracy will be facilitated, 2) the lack of protection of

186 Article 23(1) Arusha Protocol.
187 Article 23(1) Arusha Protocol.
188 Article 24(1) Arusha Protocol.
189 Article 24(1) Arusha Protocol.
190 Article 25 Arusha Protocol.
191 Article 4(3) Arusha Protocol.
192 Article 5(1) Arusha Protocol.
193 Article 4(1)–(2) Arusha Protocol.
194 Article 12(1) Arusha Protocol.
195 Article 12(3) Arusha Protocol.
196 Article 15(1) Arusha Protocol.
197 Article 16(1) Arusha Protocol.
198 Article 17 (1)(a)–(c) and (e) Arusha Protocol.
199 Articles 17(1)(d) and 18(1) Arusha Protocol.
200 Saez (2014).

farmers' rights, and 3) the non-appropriateness of the criteria for protection in the context of Sub-Saharan Africa."[201] The concern was, and remains, that the adoption of the UPOV 1991 model robs developing countries of the opportunity to nuance their PBR systems so that they better cater for farmers and their national socio-economic conditions.[202] A nuanced system might be better achieved by the adoption of a hybrid system, such as those in place in Malaysia, the Philippines and Zambia.[203] Another option would have been to borrow from the AU's African Model Legislation for the Protection of the Rights of Local Communities, Farmers and Breeders, and for the Regulation of Access to Biological Resources of 2000. This model law provides for the *sui generis* protection and has been domesticated by some African states.[204] These are valid criticisms and viable alternatives; notwithstanding, ARIPO adopted the Arusha Protocol.

Kampala Protocol

The Kampala Protocol of 2021 provides a regional system for the voluntary registration and notification of copyright and related rights[205] to meet several objectives, including ensuring "that creative industries contribute to the socio-economic development of countries."[206] The ARIPO office will establish and administer a database[207] in which it will record notifications of copyright and related rights registered by national competent authorities within contracting states.[208]

The system is predicated on contracting states first having voluntary copyright registration systems in place, registering the relevant rights nationally and then notifying the office of the said registration. Some ARIPO member states already have such registration systems in place. For example, the Botswana Copyright Office administers a database on copyright matters and on authors and their works as well as a register of works published in the jurisdiction.[209] Similarly, the Kenya Copyright Board maintains a register of copyright protected works.[210]

Contracting states also have the option of "design[ating] ARIPO to undertake the function of registering copyright and related rights on its behalf."[211] The designation to undertake these functions can be rescinded and a national competent authority can take them over should a contracting state choose to do so in the future.[212] Whether the registration is undertaken by a national competent authority or

201 De Jonge (2014) p. 101.
202 Helfer (2004) pp. 29–30, Dutfield (2008), De Jonge (2014) p. 104, Oguamanam (2015), Munyi (2015), De Jonge and Munyi (2016), Adebola (2019).
203 De Jonge (2014) pp. 106–107.
204 Feris (2004) pp. 252–253.
205 Article 2, Kampala Protocol.
206 Article 3(d) Kampala Protocol.
207 Article 5, Kampala Protocol.
208 Article 4, Kampala Protocol.
209 Section 22B(g)–(h) Chapter 68:02 Copyright and Neighbouring Rights.
210 Section 22A Copyright Act, 2001 (Act No. 12 of 2001, as amended up to Act No. 20 of 2019).
211 Article 6(1)(b) Kampala Protocol.
212 Article 6.3 Kampala Protocol.

the ARIPO office, applications for voluntary registration can be made by an author, copyright holder or any person with an interest in the copyright or related right.[213] The effect of such registration would be to provide

> *prima facie* evidence of the particulars entered in the database and documents purporting to be copies of any entries therein or extracts therefrom certified by ARIPO and sealed with the seal of ARIPO shall be admissible in evidence in all courts without further proof or production of the original.[214]

Registrations can be cancelled after grant if (1) the registration was made in error, (2) it was obtained fraudulently, (3) a court or other competent authority orders such cancellation and (4) a law of a contracting state requires it.[215] Cancelled registrations will be deleted from the database. Amendments and variations can be made to registrations.[216] The Board of Appeal will hear any appeals pertaining to registration and cancellation.[217] Disputes are to be resolved by direct negotiations between the relevant parties or through the dispute settlement mechanism that will be created by the regulations, which, as of January 2023, were still pending.[218]

4.3 OAPI

The membership of OAPI consists of 17 countries, namely Benin, Burkina Faso, Cameroon, Central African Republic, Chad, Comoros, Republic of Congo, Côte d'Ivoire, Gabon, Guinea, Equatorial Guinea, Guinea Bissau, Mali, Mauritania, Niger, Senegal and Togo. Its seat is in Yaoundé, Cameroon.[219]

Prior to their independence, the French National Patent Rights Institute (INPI) met French colonies' patent administration needs.[220] After their independence, Benin, Burkina Faso, Cameroon, Central African Republic, Chad, Republic of Congo, Cote d'Ivoire, Gabon, Malagasy, Mauritania, Niger and Senegal[221] replaced the INPI by creating the African and Malagasy Office of Industrial Property (*l'Office Africaine et Malgache de la Propriété Industrielle* in French, known as OAMPI) through the adoption of a constitutive agreement[222] at Libreville, Gabon in 1962.[223] Like the first iteration of ARIPO, OAMPI focused only on industrial property.

213 Article 7.1 Kampala Protocol.
214 Article 8.3 Kampala Protocol.
215 Article 11.1 Kampala Protocol.
216 Article 13 Kampala Protocol.
217 Articles 15–16 Kampala Protocol.
218 Article 14 Kampala Protocol.
219 Article 40 Bangui Agreement.
220 Adewopo (2005) p. 7.
221 Nwauche (2003) p. 105.
222 The Agreement Relating to the Creation of an African and Malagasy Office of Industrial Property, 1962 (Libreville Agreement).
223 Kongolo (2013) p. 82, Nwauche (2003) p. 105, Adewopo (2005) p. 7.

The OAMPI constitutive agreement, known as the Libreville Agreement, was revised on 2 March 1977 at Bangui, Central African Republic.[224] OAPI was created by this revision agreement, the agreement relating to the creation of an African Intellectual Property Organisation, known as the Bangui Agreement.[225] The 1977 Bangui Agreement came into force on 8 February 1982. It was extensively revised in 1999 to ensure compliance with the TRIPS Agreement.[226] The revised text, including Annexes I–IX, came into force on 28 February 2002. The tenth annex came into force on 1 January 2006. The agreement was next amended in 2015.[227] Subsequent to this, revised Annexes VI, VII, VII and X came into force on 14 November 2020[228] and Annexes III, IV and V on 1 January 2022.[229] The amendments to Annexes I, II and IX are yet to come into force, at the time of writing (March 2023).

OAPI's member states articulate their three-fold objective in the preamble of the Bangui Agreement as

> (1) . . . to promote the effective contribution of intellectual property to the development of their States by promoting technological innovation, technology transfer and dissemination and by promoting creativity, to the mutual advantage of those persons who generate and utilize them;
> (2) . . . affording the most effective and uniform protection of intellectual property rights on their territories as possible;
> (3) promoting training and the dissemination of knowledge of intellectual property.

The functions and responsibilities of the organisation that enable it to realise this objective are set out in full in Article 2. In summary they pertain to collaboration between the member states with regard to substantive and administrative aspects of IP.

4.3.1 Organs

Unlike ARIPO, which has four main organs, OAPI has only three, namely the Administrative Council, the High Commission of Appeal and the Office of the Director-General.[230] Each of these organs' composition and principal duties are summarised in the following sections.

224 Kongolo (2013) p. 82, Nwauche (2003) p. 105, Adewopo (2005) p. 7.

225 Bangui Agreement Relating to the Creation of an African Intellectual Property Organisation, Constituting a Revision of the Agreement Relating to the Creation of an African and Malagasy Office of Industrial Property (Bangui (Central African Republic), adopted on 2 March 1977), as amended.

226 Nwauche (2003) p. 110.

227 Bangui Agreement Revised in Bamako, Mali, on 14 December 2015.

228 OAPI Decision 003/OAPI/PCA 27 October 2020, Décision fixant la date d'entrée en vigueur de certaines annexes de l'Accord de Bangui Acte du 14 décembre 2015.

229 Hollis (2022).

230 Article 25 Bangui Agreement.

Administrative Council

The Administrative Council is OAPI's "highest authority" and as such is responsible for the organisation's "overall policy . . . and regulates and controls its activities."[231] Its membership consists of one representative from each member state,[232] and a member state may ask another to represent it subject to the limitation that a single council member may not represent more than two states.[233] The functions of the Administrative Council are:[234]

(a) drafting the regulations necessary for the application of the Bangui Agreement and its Annexes;
(b) drafting regulations pertaining to financial matters, fees, the High Commission of Appeal, the general staff and to agents;
(c) supervision of the implementation of these regulations;
(d) approval of the program of activities and the annual budgets and oversight of their implementation;
(e) auditing and approval of annual accounts and inventory
(f) approval of the annual report on the activities of OAPI;
(g) appointment of the most senior executives and designation of the auditor;
(h) ruling on applications for admission as members or as associated sates;
(i) setting the amount of any contribution to be made by member states;
(j) deciding on the creation of ad hoc committees on specific issues; and
(k) determining the working language or languages.

The Administrative Council also has powers to draft implementing regulations for specified international agreements.[235] It is required to convene one annual ordinary session,[236] and "extraordinary sessions may be convened where necessary by the Chairperson at the request of one-third of the membership, or at the request of the Director General."[237]

High Commission of Appeal

The High Commission of Appeal hears appeals relating to the "rejection of applications for titles of protection for industrial property; requests for the maintenance or extension of terms of protection; requests for restoration and decisions on oppositions."[238] Its membership consists of three members who are selected

231 Article 27 Bangui Agreement.
232 Article 26(1) Bangui Agreement.
233 Article 26(2) Bangui Agreement.
234 Article 27 Bangui Agreement.
235 Article 28 Bangui Agreement; Nwauche (2003) p. 107.
236 Article 29(1) Bangui Agreement.
237 Article 29(2) Bangui Agreement.
238 Article 31(2) Bangui Agreement.

by the drawing of lots from a list of representatives designated by the member states.[239] Each state has one designated representative on the list from which lots are drawn.[240] Unlike with the provisions pertaining to the ARIPO Board of Appeal, there is no express requirement that these members have any industrial property technical expertise. However, this may only be an illusory problem if in reality, qualified persons get put on the list.

The Office of the Director General

The Office of the Director General is under the management of the Director General, who is the most senior official of OAPI and may serve for a maximum of two fixed terms of five years each.[241] The Office of the Director General is seized with the executive work of the organisation.[242] As such it is responsible for the day-to-day management of OAPI. It implements the instructions of the Administrative Council and reports to it.

Unlike the Lusaka Agreement, which does not enumerate the duties of the Director General, the Bangui Agreement lists the following duties of the Director General:

- representing the organisation;[243]
- producing budgets, programmes, financial reports and periodic activity reports which must be conveyed to the member states;[244]
- participation, without voting rights, in all sessions of the Administrative Council at which the Director General also serves as secretary *ex officio*;[245]
- recruitment, appointment and dismissal or termination of the appointments of OAPI staff, with the exception of most senior executives;[246] and
- determining whether to issue and maintain the validity of titles, as well as, where authorised, imposing the penalties provided for in the agreement and its annexes.[247]

Ultimately, the Director General is answerable for the management of the organisation to the Administrative Council, to which the Director General reports and with whose instructions the Director General is required to comply.[248]

239 Article 31(1) Bangui Agreement.
240 Article 31(1) Bangui Agreement.
241 Article 33(1)–(2) Bangui Agreement.
242 Article 32 Bangui Agreement.
243 Article 33(2)(a) Bangui Agreement.
244 Article 33(3) Bangui Agreement.
245 Article 33(4) Bangui Agreement.
246 Article 33(5) Bangui Agreement.
247 Article 33(6) Bangui Agreement.
248 Article 33(2)(b) Bangui Agreement.

4.3.2 Regulatory Instruments

The Bangui Agreement serves as a civil code of IP and has direct application in the member states.[249] It focuses on IP (as opposed to only industrial property, as the Libreville Agreement did) and addresses its various aspects in the following ten annexes which are listed in Article 6 and constitute an integral part of the agreement:

Annex I:	Patents
Annex II:	Utility Models
Annex III:	Trademarks and Service Marks
Annex IV:	Industrial Designs
Annex V:	Trade Names
Annex VI:	Geographical Indications
Annex VII:	Literary and artistic property
Annex VIII:	Unfair Competition
Annex IX:	Layout Designs of Integrated Circuits
Annex X:	New Varieties of Plant

(See beginning of section 4.3 for dates of amendments to the agreement.) The organisation serves as an industrial property office providing the required national office services for each member state in relation to the Paris Convention, Patent Co-operation Treaty and the Protocol Relating to the Madrid Agreement Concerning the International Registration of Marks.[250] It is empowered to take "any measures for the application of the administrative procedures necessary for the implementation of the international treaties concerning intellectual property to which the Member States have acceded."[251] Application for patents, utility models, trade marks or service marks, industrial designs, trade names geographical indications or layout designs (topographies) of integrated circuits and applications for plant variety certificates can be filed directly with OAPI.[252] Alternatively, they may be filed with the ministry responsible for industrial property in member states that would then be required to transmit the application to OAPI within five days of receipt.[253] Filings with the organisation or with a ministry of a member state is effectively a national filing in each member state.[254] Similarly, when an international patent application that designates one member state is filed it is equivalent to national filing in all member states that are PCT contracting states. The same effect extends to international registrations of marks under the

249 Articles 5(2) and 6 Bangui Agreement, Kongolo (2013) p. 83.
250 Article 3.
251 Article 7 Bangui Agreement.
252 Article 8(1) Bangui Agreement.
253 Article 8(2) Bangui Agreement.
254 Article 9(1) Bangui Agreement.

Madrid Protocol[255] and the international filing of industrial designs under the Hague Agreement Concerning the International Deposit of Industrial Designs. The agreement expressly provides for the organisation's power to examine applications and carry out all the necessary procedural steps to grant patents and utility models,[256] trade marks and service marks,[257] industrial designs,[258] trade names,[259] geographical indications,[260] layout designs (topographies) of integrated circuits[261] and plant variety certificates.[262] The organisation is authorised to publish the necessary titles and procedural documents in its Official Bulletin of Industrial Property[263] and to maintain a special register of the previously listed IPRs for each member state.[264]

The following subsection outlines some of the substantive provisions relating to the IPR titles granted by OAPI. As noted in the introduction, the scope of OAPI's legal framework is much broader than that of ARIPO and for purposes of comparison, this section will outline only those annexes that have a counterpart in the ARIPO framework.

Annex I: Patents

SUBSTANTIVE REQUIREMENTS

There have been significant changes to Annex I, which have not yet entered into force. These are highlighted here since they have been passed already and are merely awaiting entry into force. The first change is an expansion of the definitions found in Article 1. Previously this article contained only two definitions, as follows:

> "Invention" means an idea that permits a specific problem in the field of technology to be solved in practice.
>
> "Patent" means the title granted for the protection of an invention.

It has been expanded by the inclusion of three more paragraphs. The first, Article 1(2), provides that an "invention may consist in, or be related to, a product,

255 Article 9(2) Bangui Agreement.
256 Article 10 Bangui Agreement.
257 Article 11 Bangui Agreement.
258 Article 12 Bangui Agreement.
259 Article 13 Bangui Agreement.
260 Article 14 Bangui Agreement.
261 Article 15 Bangui Agreement.
262 Article 16 Bangui Agreement.
263 Article 17 Bangui Agreement.
264 Article 18 Bangui Agreement.

a process or the use thereof." This had previously been contained in Article 2(2). The second change then moves the exclusion of certain subject matter from what was previously reflected in Article 6 (entitled "non-patentable subject matter") and brings it into Article 1.[265]

> (3) The following shall not be considered inventions within the meaning of paragraph (1):
>
> (a) discoveries, scientific theories and mathematical methods;
> (b) schemes, principles or methods for doing business, performing purely mental activities or playing games;
> (c) mere presentation of information;
> (d) computer programs;
> (e) purely ornamental creations; and
> (f) literary, architectural and artistic works or any other aesthetic creation.

The third change is the introduction of a qualification of this exclusion which was not previously included in Article 6. This is included in Article 1 as follows:

> (4) Paragraph (3) above only excludes the patentability of the enumerated items where the patent application contains one of these items considered as such.

This aligns the OAPI's approach to that of ARIPO found in section 3(10)(h)–(j) of the Harare Protocol, which is fashioned along the lines of Article 52(2) of the Convention on the Grant of European Patents (EPC). As noted in the first edition of this work, the OAPI approach previously differed in that it did not have the qualification now contained in paragraph 4. Therefore there was an outright prohibition of patent protection for the previously listed subject matter, which has now been qualified.

Article 2 has also been revised. It previously contained two paragraphs. The first was a statement of patentability criteria, *viz* novelty, inventive step and industrial applicability and the second paragraph provided that an "invention may consist in, or be related to, a product, a process or the use thereof."[266] As mentioned, the second paragraph has been moved to Article 1. The patentability criteria in Article 2(1) are as prescribed by the TRIPS Agreement and are therefore the same as those outlined in the Harare Protocol. The 2015 amendments revised Article 2

265 Article 1(3)–(4) Annex I, Bangui Agreement.
266 Article 2(1) Annex I Bangui Agreement (1999 version).

by moving the rest of the exclusions previously found in Article 6 to Article 2(2) as follows:

> (2) The following shall not be patentable:
>
> (a) inventions whose exploitation is contrary to public policy or morality, it being understood that the working of the invention shall not be considered contrary to public policy or morality merely because it is prohibited by law or regulation;
> (b) methods for the treatment of the human or animal body by surgery or therapy, including diagnostic methods;
> (c) inventions having as their subject matter plant varieties, animal species and essentially biological processes for the breeding of plants or animals other than microbiological processes and the products of such processes.

These are equivalent to the Harare Protocol's provisions pertaining to subject matter exclusions found in section 3 (10)(j) in relation to biotechnological inventions.

Articles 3–5 then expound on the patentability criterion of absolute novelty, inventive step and industrial applicability, in accordance with TRIPS minimum standards and in substantively the same way as ARIPO's Harare Protocol. The only differences lie in the two instruments' articulation of some of the criteria, but this is really just a matter of form rather than substance. For instance, the Harare Protocol in section 3 (10)(f) reads, "An invention shall be considered as susceptible of industrial applicability if it can be made or utilised in any kind of industry including agriculture." Annex I of the Bangui Agreement's Article 5 reads, "An invention shall be considered industrially applicable if its object can be made or used in any kind of industry. The term 'industry' shall be understood in its broadest sense and shall in particular cover handicrafts, agriculture, fishery and services."

In accordance with the TRIPS Agreement, the duration of OAPI patents is 20 years[267] and they afford their holders with the usual economic exclusivity over the invention.[268] There have been some revisions to the provisions on these rights. First, they were previously found in Article 7 but are now in Article 6. Second, the rights are encapsulated in the concept of the working invention, as was previously the case, but the definition has been revised. In the 1999 version of Annex I, Article 7(3) defined working as "manufacturing, importing, offering for sale, selling and using a patented product or a product manufactured through a patented process, holding it for the purposes of offering it for sale, selling it or using it and using a patented process." The inclusion of importation in this definition was criticised for the perceived harmful effects that would be wrought by an import monopoly, particularly in relation to essential medicines.[269] This is ameliorated by

267 Article 8 Annex I, Bangui Agreement.
268 Article 6 Annex I, Bangui Agreement.
269 Nwauche (2003) p. 111.

the adoption of the international exhaustion regime in Article 7 (1)(a). The 2015 revision has maintained the substance of the provision and merely set it out in two parts as follows:

> (3) For the purposes of this Annex, the "working" of a patented invention means any of the following acts:
>
> (a) where the patent has been granted for a product:
>
> (i) manufacturing, importing, offering for sale, selling and using the product; and
> (ii) holding the product for the purposes of offering it for sale, selling it or using it;
>
> (b) where the patent has been granted for a process:
>
> (i) using the process; and
> (ii) engaging in the acts mentioned in sub-paragraph (a) above in relation to a product resulting directly from the use of the process.

Article 7(1) of the annex provides for the following limitations:

> (a) the offer, import, holding or use of the patented product on the territory of a Member State, after the product is legally placed on the market in any country by the owner of the patent or with his express consent;
> (b) the use of objects on board foreign aircraft, land vehicles or ships that temporarily or accidentally enter the airspace, territory or waters of a Member State;
> (c) acts in relation to a patented invention that are carried out for experimental purposes in the course of scientific and technical research or for educational purposes;
> (d) studies and tests required for securing an authorisation to place a medicine on the market, as well as acts necessary for conducting such and securing the authorisation; and
> (e) acts performed by any person who in good faith on the filing date or, where priority is claimed, on the priority date of the application on the basis of which the patent is granted on the territory of a Member State, was in possession of the invention.

PROCESS

Applications can be filed directly with OAPI or with the ministry responsible for industrial property in member states[270] that would then be required to transmit the

270 Article 8(1) Annex I, Bangui Agreement.

application to OAPI within five days of receipt.[271] Where the application pertains to biotechnological inventions and it is necessary to submit a micro-organism, proof of such deposit should be submitted with the application.[272] After the allocation of a filing date,[273] a substantive examination is carried out.[274] Applications can be converted into applications for a utility model.[275]

Should the invention fail to meet patentability criteria or if the application is defective in any way, the applicant will be afforded an opportunity to rectify the application, failing which it will be rejected.[276] Appeals of a rejection of a patent application are made to the High Commission of Appeal in accordance with the rules of the organisation.[277]

An interested person may bring an application for the invalidation of a patent for sub-patentability.[278] There is provision for the application[279] for issuance of compulsory licences for non-working[280] and for dependent patents.[281] The holder of the senior patent may appeal the issue of the licence.[282] There is also provision for the grant of *ex officio* licences where the relevant patent "is of vital interest to the economy of the country, public health or national defense, or where non-working or insufficient working of such patents seriously compromises the satisfaction of the country's needs."[283] In such cases, the minister seized with IP matters or who is competent to do so on other grounds may make an "administrative enactment" subjecting the patent to the non-voluntary licence regime.[284] The enactment will detail all relevant information such as "the beneficiary administration or organisation, the conditions, term and scope of the non-voluntary licence and the amount of royalties payable."[285] Should the patent holder and the relevant ministry fail to agree on the conditions of the *ex officio* licence, they will be set by a civil court.[286] These compulsory licence provisions adopt a "TRIPS plus" stance because they exclude importation, thereby eliminating the possibility of parallel importation as a means to obtain access to patented technology such as pharmaceuticals.[287]

271 Article 8 (2) Annex I, Bangui Agreement.
272 Article 14(2) Annex I, Bangui Agreement.
273 Article 18 Annex I, Bangui Agreement.
274 Article 20 Annex I, Bangui Agreement.
275 Article 12, Annex I, Bangui Agreement.
276 Articles 23–24 Annex I, Bangui Agreement.
277 Article 33(2)(a) Annex I, Bangui Agreement.
278 Article 43 Annex I, Bangui Agreement.
279 Articles 48–49 Annex I, Bangui Agreement.
280 Article 46 Annex I, Bangui Agreement.
281 Article 47 Annex I, Bangui Agreement.
282 Article 53 Annex I, Bangui Agreement.
283 Article 56(1) Annex I, Bangui Agreement.
284 Article 56(1) Annex I, Bangui Agreement.
285 Article 56(1) Annex I, Bangui Agreement.
286 Article 56(2) Annex I, Bangui Agreement.
287 Musungu, Villanueva and Blasetti (2004) p. 55.

INFRINGEMENT

Patent infringement may be dealt with as a criminal or civil matter or both, subject to the limitation that criminal matters are brought entirely at the discretion of the Office of the Public Prosecutor.[288] Where a conviction is secured, the penalty is "a fine of 1,000,000 to 3,000,000 CFA francs, without prejudice to the right to compensation."[289] Where a second conviction is secured against the same defendant within a period of five years after the first conviction,[290] a term of imprisonment of one to six months may be imposed in addition to a fine.[291]

Annex II: Utility Models

The Bangui Agreement affords utility model protection of ten years' duration[292] that entitles its holder to economic exclusivity over the "manufacturing, offering for sale, selling and using the utility model, and importing and holding it for the purposes of offering it for sale, selling it or using it."[293]

Utility models are defined as

> implements of work or objects to be utilized or parts of such implements or objects in so far as they are useful for the work or employment for which they are intended on account of a new configuration, a new arrangement or a new component device, and are industrially applicable.[294]

This definition is much shorter than that provided for in the Harare Protocol, which, in addition to implements or objects, also expressly mentions

> any form, configuration or disposition of elements of some appliance [and] working tools . . . articles of everyday use, electrical and electronic circuitry, instrument, handicraft, mechanism or other object or any part thereof in so far as they are capable of contributing some benefit or new effect or saving in time, energy and labour or allowing a better or different functioning, use, processing or manufacture of the subject matter or that gives utility advantages, environmental benefit, and includes micro-organism or other self-replicable material, products of genetic resources, herbal as well as nutritional formulations which give new effects.[295]

288 Article 61 Annex I, Bangui Agreement.
289 Article 58 Annex I, Bangui Agreement.
290 Article 59(2) Annex I, Bangui Agreement.
291 Article 59(1) Annex I, Bangui Agreement.
292 Article 6 Annex II, Bangui Agreement
293 Article 5 Annex II, Bangui Agreement.
294 Article 1 Annex II, Bangui Agreement.
295 Section 3*ter* (1) Harare Protocol.

Another important distinction between the two protocols is the Harare Protocol's express inclusion of micro-organisms, genetic resources, and herbal and nutritional formulations as eligible subject matter for utility model protection.

In order to qualify for protection under Annex II of the Bangui Agreement, a utility model must be novel and have industrial applicability. Relative novelty is required and disclosure of a utility model in a territory beyond OAPI member states does not anticipate it for OAPI's purposes.[296] Further, a utility model will not lose its novelty where disclosure has occurred within OAPI territory by way an unauthorised person or by the applicant or an authorised person at an officially recognised international exhibition within a period of 12 months prior to the filing of the application.[297] A utility model will have industrial applicability if "it can be made or used in any kind of industry" which is "understood in its broadest sense . . . [and] cover[s] handicraft, agriculture, fishery and services."[298]

The annex excludes two categories of subject matter from eligibility for utility model protection. The first category includes objects and implements, or components thereof, that are "contrary to public policy or morality, public health, the national economy or national defense."[299] However, the mere fact that the exploitation or use of a model is prohibited by law or regulation does not render it contrary to public policy or morality.[300] There must be other substantive grounds for characterising it as such.

The second category of excluded utility models pertains to those that have "already been the subject of a patent or a utility model registration based on a prior application or an application validly claiming an earlier priority."[301]

The creator of a utility model has the sole right to its registration,[302] which will be jointly held by joint creators,[303] and applicants are deemed to be holders of such rights.[304] This right to registration may be assigned or transferred by succession.[305] The utility model registration operates on a first-to-file basis. Where the same model has been independently developed by two or more persons, the first to file or the one with the earliest validly claimed priority date will be entitled to the registration.[306] Where a model is developed or created by a person within an employment context, the default position is that the right to registration of the model belongs to the employer.[307] This default position may be varied by contract. In certain instances which are outlined herein, an employee will be entitled to additional

296 Article 2(1) Annex II, Bangui Agreement.
297 Article 2(2) Annex II, Bangui Agreement.
298 Article 3 Annex II, Bangui Agreement.
299 Article 4(1) Annex II, Bangui Agreement.
300 Article 4(1) Annex II, Bangui Agreement.
301 Article 4(2) Annex II, Bangui Agreement.
302 Article 7(1) Annex II, Bangui Agreement.
303 Article 7(2) Annex II, Bangui Agreement.
304 Article 7(2) Annex II, Bangui Agreement.
305 Article 7(4) Annex II, Bangui Agreement.
306 Article 7(3) Annex II, Bangui Agreement.
307 Article 8(1) Annex II, Bangui Agreement.

remuneration for their creation, even if it was created within the course and scope of their employment.

An employer will be entitled to the right of registration even if the relevant employment contract did not require that the employee be involved in inventive activity if the employee used "data or means" at their disposal by virtue of their employment to create the model.[308] However, in such circumstances the employee would be entitled to remuneration mutually fixed between the parties, failing which it would be fixed by a court.[309] This right to remuneration is extended to instances where a utility model is created within the course and scope of an employee's work, where the employee's utility model is "of very exceptional importance."[310]

Article 9 of the annex provides for the following exceptions:

a) once a utility model is brought into the market of an OAPI member state by its owner or with owner's consent, owner's rights are exhausted;
b) use of the utility model "on board foreign aircraft, land vehicles or ships that temporarily or accidentally enter the airspace, territory or waters of an OAPI member State";
c) experimental use of a utility model in the course of scientific and technical research;
d) any use "by any person who in good faith on the filing date of the application, or where priority is claimed on the priority date of the application on the basis of which the utility model is registered on the territory of a member State, was using the utility model or making effective and genuine preparations for such use, in so far as those acts are not different in nature or purpose from the actual or planned earlier use."

The right to rely on the fourth exception can only be transferred by its initial holder to a third party if the business or company with which the early or prior use of the model are associated is being transferred to the third party.[311]

Annex III: Trade Marks and Service Marks

OAPI acceded to the Madrid Protocol on Marks in December 2014 and the protocol entered into force for OAPI on 5 March 2015.[312] This has been a controversial move as the Bangui Agreement does not expressly provide for the accession to international

308 Article 8(2) Annex II, Bangui Agreement.
309 Article 8(3) Annex II, Bangui Agreement.
310 Article 8(4) Annex II, Bangui Agreement.
311 Article 9(2) Annex II, Bangui Agreement.
312 WIPO Madrid (Marks) Notification No. 203, Protocol Relating to the Madrid Agreement Concerning the International Registration of Marks: Accession by the African Intellectual Property Organisation, 2014.

legal instruments by OAPI. This led to some conflict between the organisation and some of its agents, which resulted in the suspension of those agents.[313]

The annex provides for both substantive and procedural aspects of trademark law. Articles 1–34 of the annex provide for trade marks and service marks. Articles 35–45 of the annex provide for collective marks and collective certification marks. As the point has already been made that OAPI administers a unitary registration system, this section does not dwell on the procedural aspects. Suffice it to say that there is provision for opposition procedures,[314] appeals against registration decisions[315] and for cancellation of registration for non-use.[316] Instead, this section summarises the substantive aspects in relation to trade marks.

Protection is provided for trade marks and service marks, upon registration, for a term of ten years, which is renewable.[317] Article 2(1) previously defined marks as

> Any visible sign used or intended to be used and capable of distinguishing the goods or services of any enterprise shall be considered a trademark or service mark, including in particular surnames by themselves or in a distinctive form, special, arbitrary or fanciful designations, the characteristic form of a product or its packaging, labels, wrappers, emblems, prints, stamps, seals, vignettes, borders, combinations or arrangements of colors, drawings, reliefs, letters, numbers, devices and pseudonyms.

The 2015 amendment introduced this new definition of marks:[318]

> Any visible or audible sign used or intended to be used and capable of distinguishing the goods or services of any natural or legal person shall be considered a trademark or service mark.
>
> The following in particular may constitute such a sign:
>
> (a) denominations in all forms such as words, combinations of words, surnames in and of themselves or in a distinctive form, special, arbitrary or fanciful designations, letters, abbreviations and numerals;
> (b) figurative signs such as drawings, labels, seals, selvedges, reliefs, holograms, logos, synthesized images; shapes, especially those of the product or its packaging or those characteristic of the service, and arrangements, combinations and shades of colors;
> (c) audible signs such as sounds and musical phrases;

313 Tita (2015).
314 Article 15, Annex III, Bangui Agreement.
315 Article 19, Annex III, Bangui Agreement.
316 Article 27, Annex III, Bangui Agreement.
317 Articles 22 and 24, Annex III, Bangui Agreement.
318 Article 2.1 Annex III Bangui Agreement.

(d) audiovisual signs; and
(e) series of signs.

The revised definition includes audible and audio-visual signs. Subsections 2 and 3 of Article 2 relate to collective and certification marks as follows:

(2) A collective mark shall consist of the mark of products or services whose conditions of use are laid down in rules approved by the competent authority and which may be used only by public enterprises, unions or groups of unions, associations, groups of producers, manufacturers, craftsmen or tradesmen, provided they are officially recognized and have legal personality.
(3) A collective certification mark shall be a mark that is applied to a product or service which by nature possesses the properties, qualities or characteristics specified in its regulations.

Article 3 then provides that a mark will not be eligible for registration if:

(a) it is not distinctive, in particular because it is composed of signs or matter constituting the necessary or genetic designation of the product or the composition thereof;
(b) it is identical to a mark that belongs to another owner and is already registered, or to a mark whose filing or priority date is earlier, and which relates to the same or similar goods or services, or it so resembles such a mark that it is liable to mislead or confuse;
(c) it is contrary to public policy, morality or the law;
(d) it is liable to mislead the public or business circles, in particular as to the geographical origin, nature or characteristics of the goods or services in question;
(e) it reproduces, imitates or incorporates armorial bearings, flags or other emblems, the abbreviated name or acronym or an official sign or hallmark indicating control and warranty of a State or intergovernmental organisation established by an international convention, save where the competent authority of that State or of that organisation has given its permission.

Article 5 provides protection for well-known marks. The owner of such a mark may file a court application for invalidation in national courts, where a registered mark is "liable to be confused" with the well-known mark. Such protection is premised on Article 6*bis* of the Paris Convention and Article 16(2)-(3) of TRIPS. However, where the mark was registered in good faith, it may not be invalidated if five years have passed since the filing of the relevant trademark application.

Rights to the registered mark, the exclusive economic acts pursuant to registration and the joint ownership of marks are provided for in Articles 4, 6 and 8, respectively. Article 7 provides two limitations to the exclusive economic rights of the right holder. The first limitation, provided for in Article 7(1), is that registering a mark would not entitle the right holder to prevent third parties from good faith use of their

> name, address, a pseudonym, a geographical name or accurate indications as to the type, quality, quantity, destination, value, place of origin or period of production of their products or the presentation of their services, provided such use is limited to the purposes of identification or information and cannot mislead the public regarding the provenance of goods or services.

The second limitation, provided for in Article 7(2), is that the right holder cannot stop "the use of the mark in relation to goods lawfully sold under the mark on the territory of a Member State or of a third-party State, provided the goods are completely unchanged."

The annex provides for border control measures,[319] criminal sanctions and civil remedies for infringement.[320] The key substantive differences between ARIPO's Banjul Protocol and OAPI's Annex III are that ARIPO leaves substantive trademark law to national legislation whilst OAPI makes provision for some aspects as shown herein.

Annex IV: Industrial Designs

Industrial designs are defined as "any arrangement of lines or colors" if it "gives a special appearance to an industrial or craft product and may serve as a pattern for the manufacture of such a product."[321] A model is similarly defined as "any three-dimensional shape, whether or not associated with lines or colors, . . . [that] gives a special appearance to an industrial or craft product and may serve as a pattern for the manufacture of such a product."[322]

Annex IV provides protection for new[323] industrial designs for a period of five years.[324] Industrial designs whose exploitation is contrary to "public policy or morality" are ineligible for protection.[325] Such protection "may be renewed for a further two consecutive periods of five years on request by the owner and on payment of a renewal fee."[326] However, such protection cannot be enforced against persons

319 Articles 66–67 Annex III, Bangui Agreement.
320 Articles 49–65 Annex III, Bangui Agreement.
321 Article 1(1) Annex IV, Bangui Agreement.
322 Article 1(1) Annex IV, Bangui Agreement.
323 Article 2(1) Annex IV, Bangui Agreement.
324 Article 19(1) Annex IV, Bangui Agreement.
325 Article 2(4) Annex IV, Bangui Agreement.
326 Article 19(2) Annex IV, Bangui Agreement.

who (a) "already owned the design" at the time the application for the registration of the industrial design was filed, (b) are authorised by the right holder, (c) use it for "private use and non-commercial purposes" or (d) reproduce it "purposes of illustration or education," as long as this is "not prejudicial to the normal exploitation of the designs and state the registration and the name of the owner of the rights."[327]

Criminal sanctions[328] and civil remedies[329] are provided for.

Annex X: Plant Varieties

The Bangui Agreement commits OAPI to implementing UPOV 1991.[330] Consequently, Annex X is in compliance with UPOV 1991.[331] This annex came into force on 1 January 2006.[332] Thereafter, in 2014, OAPI joined UPOV[333] and revised the annex in 2015 as noted previously. As they are modelled on the same international agreement, ARIPO's Arusha Protocol and OAPI's Annex X are substantively the same, so most of the commentary given here in relation to the Arusha Protocol is applicable to Annex X. OAPI's decision to adopt the UPOV model was critiqued on the same grounds that ARIPO's decision was, as outlined earlier. Further, as noted in chapter one, most OAPI member states are LDCs and were thus not required to be TRIPS-compliant at the time they made this decision,[334] as they still are. In other words, as LDCs they are not required to protect plant varieties but have chosen to forgo the benefit of the LDC transition period.

Annex X provides for the same definition of "plant variety" as found in the Arusha Protocol for "variety," with minor differences in the wording that does not alter the substantive meaning. For instance, the Arusha Protocol's definition begins: "a plant grouping within a single botanical taxon of the lowest known rank, which grouping, *irrespective of whether the conditions for the grant of a breeder's right are fully met* . . ." (emphasis added). In contrast, Annex X begins: "plant variety means a plant grouping within a single botanical taxon of the lowest known rank, which grouping, *whether or not it meets the conditions for the grant of a plant variety certificate* . . ." (emphasis added).

In keeping with UPOV, Annex X provides for breeders' rights for varieties that are "new, distinct, uniform and stable" and fall within "a denomination devised in accordance with Article 23" of the annex.[335] The provisions pertaining to the mean-

327 Article 7 Annex IV, Bangui Agreement.

328 Articles 29 and 35–38 Annex IV, Bangui Agreement.

329 Articles 32 and 33, 39–42 (on border measures) Annex IV, Bangui Agreement.

330 Article 30 Bangui Agreement; Cullet (2001) p. 103.

331 UPOV (2000) Examination of the Conformity of the Bangui Agreement on the Creation of an African Intellectual Property Organisation with the UPOV Convention, UPOV Council, Seventeenth Extraordinary Session, Geneva, 7 April, 2000, Doc. C(Extr.)/17/3.

332 Gazaro (2006) p. 129.

333 UPOV (2014).

334 Cullet (2001) p. 103.

335 Article 4.

ing of these requirements are the same as those discussed here in relation to the Arusha Protocol, so this will not be repeated.

4.5 Conclusion

From a public interest perspective, neither organisation has done as much as it could have to advance its member states' interests. For instance, OAPI member states' decision to become an early adopter of TRIPS standards notwithstanding applicable transition periods is lamentable. Similarly, the choice to adopt the UPOV 91 model instead of the AU's Model Law may be faulted for not considering African conditions and needs. However, the *sui generis* protection of traditional knowledge provided for in ARIPO's Swakopmund Protocol is a commendable development. The organisation has the requisite technical expertise amongst its staff to offer assistance to its member states and RECs on IP policy and legislation. Such advice would have the advantage of being informed by current conditions on the continent, which other sources of technical assistance often go without. This is a role that ARIPO ought to embrace in the interest of creating relevant IP systems on the continent.

As noted in the introduction, the possibility of the merger of the two sub-regional IP organisations has been raised by the organisations themselves. In addition, some scholars have also mooted this possibility. Some have considered a general merger pertaining to all aspects of IP,[336] whilst others have considered a merger only in relation to trade mark matters.[337] The advantages of such a merger would include the leveraging of economies of scale and the ease of obtaining IP protection over a broader coverage of states for applicants who use the central application system.[338]

There are two key hindrances to a general merger. First, substantively their laws are different in some respects, as shown previously. For example, Annex I of the Bangui Protocol contains patentability exclusions that the Harare Protocol does not. Another instance of substantive legal standard differences is that the LDC member states of OAPI have voluntarily become early adopters of TRIPS standards prior to the expiry of relevant transition periods. The second hindrance would be the nature of the two sub-regional IP systems. OAPI has unified its member states' IP laws in a common code, the Bangui Agreement, and has a single registration system that secures the grant of industrial property in all its member states. On the other hand, ARIPO has harmonised the IP laws of its member states through protocols to which its members voluntarily subscribe and thereafter domesticate. Its registration system is not unitary and protection is granted only in designated member states, which have an opportunity to accept or decline an application in a national process, following the initial ARIPO application stage.

336 For example, see Kongolo (2013) p. 124, Kongolo (2000), Dean (1994a) and Dean (1994b).
337 Mupangavanhu (2015), (2014) and (2013), Adewopo (2003).
338 Adewopo (2003) p. 475.

Reference List

Primary Sources: Agreements, Decisions and Official Documents

ARIPO

Agreement on the Creation of the African Regional Intellectual Property Organisation, adopted on 9 December 1976, and as amended on 13 August 2004 (Lusaka Agreement) (2016 ed.). Available at www.aripo.org/wp-content/uploads/2018/12/Lusaka-Agreement1.pdf [accessed 1 September 2022].

Arusha Protocol for the Protection of New Varieties of Plants within the Framework of the ARIPO, Approved by the Council of Ministers at Uganda, November 2013. Available at www.aripo.org/wp-content/uploads/2018/12/Arusha-Protocol_20181.pdf [accessed 1 September 2022].

Banjul Protocol on Marks within the Framework of the ARIPO, adopted by the Administrative Council of ARIPO at Banjul, The Gambia, on 19 November 1993 as amended (2022 ed.). Available at www.aripo.org/wp-content/uploads/2021/12/Banjul-Protocol-on-Marks-2022-Edition-6.pdf. [accessed 1 September 2022].

Explanatory Guide to the Swakopmund Protocol on the Protection of Traditional Knowledge and Expressions of Folklore, 2012. Available at www.aripo.org/wp-content/uploads/2020/04/Explanatory-Guide-to-the-Swakopmund-Protocol.pdf [accessed 1 September 2022].

Kampala Protocol on Voluntary Registration of Copyright and Related Rights within the Framework of the African Regional Intellectual Property Organisation (ARIPO) (Adopted On August 28, 2021 At Kampala, Uganda). Available at www.aripo.org/wp-content/uploads/2021/09/Kampala-Protocol-on-Voluntary-Registration-of-Copyright-and-Related-Rights-2.pdf [accessed 1 September 2022].

Policy Framework on Access and Benefit Sharing arising from the Use of Genetic Resources in ARIPO Member States, 2016. Available at www.aripo.org/wp-content/uploads/2018/11/Policy-Framework-on-ABS.pdf [accessed 1 September 2022].

Protocol on Patents and Industrial Designs within the Framework of the African Regional Intellectual Property Organisation (ARIPO), adopted by the Administrative Council of ARIPO at Harare, Zimbabwe on 10 December 1982, as amended (Harare Protocol) (2022 ed.). Available at www.aripo.org/wp-content/uploads/2022/01/Harare-Protocol-on-Patents-and-Industrial-Designs-2022-Edition-3.pdf [accessed 1 September 2022].

Regulations for Implementing the Arusha Protocol for the Protection of New Varieties of Plants Within the Framework of the African Regional Intellectual Property Organisation (ARIPO) [adopted by the Administrative Council of ARIPO at Lilongwe, (Malawi) on November 22, 2017].

Regulations for Implementing the Banjul Protocol on Marks Within the Framework of the ARIPO, adopted by the Administrative Council of ARIPO at Kariba, Zimbabwe on 24 November 1995, as amended.

Regulations for Implementing the Protocol on Patents and Industrial Designs Within the Framework of the ARIPO, 1984 . Available at www.aripo.org/wp-content/uploads/2020/02/Administrative-Instructions_2020-Edition.pdf [accessed 1 September 2022].

Swakopmund Protocol on the Protection of Traditional Knowledge and Expressions of Folklore Within the Framework of the ARIPO, adopted by the Diplomatic Conference of ARIPO at Swakopmund, Namibia on August 9, 2010 (2019 ed.). Available at www.

aripo.org/wp-content/uploads/2019/06/Swakopmund-Protocol-on-the-Protection-of-Traditional-Knowledge-and-Expressions-of-Folklore-2019.pdf [accessed 1 September 2022].

Guidelines and Model Laws

ARIPO Guidelines to Audiovisual Contracts (2020). Available at www.aripo.org/wp-content/uploads/2020/10/Guidelines-to-Audiovisual-Contracts-1.pdf [accessed 1 September 2022].

ARIPO Contract Guidelines: Music Genre (2017). Available at www.aripo.org/wp-content/uploads/2018/12/ARIPO-Contract-Guidelines-Digital-7.09.17_.pdf [accessed 1 September 2022].

ARIPO Guidelines for the Development of a Business Plan for CMOs in ARIPO Member States (2021). Available at www.aripo.org/wp-content/uploads/2021/03/Guidelines-for-the-Development-of-a-Business-Plan-for-CMOs-in-ARIPO-Member-States-1.pdf [accessed 1 September 2022].

ARIPO Guidelines for Ratification or Accession and Domestication of International Instruments on Copyrights and Related Rights (2019). Available at www.aripo.org/wp-content/uploads/2019/11/ARIPO-Guidelines-for-Ratification-or-Accession-and-Domestication-of-International-Instruments-on-Copyright-and-Related-Rights.pdf [accessed 1 September 2022].

ARIPO Guideline for Ratification or Accession and Domestication of the Marrakesh Treaty (2018). Available at www.aripo.org/wp-content/uploads/2018/12/ARIPO_Guidelines_for_the_Domestication_of_the_Marrakesh_Treaty.pdf [accessed 1 September 2022].

ARIPO Guidelines to Contracts: Literary Works (2018). Available at ww.aripo.org/wp-content/uploads/2019/03/ARIPO-Guidelines-to-Contracts-2018-Digital-12.11.18.pdf [accessed 1 September 2022].

ARIPO Model Law on Copyright and Related Rights (2019). Available at www.aripo.org/wp-content/uploads/2019/10/ARIPO-Model-Law-on-Copyright-and-Related-Rights.pdf [accessed 1 September 2022].

AU

African Model Legislation for the Protection of the Rights of Local Communities, Farmers and Breeders, and for the Regulation of Access to Biological Resources, 2000.

EU

Convention on the Grant of European Patents (European Patent Convention), of 5 October 1973 as revised by the Act revising Article 63 EPC of 17 December 1991 and the Act revising the EPC of 29 November 2000.

OAPI

The Agreement Relating to the Creation of an African and Malagasy Office of Industrial Property, 1962.

Bangui Agreement Relating to the Creation of an African Intellectual Property Organisation, 1977, as revised.

WIPO

Budapest Treaty on the International Recognition of the Deposit of Micro-Organisms for the Purposes of Patent Procedures, adopted at Budapest on April 28, 1977, and amended on September 26, 1980.

Madrid (Marks) Notification No. 203, Protocol Relating to the Madrid Agreement Concerning the International Registration of Marks: Accession by the African Intellectual Property Organisation, 2014.

Protocol Relating to the Madrid Agreement Concerning the International Registration of Marks, adopted at Madrid on June 27, 1989 ("Madrid Protocol (1989)"), as amended on October 3, 2006, and on November 12, 2007.

WTO

Agreement on Trade-Related Aspects of Intellectual Property Rights, Including Trade in Counterfeit Goods, adopted 15 December 1993, entered into force 1 January 1995 (1994) 33 ILM 81 (TRIPS).

UPOV

International Convention for the Protection of New Varieties of Plants of December 2, 1961, as Revised at Geneva on November 10, 1972, on October 23, 1978, and on March 19, 1991.

International Union for the Protection of New Varieties of Plants, Examination of the Conformity of the Bangui Agreement on the Creation of an African Intellectual Property Organisation with the UPOV Convention, UPOV Council, Seventeenth Extraordinary Session, Geneva, 7 April, 2000, Doc. C(Extr.)/17/3.

Secondary Sources

Adebola, T., 2019. Examining Plant Variety Protection in Nigeria: Realities, Obligations and Prospects. *The Journal of World Intellectual Property*, 22, 36–58. https://doi.org/10.1111/jwip.12113

Adewopo, A., 2003. Trademark Systems in Africa: A Proposal for the Harmonisation of the ARIPO and the OAPI Agreements on Marks. *The Journal of World Intellectual Property*, 6, 473–484.

Adewopo, A., 2005. *Developments in Intellectual Property in Africa*. ATRIP Annual Congress, Montreal, Canada, 12 July 2005. Available at http://atrip.org/wp-content/uploads/2016/06/Adewopo-Dev.-of-IP-in-Africa.doc [accessed 2 January 2023].

Aleman, M., 2012. International Legal Framework for Protection of Utility Models. *WIPO Regional Seminar on the Legislative, Economic and Policy Aspects of Utility Models Protection System*, Kuala Lumpur, Malaysia, 3–4 September 2012. WIPO/IP/KUL/12/REF/T2C.

ARIPO, 2015. *Entry into Force of the ARIPO Swakopmund Protocol on the Protection of Traditional Knowledge and Expressions of Folklore*. Available at www.aripo.org/entry-into-force-of-the-aripo-swakopmund-protocol-on-the-protection-of-traditional-knowledge-and-expressions-of-folklore/ [accessed 9 January 2023].

ARIPO, 2016a. *ARIPO: Who We Are & What We Do*. Available at www.aripo.org/publications/who-we-are-what-we-do/ [accessed 19 September 2022].

ARIPO, 2016b. *ARIPO@40: 1976–2016 40 Years of Cooperation in IP*. Harare: ARIPO. Available at https://www.aripo.org/wp-content/uploads/2020/08/ARIPO@40.pdf [accessed 19 September 2022].

ARIPO, 2018. *ARIPO's Administrative Committees Meeting in Harare*, 19 September 2018. Available at www.aripo.org/aripos-administrative-committees-meeting-in-harare/ [accessed 19 September 2022].

ARIPO, 2021a. *Notification of Amendments to Banjul Protocol 2021*. Available at www.aripo.org/wp-content/uploads/2021/12/Notification-of-Amendments-to-Banjul-Protocol-2021.pdf [accessed 17 June 2022].

ARIPO, 2021b. *Notification of Amendments to Harare Protocol 2021*. Available at www.aripo.org/wp-content/uploads/2021/12/Notification-of-Amendments-to-Harare-Protocol-2021.pdf [accessed 14 June 2022].

ARIPO, 2022. *ARIPO-OAPI 6th Joint Commission on Strengthening Cooperation Ties for the Benefit of our Member States*. Available at www.aripo.org/aripo-oapi-6th-joint-commission-on-strengthening-cooperation-ties-for-the-benefit-of-our-member-states/ [accessed 8 January 2023].

ARIPO, 2023. *Unpacking the Banjul & Harare Protocol Amendments*, 27 January 2023. Available at https://www.aripo.org/unpacking-the-banjul-harare-protocol-amendments/ [accessed 12 April 2023].

ARIPO & OAPI, 2014. *Communiqué Adopted by the Joint Meeting of the Chairmen of ARIPO AND OAPI*, held at the Headquarters of ARIPO on April 10 and 11, 2014, Harare, Republic of Zimbabwe.

Chirambo, M.H., 2002. *The African Regional Industrial Property Organisation (ARIPO) as an Example of Regional Cooperation in the Field of Patents*. Second International Forum on Creativity and Invention – A Better Future for Humanity in the 21st Century Organised by WIPO in Cooperation with the State Intellectual Property Office (SIPO) of the People's Republic of China, Beijing, May 23 to 25, 2002. WIPO/INV/BEI/02/10. Available at https://www.wipo.int/edocs/mdocs/innovation/en/wipo_inv_bei_02/wipo_inv_bei_02_10.doc [accessed 12 April 2023].

Cullet, P., 2001. Plant Variety Protection in Africa: Towards Compliance with the Trips Agreement. *Journal of African Law*, 45(1), 97–122.

Dean, O.H., 1994a. A Unified Intellectual Property Law System for Southern Africa. Part 1: International Arrangements and European Conventions. *Juta's Business Law*, 2(3), 111–114.

Dean, O.H., 1994b. A Unified Intellectual Property Law System for Southern Africa. Part 2: Multinational Registrations in Africa. *Juta's Business Law*, 2(4), 165–169.

De Jonge, B., 2014. Plant Variety Protection in Sub-Saharan Africa: Balancing Commercial and Smallholder Farmers' Interests. *Journal of Politics and Law*, 7(3), 100–111.

De Jonge, B. and Munyi, P., 2016. A Differentiated Approach to Plant Variety Protection in Africa. *World Intellectual Property*, 19, 28–52. https://doi.org/10.1111/jwip.12053

Dutfield, G., 2008. Turning Plant Varieties Into Intellectual Property: The UPOV Convention. In Tansey, G. and Rajotte, T. (eds.) *The Future Control of Food: A Guide to International Negotiations and Rules on Intellectual Property, Biodiversity and Food Security*. London and Sterling VA: Earthscan, IDRC, 27–47. Available at www.idrc.ca/en/book/future-control-food-guide-international-negotiations-and-rules-intellectual-property [accessed 8 January 2023].

Feris, L., 2004. Protecting Traditional Knowledge in Africa: Considering African Approaches. *African Human Rights Law Journal*, 4(2), 242–255.

Gazaro, W.R., 2006. Plant Variety Protection: Which System of Protection in the Member States of OAPI? *World Patent Information*, 28(2), 127–131.

Grosse Ruse-Khan, H., 2012. *The International Legal Framework for the Protection of Utility Models*. Research Paper No. 12–10. Available at http://ssrn.com/abstract=2160229 [accessed 11 April 2023].

Helfer, L.R., 2004. *Intellectual Property Rights in Plant Varieties: International Legal Regimes and Policy Options for National Governments 2004 FAO Legislative Study*. Available at www.fao.org/publications/card/en/c/121317c9-26e5-5f96-af7f-43ed915a1d02/ [accessed 23 December 2022].

Hollis, S., 2022. *OAPI: Bangui Agreement Revisions Change the Trade Mark Registration Process with Effect from 2 January 2022*. Available at www.adams.africa/oapi/oapi-bangui-agreement-revisions-change-the-trade-mark-registration-process-with-effect-from-2-january-2022/ [accessed 1 September 2022].

Kongolo, T., 2000. The African IP Organisations – The Necessity of Adopting One Uniform System for All Africa. *The Journal of World Intellectual Property*, 3(2), 265–288.

Kongolo, T., 2013. *African Contributions in Shaping the Worldwide Intellectual Property System*. Surrey and Burlington: Ashgate.

Munyi, P., 2015. Plant Variety Protection Regime in Relation to Relevant International Obligations: Implications for Smallholder Farmers in Kenya. *World Intellectual Property*, 18, 65–85. https://doi.org/10.1111/jwip.12031

Mupangavanhu, Y., 2013. The Regional Integration of African Trade Mark Laws: Challenges and Possibilities. Thesis (PhD). University of the Western Cape.

Mupangavanhu, Y., 2014. The Integration of Trade Mark Laws in the European Union: Lessons for Africa? *South African IP Law Journal*, 2, 109–130.

Mupangavanhu, Y., 2015. African Union Rising to the Need for Continental IP Protection? The Establishment of the Pan-African Intellectual Property Organisation. *Journal of African Law*, 59, 1–24.

Musungu, S.F., Villanueva, S. and Blasetti, R., 2004. *Utilizing Trips Flexibilities for Public Health Protection Through South-South Regional Frameworks*. Geneva, Switzerland: South Centre.

Nwauche, E., 2003. An Evaluation of the African Regional Intellectual Property Rights Systems. *Journal of World Intellectual Property*, 6(1), 101–118.

Oguamanam, C., 2015. Breeding Apples for Oranges: Africa's Misplaced Priority Over Plant Breeders' Rights. *World Intellectual Property*, 18, 165–195. https://doi.org/10.1111/jwip.12039

Saez, C., 2014. *African IP Body Steps Up Regional Effort to Adopt Plant Protection Protocol*.

Schneider, M. and Ferguson, V., 2020. *Enforcement of Intellectual Property Rights in Africa*. Oxford: Oxford University Press.

Tita, A.N., 2015. *OAPI Suspend Agents*, 13 April 2015. Available at http://afro-ip.blogspot.com/2015/04/oapi-suspend-agents.html [accessed 9 January 2023].

UPOV, 2014. *African Intellectual Property Organisation (OAPI) Becomes Second Intergovernmental Organisation to Join UPOV*. Geneva: UPOV Press Release, 97.

5 Key Considerations in the Development of a Continental IP System

5.1 Introduction

This chapter considers the three options of co-operation, harmonisation and unification for the IP system envisaged by the AU. It considers the prospects for IP co-operation, harmonisation and unification at regional and sub-regional levels with a view to garnering lessons for the implementation of both the PAIPO Statute and the AfCFTA IP Protocol. From its current approach to various issues, it is evident that the AU's preferred approach is harmonisation.

As argued in chapter six, at the time PAIPO was conceptualised, IP harmonisation was a challenge that the AU was not yet ready for because it was more prudent to focus on policy issues during that period and the reconciliation of PAIPO's mandate with that of ARIPO and OAPI. However, in the long term, as shown by developments discussed in chapter seven, the AU holds the view that IP harmonisation has indeed become a viable option for the continent which will be pursued through the AfCFTA IP Protocol. It is with this future prospect that this chapter is concerned. It conceptualises the available possibilities as being on a spectrum of the degrees of regional cohesiveness or conformity to IP law standards. Three nodes can be plotted on this spectrum. The first is IP co-operation that embodies concerted efforts to enable the sharing of administrative and enforcement resources without a regional substantive legal framework. It is followed by harmonisation, which aspires to such a framework in a way that leaves some room for national nuancing, and finally, at the other end of the spectrum, there is unification, which has a regional substantive legal framework that leaves no room for national divergence.

This chapter considers each of these options with reference to existing regional and sub-regional entities. IP co-operation is embodied by the approach of the Association of Southeast Asian Nations (ASEAN), the Asia-Pacific Economic Co-operation (APEC) forum and the BRICS. The Southern Common Market (MERCUSOR) and the EU use IP harmonisation. However, the EU is better classified as having a hybrid approach because it employs both harmonisation directives and unification by regulations.[1] Certain aspects of patent, design and trademark laws have been unified by the supplementary protection certificate for medicinal

1 Zirnstein (2005), Hugenholtz (2012).

DOI: 10.4324/9781003310198-5

and plant protection regulations, the Community Design Regulation and the Community Trademark Regulation, respectively.[2] To date, the EU has primarily used harmonisation with respect to copyright,[3] but there are calls to turn to unification due to the uneven regulatory landscape caused by harmonisation.[4] OHADA employs unification as does OAPI through its Bangui Agreement. OAPI's legal framework has been outlined in chapter three and only OHADA's will be discussed here.

5.2 IP Co-operation

This section presents the IP co-operation schemes chronologically rather than alphabetically because the first two regional configurations have overlapping membership and it is helpful to view their development in sequence.

5.2.1 ASEAN

ASEAN was established in 1967 and its membership comprises of the founding states of Indonesia, Malaysia, Philippines, Singapore and Thailand, together with the later joiners, Brunei Darussalam, Cambodia, Lao People's Democratic Republic (Lao PDR/Laos), Myanmar and Vietnam.[5] The ASEAN FTA (known as AFTA) was established in 1992[6] and the agreement was later upgraded, becoming in 2009 the ASEAN Trade in Goods Agreement (ATIGA), which entered into force in May 2010. Thereafter, ASEAN created an economic community, by its goal date of 2015[7] through the adoption of the Kuala Lumpur Declaration on ASEAN 2025: Forging Ahead Together in 2015.[8] Since that time, ASEAN is implementing and monitoring a blueprint to actualise the economic community.[9] ASEAN's context is very similar to that of the AU, in that both regions are developing IP frameworks within the context of a FTA. Further, it is a good comparator for the AU because the membership of the two organisations includes states at markedly different levels of development. In this respect, ASEAN's membership is classified into two groups.[10] The first is the more prosperous ASEAN-6 group of Brunei Darussalam, Indonesia, Malaysia, Philippines, Singapore, and Thailand. The second group consists of the less prosperous Cambodia, Lao PDR, Myanmar and Vietnam, commonly referred to as CMLV. The AU membership, as noted in chapter one, consists of LDCs and developing countries.

2 Kur and Drier (2013) pp. 62–63, 65–66.
3 Kur and Drier (2013) pp. 63–64.
4 New (2015), European Copyright Society (2014).
5 Ng (2013) p. 131
6 The Agreement on the Common Effective Preferential Tariff (CEPT) Scheme for the ASEAN Free Trade Area (AFTA) 28 January 1992; and the Protocol to Amend the Agreement on the Common Effective Preferential Tariff Scheme for the ASEAN Free Trade Area, 15 December 1995.
7 ASEAN (2014) p. 35, Ng (2013) p. 1, ASEAN (2008).
8 ASEAN (2015b).
9 ASEAN (2015a, 2021).
10 OECD (2013) p. 241.

ASEAN member states' work on upgrading their IP laws was necessitated by their TRIPS obligations.[11] This work soon expanded to encompass the creation of a regional IP framework. Although ASEAN was faced with significant challenges, such as the disparate national socio-economic contexts referred to earlier and the "absence of a common framework of substantive laws,"[12] it has made notable progress.[13] The ASEAN regional IP framework is grounded in its Framework Agreement on IP Co-operation of 1995.[14] The development of the framework was driven by the ASEAN Working Group on IP Co-operation (AWGIPC) which was formed in 1996.[15] ASEAN member states initially intended to fully harmonise their IP systems by 2020 but revised this goal to achieving regional co-operation by 2015. The Hanoi Plan of Action (1999–2004) contained the first iteration of how harmonisation would be achieved.[16] Further details of implementation were detailed in the ASEAN IPR Action Plan (2004–2010) and the Work Plan for ASEAN Cooperation on Copyright (2005). This plan was updated when it was realised that full harmonisation was not practicable due to the varying degrees of economic development amount member states.[17] It was realised that a more reasonable approach would be to seek co-operation in a way that allowed member states to meet their diverse national goals whilst at the same time pursuing regional interests and imperatives. In addition, the program was accelerated by five years and a new plan known as the ASEAN IPR Action Plan 2011–2015 was developed.[18] Since then, the AWGIPC has published a follow-on plan, the ASEAN IPR Action Plan 2016–2025, which states the following goals:[19]

(a) Strategic Goal 1: A more robust ASEAN IP system is developed by strengthening IP offices and building IP infrastructures in the region;
(b) Strategic Goal 2: Regional IP platforms and infrastructures are developed to contribute to enhancing the ASEAN Economic Community;
(c) Strategic Goal 3: An expanded and inclusive ASEAN IP Ecosystem is developed; and
(d) Strategic Goal 4: Regional mechanisms to promote asset creation and commercialisation, particularly geographical indications and traditional knowledge, are enhanced.

Each of these goals is then expanded with an indication of initiatives, deliverables and country champions. A mid-term review of this action plan was conducted in

11 Endeshaw (1999) p. 3.
12 Endeshaw (2004) p. 146.
13 Endeshaw (2010) pp. 7, 57–80.
14 Ng (2013) pp. 137–138.
15 Ng (2013) p. 137, Kuanporth (2013) p. 306. See the AWGIPC website at www.aseanip.org/.
16 Ng (2013) pp. 139–142.
17 Barraclough (2004–2005) p. 14.
18 Ng (2013) pp. 146–149.
19 ASEAN IPR Action Plan 2016–2025 p. 2.

2020 and a revised action plan was then published in June 2021. The revised plan noted deliverables that had been achieved and then either dropped or revised; those that were on-going or had not yet been started; added new deliverables; and earmarked some deliverables as being of higher priority than others.[20]

The essence of the ASEAN IP co-operation approach is internal co-operation between member states progressing on parallel tracks with external co-operation with significant trading partners.[21] With regard to internal co-operation, by 2015 ASEAN had achieved the following:

1 ASEAN Patent Search and Examination Co-operation (APSEC) which enables participating states to reference each other's national IP offices' findings on substantive patent examination;[22]
2 ASEAN IP Direct[23] which serves as "an online directory" of participating states' IP frameworks;[24]
3 ASEAN member states' accession to key international agreements, which include the Berne Convention, the Paris Convention, PCT and the Madrid Protocol. All the member states are bound by TRIPS, by virtue of their WTO membership.

With regard to external co-operation, Ng notes that the key achievements of ASEAN member states include co-operation with the EU[25] and Japan.[26] In addition, ASEAN has entered into an FTA with Australia and New Zealand that includes provisions on IP.[27] In particular, it requires accession to and compliance with the PCT, the Patent Law treaty and the Budapest treaty.[28] It also covers trade marks, geographical indications, traditional knowledge and folklore.[29] ASEAN has also signed these ASEAN plus FTAs: ASEAN-China FTA, ASEAN-Japan FTA, ASEAN-Korea and ASEAN–Hong Kong, China Free Trade Area. In addition, ASEAN's ten member states are party to the Regional Comprehensive Economic Partnership. However, this section's focus is internal ASEAN IP co-operation and these other FTAs are mentioned simply to make the point that the internal ASEAN IP position would have to be carried through to, or at least be compatible with, these other FTAs.

20 ASEAN IPR Action Plan 2016–2025: Updates to the ASEAN IPR Action Plan (version 2.0) 2021 pp. 2–3.
21 Ng (2013) p. 137.
22 Ng (2013) pp. 149–150, Kuanporth (2013) p. 307.
23 IP Office Singapore (2013). See website at www.ipos.gov.sg/AboutIP/IPResources/UsefulLinks/RegionalOrganisations/ASEANIPDirect.aspx
24 Ng (2013) pp. 150–151, Kuanporth (2013) pp. 307–308.
25 Ng (2013) pp. 154–155.
26 Ng (2013) pp. 157–158.
27 Kuanporth (2013) p. 309.
28 Kuanporth (2013) p. 310, Patent Law Treaty (2000), Budapest Treaty on the International Recognition of the Deposit of Microorganisms for the Purposes of Patent Procedure 1977 (as amended on September 26, 1980).
29 Kuanporth (2013) pp. 310–313.

By 2020, the mid-term review of the 2015–2016 Action Plan established that the following ten deliverables had also been achieved:[30]

(i) ASEAN Common Guidelines on Industrial Design Examination
(ii) Establishment of a regional network of patent libraries within schools and universities in [ASEAN Member States] AMS, to increase access to global scientific and technology information for research and development
(iii) Conduct a feasibility study for an ASEAN Trademark Registration System
(iv) Ensure IP offices' patent, trademark, industrial design and copyright databases and relevant information are easily accessible to their customers, partners, industry, and the public
(v) Develop a checklist to ensure that relevant information is updated regularly on the ASEAN IP Portal
(vi) Integrated searches of ASEAN IP databases can be done from the ASEAN IP Portal
(vii) National internal guidelines for enforcement consistent with the civil, criminal, and administrative structures of AMSs are drawn up based on best practices identified through information sharing among national agencies in AMSs that are tasked with IP enforcement;
(viii) Develop a coordination mechanism to enhance enforcement operations
(ix) AMS to conduct a study on supporting schemes to encourage IP protection and acquisition by [Micro, Small, and Medium Enterprises] MSMEs and the creative sectors and the effectiveness of the various schemes with the objective of adopting suitable and relevant measures
(x) Creative ASEAN

Co-operation has proven to be the more prudent option for ASEAN, following its unsuccessful attempts to harmonise. It may very well be that in the future, harmonisation may progressively be achieved from this bedrock of co-operation. The lesson, then, for the AU may be to first establish a firm co-operative framework and to thereafter build on that towards harmonisation.

5.2.2 APEC

APEC was founded in 1989[31] and has been characterised as following the contested open regionalism model because it has not adopted classic linear market integration but has chosen open economic co-operation instead.[32] This approach

30 ASEAN IPR Action Plan 2016–2025: Updates to the ASEAN IPR Action Plan (version 2.0) 2021 p. 2.
31 For a historical overview of its formation see Sutton (2007) pp. 135–138, Elek (2005) and (1991).
32 Sutton (2007) pp. 138–142, Taubman (2004) pp. 162, 189–192.

intentionally and expressly shunned the creation of a trading bloc[33] in order to appease ASEAN concerns about institutional rivalry.[34] APEC's membership consists of the following 22 member economies: Australia, Brunei, Darussalam, Canada, Chile, China, Chinese Taipei, Hong Kong, Indonesia, Japan, Republic of Korea, Malaysia, Mexico, New Zealand, Papua New Guinea, Peru, Philippines, Russia, Singapore, Thailand, United States and Vietnam.

In 1994 APEC adopted the Bogor Declaration which set out its economic co-operation aspirations. This declaration, which predates TRIPS, did not expressly mention IP. It provided two achievement deadlines, depending on the developmental status of member economies. Developing states committed to achieving free and open trade and investment in the region by 2020 whilst developed states committed to the earlier deadline of 2010.[35] APEC's Osaka Action Agenda sets out the implementation of the Bogor Declaration for IP co-operation, primarily to secure conformity with TRIPS and address the challenges faced by its member economies. The objectives are stated as follows.[36]

> APEC economies will:
>
> a in conformance with the principles of the TRIPS Agreement:
>
> - ensure adequate and effective protection, including legislation, administration and enforcement of intellectual property rights;
> - foster harmonisation of intellectual property rights systems in the APEC region;
> - strengthen public awareness activities; and
> - promote dialogue on emerging intellectual property policy issues, with a view to further improve intellectual property rights protection and use of the intellectual property rights systems for the social and economic benefit of members.
>
> b address the challenges for intellectual property rights arising from the rapid growth and developments of the New Economy by:
>
> - establishing legal frameworks to promote creative endeavour and encourage online activity;
> - ensuring a balance between the different rights and interests of copyright owners, users and distributors;

33 APEC Economic Leaders' Declaration of Common Resolve Bogor Indonesia, 15 November (1994), APEC Economic Leaders' Declaration for Action, Osaka, November (1995), APEC Osaka Action Agenda: Implementation of the Bogor Declaration (1995), APEC Ministerial Declarations (1997, 1999).

34 For a discussion of these concerns, see Akashi (1997) p. 3.

35 APEC (2010) pp. 3–4.

36 Para 7 Osaka Action Agenda (1995) p. 14.

- establishing an appropriate balance among all stakeholders, including content providers and ISPs, in terms of the liabilities for infringing intellectual property online; and
- providing incentives for innovation without sacrificing the community's interest in reasonable access to information.

In addition, the Osaka Action Agenda provides the following guidelines for individual and collective action by member economies.[37]

Guidelines

Each APEC economy will:

a ensure that intellectual property rights are granted through expeditious, simple, and cost-effective procedures;
b ensure that adequate and effective civil and administrative procedures and remedies are available against infringement of intellectual property rights; and
c provide and expand bilateral technical cooperation in relation to areas such as patent search and examination, computerisation and human resources development in order to ensure adequate intellectual property right protection in compliance with the TRIPS Agreement.

Collective Actions

APEC economies will take the following collective actions:

a Deepening the Dialogue on Intellectual Property Policy;
b Support for Easy and Prompt Acquisition of Rights:

(i) Participation in International IP-related Systems
(ii) Establishing Internationally Harmonised IPR Systems
(iii) Cooperation on Searches and Examinations;

c Electronic Processing of IPR-Related Proce-dures:

(i) Electronic Filing Systems
(ii) Dissemination of Information by Electronic Means;

d Appropriate Protection of IPR in New Fields:

(i) Protection for Biotechnology and Computer-Related Inventions
(ii) Protection for Geographical Indications
(iii) Electronic Commerce;

e Cooperation for Improvements to the Operation of IP System;

37 Para 7 Osaka Action Agenda (1995), updated 2002 pp. 14–15.

f Establishing Effective Systems for IPR Enforcement:

(i) Establishment of Enforcement Guidelines
(ii) Exchange of Information Concerning IPR Infringement
(iii) Cooperation with Other Fora/Authorities

g Promoting IP Asset Management in APEC Economies;
h Raising Public Awareness;
i Facilitation of Technology Transfer Through Ensuring IP Protection.

Pursuant to this objective and guidelines the Committee on Trade and Investment (CTI) established an Intellectual Property Rights Get Together (IPR-GT) in 1996.[38] Its objective was "to ensure adequate and effective protection, through legislative, administrative and enforcement mechanisms, of IP rights in the Asia Pacific region" as required by TRIPS "and other related agreements."[39] In 1998 the IPR-GT was converted into an official organ and renamed the IPR Experts Group (IPEG).[40] Taubman points out that this tentative evolution of IPEG is "a telling instance of the pragmatic value of APEC's constitutional flexibility in combination with a deeply-rooted consensus ethic."[41] This group's programme of action has proceeded cautiously over the years to involve a number of initiatives on IP, including an Anti-Counterfeiting and Piracy Initiative that led to the adoption of the following IPR Guidelines to:[42]

1 Reduce trade in counterfeit and pirated goods;
2 Protect against unauthorised copies;
3 Prevent the sale of counterfeit and pirated goods over the internet;
4 Provide effective public awareness campaigns on IPR;
5 Secure supply chains against counterfeit and pirated goods;
6 Strengthen IPR capacity building.

The IPEG has prepared documents, carried out studies and surveys which include a survey on PVP protection in some member economies,[43] a survey on Copyright Limitations & Exceptions Report on Copyright limitations and exceptions in APEC Economies,[44] a document on Effective Practices for Addressing Unauthorised Camcording,[45] and another on Best Practices on Intellectual Property (IP) Valuation and Financing in APEC.[46] The group holds workshops on topical matters,

38 APEC (n.d.).
39 APEC (n.d.).
40 APEC (n.d.).
41 Taubman (2004) p. 187.
42 APEC (n.d.).
43 APEC (2009).
44 APEC–IPEG (2010).
45 APEC (2011b).
46 APEC (2018).

such as one held in 2022 on ADR for IP disputes.[47] It meets twice annually, close to the first and third Senior Officials' Meeting, and reports to the Committee of Trade and Investment.[48]

In addition to the IPEG's work, the APEC Sub-Committee on Customs Procedures (SCCP), which was created in 1994, has also engaged with IP matters. In particular, it produced IP Rights Enforcement Strategies in 2006 and the APEC Guidelines for Customs Border Enforcement, Counterfeiting and Piracy, which were endorsed by the 2011 APEC Ministerial Meeting.[49]

APEC's IP activities are co-operative in nature and lack a normative basis primarily because of its nature as a regional configuration of economies, rather than states.[50] In other words, although harmonisation is referred to in the Osaka Plan of Action, that has not been actualised. Taubman's evaluation of its success is that it is "barely successful" in relation to the creation of an internal regulatory framework or providing policy direction beyond its regional reach.[51]

5.2.3 BRICS

The theorisation of regionalisation of Brazil, Russia, India, China and South Africa (BRICS) has been canvassed by other scholars[52] and is beyond the scope of this section. Suffice it to say that due to its unique features, this configuration has been characterised as a "new regionalism" of "emerging economies."[53] Tsheola argues that it should be understood as a "nominal rudimentary 'non-regionalism' grouping and [an] 'inexact' imitation, deliberate or accidental, in the management of contemporary global geopolitics and international relations."[54] The relationship between the BRICS constellation and multilaterism is not fully mapped.[55] To put it colloquially, BRICS has not fit in easily with the existing conceptualisation of regionalism. Be that as it may, what is relevant to this chapter is its approach to IP co-operation, to which the next paragraph turns.

In March 2013 the BRICS Ministers of Trade agreed on a Trade and Investment Co-operation Framework that provided for the following with respect to IP:[56]

1. Enhancing information exchange on IPR legislation and enforcement through meetings or seminars;
2. Jointly developing capacity-building programmes in the IPR area;
3. Promoting co-operation among IPR offices.

47 APEC (2022).
48 APEC (2021).
49 APEC (2011a).
50 Taubman (2004) p. 191.
51 Taubman (2004) p. 195.
52 Lagutina (2019), Naik (2019), Jayan (2012).
53 Shaw, Grant and Cornelissen (2011) p. 5.
54 Tsheola (2014) p. 195.
55 Telo (2017) p. 30.
56 Clause 4.

In addition, in May 2013 the BRICS heads of the IP offices agreed on an IP co-operation road map.[57] This road map lists the following "cooperation streams":

- Training of IP office staff;
- IP/patent processes and procedures including search, classification and translation services;
- Promotion of public awareness on IP in BRICS countries;
- National IP Strategy and IP Strategy for enterprises;
- Information services on IP, e.g., exchange of patent documentation taking account of local legislation;
- Collaboration in international forums as required and subject to consensus;
- Examiner exchange programme.

There has been a follow-on BRICS Trade and Investment Facilitation Plan which was endorsed by the Ministers of Trade at their meeting at Fortaleza in 2014. This plan does not expressly reference IP co-operation. There is no public information on how the BRICS IP offices have operationalised their co-operation streams. Due to a lack of information, it is not possible to evaluate the success of such co-operation.

In addition to these initiatives of the Ministers of Trade and the Heads of IP Offices, the BRICS Ministers of Science, Technology and Innovation have also engaged with IP matters. They signed a Memorandum of Agreement at their meeting in Brasília in March 2015. This memorandum provides for the following with regard to their management of IP:[58]

1 The parties will ensure adequate and effective protection and fair allocation of intellectual property rights of a proprietary nature that may result from the cooperative activities under this Memorandum of Understanding, according to their respective national laws and regulations and their international obligations.
2 The condition for the acquisition, maintenance and commercial exploitation of intellectual property rights over possible products and/or processes that might be obtained under this Memorandum of Understanding will be defined in the specific programmes, contracts or working plans of the activities of cooperation.
3 The specific programmes, contracts or working plans relating to the activities of cooperation mentioned in Paragraph 2 of this Article will set out the conditions regarding the confidentiality of information whose publication and/or disclosure might jeopardize the acquisition, maintenance and commercial exploitation of intellectual property rights obtained

57 New (2013), IP Cooperation Road Map (2013).
58 Clause 7, Memorandum of Understanding on Cooperation in Science, Technology and Innovation Between the Governments of the Federative Republic of Brazil, the Russian Federation, the Republic of India, the People's Republic of China and the Republic of South Africa, 2015.

under this Memorandum of Understanding. Such specific programmes, contracts or working plans related to the activities of cooperation will establish, where applicable, the rule and procedures concerning the settlement of disputes on intellectual property matters under this Memorandum of Understanding.

In 2017 BRICS states adopted IPR Co-operation Guidelines.[59] IP co-operation in the BRICS has so far been mostly on a practical level, with an emphasis on the capacity-building of IP offices, coordinated through regular meetings of the heads of IP offices (HIPO) meetings.[60] In addition to co-operation to build IP office capacity, there is some normative engagement to the extent that national IP strategies were expressly included in the IP offices' co-operation streams. They share a common prioritisation of using TRIPS health-related patent flexibilities to meet their public health needs and recently established the BRICS Vaccine Research and Development Centre.[61] Evaluations of the IP laws of BRICS states has demonstrated that there is significant congruence due to their adherence to TRIPS minimum standards.[62] This constellation of states also enriches global norm-setting because it provides a platform for these states to consolidate their positions and to then present a collective alternate view to norm-setting debates.[63]

5.3 Harmonisation

Harmonisation is an oft-cited panacea to regional and sub-regional integration challenges. The promise it offers lies in the conformity of economic and legal conditions that are expected to promote trade and foster the adoption of common positions on a variety of international matters. It is argued that a harmonised region or sub-region with a common economic and legal framework is better able to present a united front at international law-making for a. Harmonisation is pursued on a variety of levels, namely sub-regional, regional and global. In its earlier manifestations, when it was limited to certain regions, it was dubbed "regionalism in disguise"; however, as it became broader in its reach and became more globally inclusive, it was characterised as "universalism." In recent times when regional organisations have become active in international harmonisation efforts, it has been classified as "inter-regionalism"[64] or "new regionalism" when it traverses multiple regional borders.[65]

59 BRICS IPR Cooperation Guidelines, Annex V to the Seventh Meeting of the BRICS Trade Ministers Statement (2017).
60 BRICS (2022) 14th BRICS HIPO Meeting.
61 de Paula, Martins and Melo Beraldo (2022) pp. 20–21.
62 Deorsola et al. (2017).
63 Yu (2017) pp. 150–151.
64 Faria (2009) p. 7.
65 Blasetti and Correa (2021) p. 2.

Harmonisation exists across a spectrum of strictness or tightness which is determined by "the strictness of judicial review of compliance . . . and the extent to which the harmonisation instruments constrained regulatory space at both ends of the policy spectrum."[66]

5.3.1 Methods of Harmonisation

Goode enumerates the following nine ways of effecting harmonisation:[67]

1) a multilateral Convention without a Uniform Law as such;
2) a multilateral Convention embodying a Uniform Law;
3) a set of bilateral Treaties;
4) Community legislation – typically, a Directive
5) a Model Law;
6) a codification of custom and usage promulgated by an international non-governmental organisation;
7) international trade terms promulgated by such an organisation;
8) model contracts and general contractual conditions;
9) restatements by scholars and other experts.

Other classifications cluster these modes into three groups, namely:

1) legislative means through binding (hard) or non-binding (soft) law;
2) explanatory means through guidelines for practitioners; and
3) contractual means through formulating standard contractual clauses or industry norms.[68]

This tri-fold categorisation captures items 1–8 from Goode's list. The following paragraphs discuss these three clusters and Goode's item 9 in the realm of IP law.

Legislative Means

There are numerous conventions or treaties that provide for hard IP law, at global, bi-lateral, regional or community levels. These conventions and community laws may provide for the resolution of a conflict of laws or for uniform substantive law.[69] Generally, conventions and community laws are subject to an accession or ratification procedure and thereafter have to be domesticated in order to acquire force of law. The exception to this is a community instrument that is enacted to be directly applicable to community members, such as the EU's Regulations.

66 Dinwoodie (2013) p. 3 note 6.
67 Goode (1991) p. 57
68 Ndulo (1997) pp. 213–14, Faria (2009) p. 8.
69 Shumba (2014) 47.

A conflict of law convention enables the identification of the applicable substantive law in circumstances where two or more national systems are relevant, thus providing certainty for contractual parties and other affected persons. There is no IP-specific conflict of laws convention. However, WIPO has shown significant interest in the American Law Institute's project on IP: Principles Governing Jurisdiction, Choice of Law, and Judgments in Transnational Disputes (2008), as evidenced by the joint WIPO-ALI Seminar on IP and Private International Law held in January 2015.[70]

On the other hand, there are numerous IP-specific substantive law conventions that typically set minimum standards.[71] TRIPS is an example of a treaty setting a minimum standard. African RECs, such as SADC, have reinforced their member states' obligation to comply with TRIPS.[72] Similarly, the two sub-regional IP organisations' harmonisation efforts are essentially an internalisation of TRIPS. As is evident from chapter four, the two organisations use differing means to achieve this. OAPI's unification via the Bangui Agreement includes provisions that spell out substantive law. On the other hand, ARIPO's community laws, known as protocols, leave substantive law to its member states and generally provide only for a common application and administrative procedure. However, in those instances where a common position has not been reached at global level, the regional IP organisations set their own substantive standards in the relevant protocol or annex. An instance of this is ARIPO's Swakopmund Protocol, which provides for the protection of traditional knowledge.

In addition, where TRIPS leaves various options available, there have been sub-regional initiatives to settle on the adoption of a specific approach. This is evident in relation to the protection of plant varieties where TRIPS Article 27(3) b requires countries to "provide for the protection of plant varieties either by patents or by an effective *sui generis* system or by any combination thereof." ARIPO,[73] OAPI[74] and SADC[75] have opted to adopt the International Union for the Protection of New Varieties of Plants (UPOV)'s international convention for the protection of new varieties of plants (1991).[76]

Soft or model laws are not binding and are offered as templates for standards and best practices.[77] They may be drafted by a specialised international organisation

70 WIPO-ILA Seminar on IP and Private International Law, Meeting Code S/IP/GE/15, 16 January 2015.

71 Ruse – Khan (2009) pp. 57–59.

72 Article 23 of the SADC Protocol on Trade provides that member states shall "adopt policies and implement measures within the Community for the protection of Intellectual Property Rights, in accordance with the WTO Agreement on Trade-Related Aspects of Intellectual Property Rights (TRIPS)."

73 Arusha Protocol for the Protection of New Varieties of Plants (2013).

74 Bangui Agreement, Annex X: New Varieties of Plant.

75 Draft Protocol for the Protection of New Varieties of Plants (Plant Breeders' Rights) in the Southern African Development Community Region (2012).

76 For commentary on the appropriateness of this choice see De Jonge (2014).

77 Faria (2005) p. 13.

such as United Nations Commission on International Trade Law (UNCITRAL) or under the auspices of a supranational organisation like the AU, with the use of necessary expertise. States are then at liberty to domesticate the model law, either partially or wholly. An example of the use of soft law to harmonise IP standards is provided by the AU's African Model Legislation for the Protection of the Rights of Local Communities, Farmers and Breeders, and for the Regulation of Access to Biological Resources of 2000. This model law provides for the *sui generis* protection of traditional knowledge by providing for community rights in both resources and knowledge[78] and was much maligned by both UPOV and WIPO when it was adopted.[79] However, some African states have domesticated elements of this model law.[80] But as previously stated, countries that belong to OAPI are bound to the UPOV approach. Those countries that are members of ARIPO and SADC will probably adopt the same approach once these bodies finalise their draft protocols. This situation illustrates one of the major disadvantages of harmonisation through soft law, namely that of being overridden by a different approach advanced as hard law. A second example of soft law used in the field of IP is the UNESCO-WIPO Tunis Model Copyright Law for Developing Countries, 1976, mentioned in chapter one. Countries such as Ghana adopted this model law.

Explanatory

The second method of harmonisation, the provision of legislative guides, is resorted to when reaching consensus through hard or soft law, is unattainable. These guides present states with possible legislative and policy options from which they can select nationally appropriate laws and standards.[81] An example of such guides in the domain of IP law is UNCITRAL's Legislative Guide on Secured Transactions: Supplement on Security Rights in Intellectual Property (2010). It was developed in consultation with WIPO and sets out options for the legal regulation of security rights in IP.

Since the adoption of the Marrakesh Treaty[82] in 2013, several guides have been issued by various bodies and organisations for states, libraries and users. Under this category of harmonisation techniques, it is the guides prepared for states that are of interest. A case in point is ARIPO's draft domestication guide for its member states.[83] This draft guide contains recommendations pertaining to a suitable legislative approach and includes suggested provisions. Such a guide would be considered instructive by ARIPO member states due to its provenance. Guides that are

78 Feris (2004) pp. 251–53, Ekpere (2003) p. 275.

79 World Bank (2012) p. 453.

80 Feris (2004) pp. 252–253.

81 Faria (2005) p. 15.

82 Treaty to Facilitate Access to Published Works for Persons Who Are Blind, Visually Impaired, or Otherwise Print Disabled.

83 ARIPO Draft Guidelines for the Domestication of the Marrakesh Treaty to Facilitate Access to Published Works for Persons Who Are Blind, Visually Impaired or Otherwise Print Disabled (2014)

prepared by individuals may also be well received, particularly if they are penned by acknowledged experts in the area.[84]

Contractual

The third device, formulating standard contractual clauses or industry norms, has also been employed in the IP sphere. For example, WIPO has published the following:

1 Recommended WIPO Contract Clauses and Submission Agreements;[85]
2 Recommended Contract Clauses and Submission Agreements for WIPO Mediation and Expedited Arbitration for Film and Media.[86]

WIPO also maintains a database of Biodiversity-Related Access and Benefit-Sharing Agreements.[87] These draft clauses may be used by anyone. Other interested parties, such as firms of attorneys and research groupings have also prepared draft clauses.

Attempts to guide or inform industry norms are typically effected through guides for the affected community that spell out appropriate ways to beneficially utilise the law. Examples include guides prepared for libraries,[88] users[89] and academic institutions.[90]

Restatements of Law

Restatements of law are in extensive usage in the US, where the American Law Institute (ALI) has prepared the following IP-relevant restatements:

1 Restatement (Third) of Unfair Competition (1995); and
2 Restatement (First) of Torts § 757 – Liability for Disclosure or Use of Another's Trade Secret – General Principle (2010).

Since the beginning of 2015, the ALI has been working on a restatement of Copyright law.[91] Restatements of IP law are not currently in use in Africa. However, the

84 For example, Band and Jaszi (2013).
85 Available at www.wipo.int/amc/en/clauses/
86 Available at www.wipo.int/amc/en/film/clauses.html
87 Available at www.wipo.int/tk/en/databases/contracts/list.html
88 EIFL (2014).
89 Band (2013), Jaszi and Aufderheide (2015).
90 Association of Research Libraries (ARL) (2012).
91 Vanderbilt Law School (2014), ALI (n.d.).

African Institute of International Law[92] (established 2012) may in the future begin work on this front.

As is evident from the previous section, African RECs and regional IP organisations use some, but not all, of the available harmonisation modes. Indeed, some of them, such as the provision of model contractual terms and constituency guides, are not typically used by such organisations. Rather, they are prepared by specialised organisations such as UNCTRAL and UNIDRIOT. The following section discusses the pros and cons of harmonisation in general as a precursor to the section on specific IP harmonisation initiatives in various regions and regional communities.

5.3.2 Advantages of Harmonisation

Legal harmonisation is an important aspect of regional economic integration.[93] Trade is easier to conduct across borders where the legal framework is settled and congruent. Further, as argued in chapter one, it will be easier for African states to achieve their public health goals by adopting a harmonised regional approach to using patent-related TRIPS flexibilities. This section proceeds on the premise that the concept of harmonisation is generally beneficial but that issues or challenges arise with the employment of specific modes of harmonisation. In other words, the core problems lie with the *how* rather than the *what* and *why* of harmonisation. Accordingly, this section discusses the advantages that attach to the different modes of harmonisation.

Harmonisation by hard law is laudable for its ability to set binding international standards that serve the ideals of a cohesive legal environment that is expected to ease transactions across borders or regions and also to encourage the international spread of business due to confidence in a more or less uniform legal system. However, this may be at the cost of national flexibility and it may remove states' ability to nuance their legal frameworks to suit their domestic conditions. It is for this reason that the treaty negotiation process is often fraught with controversy and delays.

In view of these difficulties, harmonisation by soft norms may be more beneficial, as it enables the necessary national nuancing.[94] If a state decides to domesticate aspects of model law, it is able to adapt those aspects to suit its local conditions. It does so from a sound technical foundation because model laws are prepared with the necessary legal expertise which African states sometimes lack and do not have the financial resources to buy-in. Further, where standard contractual terms are accepted by industry and other relevant constituencies, they bring much needed clarity and certainty to contractual transactions.

92 AU Assembly Decision, Assembly/AU/14(XVIII) Add.5 (2012).
93 Ndulo (1997) p. 211.
94 Faria (2009) p. 13.

5.3.3 Disadvantages of Harmonisation

The section sets out the challenges that are raised by both hard and soft law approaches, in turn.

There are many challenges that attach to the use of hard law to harmonise the legal framework of a region or sub-region. Several of these are highlighted here. First, when the hard law or treaty model is used, the pace of harmonisation tends to be quite slow, and once agreed, tends to be uneven and may stagnate.[95] This is because reaching agreement at international or regional level on the initial text and on any future amendments is very difficult and may take decades, as is the case with negotiations at the Intergovernmental Committee (IGC) pertaining to the protection of traditional knowledge. In some cases a treaty never comes to fruition, as happened with the substantive Patent Law treaty. Where a treaty is agreed, the spread of its norms may be uneven when some target states do not ratify it.[96] For those states that choose to ratify it, there is often another lengthy process to see its norms domesticated. Party states have to go through an essentially political accession or signature and ratification process followed by the due process through the national legislature. In those areas where fast-changing technologies or innovation is occurring, it may very well be that when these processes are completed, the law is out-stripped by developments and has become obsolete.

Second, when agreement on norms is achieved, it is invariably a compromise, and some party states will be disadvantaged to the extent that their needs and preferences are not met satisfactorily – more so, when instances of legislative capture by powerful industry lobbies is evident.[97] Indeed, this has been one of the much-cited flaws of TRIPS in relation to developing countries, as discussed in chapter one. Many directives also ratchet up TRIPS minimum standards, as has been the case in the EU.[98]

A third difficulty raised by the use of hard law is the resolution of what Oppong has identified as "relational issues," namely the interface between community and national laws, conflict of laws between them, how community and national institutions interact, which of them has jurisdiction over which matters and how citizens or residents of member states can access, and participate in, community institutions.[99] These issues have to be resolved by binding legal provisions or legal precedents that apply to the community and its member states. Care has to be taken to ensure that these provisions are appropriately placed in both community and national law. Typically, such provisions will stipulate the supremacy of community law. They will also expressly state how community law acquires force of law in the member states. It is also necessary to provide guidance on how, if at all, national judicial institutions will interpret, apply and enforce community laws. One way of

95 Faria (2009) pp. 8–9.
96 Hugenholtz (2012) p. 6.
97 Faria (2009) p. 10.
98 Hugenholtz (2012) p. 6.
99 Oppong (2011) p. 8.

doing this is by making provision for a procedure through which national courts can refer questions of community law to community or regional adjudicatory bodies. Other matters that need to be resolved include provision for the circumstances under which individuals have access to regional legislatures and adjudicatory structures.[100] With regard to *locus standi* before regional courts, the available options include direct standing, as is the case in the EAC and COMESA;[101] the requirement of seeking the leave of national courts, as in the case of Caribbean; or the obligation to exhaust domestic remedies prior to advancing to the regional plane which prevails in COMESA and SADC.[102]

The fourth difficulty is the vastness and complexity of the domestication process. Community law typically impacts a host of national legislation and policies that have to be repealed or amended as appropriate to achieve the community standard. For example, it has been reported that Uganda would have to amend 54 statutes in order to conform to the EAC's Common Market Protocol and related sector-specific protocols.[103] This is an extensive and expensive exercise for which the retention of consultants is required. It is important to note that this difficulty also attaches to the internalisation of model laws. The domestication process also introduces a measure of uncertainty to the national sphere when a regional or sub-regional legal instrument introduces "new rights or novel terminology."[104] Such uncertainty persists until a national, sub-regional or regional court resolves it.

The fifth shortcoming is that the legislative process is complex, often lacks transparency and may be driven by obscured political agendas which compromise the quality of the resultant legal instrument.[105]

In addition to the previously noted disadvantages, soft law approaches are also beset by the uncertainty that follows from the high levels of flexibility extended to states. Due to this flexibility, states select different portions of model laws to adopt and a patchwork of different approaches then applies across the continent or a sub-region.[106] Further, it is not up to states to adopt or apply draft contractual terms and recommended constituency norms. The acceptance of these lies with industry or other relevant constituency. Consequently, it may be that these soft laws are rejected or ignored and that where they are accepted, it is haphazard.[107] Having laid out this context, the following section outlines EU and MECOSUR approaches to harmonisation.

100 Oppong (2011) p. 52.
101 Tino (2013) p. 151.
102 Tino (2013) p. 152.
103 ECA SRO-EA (2013) p. 22.
104 Hugenholtz (2012) p. 7.
105 Hugenholtz (2012) p. 7.
106 Shumba (2014) p. 55.
107 Shumba (2014) pp. 56–58.

5.3.4 Lessons From Existing Harmonisation Efforts

5.3.4.1 EU

The EU is a good comparator for the AU because of the significant commonalities between the two organisations.[108] As noted by Gottschalk,[109] the AEC Treaty's proposal of the creation of an African common market through a phased process spanning 34 years is modelled on the EU's evolution during the 34 years between the adoption of the Treaty of Rome[110] in 1957 and the adoption of the Maastricht Treaty[111] in 1991.

The EU achieves harmonisation primarily through the adoption of directives which set regional standards but leave some national discretion with regard to implementation within a stipulated time-frame.[112] After the expiry of this period, national laws that are contrary to community standards will be struck down, upon application, by the European Court of Justice (ECJ) (negative harmonisation) or over-ridden by the community standard. Regulations are directly binding without scope for national customisation.

For present purposes it is not necessary to itemise all EU IP instruments, and a discussion of the substantive content of the instruments is beyond the scope of this work.[113] It suffices to note that they cover almost the full spectrum of IPRs, with differing levels of success. Trade mark regulation, consisting of a directive[114] and regulation,[115] is touted as a major success.[116]

EU's Office for the Harmonisation in the Internal Market (Trademarks and Designs) (OHIM) administers the Community Trade mark (CTM) system and the community design system.[117] The patent system is administered by the European Patent Organisation, which comprises the European Patent Office (EPO) and the Administrative Council. Like ARIPO, the EPO administers a single patent application process for designated states, which if successful results in the grant of national patents in the designated states.[118] Enforcement is harmonised by the Enforcement

108 For an overview, see Olivier and Olivier (2004).
109 Gottschalk (2012) p. 16.
110 Treaty establishing the European Economic Community (TEEC), now the Treaty on the Functioning of the European Union (TFEU).
111 Treaty on European Union.
112 Woods and Watson (2014) p. 342.
113 For commentary see Pila (2022), Dinwoodie (2010) and (2013), Hugenholtz (2012), Raciti (1996), Max Planck Institute for Intellectual Property and Competition Law (2011), Blakely (2000), Askew (1999), Loewenheim (1996), Blakely (2000).
114 Directive (EU) 2015/2436 of the European Parliament and of the Council of 16 December 2015 to approximate the laws of the member states relating to trade marks.
115 Regulation (EU) 2017/1001 of the European Parliament and of the Council of 14 June 2017, EU trade mark delegated regulation (EU) 2018/625, EU trade mark implementing regulation (EU) 2018/626.
116 Pila (2022) para 1.007.
117 Kur and Drier (2013) p. 163.
118 Kur and Drier (2013) p. 88.

Directive of 2004 and infringement litigation is adjudicated by national courts with a right of appeal, ultimately, to the ECJ. In addition, national courts may also refer questions of the meaning of EU legal instruments.[119] In general, the EU's IP harmonisation efforts have been very successful due to its nature as a supranational organisation.[120] In contrast, the AU has not achieved this status and operates as an intergovernmental organisation.[121] This fundamental difference, coupled with the AU's resource constraints and weaker institutions, means that AU harmonisation attempts are likely to fall far short of the EU's.

The EU's experience with harmonising design and copyright protection has been challenging,[122] and harmonising patent law has been characterised as being part of "a history of repeated failure."[123] The lesson in this is that IP harmonisation is a huge undertaking that takes a long time and yields mixed results.

5.3.4.2 MERCUSOR

MERCUSOR's states parties are Argentina, Brazil, Paraguay, Uruguay and Venezuela. Bolivia lodged its Protocol of Accession in 2012 and is in the process of becoming a full member.[124] MERCUSOR's associate states are Bolivia, Chile, Colombia, Ecuador, Guyana, Peru and Surinam.[125] New Zealand and Mexico have observer status. MERCOSUR was established in 1991 through the adoption of the Treaty of Asunción and was operationalised in 1994 with the adoption of the Ouro Preto Protocol on Institutional Structure.[126] Its end goal is the creation of a common market[127] but it is currently a customs union. It is an appropriate comparator for the AU because its membership consists of developing countries and LDCs. Further, individually and collectively, its member states have significant trade relations with African states. For instance, Brazil and South Africa are members of BRICS and trade in that context, whilst MERCOSUR and SACU concluded a PTA in 2008.[128]

Its legal framework consists of the founding treaty and its annexes, protocols, Decisions of the Council of the Common Market (CCM),[129] Resolutions of the Common Market Group (CMG)[130] and Directives of the MERCUSOR Trade Commission (MTC).[131] The primary law, namely the founding treaty, its annexes and

119 Article 267 TFEU.
120 Fagbayibo (2013) p. 34.
121 Fagbayibo (2013) p. 34, Fagbayibo (2008) pp. 502–503.
122 Pila (2022) para 1.008–1.009.
123 Pila (2022) para 1.011.
124 Mercosur (n.d.).
125 Mercosur (n.d.), Guyana-Mercosur Framework Agreement (2013), Suriname-Mercosur Framework Agreement (2013).
126 Malamuc (2010) p. 25.
127 Article 1 Treaty of Asunción.
128 For commentary see Nkomo and Olmos (2013).
129 Article 9 Protocol of Ouro Preto (POP).
130 Article 15 POP.
131 Article 20 POP.

protocols, has to be translated into national law in dualist member states.[132] Of the MERCUSOR member states, Argentina is monist.[133] MERCUSOR secondary law, namely decisions, resolutions and directives, are binding on member states;[134] however, only directives are self-executing.[135] In addition, there are also "atypical" sources of law such as declarations.[136]

Harmonisation of IP is complicated by the differences in the domestic IP laws of the member states[137] and progress has been slow. To date the following legal instruments are in place:

1 Protocol on the Harmonisation of IP Rights in MERCUSOR, Relating to Trade Marks, Indications of Source and Appellations of Origin, 1995;
2 Protocol on the Harmonisation of Standards in the Field of Industrial Designs, 1998;
3 CCM Decision No 2/01 on Drug Policy in MERCUSOR, Bolivia and Chile, 2001.

The protocol on IP rights has been ratified only by Paraguay and Uruguay, for which it came into force on 6 August 2000.[138] This protocol provides the foundation for further regulation on IP in Article 24 which provides:

> The states parties undertake to make efforts to conclude, as soon as possible, additional agreements on patents, utility models, industrial designs, copyrights and related fields, and other matters relating to intellectual property.

The protocol on industrial designs has not been ratified by any of the MERCUSOR member states.[139] The delay in ratification seen here – 28 years since the adoption of the first protocol and 25 years since the adoption of the second – illustrates one of the key shortfalls of harmonisation, that of slow uptake of binding norms. However, this is not exclusive to IP instruments. as a study concluded in 2019 found that "from 1991 until the 15 July 2019, of all the 153 treaties already signed less than half were in force (74). More precisely, sixty-three were pending, ten derogated and six not in force."[140] A second lesson that can be drawn from this is the uneven adoption of norms across a sub-region or region. There is no legal instrument that seeks to regulate patents and copyright in MERCUSOR. The third of the listed instruments is a policy statement on access to medicines, ensuring the

132 Giupponi (2010) p. 59.
133 Giupponi (2010) p. 65.
134 Giupponi (2010) pp. 60–61; Article 41 POP.
135 Giupponi (2010) p. 63.
136 Giupponi (2010) p. 63.
137 Hicks and Holbein (1997) p. 805.
138 Ministry of Foreign Relations of Paraguay (n.d.a), Fernandez (2010) p. 321.
139 Ministry of Foreign Relations of Paraguay (n.d.b), Fernandez (2010) p. 326.
140 Caichiolo (2019) p. 253.

"quality, safety and efficacy" of medicines, rationalising their use and supporting R&D in relevant sectors of the region.[141] It expressly references patents and asserts that patent law must be nuanced to promote the health services provision goals of the region.[142] MERCUSOR does not yet have any common IP administrative structure.

Enforcement and dispute resolution is cursorily dealt with in the protocol on trade marks, indications of source and appellations of origin. Article 25 provides:

> The controversies that should arise among the Party States with respect to the application, interpretation or noncompliance of the provisions contained in the Present Protocol shall be resolved by means of direct diplomatic negotiations. If through said negotiations an agreement cannot be reached or if the controversy should be resolved only in part, the procedures established in the controversy resolution system in force in the MERCOSUR shall apply.

The reliance on diplomatic channels to resolve substantive legal issues is unsatisfactory. If this avenue does not yield results, the matter is then escalated to the ad hoc arbitration procedure and, if necessary, thereafter to the Permanent Review Court, which is the current dispute resolution framework established by the Olivos Protocol. The protocol provides that states must first attempt to resolve disputes through direct negotiations.[143] Should these fail within the prescribed period of 15 days, the matter may then be referred to the CMG that will then have 30 days to achieve resolution of the dispute.[144] If resolution is not achieved with the assistance of the CMG, the matter may then be referred to the ad hoc arbitration court,[145] from which a right of review lies to the Permanent Review Court.[146] The Permanent Review Court has jurisdiction to resolve legal disputes as a forum of last resort and deals with referrals of questions of community law from member states.[147] The key shortcoming of applying this dispute resolution mechanism to IP matters is that it is limited to disputes between member states and thus excludes private actor access.[148] Private persons are permitted to file claims only "in connection with the adoption or application, by any of the state parties, of legal or administrative measures having a limiting, discriminatory or unfair competition effect."[149] Effectively, the system is unable to deal with substantive IP disputes between private persons.

141 Fernandez (2010) p. 328.
142 Fernandez (2010) p. 329.
143 Article 4 Olivos Protocol.
144 Articles 6–8 Olivos Protocol.
145 Article 9 Olivos Protocol.
146 Article 17 Olivos Protocol.
147 Susani (2010) p. 75.
148 Susani (2010) p. 75.
149 Article 39 Olivos Protocol.

Further, the dispute resolution system lacks exclusive jurisdiction and member states may resort to other available avenues.[150]

Notwithstanding the slow uptake of MERCUSOR IP protocols, Argentina, Brazil, Paraguay and Uruguay concluded a trade agreement with the EU in 2019,[151] which includes an IP chapter that has been faulted for adopting provisions on geographical indications (GIs) that are more beneficial to the EU than to the MERCUSOR states.[152] In view of this, it is clear that in the nearly three decades following its first IP-specific protocol, through which it committed to IP harmonisation, this goal has not been achieved in MERCOSUR.

5.4 Unification in OHADA

OHADA was created in 1993 to harmonise business law in its member states, which comprises Benin, Burkina Faso, Cameroon, Central African Republic, Chad, Comoros, Côte d'Ivoire, Democratic Republic of Congo (DRC), Equatorial Guinea, Gabon, Guinea, Guinea-Bissau, Mali, Niger, Republic of Congo Senegal and Togo.[153] Whilst OHADA's legislative texts exclude IP, its member states' (with the exception of the DRC) IP regimes are unified through OAPI, as discussed in chapter four. From an IP policy perspective, there is further coverage for Comoros and the DRC through the COMESA IP policy. Nine OHADA members are also members of ECOWAS; Benin, Burkina Faso, Côte d'Ivoire, Guinea, Guinea Bissau, Mali, Niger, Senegal and Togo. None of the OHADA members are members of the EAC.

OHADA and OAPI employ the same model of unification, that of hard law with direct application in their member states. OHADA has ten Uniform Acts.[154] Although OHADA's intended scope of regulatory coverage includes IP,[155] it has yet to venture into that domain, possibly because its member states have already unified their IP laws through OAPI's Bangui Agreement. For present purposes, OHADA's law-making *modus operandi* and implementing structure is relevant.

The Permanent Secretariat, in liaison with member states and the Common Court of Justice and Arbitration, drafts OHADA's Uniform Acts.[156] Sometimes the drafting is undertaken with technical assistance from international agencies.

150 Susani (2010) pp. 75–76.
151 EU-MERCUSOR Trade Agreement (2019).
152 Blasetti and Correa (2021) pp. 13–19.
153 For an overview of its historical development see Mouloul (2009) pp. 8–19, Martor et al. (2002) pp. 4–7.
154 General Commercial Law (2010), Commercial Companies and Economic Interest Groupings (2014), Organising Securities Law (2010), Simplified Recovery Procedures and Measures of Execution (1998), Insolvency Law (2015), Arbitration Law (2017), Accounting Law and Financial Information (2017), Carriage of Goods by Road (2003), Co-operatives (2010) and Uniform Act on Mediation (2017).
155 Beauchard and Kodo (2011) p. 9.
156 Beauchard and Kodo (2011) p. 10.

For example, the OHADA draft Uniform Act on Contract Law was drafted with technical assistance from the International Institute for the Unification of Private Law (UNIDROIT).[157] Once drafts are finalised they are referred to the Council of Ministers for adoption.

OHADA's Common Court of Justice and Arbitration serves as a dispute resolution forum. It hears appeals from national courts which may be brought to it by parties to litigation or by national courts.[158] It also serves as an arbitration centre, but in its first few years, this role was characterised as being "undeveloped."[159]

OHADA's unification seems to have yielded some success.[160] However, truly serving the public interest requires the adaptation of legal norms and practices to local conditions. This imperative makes unification a less viable option than harmonisation because it excludes the policy and legislative space for national nuancing. It may be that countries from one region have significant national commonalities, but it is improbable that they would have exactly the same local conditions. For example, the member states of both OAPI and OHADA share a common Francophone heritage, and a similar colonial past and post-colonial legacy which justify the adoption of a common legal framework. However, there are significant national differences amongst the member states that make unification a contestable choice. The membership of the AU reflects even more diversity, and unification on a continental scale would face the significant hurdle of overcoming a plethora of different legal traditions and cultures. Perhaps it is due to such considerations that the AU's preferred approach is harmonisation.

5.5 Conclusion

This overview of instances of IP co-operation, harmonisation and unification from regions outside Africa provides several significant considerations for the AU and its plans for continental IP instruments and institutions. However, it should be borne in mind that a complete legal transplant of another region's scheme would be ill advised because it would overlook the variances in regional conditions. The more appropriate approach would be to evaluate what has worked and what has not worked in another region and then select aspects that may be relevant and practicable in Africa. The key learnings from the synopsis of ASEAN, APEC, BRICS, EU, MERSUCOR and OHADA approaches are summarised in this section.

First, co-operation is a good starting place. Indeed, ASEAN's experience was that seeking full harmonisation as an initial goal was overly ambitious, hence its retreat from the goal of harmonisation to co-operation. In the years since the conclusion of its Framework Agreement on IP Co-operation in 1995, ASEAN has crafted a sound co-operation system that is driven by the AWGIPC according to successive

157 Faria (2009) p. 13.
158 Fagbayibo (2009) p. 341.
159 Fagbayibo (2009) p. 341 and (2013) p. 45.
160 Mancuso (2007) p. 177.

Action Plans. The lesson for the AU in this is that creating a co-operation system is a lengthy process that requires careful negotiation and the establishment of the necessary co-ordinating unit and detailed strategic planning. Therefore, it is suggested that continental IP institutions, whether it be PAIPO or the AfCFTA IP Protocol infrastructure, should devote the first five to ten years to playing a role similar to that played by ASEAN's AWGIPC to secure regional IP co-operation. As highlighted in chapter four, a major part of this co-ordination needs to be devoted to rationalising the roles currently fulfilled by ARIPO and OAPI, because the principle of the preservation of the *acquis* required consolidation of existing frameworks and institutions.

APEC's IP co-operation model based on open regionalism has had less success than ASEAN's. APEC's nature is markedly different from any of Africa's subregional groupings, thus the wholesale adoption of its brand of IP co-operation is not the best option for the AU. The BRICS brand of IP co-operation is proven to be sustainable even though it has a limited focus on norm-setting and emphasises IP office operations. It therefore falls short of the continental vision.

Second, harmonisation must be considered on the bedrock of successful co-operation. The pros and cons of harmonisation have been canvassed in this chapter, and since the AU has committed itself to IP harmonisation, the question is no longer whether it should harmonise IP. Instead, the main consideration is really how to harmonise to the best effect in a way that minimises the disadvantages of harmonisation. This requires a careful consideration of which instruments to use and how to craft the regional harmonised system. As pointed out previously, regional legal instruments have to provide for relational aspects and it would be necessary for the AU to provide appropriate technical legal assistance to its member states for the domestication of community IP norms.

Generally speaking, the adoption of a hard law instrument such as a protocol is preferable to a soft law approach (e.g., model law) for the galvanising effect it would have on AU member states.[161] In addition, if the AU adopted a loose, rather than tight, approach, in its binding instruments, it would leave the necessary scope for national divergence to suit local conditions. The EU's experience has shown that the development of a harmonised IP system is a long and expensive process.[162] This is also evident from MERCUSOR's experience, which has spanned three decades to date and the region has yet to achieve harmonisation. It also has IP-right-specific instruments so that the system caters separately for each IP right through a series of annexes to a protocol. Indeed, there have been calls for Africa to harmonise its trademark laws per the EU model.[163] It may be possible to rationalise the implementation of the system through one or two administrative structures as the EU does with the EPO and OHIM.

161 Mupangavanhu (2013) p. 303.
162 Mupangavanhu (2013) p. 306.
163 Mupangavanhu (2013, 2014, 2015), Adewopo (2003) and Dean (1994a, 1994b).

The AU's internalisation of these considerations must be taken in the context of the ARIPO and OAPI IP systems' substantive legal norms, administrative and enforcement systems. This distinguishes the AU from the EU. The EU system was not built on top of existing sub-regional systems; it only had to contend with national systems. The AU, on the other hand, has to rationalise two entrenched sub-regional IP organisations that intend to continue their IP right registration functions.

Enforcement would also need to be provided for through a hard law instrument. Such an instrument would have to establish a regional judicial structure to adjudicate infringement and other IP-related matters, such as dealing with the referral of questions on community IP law from national courts. The existing AU adjudication arrangements are likely to be ill suited for IP matters due to the technical expertise required of the bench. However, a permanent IP-specific regional court may be under-utilised because, in reality, IP is not a priority for many African states that are seized with other issues such as food security, security threats and political instability. Therefore, a periodic IP Court would be the most prudent option.[164] It would allow for IP judges and experts from across Africa to be seconded to the periodic court for brief periods that would ensure their expertise is not restricted to their home countries but is also extended to the continental plane. However, Africa has had mixed results with sub-regional judiciaries, the most-cited failure being that of the SADC Tribunal, whilst it has been somewhat successful with COMESA and EAC courts.[165]

Reference List

Primary Sources

AU

African Model Legislation for the Protection of the Rights of Local Communities, Farmers and Breeders, and for the Regulation of Access to Biological Resources 2000.

AU Assembly Decision, Assembly/AU/14(XVIII) Add.5. On the Establishment of an African Institute of International Law in Arusha, the United Republic of Tanzania. Eighteenth Ordinary Session, 29–30 January 2012. Addis Ababa, Ethiopia.

APEC

APEC Economic Leaders' Declaration for Action, Osaka, November 1995.

APEC Economic Leaders' Declaration of Common Resolve Bogor Indonesia, 15 November 1994.

APEC Eleventh APEC Ministerial Meeting, Auckland, New Zealand, 9–10 September 1999.

APEC Intellectual Property Rights (IPR) Enforcement Strategies, 2006.

164 Mupangavanhu (2013) pp. 310–311.
165 For commentary see Tino (2013).

APEC Ninth APEC Ministerial Meeting Joint Statement, Vancouver, 21–22 November 1997.
APEC Osaka Action Agenda: Implementation of the Bogor Declaration, 1995.

ARIPO

ARIPO Draft Guidelines for the Domestication of the Marrakesh Treaty to Facilitate Access to Published Works for Persons Who Are Blind, Visually Impaired or Otherwise Print Disabled, 2014.
Arusha Protocol for the Protection of New Varieties of Plants, 2013.

ASEAN

Agreement on the Common Effective Preferential Tariff (CEPT) Scheme for the ASEAN Free Trade Area (AFTA) 28 January 1992.
ASEAN Framework Agreement on Intellectual Property Cooperation, Bangkok, 15 December 1995.
ASEAN Hanoi Plan of Action 1999–2004.
ASEAN IP Rights Action Plan 2016–2025.
ASEAN IPR Action Plan 2004–2010.
ASEAN IPR Action Plan 2016–2025: Updates to the ASEAN IPR Action Plan (version 2.0) 2021.
ASEAN IPR Action Plan 2011–2015.
ASEAN Trade in Goods Agreement (ATIGA) 2009.
Kuala Lumpur Declaration on ASEAN 2025: Forging Ahead Together, 22 November 2015.
Protocol to Amend the Agreement on the Common Effective Preferential Tariff Scheme for the ASEAN Free Trade Area, 15 December 1995.
Work Plan for ASEAN Cooperation on Copyright 2005.

BRICS

BRICS IPR Cooperation Guidelines, Annex V to the Seventh Meeting of the BRICS Trade Ministers Statement (2017). Available at www.brics.utoronto.ca/docs/170831-ipr.html [accessed 8 January 2023].
IP Cooperation Road Map, 2013.
Memorandum of Understanding on Cooperation in Science, Technology and Innovation Between the Governments of the Federative Republic of Brazil, the Russian Federation, the Republic of India, the People's Republic of China and the Republic of South Africa, 2015.
Trade and Investment Cooperation Framework, 2013.

EU

Commission Delegated Regulation (EU) 2018/625 of 5 March 2018 Supplementing Regulation (EU) 2017/1001 of the European Parliament and of the Council on the European Union Trade Mark, and Repealing Delegated Regulation (EU) 2017/1430, C/2018/1231, OJ L 104, 24.4.2018, pp. 1–36.
Commission Implementing Regulation (EU) 2018/626 of 5 March 2018 Laying Down Detailed Rules for Implementing Certain Provisions of Regulation (EU) 2017/1001 of the

European Parliament and of the Council on the European Union Trade Mark, and Repealing Implementing Regulation (EU) 2017/1431, C/2018/1225, OJ L 104, 24.4.2018, pp. 37–56.
Directive (EU) 2015/2436 of the European Parliament and of the Council of 16 December 2015 to Approximate the laws of the Member States Relating to Trade Marks (Recast) OJ L 336, 23.12.2015, pp. 1–26.
EU-MERCUSOR Trade Agreement (2019).
Regulation (EU) 2017/1001 of the European Parliament and of the Council of 14 June 2017 on the European Union Trade Mark (Codification) (Text with EEA Relevance). OJ L 154, 16.6.2017, pp. 1–99.

MERCUSOR

CCM Decision No 2/01 on Drug Policy in MERCUSOR, Bolivia and Chile, Montevideo, 27 November 2001.
Protocol of Ouro Preto, 1994.
Protocol on the Harmonisation of IP Rights in MERCUSOR, Relating to Trademarks, Indications of Source and Appellations of Origin, Asuncion, 5 August 1995, CCM Decision No 08/98.
Protocol on the Harmonisation of Standards in the Field of Industrial Designs, Rio de Janeiro, 10 December, CCM Decision No 16/98.
Treaty of Asuncion, 1991.
Olivos Protocol for the Settlement of Disputes in MERCOSUR
Guyana-Mercosur Framework Agreement, 2013.
Suriname-Mercosur Framework Agreement, 2013.

OHADA

Uniform Act on Arbitration Law, adopted 23 November 2017 at Conakry, Guinea entry into force 15 March 2018 (replacing a 1999 version).
Uniform Act on Commercial Companies and Economic Interest Groupings, adopted 30 January 2014 at Ouagadougou, Burkina Faso, entry 5 May 2014.
Uniform Act on Contracts for the Carriage of Goods by Road adopted 22 March 2003 at Yaoundé, Cameroon entry 1 January 2004.
Uniform Act on Co-operatives adopted 15 December 2010 at Lomé, Togo entry 15 May 2011.
Uniform Act on General Commercial Law, adopted 15 December 2010 at Lomé, Togo entry 15 May 2011.
Uniform Act on Insolvency Law, adopted 10 September at Grand-Bassam, Côte d'Ivoire, entry into force 24 December 2015.
Uniform Act on Mediation, adopted 23 November 2017 at Conakry, Guinea entry into force 15 March 2018.
Uniform Act on Organising Securities law, adopted 15 December 2010 at Lomé, Togo entry 15 May 2011.
Uniform Act Organising Simplified Recovery Procedures and Measures of Execution, adopted 10 April 1998 at Libreville, Gabon entry into force 31 August 1998.
Uniform Act Relating to Accounting Law and Financial Information, adopted 26 January 2017 entry into force 15 February 2017 (for entities personal accounts) and 1 January 2019 (for the consolidated accounts, combined accounts and financial statements produced under IFRS) (replacing the 2000 version).

UPOV

International Convention for the Protection of New Varieties of Plants (1991).
UNCITRAL's Legislative Guide on Secured Transactions: Supplement on Security Rights in Intellectual Property (2010).

WIPO

Budapest Treaty on the International Recognition of the Deposit of Micro-Organisms for the Purposes of Patent Procedures, adopted at Budapest on April 28, 1977, and amended on September 26, 1980.
Patent Law Treaty adopted at Geneva on June 1, 2000.
UNESCO-WIPO Tunis Model Copyright Law for Developing Countries, 1976.

Secondary Sources

Adewopo, A., 2003. Trademark Systems in Africa: A Proposal for the Harmonisation of the ARIPO and the OAPI Agreements on Marks. *The Journal of World Intellectual Property*, 6, 473–484.
Akashi, Y., 1997. *An ASEAN Perspective on APEC*. The Helen Kellogg Institute for International Studies Working Paper 240. Notre Dame. Hellen Kellogg Institute for International Studies.
ALI, n.d., *Annual Meeting Project Restatement of the Law: Copyright*. 2023 Annual Meeting, 22–24 May 2023. Available at https://www.ali.org/projects/show/copyright/ [accessed 17 April 2023].
APEC, 2009. *Report on Survey of Plant Variety Protection Regimes in APEC Economies*. Singapore: APEC.
APEC, 2010. *The Report on APEC's 2010 Economies' Progress Towards the Bogor Goals*. Singapore: APEC Policy Unit.
APEC, 2011a. Ministerial Statement. *APEC Ministerial Meeting*, Honolulu 11 November 2011.
APEC, 2011b. *Effective Practices for Addressing Unauthorized Camcording*. 23rd APEC Ministerial Meeting, Hawaii, United States, 11 November 2011, Agenda item: 1a, Doc 2011/AMM/014app05. Available at https://www.apec.org/docs/default-source/groups/ip/11_amm_014app05.doc [accessed 17 April 2023].
APEC, 2018. *Best Practices on Intellectual Property (IP) Valuation and Financing in APEC*. Singapore: APEC Secretariat.
APEC, 2022. *Final Report on 2021 APEC Workshop on the Potential for Use of Alternative Dispute Resolution (ADR) in the Field of IPR Taipei, Chinese Taipei | 29–30 July 2021*. Singapore: APEC Secretariat.
APEC, n.d. *Intellectual Property Rights Group* (last updated March 2021) Available at www.apec.org/groups/committee-on-trade-and-investment/intellectual-property-rights-experts-group [accessed 7 October 2022].
APEC–IPEG, 2010. *Survey on Copyright Limitations & Exceptions Report on Copyright L&E in APEC Economies*. Singapore: APEC Secretariat.
ASEAN, 2008. *ASEAN Economic Community Blueprint*. Jakarta: ASEAN Secretariat.
ASEAN, 2014. *Thinking Globally, Prospering Regionally–ASEAN Economic Community 2015*. Jakarta: ASEAN Secretariat.
ASEAN, 2015a. *ASEAN Economic Community Blueprint 2025*. Jakarta: ASEAN Secretariat.

ASEAN, 2015b. *ASEAN 2025: Forging Ahead Together*. Jakarta: ASEAN Secretariat.
ASEAN, 2021. *Mid-Term Review ASEAN Economic Community Blueprint 2025*. Jakarta: ASEAN Secretariat.
Askew, L.A., 1999. The CJEU, the ICJ and Intellectual Property: Is Harmonisation the Key? *Tulsa Journal of Comparative and International Law*, 7, 375–412.
Association of Research Libraries (ARL), 2012. *Code of Best Practices in Fair Use for Academic and Research Libraries*. Washington, DC: ARL.
AWGIPC, n.d. *The ASEAN IPR Action Plan 2016–2020*. Available at www.aseanip.org/About-Us/ASEAN-IPR-Action-Plan-2016-2020 [accessed 1 March 2015].
Band, J., 2013. *A User Guide to the Marrakesh Treaty*. Available at https://www.llrx.com/2013/08/a-user-guide-to-the-marrakesh-treaty/ [accessed 1 March 2023].
Band, J. and Jaszi, P., 2013. *Model Statute for Implementation of the Marrakesh Treaty to Facilitate Access to Published Works for Persons Who Are Blind, Visually Impaired, or Otherwise Print Disabled*. Available at http://infojustice.org/wp-content/uploads/2013/09/MODEL-STATUTE-FOR-MARRAKESH-IMPLEMENTATION.pdf [accessed 1 March 2023].
Barraclough, E., 2004–2005. *ASEAN Scales Back IP Plans. Managing Intellectual Property. 1 December 2004*. Available at www.managingip.com/Article/1255213/News-focus-Asean-scales-back-IP-plans.html [accessed 1 March 2023].
Beauchard, R. and Kodo, M.J.V., 2011. *Can OHADA Increase Legal Certainty in Africa?* World Bank Justice and Development Working Paper Series. Washington, DC: The World Bank.
Blakely, T.W., 2000. Beyond the International Harmonization of Trademark Law: The Community Trade Mark as a Model of Unitary Transnational Trade Mark Protection. *University of Pennsylvania Law Review*, 149(1), 313.
Blasetti, R. and Correa, J.I., 2021. *Intellectual Property in the EUMERCOSUR FTA: A Brief Review of the Negotiating Outcomes of a Long-Awaited Agreement*. Research Paper, No. 128, South Centre, Geneva.
BRICS, 2022. *14th BRICS HIPO Meeting Successfully Held*. Available at http://brics2022.mfa.gov.cn/eng/dtxw/202209/t20220930_10775638.html [accessed 8 January 2023].
Caichiolo, R., 2019. Mercosur: Limits of Regional Integration. *Erasmus Law Review*, 3, 246–268.
Dean, O.H., 1994a. A Unified Intellectual Property Law System for Southern Africa. Part 1: International Arrangements and European Conventions. *Juta's Business Law*, 2(3), 111–114.
Dean, O.H., 1994b. A Unified Intellectual Property Law System for Southern Africa. Part 2: Multinational Registrations in Africa. *Juta's Business Law*, 2(4), 165–169.
De Jonge, B., 2014. Plant Variety Protection in Sub-Saharan Africa: Balancing Commercial and Smallholder Farmers' Interests. *Journal of Politics and Law*, 7(3), 100–111.
Deorsola, A.B., Leal, M.C.M.R., Milene, D.C., Schmidt, I.J. and Braga, E.J., 2017. Intellectual Property and Trademark Legal Framework in BRICS Countries: Comparative Study. *World Patent Information*, 49, 1–9. https://doi.org/10.1016/j.wpi.2017.03.001
de Paula Bueno, E., Martins, L.M. and Melo Beraldo, M.A. (2022). Health Diplomacy and Intellectual Property Cooperation Within BRICS: From Beijing Declaration to the BRICS Vaccine Research and Development Centre. *Journal of BRICS Studies*, 1(1), 16–25. https://doi.org/10.36615/jbs.v1i1.650
Dinwoodie, G.B., 2010. Editorial: Trade Mark Harmonisation: National Courts and the European Court of Justice. *Int'l Review of Industrial Property and Copyright Law*, 41, 1–3.

Dinwoodie, G.B., 2013. *The Europeanisation of Trademark Law*. University of Oxford Legal Research Paper Series Paper No 54/2013 April 2013. Oxford. Available at http://ssrn.com/abstract=2260908 [accessed 1 March 2015].

ECA SRO-EA, 2013. *Domestication and Mainstreaming of Regional Integration Processes Instruments and Decisions into National Policies, Legal and Regulatory Frameworks: Issues, Challenges and Opportunities – The Case of Uganda*. Kigali: ECA SRO-EA.

EIFL, 2014. *The Marrakesh Treaty: An EIFL Guide for Libraries*. Available at www.eifl.net/news/marrakesh-treaty-eifl-guide-libraries [accessed 1 March 2015].

Ekpere, J., 2003. African Model Law on the Protection of the Rights of Local Communities, Farmers and Breeders, and for the Regulation of Access to Biological Resources. In Nnadozie, K., et al. (eds.) *African Perspectives on Genetic Resources, a Handbook on Law, Policies and Institutions*. Washington, DC: Environmental Law Institute, 275–286.

Elek, A., 1991. Asia Pacific Economic Cooperation (APEC). *Southeast Asian Affairs*. Singapore: Institute of Southeast Asian Studies.

Elek, A., 2005. Back to Canberra: Founding APEC. In Elek, A. (ed.) *The Evolution of PECC: The First 25 Years*. Singapore: Pacific Economic Cooperation Council (PECC), 65–92.

Endeshaw, A., 1999. Harmonisation of Intellectual Property Laws in ASEAN. *The Journal of World Intellectual Property*, 2, 3–23.

Endeshaw, A., 2004. The Momentum for Review of TRIPS and Harmonisation of Intellectual Property in ASEAN. In Antons, C., Blakeney, M. and Heath, C. (eds.) *Intellectual Property Harmonisation Within ASEAN and APEC*. The Hague: Kluwer Law International, 139–158.

Endeshaw, A., 2010. *Intellectual Property in Asian Emerging Economies: Law and Policy in the Post-TRIPS Era*. Surrey and Burlington: Ashgate Publishing.

European Copyright Society, 2014. *Letter to Commissioner for Digital Economy and Society*. Unification of Copyright Law, 19 December 2014. Available at www.ivir.nl/syscontent/pdfs/78.pdf [accessed 1 March 2015].

Fagbayibo, B., 2008. A Supranational African Union? Gazing Into the Crystal Ball. *De Jure*, 3, 493–503.

Fagbayibo, B., 2009. Towards the Harmonisation of Laws in Africa: Is OHADA the Way to Go? *CILSA*, 309–322.

Fagbayibo, B., 2013. Common Problems Affecting Supranational Attempts in Africa: An Analytical Overview. *PER/PELJ*, 16(1), 32–69.

Faria, J.A.E., 2005. Model Laws as an Instrument of Legal Harmonisation: The Experience of UNCITRAL. *ALRAESA Conference*, South Africa, 15–17 March. Available at www.justice.gov.za/alraesa/conferences/2005sa/papers/s5_faria2.pdf [accessed 1 March 2023].

Faria, J.A.E., 2009. Future Directions of Legal Harmonisation and Law Reform: Stormy Seas or Prosperous Voyage? *Uniform Law Review*, 14, 5–34.

Feris, L., 2004. Protecting Traditional Knowledge in Africa: Considering African Approaches. *African Human Rights Law Journal*, 4(2), 242–255.

Fernandez, F.V., 2010. The Protection of Intellectual Property in MERCUSOR. In Filho, M.T.F., Lixinski, L. and Giupponi, M.B.O. (eds.) *The Law of Mercusor*. Oxford: Hart Publishing, 317–330.

Giupponi, M.B.O., 2010. Sources of Law in MERCUSOR. In Filho, M.T.F., Lixinski, L. and Giupponi, M.B.O. (eds.) *The Law of Mercusor*. Oxford: Hart Publishing, 57–71.

Goode, R., 1991. Reflections on the Harmonisation of Commercial Law. *Uniform Law Review*, os-19(1), 54–74.

Gottschalk, K., 2012. The African Union and its Sub-Regional Structures. *Journal of African Union Studies*, 1(1), 9–39.

Hicks, L.L. and Holbein, J.R., 1997. Convergence of National Intellectual Property Norms in International Trading Agreements. *American University Journal of International Law & Policy*, 12(5), 770–814.

Hugenholtz, P.B., 2012. Harmonisation or Unification of EU Copyright Law. *Monash University Law Review*, 38(1), 4–16.

IP Office Singapore, 2013. *Asean IP Direct*. Available at www.ipos.gov.sg/AboutIP/IPResources/UsefulLinks/RegionalOrganisations/ASEANIPDirect.aspx [accessed 1 March 2023].

Jaszi, P. and Aufderheide, J., 2015. *Code of Best Practices in Fair Use for the Visual Arts*. Washington, DC: College Art Association.

Jayan, P.A., 2012. BRICS: Advancing Cooperation and Strengthening Regionalism. *India Quarterly*, 68(4), 363–384.

Kuanporth, J., 2013. Patents and the Emerging Markets of Asia: ASEAN and Thailand. In Abbott, F.M., Correa, C.M. and Drahos, P. (eds.) *Emerging Markets and the World Patent Order*. Cheltenham: Edward Elgar, 305–326.

Kur, A. and Drier, T., 2013. *European IP Law: Text, Cases & Materials*. Cheltenham: Edward Elgar.

Lagutina, M.L., 2019. BRICS in a World of Regions. *Third World Thematics: A TWQ Journal*, 4(6), 442–458. http://doi.org/10.1080/23802014.2019.1643781

Loewenheim, L., 1996. Harmonisation and Intellectual Property in Europe. *Columbia Journal of European Law*, 2, 481–490.

Malamuc, A., 2010. Theories of Regional Integration and the Origins of MERCUSOR. In Filho, M.T.F., Lixinski, L. and Giupponi, M.B.O. (eds.) *The Law of Mercusor*. Oxford: Hart Publishing, 9–27.

Mancuso, S., 2007. Trends on the Harmonisation of Contract Law in Africa. *Annual Survey of International & Comparative Law*, 13(1), 157–178.

Martor, B., et al., eds., 2002. *Business Law in Africa: OHADA and the Harmonisation Process*. London and Sterling: Kogan Page Limited.

Max Planck Institute for Intellectual Property and Competition Law, 2011. *Study on the Overall Functioning of the European Trademark Systems*. Available at https://op.europa.eu/en/publication-detail/-/publication/5f878564-9b8d-4624-ba68-72531215967e [accessed 1 March 2023].

Mercosur, n.d. *Mercusor Countries*. Available at www.mercosur.int/en/about-mercosur/mercosur-countries/ [accessed 8 January 2023].

Ministry of Foreign Relations of Paraguay, n.d.a. *Protocol on the Harmonisation of Rules on Intellectual Property in Mercosur, Regarding Trademarks, Indications of Origin and Appellations of Origin*. Available at www.mre.gov.py/tratados/public_web/DetallesTratado.aspx?id=2ooBwPZqYBYDyHTjMx+HmQ== [accessed 8 January 2023].

Ministry of Foreign Relations of Paraguay, n.d.b. *Protocol for the Harmonisation of Standards on Industrial Designs*. Available at www.mre.gov.py/tratados/public_web/DetallesTratado.aspx?id=4+6APUUoU6ON0zDqSAxQxw== [accessed 8 January 2023].

Mouloul, A., 2009. *Understanding the Organisation for the Harmonisation of Business Laws in Africa (OHADA)* (2nd ed.). Available at www.ohada.com/content/newsletters/1403/Comprendre-l-Ohada-en.pdf [accessed 1 March 2023].

Mupangavanhu, Y., 2013. The Regional Integration of African Trade Mark Laws: Challenges and Possibilities. Thesis (PhD). University of the Western Cape.

Mupangavanhu, Y., 2014. The Integration of Trade Mark Laws in the European Union: Lessons for Africa? *South African IP Law Journal*, 2, 109–130.

Mupangavanhu, Y., 2015. African Union Rising to the Need for Continental IP Protection? The Establishment of the Pan-African Intellectual Property Organisation. *Journal of African Law*, 59, 1–24.

Naik, S., 2019. The Emergence of BRICS: An Extension of Interregionalism to the Global South. In Féron, É., Käkönen, J. and Rached, G. (eds.) *Revisiting Regionalism and the Contemporary World Order: Perspectives from the BRICS and Beyond* (1st ed.). Verlag Barbara Budrich, 61–82. https://doi.org/10.2307/j.ctvr00xjn.8

Ndulo, M., 1997. The Need for the Harmonisation of Trade Laws in the Southern Africa Development Community (SADC). In Yusuf, A.A. (ed.) *African Yearbook of International Law*. Leiden, The Netherlands: African Association of International Law, 195–225.

New, W., 2013. *BRICS Launch Their Own Plan for IP Cooperation; India Defends Itself.* IP Watch 27 November 2013.

New, W., 2015. *Top European Copyright Experts Urge Reform, Unification of Copyright.* IP Watch 5 January 2015.

Ng, E.S.K., 2013. ASEAN IP Harmonisation: Striking the Delicate Balance. *Pace International Law Review*, 25, 129–160.

Nkomo, M. and Olmos, B., 2013. The MERCOSUR-SACU Preferential Trade Agreement: A Step Forward in South-South Relations? In du Pisani, A., Erasmus, G. and Hartzenberg, T. (eds.) *Monitoring Regional Integration in Southern Africa Yearbook 2012*. Stellenbosch: Trade Law Centre and the Konrad-Adenauer-Stiftung, 194–211.

OECD, 2013. Overview of Development Gaps in Southeast Asia: Gaps between ASEAN – 6 and CLM V Countries. In *Southeast Asian Economic Outlook 2013: With Perspectives on China and India.* Paris: OECD Publishing, 241–290.

Olivier, G. and Olivier, M., 2004. Models of Regional Integration: The European Union and the African Union. *SA Public Law*, 19, 351–364.

Oppong, R.F., 2011. *Legal Aspects of Economic Integration in Africa.* Cambridge: Cambridge University Press.

Pila, J., 2022. *Seville's EU Intellectual Property Law and Policy*. Cheltenham: Edward Elgar.

Raciti, E.P., 1996. The Harmonisation of Trademarks in the European Community: The Harmonisation Directive and the Community Trademark. *Journal of the Patent and Trademark Office Society*, 78, 51–68.

Ruse-Khan, H.G., 2009. Time for a Paradigm Shift? Exploring Maximum Standards in International Intellectual Property Protection. *Trade, Law and Development*, 1(56), 56–102.

Shaw, T.M., Grant, J.A. and Cornelissen, S., 2011. Introduction and Overview: The Study of New Regionalism(s) at the Start of the Second Decade of the Twenty-First Century. In Shaw, T.M., Grant, J.A. and Cornelissen, S. (eds.) *The Ashgate Research Companion to Regionalisms*. Surrey and Burlington: Ashgate Publishing, 3–30.

Shumba, T., 2014. Harmonising the Law of Sale in the Southern African Development Community (SADC): An Analysis of Selected Models. Thesis (PhD). Stellenbosch University.

Susani, N., 2010. Dispute Settlement. In Filho, M.T.F., Lixinski, L. and Giupponi, M.B.O. (eds.) *The Law of Mercusor*. Oxford: Hart Publishing, 73–85.

Sutton, M., 2007. Open Regionalism and the Asia Pacific: Implications for the Rise of an East Asian Economic Community. *Ritsumeikan International Affairs*, 5, 133–152.

Taubman, A.S., 2004. Collective Management of TRIPS: APEC, New Regionalism and Intellectual Property. In Antons, C., Blakeney, M. and Heath, C. (eds.) *Intellectual Property Harmonisation within ASEAN and APEC*. The Hague, The Netherlands: Kluwer Law International, 161–202.

Telo, M., 2017. Les BRICS et la coopération régionale entre États voisins. *Hermès, La Revue*, 79, 29–30. https://doi.org/10.3917/herm.079.0027

Tino, E., 2013. The Role of Regional Judiciaries in Eastern and Southern Africa. In du Pisani, A., Erasmus, G. and Hartzenberg, T. (eds.) *Monitoring Regional Integration in Southern Africa Yearbook 2012*. Stellenbosch: Trade Law Centre and the Konrad-Adenauer-Stiftung, 140–174.

Tsheola, J., 2014. Groping in the Dark with the "Non-Places" BRICS: Geopolitics of the Emergence of an Empire or States Racing to the Bottom? *Mediterranean Journal of Social Sciences*, 5(25), 187–197.

Vanderbilt Law School, 2014. *Daniel Gervais to Serve as Associate Reporter of the American Law Institute's Restatement of Law Copyright*, 4 December 2014.

WIPO-ILA Seminar on IP and Private International Law, *Meeting Code S/IP/GE/15*, 16 January 2015.

Woods, L. and Watson, L., 2014. Harmonisation. In Woods, L., Watson, P. and Steiner, J. (eds.) *Steiner & Woods EU Law* (25th ed.). Oxford: Oxford University Press, 341–360.

World Bank, 2012. *Agricultural Innovation Systems: An Investment Sourcebook*. Geneva: World Bank.

Yu, P., 2017. Intellectual Property Negotiations, the BRICS Factor and the Changing North-South Debate. In Neuwirth, R., Svetlicinii, A. and De Castro Halis, D. (eds.) *The BRICS-Lawyers' Guide to Global Cooperation*. Cambridge: Cambridge University Press, 123–147.

Zirnstein, E., 2005. Harmonisation and Unification of IP in the EU. In Vodov, Z. (ed.) *Intellectual Capital and Knowledge Management: Proceedings of the 5th International Conference of the Faculty of Management*, Koper, University of Primorska 18–20 November 2004. Koper: University of Primorska Faculty of Management, 293–308.

6 Continental IP Co-operation

PAIPO

To register or not to register: that is the question.

6.1 Introduction

This chapter considers developments pertaining to the establishment of PAIPO (A discussion of the AfCFTA IP Protocol appears in chapter seven.) It provides a historical outline of events that have been publicly disclosed. There are likely to be events and stages in the process that are not canvassed, simply because they have not been publicly disclosed by the AU and other relevant parties. The reason for any such non-disclosure is probably that creation of a new organisation on a continent where there are already two sub-regional institutions, whose future will be impacted significantly by the new organisation, is highly political and involves a lot of diplomacy, which requires confidentiality. Secondly, the negotiation of AU regulatory instruments has both open and restricted aspects. The open aspects include national and continental stakeholder consultations and public meetings. The restricted aspects include the relevant committee meetings and negotiation sessions. Accordingly, this chapter engages only with the open aspects.

The first section of this chapter focuses on the creation of PAIPO as a specialised AU agency and includes a historical overview. It is followed by an outline of how PAIPO will function. This section sets out the organisation's organs, its objectives and functions. It then discusses how ARIPO, OAPI and PAIPO can co-operate in the future, in a way that respects their distinct mandates and maximises efficiency. It suggests that PAIPO may be best placed to lead on the formulation of continental policy direction. Therefore, it advances some views on the key considerations PAIPO of which ought to be aware, with respect to such policy. Specifically, developmental and human rights aspects are singled out as fundamental.

6.2 Historical Overview of the AU's Efforts to Establish PAIPO

Suggestions for the creation of a continental IP organisation have been made since the mid-1990s.[1] One of the earliest calls was Kongolo's proposal for the formation

1 For example, see Dean (1994a) and (1994b).

DOI: 10.4324/9781003310198-6

of the Folklore and IP Organisation of Africa.[2] In more recent years, the proposals have centred on a unified continental trademark system.[3] As will be shown, the PAIPO Statute does not envisage any industrial property registration function for PAIPO.

The proposal for the establishment of PAIPO was one of the outcomes of the Pan-African agenda, over which the AU has oversight. A brief overview of the historical development of the AU was given in chapter three. This chapter only outlines developments in the AU that catapulted its conceptualisation of PAIPO. As noted in chapter three, the AU's mandate includes the promotion of sustainable socio-economic and cultural development and the integration of African economies.[4] It also extends to "co-ordinat[ing] and harmonis[ing] the policies between the existing and future RECs" and promoting research in science and technology, amongst other fields.[5] A large part of this mandate is being pursued through AUDA-NEPAD. In keeping with its objectives, the then NEPAD began working on initiatives to promote science and technology which included co-hosting a workshop in 2003 with South Africa's then Department of Science and Technology, now known as the Department of Science and Innovation.[6] One of the outcomes of this workshop was the creation of African Ministerial Conference on Science and Technology (AMCOST). At its first conference, in November 2003, related AMCOST structures and an outline of a plan of action were agreed upon.[7] Following this, AUDA-NEPAD and the AU Commission's 2004–2007 Strategic Plan for Human Resources, Science and Technology provided for a series of workshops that were hosted in each of the AU's five regions during the period November 2004 to March 2005.[8] The findings of these workshops together with experts' consultations and studies[9] informed the AU's Science and Technology Consolidated Plan of Action which the AU adopted in November 2006. This plan constituted a blueprint for science and technology related activities.

The AU Human Resources, Science and Technology (HRS&T) department together with the AU's General Office and WIPO arranged a meeting of the African Group on IP in May 2006 that recommended the establishment of PAIPO.[10] This led to the preparation of a concept paper for consideration at the AMCOST extraordinary conference held in November that year.[11] The four-page concept pa-

2 Kongolo (2013) p. 124, Kongolo (2000).
3 Adewopo (2003), Mupangavanhu (2014) and (2013).
4 Article 3(j) Constitutive Act of the African Union.
5 Article 3(l)–(m) Constitutive Act of the African Union.
6 National Advisory Council on Innovation (NACI) (2007) p. 20, NEPAD (2006) p. 6, Dountino (2013).
7 NACI (2007) p. 20, NEPAD (2006) p. 6, Dountino (2013).
8 NEPAD (2006) p. 6.
9 For example, van Gardingen and Karp (2006a), (2006b), (2006c), Oldham, Adeoti and Thomas (2006).
10 AU HRS&T (2006) p. 1, Kongolo (2013) p. 125.
11 AU HRS&T Establishing a Pan-African Intellectual Property Organisation (PAIPO). A Concept Paper. Extraordinary Conference of the AMCOST. 20–24 November 2006. Cairo, Egypt. EXT/AU/EXP/ST/8(II) p. 1 (Concept Paper).

per identified the key motivations for establishing the organisation as "the lack of continental inclusiveness"[12] and the need to "sharpen the visibility of IP issues as they relate to economic development . . . [to] add impetus to the leaders'" political will and commitment to inventiveness and innovation, thus emphasising the significance of political leadership in such a "strategic field of development."[13] It noted that the benefits that would accrue to AU member states upon the establishment of PAIPO would include cost saving, information sharing and the availability of a platform on which to deliberate IP issues and reach consensus on a continental position on these issues.

The concept paper emphasised that what was being sought at that stage was a high-level expression of interest and commitment from the AU, ARIPO and OAPI. It was envisaged that the two sub-regional bodies would continue to exist under the "umbrella" of PAIPO after its establishment, the practicalities of which would be ironed out at a later stage through a series of meetings between these key stakeholders. The objectives of the continental organisation would be to:[14]

1 Set IP standards that reflect the needs of Member States;
2 Set benchmarks for best practices on intellectual property;
3 Promote the growth of knowledge-based economies in Africa;
4 Facilitate the rationalisation and harmonisation of IP standards;
5 To collect, process and disseminate relevant information on intellectual property to Member States;
6 Facilitate the utilisation of relevant IP information by Member States;
7 Assist Member States in training and capacity building on a wide range of IP matters.

These references to standards hinted at a normative angle to PAIPO's work that could be implemented through hard or soft law approaches. After the presentation and discussion of the concept paper at an experts' meeting at the extraordinary conference, it was agreed that PAIPO "would help Africa participate more effectively in IP production and management of IP processes" and that the "AU should proceed and accelerate the formation of PAIPO with full participation of ARIPO and OAPI."[15]

In January 2007 the AU Assembly endorsed work on the creation of PAIPO, which had already commenced, by calling for the AU Commission, RECs, WIPO, OAPI and ARIPO "to submit to it the texts relevant to the establishment of" the organisation.[16] According to a progress report tabled at AMCOST III, in November

12 AU HRS&T Concept Paper p. 2.
13 AU HRS&T Concept Paper p. 2; Kongolo (2013) pp. 125–126.
14 AU HRS&T Concept Paper pp. 2–3.
15 AU Report of the Meeting of Experts Extraordinary Conference of the AMCOST 20–24 November 2006. Cairo, Egypt. EXT/AU/EXP/ST/Rpt.(II) p. 9.
16 AU Assembly Decision on the Establishment of PAIPO. Assembly of the African Union Eighth Ordinary Session 29–30 January 2007. Addis Ababa, Ethiopia. Assembly/AU/Dec.138 (VIII) para 2.

2007, the HRS&T department appointed the Scientific, Technical and Research Commission (AU-STRC) as the lead office on all matters relating to PAIPO.[17] In addition, a consultant was also appointed to conduct a situation analysis[18] and to draft the Constitutive Articles of PAIPO that would be discussed by stakeholders in 2008. Such discussions took place thereafter with WIPO participation.[19] In March 2010 the draft constitutive articles were discussed at AMCOST IV, in Cairo, Egypt.[20] After such consideration, the conference recommended that the draft should be revised and further consultations undertaken.

The AU-STRC reports that it then retained two consultants to undertake the review that was followed by a stakeholders' meeting in Dakar, Senegal, in September 2011.[21] It is reported that part of the consultants' work entailed drafting an Agreement on the Establishment of the PAIPO and a business plan for PAIPO that spans 25 years.[22] Neither of these two documents are publicly available, therefore it is not possible to comment on their content and import. However, the length of the development period reportedly provided for in the business plan shows that this is a long-term endeavour. In mid-2012 a draft statute became public and reports were that it was intended to be approved by AMCOST V in November of that year. It became the centre of much scrutiny as it was the first concrete manifestation of how PAIPO would be operationalised.

Several concerns were raised about the draft statute in online critiques authored by scholars and practitioners, the main of which will be discussed later.[23] In addition, concerns about the Draft PAIPO Statute were communicated to the AU member states through a petition.[24] In view of these concerns, when AMCOST V met in Congo Brazzaville on 12–16 November 2012 the draft was not approved, as had been intended, but it was referred back for further consultation. To this end, a Ministerial Decision was taken, urging the finalisation and operationalisation of PAIPO by 2013.[25] However, this did not eventuate due to strong opposition based on policy considerations (discussed later). The 20th Ordinary Session of the AU

17 AU Progress Report on Research Policy Framework, Capacity Building for the African Policymakers and the Formation of the PAIPO. AMCOST III Third Ordinary Session 12–16 November 2007. Mombasa, Republic of Kenya. AU/EXP/ST/11(III) p. 1.

18 Sibanda (2009).

19 WIPO Technical Assistance Database: Experts Group Meeting on PAIPO, Addis Ababa, Ethiopia. 18 May 2009; WIPO Support to NEPAD Period of Report: July 2008 to June 2009.

20 AU Ministerial Decisions. AU/MIN/ST/Dec.(IV). Fourth Ordinary Session of the AMCOST (AMCOST IV), 10 March 2010, Cairo, Egypt.

21 AU-STRC. Progress report to AMCOST V.). Fifth Ordinary Session of the AMCOST (AMCOST V), 12–15 December 2012, Brazzaville, Congo p. 2, WIPO (2011), Kongolo (2013) p. 127.

22 Kongolo (2013) p. 127, ARIPO Recent IP Developments in the Africa Region and Proposal for the Harmonization of ARIPO and OAPI. Council of Ministers 13th Session, Accra, Ghana, 1–2 December 2011. ARIPO Doc. No. ARIPO/AC/XIII/13 pp. 2–3.

23 For example see Baker (2012), Olivier (2012), Egbuonu (2012), Ncube (2012), Moyo (2012) and Karjiker (2012).

24 Kawooya and Latif (2012).

25 AU Ministerial Decisions. AU/MIN/ST/Dec.(V). Fifth Ordinary Session of the AMCOST (AMCOST V), 12–15 December 2012, Brazzaville, Congo.

Summit held in Addis Ababa in January 2013 confirmed AMCOST V's position and indicated that a stakeholders' meeting would be held in May 2013.[26] However, the programme of the 21st Ordinary Session of the AU Summit held in May 2013 did not include this meeting. A year later, in April 2014, the ARIPO and OAPI Secretariats issued a joint communiqué calling for this meeting to be convened, with their participation.[27]

ARIPO and OAPI made this call after a meeting they held on 10–11 April 2014, in Harare, at which they discussed their concerns about the creation of PAIPO. This meeting was strategically timed to precede the AMCOST meeting scheduled for 15–18 April 2014. In addition to calling for the stakeholders' meeting, ARIPO and OAPI recommended that the ministries responsible for IP be afforded a leading role in the process of establishing PAIPO. The process had been driven by the ministries of science and technology. The communiqué also suggested the possibility of an amalgamation of the two organisations under the oversight of a unit of the AU Commission, which would be created for that purpose. It emphasised that ARIPO and OAPI should continue to be the sole registrants of IP rights in Africa. Its parting shot was a request that "the Heads of State and Government should be sensitised on the role ARIPO and OAPI play in the management and coordination of IP in Africa." This comment is indicative of their sentiment that the work of these two organisations is being undervalued and not given its due weight in the considerations of the necessity and viability of PAIPO.

When AMCOST met at Brazzaville a few days after the release of this communiqué, it considered a revised draft of the PAIPO Statute and approved it. A related development at that meeting was the approval of the Science, Technology and Innovation Strategy for Africa 2024 (STISA 2024). The STISA 2024 followed the AU's Consolidated Plan of Action and is part of the AU's Agenda 2063, which is a 50-year developmental plan for the continent. It lists PAIPO as one of the bodies under the AU Commission and describes it as follows:

> PAIPO is in the process of being established to implement AU policy in the field of Intellectual property. It will ensure dissemination of patent information, provide technical and financial support to invention and innovation and promote protection and exploitation of research results.[28]

Both the 2013 Draft PAIPO Statute and STISA 2024 were then referred to the AU Assembly's 23rd Ordinary Session, held in June 2014. STISA 2024 was adopted[29] and the AU Assembly requested the AU Commission to submit the Draft PAIPO

26 AU Assembly Decision on the Creation of PAIPO. **DOC. EX.CL/766(XXII). Twentieth Ordinary Session, 27–28 January 2013. Addis Ababa, Ethiopia Assembly/AU/Dec.453(XX).

27 ARIPO and OAPI (2014).

28 AU STISA (2024) p. 36.

29 Assembly Decision on Strategy for Science Technology and Innovation in Africa 2024. Doc. EX.CL/839(XXV). Assembly of the Union Twenty-Third Ordinary Session 26–27 June 2014. Malabo, Equatorial Guinea. Assembly/AU/Dec.520(XXIII).

Statute to the Specialised Technical Committee (STC) on Justice and Legal Affairs for its consideration.[30] The assembly also re-affirmed the pivotal role of ARIPO and OAPI as constituent elements of PAIPO whose support of the endeavour is both necessary and desirable. It endorsed Tunisia as the host of the headquarters and secretariat of PAIPO.[31] Finally, it requested the AU to "prepare [a] road map for [the] implementation of PAIPO in coordination with the host country and to report progress in this regard to the [next] Summit." The next session of the assembly to which reference was being made was the 2015 summit that was held in Addis Ababa in January 2015. It appears that the report was not tabled at the 2015 assembly because the STC on Justice and Legal Affairs had not yet made recommendations on the draft statute. This seems to have been done in time for the 2016 AU Summit because the final PAIPO Statute was adopted at that summit.[32] The events and decisions outlined here are summarised in Table 6.1.

6.2.1 Entry Into Force

Article 5 of the PAIPO Statute provides that membership shall be "open to AU Member States. Each Member State shall enjoy equal rights in terms of participation and representation at PAIPO meetings." Article 23 sets out the process for signature and ratification or accession. The 2012 draft of the statute had provided that the statute would enter into force on the date of its endorsement by the Assembly of Heads of State and Government of the AU. As noted by Moyo, in that draft there was no provision for the signature and ratification of, or accession to, the statute by member states.[33] Whilst it was clear which states would be eligible for membership, it was not clear how this membership would be acquired. This approach was in stark contrast to the Lusaka and Bangui Agreements, which provide for these aspects in relation to ARIPO and OAPI, respectively. Similarly, the convention establishing the WIPO also provides for signature and ratification or accession to the convention. The lack of a provision on how membership could be taken up raised concerns. Therefore, the inclusion of Article 23 in the final statute is very welcome.

Article 24 provides that the statute will enter into force 30 days after the 15th ratification. In 2019 the AU last updated the list of AU member states which have signed the PAIPO Statute.[34] This would indicate that there have been no further signatures. The following states have signed the agreement (date of sig-

30 Assembly Decision on the Pan African Intellectual Property Organisation (PAIPO) Doc. EX.CL/839(XXV). Assembly of the Union Twenty-Third Ordinary Session, 26–27 June 2014. Malabo, Equatorial Guinea. Assembly/AU/Dec.522(XXIII).

31 AU (2014), WIPO (2015) p. 58.

32 Statute of the Pan-African Intellectual Property Organisation (PAIPO), adopted by the 26th Ordinary Session of the Assembly, held in Addis Ababa, Ethiopia, 31 January 2016 (PAIPO Statute), Assembly Decision on the Specialised Technical Committees Twenty-Sixth Ordinary Session, 30–31 January 2016. Addis Ababa, Ethiopia. Assembly/AU/Dec.589(XXVI) p. 1, para 2(x).

33 Moyo (2012).

34 AU (2019), (2022) p. 235.

Table 6.1 PAIPO Timeline: Known Key Events and Decisions

2006	*2007*	*2008*	*2010*	*2011*	*2012*	*2013*	*2014*	*2016*
	AU Assembly decision on PAIPO Assembly/ AU/Dec.138 (VIII)					AU Assembly Decision to create PAIPO Assembly/AU/ Dec.453(XX)	AU Assembly Referral to STC Assembly/ AU/Dec.522 (XXIII)	Assembly/ AU/Dec.589 (XXVI)
AMCOST extraordinary session PAIPO Concept Paper EXT/ AU/EXP/ ST/8(II)	AMCOST III PAIPO Progress Report AU/EXP/ ST/11(III)		AMCOST IV Ministerial Decision AU/ MIN/ST/Dec. (IV)		AMCOST V Ministerial Decision AU/MIN/ST/ Dec.(V)		AMCOST extraordinary session approves draft	Adoption of PAIPO Statute
		Preparation of draft, stakeholder consultations		Revision of draft, stakeholder consultation				

nature in brackets): Chad (1 July 2018), Comoros (29 January 2018), Ghana (4 July 2017), Guinea (13 December 2018), Sierra Leone (14 July 2016) and Tunisia (19 June 2019). None have ratified. Therefore, the statute has not yet come into force.

6.3 How PAIPO Will Function

It is necessary to outline in some detail how it is envisaged that PAIPO will function, in order to contextualise the issues that have been raised pertaining to its mandate and role. The outline that follows is based on the adopted statute. Cross-reference will be made to the 2013 draft and an earlier version published in November 2012 (AU/STRC/522), where appropriate, to show development of the statute. The drafts will be differentiated by their year of publication.

6.3.1 The Legal Nature of PAIPO

This section considers the legal nature of PAIPO as a specialised agency of the AU.[35] Specialised agencies are one of the institutional organs of the AU, which it has authority to establish through Article 5(2) of the Constitutive Act of the AU. A specialised agency is defined as

> an independent body established by Member States of the Union outside the managerial and budgetary rules and regulations as well as control of the AU or the Commission to carry out a specific or specialised but related function of the mandate of the AU.[36]

Specialised agencies have autonomy, legal personality, their own budget, managerial independence and separate governance structures, as well as staff and financial rules and regulations.[37] PAIPO will be required to raise its own funds through members' dues and it may accept donations.[38] In addition, the AU may grant it seed funding for a period of five years.[39] In contrast, it had been proposed in the 2013 draft that the AUC will fund it "in its first two phases or to the time that PAIPO is capable to generate resource to sustain itself."[40] PAIPO, like other specialised agencies, will interface with the AU through a department of the AU Commission or an organ of the AU.[41]

35 Article 2 PAIPO Statute and Article 2(2) of the 2013 Draft Statute.
36 AU (n.d.) p. 2.
37 AU (n.d.) p. 5, Article 6 PAIPO Statute.
38 Article 17(1)–(2) PAIPO Statute.
39 Article 17(3) PAIPO Statute.
40 Article 17(iii) of the 2013 Draft Statute.
41 AU (n.d.) p. 3.

The methodology of the creation of AU specialised agencies consists of the following three modes:[42]

a) an agency set up by AU member states, which is then approved by the AU Assembly prior to its operationalisation;
b) an agency set up by decision of the AU Assembly;
c) an already existing agency that is linked to the AU system post its creation by member states.

PAIPO falls into the second category. As stated, the AU Assembly passed decisions pertaining to the process of its creation and its establishment in 2007 and 2013, respectively. The specifics of operationalisation of the organisation were not spelt out in the 2013 decision and were later included in the PAIPO Statute.

6.3.2 Objectives, Principles and Functions

As stated previously, PAIPO is intended to be a specialised agency of the AU. Expectations are that its future work would contribute to an appropriately nuanced IP system that meets the continent's developmental goals.[43] The final statute does not have provisions setting out PAIPO's objectives and principles, in a manner akin to Articles 7 and 8 of the TRIPS Agreement, which is regrettable because these would have served as important interpretative and guiding tools. One of the draft statutes had enumerated objectives including giving policy direction to the continent on IP matters; promoting the harmonisation of IP systems; the provision of unstipulated common services to member states and/or RECs in relation to the administration and management of IP rights; serving as a platform for IP policy discussion and formulation; and promoting the use of the IP system "as a tool for economic, cultural, social and technological development of the continent."[44] It is unclear why the objectives were ultimately excluded from the final statute and why principles were never articulated, even in a draft.

Article 4 sets out 18 functions in paragraphs (a)–(r). These include the harmonisation of IP standards "that reflect the needs of the AU, its Member States and RECs; ARIPO and OAPI";[45] assisting member states, upon request, in their IP policy formulation;[46] strengthening regional organisations and similar organisations, as may be necessary;[47] and establishing or strengthening existing collective management organisations.[48] In addition to these functions, PAIPO was also

42 AU (n.d.) p. 3; Articles 5(2) and 9(1)(d) of the Constitutive Act of the AU.
43 OseiTutu (2021) p. 112.
44 Article 5 Draft PAIPO Statute (2013).
45 Article 4(a) PAIPO Statute.
46 Article 4(d) PAIPO Statute.
47 Article 4(f) PAIPO Statute.
48 Article 4(g) PAIPO Statute.

initially intended to serve as a registration office for industrial property rights.[49] However due to the concerns expressed by the OAPI and ARIPO Secretariats, this function, together with the related provisions for the Board of Appeal to hear appeals against registration decisions, was excised from the 2013 draft statute and the final statute. The Board of Appeals remains but its function is not related to registration appeals.

It is appropriate that the final PAIPO Statute does not include an IP standard or norm-setting function, which had been included in the drafts. This inclusion had raised several questions: Which matters would these standards pertain to, since IP standards have been comprehensively set by several existing international and sub-regional agreements such as TRIPS, the Bangui Agreement and the various ARIPO Protocols? What would be the exact nature of the instruments which would contain these standards? Would they have force of law? Would PAIPO have legislative competence, and if so, which of its organs would exercise such competence? What form would they take? Would PAIPO craft agreements, protocols and regulations? Since the norm-setting function has been excluded from the final statute, these questions have fallen away.

As there are already various national and sub-regional IP laws in force, PAIPO has been set the ambitious function of harmonising these. The various modes of harmonisation of IP laws and standards that PAIPO would have to consider have been canvassed in chapter five.

6.3.3 Organs of PAIPO

Article 9 of the PAIPO Statute lists these four organs: Conference of State Parties, Council of Ministers, the Secretariat and the Board of Appeal. The structure of the organisation as set out by Article 7 of the 2013 draft consisted of a Council of Ministers and its bureau; an Experts Committee and its bureau; and the Secretariat or office.[50] As stated, the 2012 version of the draft statute also included a Board of Appeal which had functions related to IPR registration decisions. The final structure is significantly different from what was envisaged in the drafts. These differences have been mentioned to show the evolution of the PAIPO Statute. The functions of the PAIPO organs provided for in the final statute is summarised in the next section.

The Conference of State Parties

Article 10 of the PAIPO Statute provides that the Conference of State Parties is the supreme policy-making organ. It is to meet every three years[51] and will have

49 Article 6(ii) Draft PAIPO Statute (2012).
50 Article 7 Draft PAIPO Statute (2013).
51 Article 10(5) PAIPO Statute.

a bureau composed of a president, three vice-presidents and a rapporteur.[52] It will formulate and adopt procedural and financial rules. Its functions are to

(a) provide strategic leadership and ensure oversight for the implementation of the PAIPO Statute . . .;
(b) consider and adopt, as appropriate, recommendations of the Council of Ministers;
(c) Consider the reports and activities of the Bureau and take appropriate action in regard thereto; and
(d) Perform any other function consistent with PAIPO's Statute or the Rules of Procedure of the Conference of State Parties.

The Council of Ministers

Article 11(1) provides that the Council of Ministers is the "highest decision-making Organ and shall constitute the General Assembly of PAIPO." As indicated, it comprises ministers in charge of intellectual property. Further, it will have a committee of experts made up of senior officials representing these ministries[53] and may create any other appropriate working groups or subsidiary bodies.[54] The Council of Ministers will also have a bureau of five members, with a president, three vice-presidents and a rapporteur elected from the five AU geographical regions, plus one observer member, namely the AUC Commissioner, who is responsible for intellectual property.[55]

Article 11(6) lists nine functions of this organ. Among these are giving "policy direction to the PAIPO and address[ing] policy matters relating to the Organisation"; "decid[ing] and prioritis[ing] the activities of PAIPO relating to intellectual property"; financial aspects such as setting member states' contributions and approving budgets; electing the members of its bureau; electing the director general; and developing rules and guidelines for the Secretariat and the Board of Appeal.

The Council of Ministers will have meetings every two years[56] and its bureau will meet once a year in ordinary session, with extraordinary sessions being held as necessary.[57]

The Director General and Secretariat

The Director General's term will be for three years and will only be renewable once.[58] The Council of Ministers' election of the Director General will be "based on geographical rotation."[59] The Council of Ministers make the staff rules and regula-

52 Article 10(4) PAIPO Statute.
53 Article 11(4) PAIPO Statute.
54 Article 11(5) PAIPO Statute.
55 Article 11(6)(f).
56 Article 11(3) PAIPO Statute.
57 Article 11(7) PAIPO Statute.
58 Article 12(1) PAIPO Statute.
59 Article 12(1) PAIPO Statute.

tions which contain the powers, duties and conditions of service for this role.[60] The main function of the Director General is to serve as "Head of the Secretariat,"[61] which includes the appointment of its staff[62] and requires independence from external parties.[63]

The Secretariat is assigned the following duties by Article 12(2):

(a) implementation of PAIPO decisions;
(b) drafting policies and strategies for adoption by the Council of Ministers;
(c) intellectual property capacity building for Member States;
(d) taking "necessary actions to ensure the protection of intellectual property rights including indigenous knowledge systems, genetic resources and associated traditional knowledge, geographical indications, expressions of folklore among others";
(e) advocacy and community awareness;
(f) drafting policies and strategies on international cooperation for adoption by the Council of Ministers;
(g) preparing strategic plans, work programmes, budgets, financial statements and annual reports;
(h) day-to-day management of the organisation; and
(i) any other duties, as assigned by the Council of Ministers.

The Board of Appeal

Article 14 is the shortest provision on organs and has only two paragraphs. The first paragraph provides that the Council of Ministers will establish a Board of Appeal. The second paragraph provides that the board will hear disputes and litigation arising from the activities of PAIPO. It is difficult to conceive what litigation and disputes may arise from PAIPO fulfilling its functions and seems as if the board is a relic from when a registration function was envisaged for PAIPO. There are no details as to the composition of the board and the qualification or other eligibility requirements for its members. Neither is there any mention of the length of their term of office nor of applicable procedural rules. This lack of detail means it is a shell of an organ.

The following section considers how PAIPO is intended to interface with the existing sub-regional IP organisations.

6.3.4 Organisational Issues (PAIPO, OAPI and ARIPO)

It has been noted that ARIPO and OAPI were not consulted during the early stages of the formulation of the PAIPO proposal so they were opposed to the concept.[64] It would appear that they were not invited to certain crucial consultative meetings.

60 Article 12(2) PAIPO Statute.
61 Article 12(3) PAIPO Statute.
62 Article 12(4) PAIPO Statute.
63 Article 12(5) PAIPO Statute.
64 Blakeney and Mengistie (2011) p. 251.

However, with the passage of time and a change of leadership at ARIPO, the two organisations have found ways of making their views known to the AU, primarily through private diplomatic channels but also publicly, through the joint communiqué they issued in April 2014.

The key concerns of the two sub-regional IP organisations pertain to the overlapping of their mandates with PAIPO: duplication of the industrial property registration and other functions and the nature of the relationship between themselves and the continental organisation. Each of these, in turn, is briefly addressed, with the caveat that they are difficult to separate because they are interconnected and cascade into each other. The general question of mandate solidifies into concerns about registration of industrial property and policy formulation issues which ultimately goes to the crux of the relationship between the three organisations.

Overlapping Mandates

According to the 2013 Draft PAIPO Statute, PAIPO was intended to give continental IP policy, law and administrative direction. To all intents and purposes, it would seek to do what the sub-regional organisations currently do but on the larger, continental platform, with what the concept paper dubbed "continental inclusiveness." The obvious issue that such an ambition immediately raises is that of "turf" – what, if any, role would remain for the sub-regional IP organisations after the establishment of PAIPO? The resolution of this issue indisputably involves careful consultation and negotiation.

Another mandate in which PAIPO would be seeking to involve itself is the provision of a platform or forum where African states can jointly arrive at common positions they wish to advance at international IP law-making fora. African states have already successfully organised themselves into influential groups through which they jointly advance their views. The African Group has established itself as one of the most active groups at both the WTO[65] and WIPO.[66] Its contributions towards the adoption of the WIPO Development Agenda (WIPO DA 2007) have been outlined in chapter one. As there is already a working mechanism for this aspect of PAIPO's intended mandate, it is important to have clarity on how PAIPO would complement or substitute that mechanism. An even more fundamental question was whether there is any need for a formal organisational platform in the first place. However, that enquiry has been rendered academic by events, and as the PAIPO Statute has been adopted, the more relevant question would be the first issue raised – that of alignment with the African Group. The 2012 Draft PAIPO Statute completely overlooked the pro-development position of the African Group and failed to reference the WIPO DA, which it had been instrumental in securing.

65 May (2007) p. 74.
66 Shabalala (2007) p. 32.

The 2013 draft expressly referenced the WIPO DA in its preamble. Among its mandates, the draft stated:

> Realising the need to strengthen the capacity of national Intellectual Property institutions and boosting manpower development in Intellectual Property management; affirming the 45 recommendations of the Development Agenda under world Intellectual Property rights programmes.

However, the lingering concern is whether this was lip service or whether it embodied a real commitment to the imperatives of the WIPO DA Agenda. This, and other policy matters, are canvassed at section 6.4. Prior to that discussion, it is important to address issues of functional overlap between ARIPO, OAPI and PAIPO.

As outlined in chapter four, OAPI and ARIPO register industrial property rights. In OAPI's case, its members all subscribe to one body of IP law, contained in the Bangui Agreement and its annexes. When an application is made for registration, the granted rights extend to all the member states' territories. ARIPO's protocols are not automatically binding on its member states and domestication is required to give them force of law in member states. Further, the ARIPO industrial property registration system does not necessarily result in the grant of rights in every member state's territory. An applicant is required to designate countries in which protection is sought. Thereafter, each designated country is afforded an opportunity to indicate whether or not it wishes to grant the said industrial property rights in its territory. Therefore, once operationalised, PAIPO would be seeking to sit atop two asymmetrical sub-regional organisations.

Whilst there have been suggestions for the merger of the two sub-regional organisations, such a merger would be complicated by the stated differences between them and the more fundamental common law and civil law distinction between them. However, as discussed in chapter four, they are already successfully co-operating to a significant extent. ARIPO and OAPI have stressed their view that they ought to remain the sole regional registrants of industrial property rights. Several commentators agree that PAIPO would be ill suited to the industrial property registration function.[67] The AU has conceded this point through the revision of the Draft PAIPO Statute, as previously explained, and the registration function was not included in the 2013 draft and in the final statute.

The remaining functions of PAIPO pertain to activities that currently fall within the purview of ARIPO and OAPI. For instance, in relation to IP policy formulation, Article 6 of the 2012 Draft PAIPO Statute listed the following functions:

> (iv) Assist its Member States upon request in formulating policies and addressing current and emerging Intellectual Property issues in conformity with the Objectives of the Organisation;

67 Ncube and Laltaika (2013) p. 117, Kongolo (2013) p. 130, Baker (2012).

(x) To develop updated policy guidelines using best practices and training modules to support Member States to achieve world-class IP systems;

The sub-regional IP organisations also render IP policy formulation technical assistance to their member states, although their performance has been faulted. In this regard, it has been pointed out that their policy formulation assistance is hampered because

> they tend to operate outside the broad policy framework on research, technology development and innovation that should inform intellectual property policy formulation . . . [and] the mandates of these organisations are mostly limited to matters of patent grants and examination or registration and do not include issues relating to the exercise of patent rights.[68]

Consequently, it has been suggested that African RECs create an Advisory Council on Trade-Related Innovation Policies (ACTRIPS) that would be better suited to lead on policy matters because it would not be constrained by the stated limitations that apply to ARIPO and OAPI.[69] The original ACTRIPS proposal was that countries develop their own domestic ACTRIPS which would then engage in dialogue at regional level through REC-hosted ACTRIPS.[70] Against this backdrop, the PAIPO proposal can be viewed as a continental, rather than regional, ACTRIPS. Indeed, it has been persuasively suggested that a better approach to the conceptualisation of PAIPO would be to limit it to policy oversight and capacity building at its initial stages and to thereafter consider expanding its functions.[71] It would still be possible to build in the national and regional ACTRIPS concept into the continental PAIPO model. As stated earlier, the AU already organises its members into five geographical regions. These regions, the regional IP organisations or RECs could be the sponsor of regional ACTRIPS.

In view of its important continental policy direction function, it is necessary to interrogate the indicators of PAIPO's policy approach, which is done in section 6.4, after the discussion of the relationship between PAIPO, ARIPO and OAPI.

Relationship Between PAIPO, ARIPO and OAPI

The relationship between PAIPO and the two sub-regional IP organisations is also a point of concern. The preambles of both the 2012 and June 2013 versions of the Draft PAIPO Statute stated that the AU Heads of State and Government both appreciate and respect the autonomy of ARIPO and OAPI and are "desirous of

68 Musungu, Villanueva and Blasetti (2004) pp. 55–56.
69 Musungu, Villanueva and Blasetti (2004) pp. 53–54. Also see Reichman (2003) pp. 5–8, Musungu and Dutfield (2003) p. 22.
70 Reichman (2003) p. 5.
71 Blakeney and Mengistie (2011) p. 252.

supplementing and complementing the role played" by them. However, the initial overlooking of the regional organisations in the early consultative stages sent out the unfortunate message that the AU undervalued them and did not fully appreciate their contribution. This impression was compounded by the provision for duplication of the registration function by PAIPO, which as discussed previously, has now been removed. However, ARIPO and OAPI sought to ensure that such an oversight would not be repeated by their call in their joint communiqué for the sensitisation of AU heads of state to their significance, as quoted herein.

Consequently, the final statute's preamble rectifies this by stating:

> APPRECIATING the crucial role played by national intellectual property offices of Member States and taking note of the autonomy of ARIPO and OAPI, in recognising the need to modernise and harmonise intellectual property legislation throughout Africa and to render more efficient the administration of intellectual property rights . . .
>
> RECOGNISING ARIPO and OAPI as building blocks for the creation of a PanAfrican Intellectual Property Organisation as well as welcoming their support in the implementation of the Heads of State and Government decisions on PAIPO Assembly/AU/Dec. 522(XXIII)

Another sore point is the exclusion of ministers of IP in the PAIPO formulation process. As it is a creature of AMCOST, its design has been the province of ministers of science and technology. These ministries, whilst being *au fait* with innovation, science and technology, may miss certain IP nuances. Hence the call by ARIPO and OAPI, in their communiqué, for the inclusion of IP ministries in PAIPO deliberations. It goes without saying that these are the ministries with which the two organisations are accustomed to working and that their involvement, alongside the ministries of science, technology and innovation, would have eased the consultative process. This is necessary because "the policy impacts of IP go far beyond the realm of science and technology."[72] Ironically, whilst they were not included in the formulation process, the PAIPO Statute places the implementation of PAIPO under ministries of IP who constitute the Council of Ministers, the organisation's highest decision-making organ.

Both the 2012 and 2013 versions of the Draft PAIPO Statute provide some indicators of how the AU conceives of the relationship between PAIPO and the regional organisations going forward in the following provision:

> The Organisation shall establish and maintain close and continuous working relationships with ARIPO, OAPI, World Intellectual Property Organisation (WIPO) the International Confederation of Authors and Composers Societies (CISAC) and World Trade Organisation (WTO).[73]

72 de Beer (2013) p. 895.

73 Article 15 Draft PAIPO Statute (June 2013); Article 16 Draft PAIPO Statute (2012).

This language was altered in the final statute's Article 16 to exclude naming any institutions and it now reads:

> The PAIPO shall establish and maintain working relationships with any intergovernmental, international, regional or national institutions that may assist PAIPO to achieve its objectives.

In practice such relationships would have to be brokered through co-operation agreements. It is currently unclear as to what such agreements with ARIPO and OAPI would pertain. However, like Article 6(vi) of the June 2013 draft statute, Article 4(f) of the final PAIPO statute lists the strengthening of existing regional organisations as one of PAIPO's functions. It is unclear what form such strengthening may take. However, as shown, it is likely to relate to policy matters.

6.4 Policy Imperatives: The PAIPO Statute, Development and Human Rights

This section considers the IP policy stance as it relates to development and human rights, as articulated in the PAIPO statute's preamble. This is an important aspect to consider because of PAIPO's focus on policy matters and because "ideally, a Pan-African IP policy will account for human rights and promote human development on the African continent."[74] The extensive analysis of the 2012 Draft PAIPO Statute referred to earlier flagged the main concern that its wording reflected little regard for the development imperatives of African states and the hard-won victory of the WIPO DA.[75] For example, I have argued elsewhere that references to effective IP systems juxtaposed with the intent to combat piracy and counterfeiting give the impression of a right-holder-focused position that is concerning to those who seek a more equitable position that takes due consideration of user and societal interests.[76]

Similarly, several commentators pointed out that the 2012 Draft PAIPO Statute's failure to expressly reference the WIPO DA and the issues that confront Africa was a major shortcoming.[77] Fortunately, the 2013 draft included some of these aspects and the final PAIPO Statute's preamble now states the following:

> REALISING the need to strengthen the capacity of national intellectual property institutions and boosting manpower development in intellectual property management as well as affirming the the 45 recommendations of the WIPO DA adopted in 2007 . . .

74 Osei-Tutu (2021) p. 112.

75 For example, see Ncube and Laltaika (2013), Kawooya and Latif (2012), Baker (2012), Olivier (2012), Egbuonu (2012), Ncube (2012), Moyo (2012), Karjiker (2012).

76 Ncube and Laltaika (2013).

77 Ncube and Laltaika (2013) p. 116, de Beer (2013) p. 896, Kawooya and Latif (2012).

> RECOGNISING international human rights law and international agreements on sustainable development and the protection of indigenous knowledge, that provides ligament right of indigenous and local communities . . .
> RECALLING the United Nations Resolution A/RES/70/1 entitled: Transforming our world: The 2030 Agenda for Sustainable Development adopted on 25 September and the African Union Agenda 2063.

However, as far as IP and public health are concerned, the 2012 and 2013 draft statutes and the final statute neglect to reference the TRIPS flexibilities, the WTO Doha Declaration on the TRIPS Agreement and Public Health and other important decisions, such as the Global Strategy and Plan of Action on Public Health, Innovation and IP. It is accepted that the PAIPO statute cannot be expected to go beyond a general contextualisation of public interest and policy considerations.[78] However, explicit reference to some of these instruments would signal the commitment of the AU to build on existing work in this area. There is solace in the fact that PAIPO ought to be consolidating REC efforts on IP and public health and in this way, some of these considerations will be incorporated. As shown in chapters two and three, RECs have made significant progress on this front which hopefully will be taken on board by PAIPO. In his close human rights analysis of the statute, Oke argues that these paragraphs in the preamble are paying lip service to human rights because they are not backed up by any further provisions, specifically in Article 4, which itemises the functions of PAIPO, which then means the statute is lacking the necessary balance.[79] It is worth noting that the final statute was finalised at about the same time that the Dakar Declaration on IP for Africa was written; however, the perspectives taken in the declaration do not seem to be fully articulated in the PAIPO statute. Granted, the declaration was not adopted by the assembly but, being authored by the ministers responsible for IP on the continent, its aspirations and expectations are important considerations that ought to be reflected in continental IP instruments.

6.5 Conclusion

Several arguments were made for and against the establishment of PAIPO.[80] Three of each are recounted here. First, one of the main arguments made in favour of the creation of the organisation pertains to continental geographic, economic and linguistic inclusivity, which would be achieved by the creation of an AU organ that potentially would draw in all AU member states.[81] Secondly, the desirability of a continental platform for the consolidation of AU member states' views to formulate continental positions on matters of significance has been forwarded as another supportive argu-

78 de Beer (2013) p. 896.
79 Oke (2021) p. 162.
80 Mupangavanhu (2015).
81 Ncube and Laltaika (2013) p. 115.

ment. This would be to build on African states' effective organisation to formulate shared positions at various international fora, such as WTO, WIPO and WHO.

Thirdly, it is argued that having a specialised agency of the AU devoted to IP would elevate IP matters to be a focal point of regional integration efforts.[82] This would be beneficial because it might overcome the challenges faced by ARIPO and OAPI when it comes to crafting policy frameworks that are informed by broader research, technology, innovation and regional economic development concerns. As shown in chapter two, to date, some RECs have concerned themselves with IP. Significant progress has been made in relation to IP in the EAC, ECOWAS and COMESA, which have all formulated IP policies. Further, as shown in chapter three, IP was one of the key concerns of the TFTA between COMESA, EAC and SADC, as evidenced by the annex on IP rights which would have formed part of the TFTA Agreement, after successful negotiation. This focus on IP has been carried through to the AfCFTA, which was intended to progress initially through the merger of the TFTA and ECOWAS.[83] PAIPO would then be well placed to rationalise existing REC initiatives and to stimulate similar activities in the other RECs.

On the other hand, credible concerns have been raised about procedural, institutional and substantive issues. It has been noted that there is a need to resolve outstanding organisational and relational matters between PAIPO and the existing sub-regional IP organisations. The actual mechanics of the operationalisation of PAIPO are not yet clear, although they are reportedly detailed in a 25-year business plan, which is not publicly available. A phased and incremental approach would be prudent.[84] In addition, the creation of PAIPO will require significant financial outlay which may be beyond the AU and its member states' current economic realities. It would also be vital to ensure that there is no wastage of resources through the unnecessary duplication of functions that are already fulfilled by existing entities. Finally, the nature and status of PAIPO standard-setting instruments is not yet clear, nor is its efficacy and value as a policy formulation platform indisputable due to its inadequate attention to developmental and human rights aspects. However, since the AU has already established PAIPO, the real challenge is the efficient operationalisation of the organisation. It is significant that seven years after the adoption of the statute, there are still very few signatures and no ratifications, and consequently the initiative is stalled.

Reference List

ARIPO

ARIPO & OAPI, 2014. Communiqué Adopted by the Joint Meeting of the Chairmen of ARIPO AND OAPI, held at the Headquarters of ARIPO on 10–11 April 2014, Harare, Republic of Zimbabwe.

82 Mupangavanhu (2015) p. 4.
83 Ngwenya (2015).
84 Mupangavanhu (2015) p. 24, Blakeney and Mengistie (2011) p. 252.

Lusaka Agreement on the Creation of the African Regional Intellectual Property Organisation as Amended, 2004.

Recent IP Developments in the Africa Region and Proposal for the Harmonization of ARIPO and OAPI. Council of Ministers 13th Session, Accra, Ghana, 1–2 December 2011. ARIPO Doc. No. ARIPO/AC/XIII/13.

Swakopmund Protocol on the Protection of Traditional Knowledge and Expressions of Folklore within the Framework of the ARIPO, adopted by the Diplomatic Conference of ARIPO at Swakopmund, Namibia on 9 August 2010.

AU

Assembly Decision on the Creation of PAIPO. DOC. EX.CL/766(XXII). Assembly/AU/Dec.453(XX). Twentieth Ordinary Session, 27–28 January 2013. Addis Ababa, Ethiopia.

Assembly Decision on the Establishment of PAIPO. Assembly of the African Union Eighth Ordinary Session, 29–30 January 2007. Addis Ababa, Ethiopia. Assembly/AU/Dec.138 (VIII).

Assembly Decision on PAIPO Doc. EX.CL/839(XXV). Assembly/AU/Dec.522(XXIII). Assembly of the Union Twenty-Third Ordinary Session, 26–27 June 2014. Malabo, Equatorial Guinea.

Assembly Decision on the Specialised Technical Committees. Twenty-Sixth Ordinary Session, 30–31 January 2016. Addis Ababa, Ethiopia. Assembly/AU/Dec.589(XXVI).

Assembly Decision on Strategy for Science Technology and Innovation in Africa 2024. Doc. EX.CL/839(XXV). Assembly/AU/Dec.520(XXIII). Assembly of the Union Twenty-Third Ordinary Session, 26–27 June 2014. Malabo, Equatorial Guinea.

AU HRS&T. Establishing a Pan-African Intellectual Property Organisation (PAIPO), AU, 2002. Declaration on the Implementation of NEPAD (Assembly/AU/Decl. 1 (I)).

AU-STRC Progress Report to AMCOST V. Fifth Ordinary Session of the AMCOST (AMCOST V), 12–15 December 2012, Brazzaville, Congo.

A Concept Paper. Extraordinary Conference of the AMCOST, 20–24 November 2006 Cairo, Egypt. EXT/AU/EXP/ST/8(II). Report of the Meeting of Experts Extraordinary Conference of the AMCOST 20–24 November 2006 Cairo, Egypt. EXT/AU/EXP/ST/Rpt.(II).

Constitutive Act of the African Union, 2000.

Draft Statute of the Pan-African Intellectual Property Organisation (PAIPO), As of 4 June 2013.

Final Draft Statute of the Pan-African Intellectual Property Organisation (PAIPO), 2012 Ref No: AU/STRC/522.

Ministerial Decisions. AU/MIN/ST/Dec.(IV). Fourth Ordinary Session of the AMCOST (AMCOST IV), 10 March 2010, Cairo, Egypt.

Ministerial Decisions. AU/MIN/ST/Dec.(V). Fifth Ordinary Session of the AMCOST (AMCOST V), 12–15 December 2012, Brazzaville, Congo.

Progress Report on Research Policy Framework, Capacity Building for the African Policymakers and the Formation of the PAIPO. AMCOST III Third Ordinary Session 12–16 November 2007, Mombasa, Republic of Kenya. AU/EXP/ST/11(III).

Science, Technology and Innovation Strategy for Africa 2024 (STISA 2024). Available at https://au.int/sites/default/files/newsevents/workingdocuments/33178-wd-stisa-english_-_final.pdf [accessed 16 April 2023].

Statute of the Pan-African Intellectual Property Organisation (PAIPO), adopted by the 26th Ordinary Session of the Assembly, held in Addis Ababa, Ethiopia, 31 January 2016. Available at https://au.int/sites/default/files/treaties/32549-treaty-0053_-_paipo_e.pdf [accessed 16 January 2023].

WIPO

Development Agenda, 2007. WIPO General Assembly Thirty-Fourth (18th Ordinary) Session Geneva, 24 September to 3 October 2007.

WIPO, 2009a. Technical Assistance Database: Experts Group Meeting on PAIPO, Addis Ababa, Ethiopia, 18 May 2009. Available at www.wipo.int/tad/en/activitydetails.jsp?id=787 [accessed 9 January 2023].

WIPO, 2009b. Support to NEPAD Period of Report: July 2008 to June 2009.

WIPO, 2011. Technical Assistance Database: PAIPO Stakeholders Workshop, Dakar, Senegal, 7–8 September 2011. Available at www.wipo.int/tad/en/activitydetails.jsp?id=2008 [accessed 9 January 2023].

WIPO, 2015. Assemblies of the Member States of WIPO Fifty-Fourth Series of Meetings, Geneva, 22–30 September 2014. General Report. A/54/13.

WTO

Doha WTO Ministerial Declaration (adopted 14 November 2001) Doc. WT/MIN(01)/DEC/1 20 November 2001.

Secondary Sources

Adewopo, A., 2003. Trademark Systems in Africa: A Proposal for the Harmonization of the ARIPO and the OAPI Agreements on Marks. *The Journal of World Intellectual Property*, 6, 473–484.

AU, 2019. *List of Countries Which Have Signed, Ratified/Acceded to the Statute of the Pan African Intellectual Property Organisation (PAIPO)*, 28 June 2019. Available at https://au.int/sites/default/files/treaties/32549-sl-STATUTE%20OF%20THE%20PAN%20AFRICAN%20INTELLECTUAL%20PROPERTY%20ORGANISATION%20%28PAIPO%29%20%281%29.pdf [accessed 28 September 2022].

AU, n.d., *Concept Note on Specialized Institutions and Agencies of the African Union*. Available at https://au.int/sites/default/files/newsevents/conceptnotes/14601-cn-olc_conecpt_note_specialized_agencies_and_institutions.pdf [accessed 16 January 2023].

AU Commission (AU), New Zealand Ministry of Foreign Affairs and Trade/Manatu Aorere, 2022. *AU Handbook 2022: A Guide for Those Working with and Within the African Union* (9th ed.), first published 2014. Addis Ababa: AUC and Wellington: Ministry of Foreign Affairs and Trade/Manatu Aorere. Available at https://au.int/sites/default/files/documents/31829-doc-2022_AU_Hanbook_ENGLISH.pdf [accessed 16 January 2023].

Baker, B., 2012. *Proposed Pan-African IP Organisation a Terrible Idea*, 28 September 2012. Available at http://infojustice.org/archives/27392?doing_wp_cron=1349607009.5964870452880859375000 [accessed 6 February 2023].

Blakeney, M. and Mengistie, G., 2011. Intellectual Property and Economic Development in Sub-Saharan Africa. *Journal of World Intellectual Property*, 14(3/4), 238–264.

Dean, O.H., 1994a. A Unified Intellectual Property Law System for Southern Africa. Part 1: International Arrangements and European Conventions. *Juta's Business Law*, 2(3), 111–114.

Dean, O.H., 1994b. A Unified Intellectual Property Law System for Southern Africa. Part 2: Multinational Registrations in Africa. *Juta's Business Law*, 2(4), 165–169.

de Beer, J., 2013. Applying Best Practice Principles to International Intellectual Property Lawmaking. *International Review of Intellectual Property and Competition Law*, 44, 884–901.

Dountino, J., 2013. *Some Key Events in the Early Development of the Proposal for a PAIPO* [online]. Available at www.keionline.org/paipo [accessed 31 January 2023].
Egbuonu, K., 2012. *Pan-Africa Intellectual Property Organisation (PAIPO)*, 8 October 2012. Available at http://afro-ip.blogspot.com/2012/10/a-review-of-african-official-ip_8.html [accessed 6 February 2023].
Karjiker, S., 2012. Sizing Up the "Ill-Conceived" PAIPO Draft Statute 6 November 2012. *IP Watch Insider Views*.
Kawooya, D. and Latif, A.A., 2012. *A New Course for the Pan African Intellectual Property Organisation Is Urgently Needed*, 18 October 2012.
Kongolo, T., 2000. The African IP Organisations: The Necessity of Adopting One Uniform System for All Africa. *The Journal of World Intellectual Property*, 3(2), 265–288.
Kongolo, T., 2013. *African Contributions in Shaping the Worldwide IP System*. Surrey and Burlington: Ashgate Publishing.
May, C., 2007. *The World Intellectual Property Organisation: Resurgence and the Development Agenda*. Oxford: Routledge.
Moyo, C., 2012. *Furthering Debate on PAIPO*, 31 October 2012. Available at http://afro-ip.blogspot.com/2012/10/moyo-furthers-debate-on-paipo_31.html [accessed 6 February 2023].
Mupangavanhu, Y., 2013. The Regional Integration of African Trade Mark Laws: Challenges and Possibilities. Thesis (Ph.D.). University of the Western Cape.
Mupangavanhu, Y., 2014. The Integration of Trade Mark Laws in the European Union: Lessons for Africa? *South African IP Law Journal*, 2, 109–130.
Mupangavanhu, Y., 2015. African Union Rising to the Need for Continental IP Protection? The Establishment of the Pan-African Intellectual Property Organisation. *Journal of African Law*, 59, 1–24.
Musungu, S.F. and Dutfield, G., 2003. *Multilateral Agreements and a TRIPS-Plus World: The World Intellectual Property Organisation (WIPO)*. QUNO, Geneva/QIAP, Ottawa.
Musungu, S.F., Villanueva, S. and Blasetti, R., 2004. *Utilizing TRIPS Flexibilities for Public Health Protection Through South-South Regional Frameworks*. Geneva: South Centre.
NACI, 2007. *Corporate Business Plan 2007/8*. Pretoria: NACI.
Ncube, C.B., 2012. *Piping Up on PAIPO*, 16 October 2012. Available at http://afro-ip.blogspot.com/2012/10/piping-up-on-paipo.html [accessed 6 February 2023].
Ncube, C.B. and Laltaika, E., 2013. A New Intellectual Property Organisation for Africa? *Journal of Intellectual Property Law and Practice*, 8(2), 114–117.
Oke, E.K., 2021. The Statute of the Pan-African Intellectual Property Organisation: A Human Rights Perspective. In Amao, O., Olivier, M. and Magliveras, K.D. (eds.) *The Emergent African Union Law Conceptualisation, Delimitation, and Application*. Oxford: Oxford University Press.
Oldham, G., Adeoti, J. and Thomas, S.M., 2006. *Designing a Model for the African Science and Innovation Facility to Implement the Science and Technology Consolidated Plan of Action*. Pretoria: NEPAD Office of Science and Technology.
Olivier, D., 2012. *South-South Agenda Timely as PAIPO Receives Criticism*, 8 October 2012. Available at http://afro-ip.blogspot.com/2012/10/south-south-agenda-timely-as-paipo.html [accessed 6 February 2023].
Osei-Tutu, J.J., 2021. African Union Continental Free Trade Area: Opportunities for New Regional Discourse? In Ragavan, S. and Vanni, A. (eds.) *A Intellectual Property Law and Access to Medicines: TRIPS Agreement, Health and Pharmaceuticals*. Abingdon: Routledge, 111–132.
Reichman, J., 2003. Managing the Challenges of a Globalized Intellectual Property Regime. *The Second Bellagio Series of Dialogues* 18–21 September 2003 Bellagio. Available at

www.iprsonline.org/unctadictsd/bellagio/docs/Reichmann_Bellagio2.pdf [accessed 8 January 2023].

Shabalala, D., 2007. *Citizen's Guide to WIPO*. Geneva: Center for International Environmental Law.

Sibanda, M., 2009. *IP Situation in Africa: A Profile*. Techno Africa Policy Monitor (4), AU-STRC.

van Gardingen, P.R. and Karp, A., 2006a. *International Experience on Regional Programmes for Science and Technology: Lessons for Africa's Science and Technology Consolidated Plan of Action*. Edinburgh: The University of Edinburgh.

van Gardingen, P.R. and Karp, A., 2006b. *International Overview of Arrangements for National Support of R&D. Options for African Nations*. Edinburgh: The University of Edinburgh.

van Gardingen, P.R. and Karp, A., 2006c. *International Survey of Options to Fund Regional Science and Technology in Africa*. Edinburgh: The University of Edinburgh.

7 Intellectual Property in the African Continental Free Trade Area

7.1 Introduction

The historical development of the AfCFTA is embedded in the AU's predecessor, the OAU, and its aspirations articulated in the Lagos Plan of Action for the Economic Development of Africa, 1980–2000 (Lagos Plan of Action), with its accompanying Final Act of Lagos, the Treaty Establishing the African Economic Community (Abuja Treaty, 1991) and other continental integration efforts. Progress on some of these early efforts was sub-optimal due to several significant factors such as the lack of a monitoring and evaluation process for the Lagos Plan of Action.[1] The Abuja Treaty has the ultimate goal of creating an African Economic Community through a phased process including six identified milestones.[2] Another notable integration initiative is the AU's Minimum Integration Programme.[3] Further, agenda efforts to establish the AfCFTA were re-energised in January 2011 when the AU Summit adopted a decision[4] which endorsed the Sixth Ordinary Session of the AU Ministers of Trade's recommendation to expediate the process.[5] Thereafter, in 2012, the assembly passed a decision on the *Framework, Road Map and Architecture for Fast Tracking the AfCFTA and the action plan for Boosting Intra-African Trade*, which is referenced in the preamble of the AfCFTA Agreement.

When Agenda 2063 was adopted, in 2013, its aspirations cumulatively aspired to an integrated continent,[6] and unsurprisingly, the AfCFTA is one of its flagship projects.[7] This gave impetus to efforts to create the AfCFTA, as did STISA 2024. As noted in chapter one, the agreement establishing the AfCFTA (AfCFTA Agreement) was concluded in 2018 following the launch of negotiations in 2015. The

1 United Nations (UN). Economic and Social Council; ECA (1991–04), UN. Economic and Social Council; ECA (1991–03) p. 3.
2 Article 6 Abuja Treaty.
3 AU (2009).
4 Assembly/AU/Dec.394(XVIII) Decision on Boosting Intra-African Trade and Fast Tracking the Continental Free Trade Area Doc. EX.CL/700(XX).
5 ECA and AU (2012) p. 5.
6 AU (2019) p. 5.
7 AU (2019) p. 17.

DOI: 10.4324/9781003310198-7

agreement was adopted on 21 March 2018 and signed by 44 AU member states at the Extraordinary AU Summit, held in Kigali, Rwanda, from 17 to 21 March 2018. Since then, ten more states have signed, and by March 2023, 54 member states had signed, 46 of which had also ratified the agreement.[8] This makes the AfCFTA the world's largest by number of countries participating.[9]

Article 23 of the agreement provides for its entry into force 30 days after the lodgement of the 22nd ratification. This was achieved in April 2019, and on 30 May 2019 the agreement duly came into force.[10] It was formally launched at Niamey, Niger, in July 2019 at the 12th Extraordinary Session of the Assembly on the AfCFTA.[11] The declared date of the start of trading was 1 January 2021,[12] and trade commenced, facilitated by the Guided Trade Initiative which was launched on 7 October 2022.[13] This initiative pairs suppliers and buyers in AfCFTA member states for a specified range of goods, including tea and coffee. The first Certificate of Origin was issued on 30 September 2022 to a women-led Rwandese enterprise, Igire Coffee, and the shipment was flown to Accra.[14]

This chapter proceeds as follows: It sets the context by outlining the general trajectory of the AfCFTA, an overview of the developmental underpinnings of the AfCFTA, then explains the role and function of AfCFTA institutions. Thereafter, it explains the importance of IP with the AfCFTA. Then it outlines the development, negotiation and adoption of the IP Protocol. It then briefly sets out its provisions and assesses them against the AU's stated goals for a continental IP system. Specifically, it examines whether the protocol consolidates the collective African vision for IP that furthers developmental goals, contributes to the protection and promotion of human rights and generally furthers the public interest.

7.2 Developmental Underpinnings of the AfCFTA

The developmental underpinnings of the AfCFTA Agreement presented a significant opportunity for AU member states to put forth a developmentally orientated IP Protocol.[15] The AfCFTA is firmly embedded within the bedrock of sustainable and inclusive development as a flagship project of Agenda 2063, which is a 50-year developmental plan supported by various other implementation plans such as the

8 AfCFTA Secretariat (2023) p. 4.
9 World Bank (2020).
10 AfCFTA Secretariat (2023) p. 10.
11 Niamey Declaration on the Launch of the Operational Phase of the AfCFTA. Twelfth Extraordinary Session, 7 July 2019. Niamey, Niger. Ext/Assembly/AU/Dec.1(XII).
12 Assembly Decision on the Start of Trading Under the African Continental Free Trade Area (AfCFTA); Johannesburg Declaration on the Start of Trading Under the Agreement Establishing the African Continental Free Trade Area. Thirteenth Extraordinary Session (on the AfCFTA) 5 December 2020, Johannesburg, South Africa (virtual). EXT/Assembly/AU/Dec.1 (XIII).
13 AfCFTA Secretariat (2022).
14 Pan African Chamber of Commerce and Industry (2022).
15 Osei-Tutu (2021b) pp. 119, 128–132, Adebola (2020) pp. 234–235.

Shared Strategic Framework for Inclusive Growth and Sustainable Development First Ten-Year Implementation Plan 2014–2023[16] and STISA 2024. Therefore, the AfCFTA's aspirations are to contribute to the continental developmental plan for sustainable and inclusive development in Africa.

Agenda 2063 has seven aspirations, supported by 20 goals which in turn are linked to 40 priority areas. The seven priorities are:

1 A prosperous Africa based on inclusive growth and sustainable development.
2 An integrated continent, politically united and based on the ideals of Pan-Africanism and the vision of Africa's Renaissance.
3 An Africa of good governance, democracy, respect for human rights, justice and the rule of law.
4 A peaceful and secure Africa.
5 An Africa with a strong cultural identity, common heritage, shared values and ethics.
6 An Africa whose development is people-driven, relying on the potential of African people, especially its women and youth, and caring for children.
7 Africa as a strong, united, resilient and influential global player and partner.

Of these, aspirations 1 and 6 are most readily identifiable with the AfCFTA Agreement and are echoed in some of its provisions, specifically in Article 3, which provide for the general objectives of the AfCFTA, as follows:

(a) create a single market for goods, services, facilitated by movement of persons in order to deepen the economic integration of the African continent and in accordance with the Pan African Vision of "An integrated, prosperous and peaceful Africa" enshrined in Agenda 2063;
(b) create a liberalised market for goods and services through successive rounds of negotiations;
(c) contribute to the movement of capital and natural persons and facilitate investments building on the initiatives and developments in the State Parties and RECs;
(d) lay the foundation for the establishment of a Continental Customs Union at a later stage;
(e) promote and attain sustainable and inclusive socio-economic development, gender equality and structural transformation of the State Parties;
(f) enhance the competitiveness of the economies of State Parties within the continent and the global market;
(g) promote industrial development through diversification and regional value chain development, agricultural development and food security; and

16 AU (2015)

(h) resolve the challenges of multiple and overlapping membership and expedite the regional and continental integration processes.

As is evident, paragraph (a) is an articulation of aspiration 1 of Agenda 2063, paragraph (e) resonates strongly with aspiration 6 and paragraph (f) recalls aspiration 7. Further, all of Agenda 2063's aspirations are clearly required for trade to occur. A shared vision of an "integrated continent" facilitated and supported by "good governance, democracy, respect for human rights, justice and the rule of law" in "a peaceful and secure Africa" that has a "a strong cultural identity, common heritage, shared values and ethics" is the necessary context for the success of the envisioned single market. In turn, this will make the continent "a strong, united, resilient and influential global player and partner." Similarly, scrutiny of Agenda 2063's 20 goals and their accompanying priority areas shows strong affinity and linkage to the AfCFTA.

Whilst they are distinct in significant ways, Agenda 2063 and the sustainable development goals (SDGs) converge to a great extent.[17] Both speak to sustainability and have the three priority areas of "economic development, social inclusion and responsible environmental stewardship."[18] Indeed, all 17 SDGs are covered in Agenda 2063's 20 goals, and therefore also find resonance with the AfCFTA. For instance, in relation to Agenda 2063 Goal 1 (a high standard of living, quality of life and well-being for all citizens) and SDG 1 (no poverty), the World Bank has estimated, if the AfCFTA is fully implemented, "30 million people, or 1.5 percent of the continent's population [would be lifted] out of extreme poverty [and] 67.9 million [people] in the continent [would be lifted] out of moderate poverty (at US$5.50, PPP-adjusted, a day)."[19] This is closely related to SDG 8 (decent work and economic growth) and SDG 10 (reduced inequalities) which targets income equality (target 10.1) and economic inclusion (target 10.2).

The AfCFTA goal to "promote industrial development through diversification regional value chain development, agricultural development and food security"[20] is readily linked to SDG 2 (zero hunger) and Agenda 2063 goal 1 (a high standard of living, quality of life and well-being for all citizens), Goal 3 (healthy and well-nourished citizens) and Goal 5 (modern agriculture for increased productivity and production). The ten regional value chains that have been prioritised are (1) automotive, (2) leather and leather products, (3) cocoa, (4) soya, (5) textiles and apparel, (6) pharmaceuticals, (7) vaccine manufacturing, (8) lithium-ion batteries, (9) mobile financial services and (10) cultural and creative industries.[21]

These value chains have clear significance for several developmental goals and a mapping exercise has been conducted for most of them, linking them with the relevant SDGs.[22] For present purposes, it is not necessary to replicate that exercise.

17 Ncube (2021) p. 26.
18 Ibid.
19 World Bank (2020) p. 58.
20 AfCFTA Agreement Article 3(g).
21 UNDP and AfCFTA Secretariat (2021) p. 19.
22 UNDP and AfCFTA Secretariat (2021) pp. 20–65.

Two examples will suffice to make the point. For instance, the pharmaceuticals and vaccine manufacturing value chains are critical to health-related goals, so Agenda 2063's Goal 1 (A high standard of living, quality of life and well-being for all citizens), Goal 3 (healthy and well-nourished citizens) and SDG 3 (good health and well-being) are relevant. In addition, they relate to these economic goals: Agenda 2063 Goal 4 (transformed economies), Agenda 2063 Goal 10 (world-class infrastructure across Africa), SDG 8 (decent work and economic growth) and SDG 9 (industry, innovation and infrastructure). Each regional value chain is clearly affected by IP, which is further discussed in the following sections.

7.3 AfCFTA Institutions

The AfCFTA Agreement provides for an institutional framework composed of four organs, namely the Assembly, Council of Ministers (COM), the Committee of Senior Trade Officials (STOs), and the Secretariat.

The assembly is "the highest decision-making organ of the AU" and as such is the apex organ overseeing the AfCFTA, through the provision of "strategic guidance."[23] Further, it has "the exclusive authority to adopt interpretation of this Agreement on the recommendation of the Council of Ministers," taking such decisions by consensus.[24]

The COM comprises "Ministers responsible for Trade or such other ministers, authorities or officials designated by State Parties"[25] and "reports to the Assembly through the Executive Council."[26] Its functions are wide ranging and include the following:

1 "Implementation and enforcement of the Agreement";[27]
2 Promotion of the Agreement's objectives;[28]
3 Promotion of "the harmonisation of appropriate policies, strategies and measures" for effective implementation of the Agreement;[29]
4 Considering Secretariat activities and reports as well as taking "appropriate actions";
5 Proposing staff and financial regulations and the organisational structure of the Secretariat for adoption by the Assembly;[30]
6 Making "recommendations to the Assembly for the adoption of authoritative interpretation of this Agreement."[31]

The COM convenes two ordinary sessions a year and may convene extraordinary sessions as needed.[32] Its decisions are binding on state parties and "decisions that

23 Article 10(1) AfCFTA Agreement.
24 Article 10(2) AfCFTA Agreement.
25 Article 11(1) AfCFTA Agreement.
26 Article 11(2) AfCFTA Agreement.
27 Article 11(3)(b) AfCFTA Agreement.
28 Article 11(3)(c) AfCFTA Agreement.
29 Article 11(3)(e) AfCFTA Agreement.
30 Article 11(3) (l)–(m) AfCFTA Agreement.
31 Article 11(3)(o) AfCFTA Agreement.
32 Article 11(4) AfCFTA Agreement.

have legal, structural or financial implications" become binding only upon adoption by the assembly.[33] State parties are enjoined to "take such measures as are necessary to implement" the COM's decisions.[34]

The Committee of STOs is the next organ in this institutional hierarchy. It reports to the COM.[35] Each state party deploys permanent or principal secretaries or other designated officials to represent them at the committee.[36] REC representatives sit on the committee in an advisory capacity.[37] Article 12(2) sets out the mandate of the Committee of STOs as follows, to:

(a) implement the decisions of the Council of Ministers as may be directed;
(b) be responsible for the development of programmes and action plans for the implementation of the Agreement;
(c) monitor and keep under constant review and ensure proper functioning and development of the AfCFTA in accordance with the provisions of this Agreement;
(d) establish committees or other working groups as may be required;
(e) oversee the implementation of the provisions of this Agreement and for that purpose, may request a Technical Committee to investigate any particular matter;
(f) direct the Secretariat to undertake specific assignments; and
(g) perform any other function consistent with this Agreement or as may be requested by the Council of Ministers.

One level below the Committee of STOs lies the Secretariat, which was established by the Assembly, which also set its nature and location in addition to approving its structure and budget.[38] Initial developments, negotiations and adoption-related AfCFTA developments were coordinated by the African Union Commission (AUC)'s specialised unit, the AfCFTA Negotiations Support Unit. Thereafter, once the AfCFTA Agreement came into force, the AUC served as interim secretariat.[39] In February 2020 the Secretary-General of the AfCFTA Secretariat was appointed, and he was sworn in on 31 March 2020, on which day the secretariat was established.[40] It subsequently moved into its headquarters at Africa Trade House in Accra, Ghana, and started its work in August of that year. The instalment of the Secretary-General and the commencement of work by the secretariat was the catalyst for developments that have occurred in the since 2020, which include the negotiation of the IP Proto-

33 Article 11(5) AfCFTA Agreement.
34 Article 11(6) AfCFTA Agreement.
35 Article 12(4) AfCFTA Agreement.
36 Article 12(1) AfCFTA Agreement.
37 Article 12(5) AfCFTA Agreement.
38 Article 13(1) AfCFTA Agreement.
39 Article 13(2) AfCFTA Agreement.
40 Assembly/AU/Dec.751(XXXIII) 33rd Ordinary Session of the Assembly of the Union, 9–10 February 2020, Addis Ababa, Ethiopia Decision on the African Continental Free Trade Area (AfCFTA) Doc. Assembly/AU/4(XXXIII) paras 6–8.

col. The secretariat is "a functionally autonomous institutional body" with "an independent legal personality."[41] It is "autonomous of the AUC"[42] and is funded from the AU's "overall annual budgets."[43] The AfCFTA agreement is member driven, and the secretariat serves as a coordinating unit. It undertakes whatever tasks are necessary to implement the agreement, including the completion of outstanding negotiations and seeing to it that trade occurs. Its roles and responsibilities are set by the COM.[44]

7.4 IP in the AfCFTA

The relevance of IP to trade generally and within the AfCFTA cannot be overemphasised. Being a non-tariff barrier,[45] it is relevant to every aspect of intra-Africa and inter-Africa trade because IP rights afford their holders economic exclusivity upon which they build market share. It is illustrative to refer back to the regional value chains that are prioritised in the AfCFTA to underscore the relevance of IP. A cursory evaluation of each of the ten prioritised value chains shows that a variety of IPRs would be relevant to them. These industries are the (1) automotive, (2) leather and leather products, (3) cocoa, (4) soya, (5) textiles and apparel, (6) pharmaceuticals, (7) vaccine manufacturing, (8) lithium-ion batteries, (9) mobile financial services and (10) cultural and creative Industries. A few examples in relation to each of the ten will suffice to support this point. For the automotive, pharmaceuticals, vaccine manufacturing, lithium-ion and mobile financial services industries, copyright, designs, patents, trade secrets and trade marks would be relevant. Due to the COVID-19 pandemic, the relevance of IP for pharmaceuticals and vaccine manufacturing received significant scholarly attention, specifically around the TRIPS Waiver proposal co-sponsored by India and South Africa[46] with wide support including that of the AU member states.[47] In relation to the prioritised agricultural products, cocoa and soya, trade marks, collective marks, certification marks, GIs and plant breeders' rights may be relevant, depending on the product and entrepreneurs involved. For instance, research has shown that GIs can be both "successfully and sustainably" used to protect coffee and cocoa by local communal producers in Ethiopia and Ghana, respectively.[48] For leather and leather products, as well as the textiles and apparel industries, trade marks are routinely employed, especially by medium and large enterprises in the formal sector, and research has demonstrated that small enterprises including those in the informal sector in Nigeria can benefi-

41 Article 13(3) AfCFTA Agreement.
42 Article 13(4) AfCFTA Agreement.
43 Article 13(5) AfCFTA Agreement.
44 Article 13(6) AfCFTA Agreement.
45 UNCTAD (2019) pp. 65–69.
46 WTO Council for TRIPS (2020) and (2021).
47 Dos Santos, Ncube and Ouma (2022), Adewopo (2021). For commentary on African approaches to global health diplomacy, see Loewenson, Modisenyane and Pearcey (2014).
48 Oguamanam and Dagne (2013), AU Continental Strategy for Geographical Indications in Africa 2018–2023 pp. 2–3.

cially use certification marks, collective marks and/or GIs.[49] For the creative and cultural industries, designs, copyright and related rights and trade secrets would be relevant.

Further, it is important to emphasise that IP acquires greater significance in the context of cross-border trade, the main goal of the AfCFTA, because businesses would now need to be knowledgeable about the IP laws of all the countries in which they conduct trade. A related aspect is the focus on growing digital trade, which also invokes IP aspects in that an enterprise that trades online would also consider as relevant a variety of IP rights, such as copyright protection for a website, trademark protection for its brand and perhaps patent protection for eligible processes and underlying technologies. Finally, the relevance of IP needs to be understood within the context of inclusive trade, which seeks to ensure that entrepreneurs of all sizes, including the informal sector and enterprises owned by significant constituencies such as youth and women, are not left behind. Consequently, there are three protocols in the AfCFTA agreement that relate to these aspects, namely the protocol on IPRs, the protocol on digital trade and the protocol on youth and women in trade. The latter two are yet to be concluded.

AfCFTA Agreement protocols become "an integral part of the agreement upon adoption and form part of the single undertaking upon entry into force."[50] Article 23 (1)–(2) of the agreement provides the formula for their entry into force as follows: "thirty (30) days after the deposit of the twenty second (22nd) instrument of ratification." Further, Article 23(4) reads:

> For Member States acceding to the Protocols on Investment, Intellectual Property Rights, Competition Policy, and any other Instrument within the scope of this Agreement deemed necessary, shall enter into force on the date of the deposit of its instrument of accession.

The following sections consider the process of development and adoption of the Protocol on IPRs, its structure, scope and content.

7.5 Negotiation and Adoption of the Protocol on IPRs

The negotiation of the Protocol on IPRs was part of the second phase, which also included competition, investment and, by later addition, digital trade.[51] The date for the conclusion of negotiations set by the COM had to be shifted several times, from

49 Adewopo, Chuma-Okoro and Oyewunmi (2014), Oguamanam and Dagne (2014) p. 77, AU Continental Strategy for Geographical Indications in Africa 2018–2023 ibid.

50 Article 8 AfCFTA Agreement.

51 Article 7 AfCFTA Agreement; AU Decision on the African Continental free trade area (AfCFTA) Assembly/AU/Dec751(XXXIII) para 22.

December 2020 to 31 December 2021 and later to September 2022.[52] The negotiations for the Protocol on IPRs were conducted by the Committee on IP, established by the COM at its fifth meeting on 3 May 2021.[53] The committee undertook the negotiations in accordance with its terms of reference, the AU Statement of the Objectives and Guiding Principles for Negotiating the Continental Free Trade Area[54] and the modalities for the negotiations of the AfCFTA Protocol on IPRs.[55] The modalities set the scope of negotiations to include:

> all categories of IPRs . . . traditional knowledge, traditional cultural expressions and genetic resources . . . the support, promotion, facilitation, protection, enhancement and enforcement of IPRS that would promote intra-African trade, while maintaining flexibility to AU member states to promote and protect the public interest; and the means for co-operation among African States to address shared IPR challenges.[56]

In addition, the negotiation covered both norm-setting co-operation and implementation.[57]

A series of four Committee on IP meetings were held in 2021 and 2022. Several other related meetings and consultations took place, including a high-level brainstorming session hosted by the AfCFTA Secretariat in February 2022 at which the regional IP organisations were represented by their directors general. Following the fourth Committee on IP meeting, the protocol was considered by the 13th meeting of STOs, held on 25 October 2022, The first extraordinary meeting of the COMs responsible for trade, held in in Libreville, Gabon, from 27–28 October 2022, revised the draft protocol before it, then approved the revised protocol and recommended its adoption by the assembly.[58] Following this, the 17th Extraordinary Assembly, held 20–25 November 2022 in Niamey, Niger, noted the adoption of the protocol by the COM and requested the STC on Justice and Legal Affairs to consider it at an extraordinary session in January 2023, following which further adoption processes would commence.[59] As indicated earlier, the protocol was adopted by the 36th

52 AU Decision on the African Continental Free Trade Area (AfCFTA) Assembly/AU/Dec.751(XXXIII) para 23; Assembly of the African Union Thirteenth Extraordinary Session (on the AfCFTA) 5 December 2020 Johannesburg, South Africa Ext/Assembly/AU/Decl.1(XIII) para 15; Maurice.Info, 2022.

53 AfCFTA/COM/5/REPORT/FINAL/27(a).

54 Report of the Chairperson of the High-Level African Trade Committee (HATC) Assembly of the Union Twenty-Fifth Ordinary Session 14–15 June 2015, Johannesburg, South Africa Assembly/AU/11(XXV) Annex I.

55 AfCFTA/DTIID/IPRs/1/M/FINAL (27 January 2022).

56 Paras 15–17.

57 Paras 18–19.

58 First Extraordinary Session of the African Continental Free Trade Area (AfCFTA) Council of Ministers Responsible for Trade Report AfCFTA/COM/EX/REPORT/FINAL (2022) paras 39–42.

59 17th Extraordinary Session of the Assembly of the AU on the AfCFTA, 25 November 2022 Draft Decision Ext/Assembly/AU/Draft/Dec.2(XVII).

Ordinary Session of the AU Assembly of Heads of State and Government in February 2023. This is the same route that the PAIPO Statute followed prior to its adoption by the assembly. The following sections discuss the protocol. It is important to stress that whilst the negotiators started off with a zero-draft prepared by the drafting task force convened and led by the Secretariat, the final instrument is the output of state negotiators' deliberations and decisions. It is the member states' instrument as negotiated and finalised by them.

7.6 Structure, Scope and Content of the Protocol on IPRs

The structure of the IP Protocol conforms to the structure of other AfCFTA protocols and mirrors, to a certain extent, the main agreement itself. Its Preamble is organised as follows, and is discussed in the following sections; Part I: Definitions, Objectives and Scope (Articles 1–3); Part II: Principles (Articles 4–7); Part III: Standards on IPRs (Articles 8–21); Part IV: Co-operation on IPRs (Articles 22–24); Part V: Enforcement of IPRs (Articles 25–29); Part VI: Institutional Arrangements (Articles 30–34); and Part VII: Final Provisions (Articles 35–42).

7.6.1 Preamble

As I have argued elsewhere, the preamble ought to set "an appropriate tone for the protocol with regard to the developmental priorities on the continent"[60] and I evaluate it from that perspective. It begins with a reaffirmation of Agenda 2063 aspirations and mandate given by Article 7(1) of the AfCFTA Agreement, then states the protocol's goal as being "to establish harmonised rules and principles on intellectual property rights to boost intra-African trade" and "promoting economic growth and development within the continent." This signals that the protocol will have rules or standards on IP that harmonise prevailing standards or create new ones. Significantly, the preamble notes the commitment of state parties to crafting a protocol that has "an inclusive, balanced and development-oriented" approach that "centres African interests and prioritises African-driven innovation and creativity." This means the standards set by the protocol ought to be aligned with, or at least not impede, such innovation and creativity. Intellectual property impacts development[61] and the preamble's foregrounding of a developmental approach to IP is welcome.

Research has shown that innovation unfolds in unique ways on the continent, and IP systems have to be carefully calibrated to support this.[62] It is thus fitting that the preamble then proceeds to reference the role of IPRs in "the promotion of access to knowledge, innovation and creativity, and the transfer and diffusion of technology" and "the need to ensure that that measures to protect and enforce of IPRs

60 Ncube (2022) p. 108.

61 Adebola (2020) p. 235, Osei-Tutu (2021a) and (2021b), Chidede (2022), Ncube (2013), Barbosa, Chon and von Hase (2007).

62 Adebola (2020) p. 235, Ncube et al. (2019) p. 178, Ncube et al. (2017), de Beer et al. (2013) p. 1 and (2020).

do not constitute barriers to trade." Regarding a common African policy position, the preamble references "policy coherence" and acknowledges the importance of co-operation and the need for meaningful use of flexibilities found in international IP instruments. Next, based on the AfCFTA principle of preservation of the *acquis*, the preamble recognises national IP systems and the achievements of the RECs and the regional IP organisations. This means that the continental IP framework seeks to build upon, not to replace or redo, existing frameworks.

Finally, in keeping with its Afro-centric focus, the preamble closes by stating that the protocol seeks "to ensure that the implementation of multilateral and bilateral treaties or agreements relating to intellectual property rights prioritises African interests and the protection of African innovation and creativity and deepens intellectual property culture in Africa." This is an important note to end on in view of Kenya's bilateral negotiations with the US, which if they ultimately result in a FTA will have significant impact on the EAC, COMESA and the AfCFTA.[63]

The preamble does not reference any IP instruments by name, nor does it reference any other relevant normative instruments, such as the UNDHR. I and other scholars[64] have argued that express reference to these instruments would send an unequivocal message about the policy direction. The argument against doing this, which prevailed, was that to expressly list instruments would mean that the list would have to be revised with any new relevant instrument adopted in the future and that this would be undesirable because of the lengthy process of negotiation and adoption of such revisions.

7.6.2 Part I: Definition, Objectives and Scope

The definition section is very lean, consisting of two definitions, those of "protocol" and of "intellectual property rights." The logic behind this was that the definitions in the AfCFTA Agreement apply to the protocol and therefore should not be repeated. Similarly, the provision of an elaborate definition of IPRs is obviated by the definitions found in all the relevant IP instruments to which state parties are party and are likely to be provided in the accompanying annexes. There would have been value in replicating some of the definitions here, as I have argued elsewhere, drawing from treaty language, the regional IP organisations' instruments and national legislation, to make the protocol self-contained.[65]

The objectives of the protocol are stated in Article 2. First the general objective is stated in Article 2(1) as being "to support the realisation of the objectives of the AfCFTA as set out in Article 3 of the AfCFTA Agreement by establishing harmonised rules and principles on the promotion, protection, co-operation and enforcement of intellectual property rights." This is in keeping with the way other protocols under the agreement are founded within the agreement. Each protocol

63 Ncube (2021) pp. 63–64, Gathii (2020), Naumann (2020).
64 Ncube (2022) p. 108, Osei-Tutu (2021a, 2021b) pp. 118–122.
65 Ncube (2022) p. 108.

then has specific objectives in keeping with its subject matter. Accordingly, the Protocol on IPRs then sets out its own specific objectives in Article 2(2). These are drawn largely from the modalities and are listed as follows:

(a) Support intra-African trade;
(b) Promote African innovation and creativity and deepen intellectual property culture in Africa;
(c) Promote coherent intellectual property rights policy in Africa;
(d) Contribute to the promotion of science, industrialisation, investment, digital trade, technology and technology transfer and regional value chains;
(e) Promote and ensure a harmonised system of intellectual property protection throughout the continent;
(f) Encourage African positions on intellectual property rights;
(g) support and promote creative and cultural industries by setting up a legal framework while securing and giving incentives that would help in their development;
(h) contribute to access to knowledge; and
(i) support public health needs and priorities of State Parties.

These are noble objectives that heed the call of a large body of scholarship on the kind of IP framework that is most appropriate for Africa. For instance, whilst the African Group's position developed in Geneva is strong, it lacks longevity because it was developed for specific circumstances, such as the negotiation of an instrument. This would be rectified by the protocol aiming to provide a coherent and comprehensive IP policy approach which can then be applied to various settings and circumstances (specific objectives (c) and (f)). The objectives also closely align with the expectations and commitments of the Dakar Declaration, outlined in chapter two, which will be recalled, as needed, throughout this chapter.

Much scholarship has been devoted to detailing how innovation unfolds on the continent, with recommendations for the type of IP approach which would best support this.[66] This is not to say that African innovation is any less than innovation elsewhere but to highlight its unique features, specifically the collaborative dynamics that drive it. Further, the incremental innovation found in traditional contexts and informal settings is not readily afforded IP protection, because it does not meet protection criteria.[67] Specific objective (b) is an express acknowledgement of that reality and an undertaking to customise IP frameworks to suit an African setting. Similarly, the fact that there several layers of IP protection – national, regional (RECs, ARIPO, OAPI) and continental – means that the system is fragmented, and in a continental FTA, such as the AfCFTA, it is desirable to cohere these different parts and consolidate them into a continental system, as is the case with

66 de beer et al. (2020), de Beer et al. (2013).
67 de Beer, Fu and Wunsch-Vincent (2013).

other regional trading blocs (specific objective [e]). This is intended to facilitate intra-African trade (specific objective (a)).

Access to knowledge is important in several respects, including for educational purposes, and research has highlighted some ways in which copyright hinders it.[68] Public health priorities rank very high for the continent, which has a high disease burden, including neglected diseases as well as endemics. It has been severely affected by pandemics including COVID-19.[69] Access to medicines and patents from a human rights perspective is a subject that has also spurred much scholarship with specific reference to Africa. These two priorities, and others, have compelling human rights underpinnings[70] and it is fitting that the preamble has expressly referenced them.

Article 3 states that the protocol applies to all categories of IPRs, then includes a non-exhaustive list. Specifically, the list includes TK, TCEs, genetic resources, emerging technologies and other emerging issues on IPRs.

7.6.3 Part II: Principles

This section consists of three articles. Article 4, on guiding principles, provides that the protection of IPRs shall adhere to eight principles as follows:

1. Promote intra-African trade;
2. Promote coherence between IP policies and other policies for socio-economic development;
3. create a balance between public and private interests;
4. Promote the public interest in sectors of vital importance to socio-economic and technological development including education, public health, agriculture, food security and nutrition;
5. Facilitate access to medicines, vaccines, diagnostics, therapeutics, and other healthcare essential tools consistent with the relevant treaties on intellectual property rights;
6. Facilitate access to clean and efficient energy as well as promote just and fair energy transition and environmental sustainability;
7. Promote digital trade along with new and emerging technologies to foster Africa's digital transformation;
8. Prevent the abuse of intellectual property rights or the resort to practices that unreasonably restrain trade or adversely affect the transfer of technology.

As indicated earlier, much of the content of the IP Protocol remains true to the vision and commitments of the Dakar Declaration on IP. The commitments listed in the declaration are depicted in the extract:

68 Armstrong et al. (2010), Štrba (2012), Shabalala (2011).

69 dos Santos, Ncube and Ouma (2022).

70 Oke (2021, 2022), Adewopo (2021),Yu (2019, 2021), Velásquez, Correa and Ido (2020), Ncube (2017), Štrba (2012), Armstrong et al. (2010).

We hereby declare our commitment to:

- Enhance innovative and creative capacities by providing a conducive environment with dynamic IP systems that propel creativity, innovation and inventiveness and effectively guide the promotion, acquisition and commercialisation of intellectual property for sustainable growth and development and for the wellbeing of African populations, and to enhance social recognition of creators;
- Build an enabling environment for innovation and creativity by strengthening the financial and regulatory environment to support innovation and creativity through strengthening African institutions; promoting and protecting intellectual property; establishing and strengthening collective management systems; increasing funding for science and technology; and enhancing collaboration among African countries;
- Foster the development and utilisation of copyright and related rights to support the development of new business models for the legal distribution of works and move towards realising through effective management of rights, effective contractual practices, and new revenue models their potential role as drivers for and contributors to economic, social and cultural development;
- Increase support for research and development (R&D) through promoting links among academia, industry, government and civil society organisations with a view to improving marketing and commercialisation of R&D; scaling up investments in science and technology parks; and encouraging action-oriented research at all levels of education;
- Nurture the culture of innovation and creativity by reviewing and strengthening the present education systems enhancing business competitiveness through strategic use of IP tools;
- Encourage public private partnerships for promoting production, exploitation and monetisation of domestic innovation and all creative works;
- Document, protect and promote the use and management of traditional/indigenous knowledge systems for development in Africa;
- Promote IP education in schools and higher education institutions;
- Take advantage of opportunities available within WIPO technical assistance and capacity building programs including access to data, multi-stakeholder platforms, and scientific and technological information; and
- Consider joining relevant WIPO-Administrated Treaties to which we are not yet Parties, including the recent Beijing Treaty on Audio-visual Performances and Marrakesh Treaty to Facilitate Access to Published Works for Persons Who Are Blind, Visually Impaired or Otherwise Print Disabled.

(Dakar Declaration on IP, 2015, pp. 2–3)

These principles are to be understood within the context of the AfCFTA Agreement of which the protocol is an integral part, consequently the principles listed in Article 5 of the AfCFTA Agreement are applicable.[71] Accordingly, the protocol articulates only the principles of most-favoured nation treatment (Article 5), national treatment (Article 6) and exhaustion of IPRs (Article 7) and draws these from the TRIPS Agreement. It provides for the principle of regional exhaustion as is to be expected in a CFTA and as had been the preferred approach of the TFTA IP agenda.[72] It then provides that the annexes on IPRs may include conditions for the applicability of exhaustion of that IPR.[73]

7.6.4 Part III: Standards on IPRs

In keeping with the objectives stated in the modalities and the protocol's Article 4, Part III's provisions are intended to contribute to the crafting of an IP framework that serves the African continent by addressing aspects that are of priority to AU member states. Consequently, it leads with provisions on plant variety protection (Article 8) and geographical indications (Article 9). Thereafter it addresses the following: marks (Article 10), copyright and related rights (Article 11), patents (Article 12), utility models (Article 13), industrial designs (Article 14), protection of undisclosed information (Article 15), layout designs (topographies) and integrated circuits (Article 16), emerging technologies (Article 17), traditional knowledge (Article 18), traditional cultural expressions and folklore (Article 19), genetic resources (Article 20) and addressing public health emergencies and promoting local production of pharmaceuticals (Article 21).

As can be seen from this list, these provisions are comprehensive in their coverage and include IPRs that are linked to the regional value chains that are being prioritised. They also accord directly with the principles listed in Article 4. This section does not outline the content of all these provisions as that is not necessary for the present purpose, which is to give a broad overview of the substantive content of the protocol and highlight the approach taken. Consequently, the regulation of only two IPRS, copyright and patents, will be considered in some detail.

Most of the provisions begin with an undertaking by the state parties to provide protection for the relevant IPR and include an emphasis on taking developmental priorities into account in crafting such protection. In some cases that is the extent of the article, and the details are deferred to an annex to be developed by the state parties. This is the general approach, and the protocol provides that annexes shall be adopted for plant variety protection, geographical indications, trade marks, copyright and related rights, patents, utility models, industrial designs and TK, TCEs, folklore and genetic resources.[74] The development of an annex is not required for

71 See Ncube (2022) pp. 109–110 for an explanation of these.

72 Ncube (2022) p. 112.

73 Article 7(2).

74 Articles 8(3), 9(3), 10(4), 11(7), 12(4), 13(4), 14(4), 18(10), 19(10), 20(9), 42(1).

the protection of undisclosed information and is optional for addressing matters to do with emerging technologies. Article 42 provides that annexes will be negotiated "immediately upon the adoption of this Protocol"[75] and "upon adoption these Annexes shall form part of this Protocol."[76] State parties may negotiate any further annexes on any IP aspects as they deem appropriate in the future.[77]

As indicated, all the provisions centre development concerns and in some cases there is express mention of public interest mechanisms. This is the case for copyright where "exceptions and limitations for educational and research purposes in national contexts, online cross-border contexts, and multi-country research collaborations" are required.[78] In addition, state parties are required to "provide for exceptions that support the preservation of cultural heritage and for the reproduction of a reasonable portion of any published work in their collection upon request for use for research purposes or private study of the requesting party."[79] Finally, state parties agree to comply with the Marrakesh Treaty.[80] All these commitments are in keeping with the oft-repeated position of African states, for example at the WIPO Standing Committee on Copyright and Related Rights,[81] in the IP Agenda of the TFTA and in the Dakar Declaration. They are appropriately aligned with developmental, human rights and public interest perspectives.

Similarly, the patent provisions make appropriate reference to exceptions to permit "research, experimentation and testing for obtaining information about the subject matter of a patented invention,"[82] amongst others. For instance, it requires state parties to "ensure that their patent law does not hinder access to medicines, vaccines, diagnostics, therapeutics and other healthcare essential tools consistent with intellectual property treaties to which they are party."[83] Again these requirements are in accordance with the public policy commitments of African states as articulated in national IP policies, some REC policies, the TFTA IP Agenda and the African position on patents and public health most recently demonstrated in the context of the AU's position regarding the COVID-19 pandemic and IP. In alignment with this, Article 21(1) sets out that "States Parties may take any action which [they] consider necessary for the protection of its essential public health interests during any emergency; including epidemics [and] pandemics." Then Article 21(2) enjoins state parties to ensure policy coherence in relation to "IPRs, innovation, trade, industry and health to promote local production of pharmaceutical prod-

75 Article 41.
76 Article 42(3).
77 Article 42(2).
78 Article 11(4).
79 Article 11(5).
80 Article 11(6).
81 WIPO Standing Committee on Copyright and Related Rights Forty-Second Session Geneva, 9–13 May 2022 Proposal by the African Group for a Draft Work Program on Exceptions and Limitations SCCR/42/4 REV.
82 Article 11(3)(d).
83 Article 12(3)(a).

ucts, and vaccines, diagnostics, therapeutics and other healthcare essential tools." Finally, Article 21(3) requires that state parties "ensure regional co-operation to provide for greater economies of scale and to develop regional value chains critical for the competitiveness and sustainability of pharmaceutical and vaccines sector development in Africa."

Another notable area of regulation is Article 17(1) on emerging technologies, which is a light touch as it does not require anything of states but merely provides that they may adopt measures to (1) protect these technologies "through existing categories of intellectual property rights or *sui generis* systems to facilitate trade under the AfCFTA," and (2) "promote access and use of new and emerging technologies" and "support and encourage use of emerging technologies to facilitate industrialisation and the development of value chains" and "promote environmentally friendly use." As indicated, an annex is not required for this aspect. Global debates are ongoing on the appropriate IP protection of fourth industrial revolution technologies, such as through the WIPO conversations on IP and AI,[84] and on the continent there is a growing body of work on the topic.[85]

Similarly the detailed engagement with TK, TCEs and genetic resources which will be supported by a mandatory annex is very important because the African continent is extremely well endowed with these resources and global norm-setting for the protection of TK and TCEs has been an inordinately long process. Further, the approach on the continent has so far been uneven at both national and regional levels, so it is fitting that the protocol leads on this. As indicated previously, a detailed overview of the whole of Part II cannot be given and what appears here is only illustrative and non-exhaustive.

7.6.5 Parts IV–VII: Co-operation on Enforcement, Institutional Arrangements and Final Provisions

The IP Protocol provides in Part IV a general obligation for state parties to co-operate to meet the objectives of the protocol in Article 22, then sets out a list of areas of co-operation Article 23, which are primarily normative in their nature and are for the beneficial use of IP, including through the use of public interest mechanisms such as TRIPS flexibilities. Article 24 specifically addresses co-operation in relation to administration of IPRs and includes aspects such as "automation and streamlining of intra-agency communications," sharing of experience and joint capacity building of IP Offices.

Enforcement is the subject of Part V and addresses the following: General Provisions (Article 25), Responsibilities of States Parties (Article 26), Injunction (Article 27), Transit Trade (Article 28) and Border Measures (Article 29). These are all critically important aspects within the context of a regional market.

84 AI and IP Policy: The WIPO Conversation. www.wipo.int/about-ip/en/frontier_technologies/ai_and_ip_policy.html

85 For example Ncube and Rutenberg (2020).

Part VI, on institutional arrangements, covers the Committee on IPRs (Article 30), the AfCFTA IP Office (Article 31), Transition and Roadmap (Article 32), Transparency and Notification (Article 33) and Technical Assistance and Capacity Building (Article 34). The committee is the structure through which the protocol was negotiated and its future functions will be as assigned by the COM to "facilitate the implementation" of the protocol and to "further its objectives."[86] The AfCFTA IP office will comprise "the AfCFTA Secretariat, Africa Centre for Disease Control and Prevention (Africa CDC) and the African Medicinal Agency (AMA)."[87] An annex will be developed by the COM on "the governance and administrative structures, [and] functions of the office" and all other related institutional arrangements. The office's operationalisation timeline (road map) will be adopted by the COM and in the interim operationalisation period the office will be supported by the AfCFTA Secretariat.[88] Similarly the Secretariat will play a supporting role to state parties by serving as a point for notifications of relevant normative instruments as required by Article 33 and also by providing technical assistance to state parties in collaboration with state parties, RECS, regional IP organisations and relevant stakeholders. The provisions on the IP office do not include details at this point on function and mandate so it is not yet possible to comment on operational issues and mandate overlap, if any. Once these details are concluded in the relevant annex, it will be possible to do so.

The final provisions in Part VII cover Entry Into Force (Article 35), Application (Article 36), Conflict and Inconsistency with other Agreements (Article 37), Dispute Settlement (Article 38), Review (Article 39), Amendment (Article 40), Negotiation of Annexes (Article 41) and Annexes (Article 42). The protocol will enter into force in accordance with the formula in Articles 23(2) and 23(4) of the AfCFTA Agreement, meaning that it will enter into force "thirty (30) days after the deposit of the twenty-second (22nd) instrument of ratification" and for any state acceding, the protocol "shall enter into force on the date of the deposit of its instrument of accession."

7.7 Evaluation and Conclusion

The institutional arrangements are not yet known in their full detail so it is not possible to provide full commentary. The regional IP organisations have been referred to in both the preamble and the capacity building provisions but it is not yet clear whether there would be mandate overlap between them and the AfCFTA IP Office. Regarding the scope of the substantive provisions of the IP Protocol found in Part II, it is important to keep in mind that IP is already extensively regulated at multiple levels, (national, sub-regional by the regional economic communities, and by the regional IP organisations) and to some extent continentally by some AU instruments.

86 Article 30(1).
87 Article 31(1).
88 Article 32.

Therefore, the IP Protocol would not seek to regulate every aspect of IP to the extent of replicating what already exists; the more prudent approach would be to look for gaps and policy space opportunities to take advantage of, so its provisions are not just a replication of the TRIPS. Further, the protocol on IP needed to be a manageable document, so it is a framework agreement, setting out the core approach and leaving to be fleshed out in annexes further details that are yet to be negotiated.

The protocol centres African priorities as shown by its inclusion of provisions on plant varieties, geographical indications, TK, TCEs and genetic resources. It is also forward-looking in its engagement with emerging technologies, a currently topical matter globally, with debates still on-going on how best to regulate fourth industrial revolution technologies. These debates are already entrenched on the continent and it is appropriate that the protocol seeks to contribute.

The IP Protocol's provisions are what one would expect to see in the surfacing of an African approach to IPRs, and as has been shown in the few examples given here, this seems to have been achieved by the consolidation of oft-stated African positions. This entails harmonisation of standards that will enable trade in the AfCFTA to meet African priorities, so, for example, if the pharmaceuticals and vaccines manufacturing sector are prioritised regional value chains, the provisions of Article 7 (regional exhaustion) and Articles 15 and 21 on patents and addressing public health emergencies make sense.

The IP Protocol is an instrument born from the negotiations of more than 50 states from different legal traditions and contexts, which share common developmental aspirations and are guided by some shared instruments like Agenda 2063. The final wording of this legal text is thus a complex document, based on a compromise reached as the outcome of negotiations. Therefore, it may look nothing like what a technician or an academic or researcher might draft within the confines of their ivory towers. What then becomes the prime useful engagement point is how it may best be implemented to achieve its noble objectives to harness IP for the benefit of Africa. It remains to be seen how soon it will come into force and how its implementation will be undertaken.

Reference List

Decisions, Declarations, Reports and Statements

AU

Assembly/AU/Dec.394(XVIII) Decision on Boosting Intra-African Trade and Fast Tracking the Continental Free Trade Area Doc. EX.CL/700(XX). Seventeenth Extraordinary Session of the Assembly of the AU on the AfCFTA, 25 November 2022. Draft DecisionExt/Assembly/AU/Draft/Dec.2(XVII).

Assembly Decision on the Start of Trading Under the African Continental Free Trade Area (AfCFTA). Ext/Assembly/AU/Dec.1 (XIII). Johannesburg Declaration on the Start of Trading Under the Agreement Establishing the African Continental Free Trade Area. Thirteenth Extraordinary Session (on the AfCFTA), 5 December 2020. Johannesburg, South Africa (virtual).

AU, 2015. *A Shared Strategic Framework for Inclusive Growth and Sustainable Development First Ten-Year Implementation Plan. 2014–2023*. AUC. Addis Ababa, Ethiopia. Available at https://au.int/sites/default/files/documents/33126-doc-ten_year_implementation_book.pdf [accessed 9 January 2023]

AU Continental Strategy for Geographical Indications in Africa 2018–2023.

AU Minimum Integration Programme (MIP) May 2009. Available at https://au.int/sites/default/files/pages/32825-file-minimumintegrationprogrammeeng.pdf [accessed 9 January 2023].

AU Statement of the Objectives and Guiding Principles for Negotiating the Continental Free Trade Area AfCFTA/COM/5/REPORT/FINAL/27(a).

First Extraordinary Session of the African Continental Free Trade Area (AfCFTA) Council of Ministers responsible for Trade Report AfCFTA/COM/EX/REPORT/FINAL (October 2022).

Modalities for the negotiations of the AfCFTA Protocol on IP AfCFTA/DTIID/IPRs/1/M/FINAL, 27 January 2022.

Niamey Declaration on the Launch of the Operational Phase of the AfCFTA. Ext/Assembly/AU/Dec.1(XII). Twelfth Extraordinary Session, 7 July 2019. Niamey, Niger.

UNCTAD

International Classification of Non-Tariff Measures 2019 Version. UNCTAD/DITC/TAB/2019/5.

ECA

ECA and AU, 2012. Boosting Intra-African Trade: Issues Affecting Intra-African Trade, Proposed Action Plan for Boosting Intra-African Trade and Framework for the Fast Tracking of a Continental Free Trade Area, 8 October 2012.

UN Economic and Social Council

United Nations. Economic and Social Council; ECA (1991–03). Appraisal and Review of the Impact of the Lagos Plan of Action on the Development and Expansion of Intra-African Trade. ECA Conference of African Ministers of Trade Meeting (11th session: 15–19 April 1990: Addis Ababa, Ethiopia). Addis Ababa: ECA. Available at https://hdl.handle.net/10855/14129 [accessed 9 January 2023].

United Nations. Economic and Social Council; ECA (1991–04). Decennial Review and Appraisal of the Lagos Plan of Action and the Final Act of Lagos. ECA Technical Preparatory Committee of the Whole Meeting (12th: 29 April–7 May 1991: Addis Ababa, Ethiopia); ECA Session of the Commission (26th: 9–13 May 1991: Addis Ababa, Ethiopia); ECA Conference of Ministers Meeting (17th: 9–13 May 1991: Addis Ababa, Ethiopia). Addis Ababa: ECA. Available at https://hdl.handle.net/10855/12217 [accessed 9 January 2023].

WIPO

WIPO Standing Committee on Copyright and Related Rights Forty-Second Session Geneva, 9–13 May 2022 Proposal by the African Group for a Draft Work Program on Exceptions and Limitations SCCR/42/4 REV.

WTO

WTO Council for TRIPS, 2020. Waiver from Certain Provisions of the TRIPS Agreement for the Prevention, Containment and Treatment of Covid-19 – Communication from India and South Africa IP/C/W/669, 2 October 2020.

WTO Council for TRIPS, 2021. Waiver from Certain Provisions of the TRIPS Agreement for the Prevention, Containment and Treatment of Covid-19 – Revised Decision Text Communication from the African Group, The Plurinational State of Bolivia, Egypt, Eswatini, Fiji, India, Indonesia, Kenya, The LDC Group, Maldives, Mozambique, Mongolia, Namibia, Pakistan, South Africa, Vanuatu, The Bolivarian Republic of Venezuela and Zimbabwe IP/C/W/669/Rev.1, 25 May 2021.

Secondary Sources

Adebola, T., 2020. Mapping Africa's Complex Regimes: Towards an African Centred AfCFTA Intellectual Property (IP) Protocol. *Journal of International Economic Law*, 23(4), 233–289.

Adewopo, A., 2021. Access to Pharmaceutical Patents in the COVID-19 Emergency: A Case for Government Use in Nigeria. *Journal of African Law*, 65(S2), 259–286. http://doi.org/10.1017/S0021855321000334

Adewopo, A., Chuma-Okoro, H. and Oyewunmi, A., 2014. A Consideration of Communal Trademarks for Nigerian Leather and Textile Products. In Jeremy de Beer, J., Armstrong, C., Oguamanam, C. and Schonwetter, T. (eds.) *Innovation & Intellectual Property Collaborative Dynamics in Africa*. Cape Town: UCT Press, 109–131.

AfCFTA Secretariat, 2022. *What Is the AfCFTA Guided Trade Initiative All About*? Available at https://au-afcfta.org/2022/10/what-is-the-afcfta-guided-trade-initiative-all-about/ [accessed 8 January 2023].

AfCFTA Secretariat, 2023. *AfCFTA Fact Sheet*, April 2023. Accra, Ghana: AfCFTA Secretariat.

Armstrong, C., de Beer, J., Kawooya, D., Prabhala, A. and Schonwetter, T. (eds.), 2010. *Access to Knowledge in Africa: The Role of Copyright*. Claremont, CPT: UCT Press.

AU, 2015. *A Shared Strategic Framework for Inclusive Growth and Sustainable Development First Ten-Year Implementation Plan. 2014–2023*. AUC. Addis Ababa, Ethiopia. Available at https://au.int/sites/default/files/documents/33126-doc-ten_year_implementation_book.pdf

AU, 2019. *African Integration Booklet*. Department of Economic Affairs, AUC. Addis Ababa, Ethiopia.

Barbosa, D.B., Chon, M. and von Hase, A.M., 2007. Slouching Towards Development in International Intellectual Property. *Michigan State Law Review*, 71–141.

Chidede, T., 2022. The Role of Intellectual Property Rights Protection in Advancing Development in South Africa. *Law, Democracy and Development*, 26, 168–189. https://doi.org/10.17159/2077-4907/2021/ldd.v26.7

de Beer, J., Armstrong, C., Elahi, S., Kawooya, D., Kramer-Mbula, E., Ncube, C., Oguamanam, C., Rizk, N., Rutenberg, I. and Schonwetter, T., 2020. Open Innovation in Africa: Current Realities, Future Scenarios, and Scalable Solutions. In Matthew, L., Smith, M.L. and Seward, R.K. (eds.) *Making Open Development Inclusive: Lessons from IDRC Research*. Cambridge, MA: MIT Press, IDRC, 403–430.

de Beer, J., Armstrong, C., Oguamanam, C. and Schonwetter, T. (eds.), 2013. *Innovation and Intellectual Property: Collaborative Dynamics in Africa*. Claremont, CT: University of Cape Town Press.

de Beer, J., Fu, K. and Wunsch-Vincent, S., 2013. *The Informal Economy, Innovation and Intellectual Property: Concepts, Metrics and Policy Considerations*. WIPO Economics & Statistics Series. Economic Research Working Paper No. 10. Geneva: WIPO. Available at https://www.wipo.int/publications/en/details.jsp?id=3954 [accessed 8 January 2023].

dos Santos, F., Ncube, C. B. and Ouma, M., 2022. Intellectual Property Framework Responses to Health Emergencies: Options for Africa. *South African Journal of Science*, 118(5/6). https://doi.org/10.17159/sajs.2022/12775

Gathii, J.T., 2020. An Early Assessment of the Prospective Kenya–United States Trade Agreement. *Afronomics Law*, 13 February 2020. www.afronomicslaw.org/2020/02/13/an-early-assessment-of-the-prospective-kenya-united-states-trade-agreement [accessed 8 January 2023].

Loewenson, R., Modisenyane, M. and Pearcey, M., 2014. African Perspectives in Global Health Diplomacy. *Journal of Health Diplomacy*, 1(2), 1–19.

Maurice.Info, 2022. *Outcome of the 9th Meeting of the AfCFTA Council of Ministers of Trade*. Available at www.maurice-info.mu/2022-07-28-outcome-of-the-9th-meeting-of-the-afcfta-council-of-ministers-of-trade.html [accessed 1 December 2022].

Naumann, E. The United States-Kenya Free Trade Area (FTA): Insights into the Bilateral Trade Relationship and Early Progress on Setting Terms for an FTA (June 2020) *Tralac Working Paper No. US20WP03/2020*.

Ncube, C.B., 2013. Harnessing Intellectual Property for Development: Some Thoughts on an Appropriate Theoretical Framework. *Potchefstroom Electronic Law Journal*, 16(4), 370–396.

Ncube, C.B., 2017. Using Human Rights to Move Beyond Reformism to Radicalism: A2K for Schools, Libraries and Archives. In Callahan, M. and Rogers, J. (eds.) *A Critical Guide to Intellectual Property*. London and New York: Zed Books, 117–143.

Ncube, C.B., 2021. *Science, Technology & Innovation and Intellectual Property: Leveraging Openness for Sustainable Development in Africa*. Cape Town: Juta.

Ncube, C.B., 2022. Intellectual Property and the African Continental Free Trade Area: Lessons and Recommendations for the IP Protocol. *Journal of International Trade Law and Policy*, 21(2), 105–121. https://doi.org/10.1108/JITLP-09-2021-0051

Ncube, C.B. and Laltaika, E., 2013. A New Intellectual Property Organisation for Africa? *Journal of Intellectual Property Law and Practice*, 8(2), 114–117.

Ncube, C.B. and Rutenberg, I., 2020. Intellectual Property and Fourth Industrial Revolution Technologies. In Mazibuko-Makena, Z. and Kraemer-Mbula, E. (eds.) *Leap 4.0: African Perspectives on the Fourth Industrial Revolution*. Johannesburg: The Mapungubwe Institute for Strategic Reflection (MISTRA), 393–416.

Ncube, C.B., Schonwetter, T., de Beer, J. and Oguamanam, C., 2019. A Principled Approach to Intellectual Property Rights and Innovation in the African Continental Free Trade Agreement. In David, L. and Macleod, J. (eds.) *Inclusive Trade in Africa: The African Continental Free Trade Area in Comparative Perspective*. Abingdon: Routledge, 177–194.

Ncube, C.B., Schonwetter, T., de Beer, J. and Oguamanam, J., 2017. *Intellectual Property Rights and Innovation: Assessing Regional Integration in Africa (ARIA VIII) Open AIR Working Paper Series*. Available at https://openair.africa/intellectual-property-rights-and-innovation-assessing-regional-integration-in-africa-aria-viii/ [accessed 8 January 2023].

Oguamanam, C. and Dagne, T., 2013. Geographical Indication (GI) Options for Ethiopian Coffee and Ghanaian Cocoa. In Jeremy de Beer, J., Armstrong, C., Oguamanam, C. and Schonwetter, T. (eds.) *Innovation & Intellectual Property Collaborative Dynamics in Africa*. Cape Town: UCT Press, 77–108.

Oguamanam, C. and Dagne, T., 2014. A Consideration of Communal Trademarks for Nigerian Leather and Textile Products. In Jeremy de Beer, J., Armstrong, C., Oguamanam, C. and Schonwetter, T. (eds.) *Innovation & Intellectual Property Collaborative Dynamics in Africa*. Cape Town: UCT Press, 77–108.

Oke, E.K., 2021. The Statute of the Pan-African Intellectual Property Organisation: A Human Rights Perspective. In Amao, O., Olivier, M. and Magliveras, K.D. (eds.) *The Emergent African Union Law Conceptualisation, Delimitation, and Application*. Oxford: Oxford University Press.

Oke, E.K., 2022. *Patents, Human Rights and Access to Medicines*. Cambridge: Cambridge University Press.

Osei-Tutu, J.J., 2021a. A Human Development Approach to Intellectual Property Law. In Calboli, I. and Montagnani, M.L. (eds.) *Handbook of Intellectual Property Research: Lenses, Methods, and Perspectives*. Oxford: Oxford University Press, 640–653.

Osei-Tutu, J.J., 2021b. African Union Continental Free Trade Area: Opportunities for New Regional Discourse? In Ragavan, S. and Vanni, A. (eds.) *Intellectual Property Law and Access to Medicines: TRIPS Agreement, Health and Pharmaceuticals*. Abingdon: Routledge, 111–132.

Pan African Chamber of Commerce and Industry, 2022, 1 October. *Rwanda Begins Trade Under the AfCFTA*. Available at www.newtimes.co.rw/article/1453/news/africa/rwanda-begins-trade-under-afcfta [accessed 8 January 2023].

Shabalala, D.B., 2011. Knowledge and Education: Pro-Access Implications of New Technologies. In Wong, T. and Dutfield, G. (eds.) *Intellectual Property and Human Development: Current Trends and Future Scenarios*. Cambridge: Cambridge University Press, 2010, 250–274.

Štrba, S., 2012. *International Copyright Law and Access to Education in Developing Countries*. Lieden: Martinus Nijhoff.

UNDP and AfCFTA Secretariat, 2021. *The African Continental Free Trade Area (AfCFTA) Futures Report – Which Value Chains for a Made in Africa Revolution?* Available at https://www.undp.org/africa/publications/futures-report-2021 [accessed 8 January 2023].

Velásquez, G, Correa C.M. and Ido, V., 2020. *Intellectual Property, Human Rights and Access to Medicines: A Selected and Annotated Bibliography* (3rd ed). Geneva: South Centre.

World Bank, 2020. *The African Continental Free Trade Area: Economic and Distributional Effects*. Washington, DC: World Bank. http://doi.org/10.1596/978-1-4648-1559-1. License: Creative Commons Attribution CC BY 3.0 IGO.

Yu, P.K., 2019. Intellectual Property and Human Rights 2.0. *University of Richmond Law Review*, 53, 1375.

Yu, P.K., 2021. Intellectual Property, Human Rights, and Methodological Reflections. In Calboli, I. and Montagnani, M.L. (eds.) *Handbook of Intellectual Property Research: Lenses, Methods, and Perspectives*. Oxford: Oxford University Press, 182–197.

8 Harmony or Discord? Lessons for the Future African Continental IP System

8.1 The Status Quo

The discussion in previous chapters has shown that African states have embarked on a drive to harmonise their IP regimes within the framework of sub-regional IP organisations, at REC and at AU level. On a continental level, the AU's progress towards the operationalisation of PAIPO seems to have stalled due to a lack of the requisite ratification numbers and it has been overtaken by the AfCFTA's IP Protocol–related plans. Similarly, at REC level, the COMESA-EAC-SADC TFTA has stalled, with the required number of ratifications still unachieved. Its intended second phase IP negotiations have been trumped by the negotiation of the IP Protocol. Therefore, it would be prudent for African states to focus their collective energy and attention on the AfCFTA IP Protocol, which so far has proven to have more momentum than the earlier attempts at IP harmonisation.

8.2 Pursuing the Public Interest

The focal point of analysis of these REC and AU level developments has been whether they serve individual states' public interest. For purposes of the discussion, the public interest has been characterised as a complex, but useful, concept that seeks to identify a state's socio-economic and human rights or constitutional priorities and then to use them as a guide for policy, legislative and state action decisions. Whilst African states have a lot of commonalities, they are also incredibly diverse, which mitigates against any attempt to coin "one size fits all" solutions or systems. The adoption of the WIPO DA at global level was motivated by the need to appropriately nuance IP systems in order to meet the needs of such diversity in Africa, and elsewhere, in both the global north and south. As noted previously, African states, together with other developing countries, were instrumental in the adoption of the WIPO DA. The adoption of the Dakar Declaration of IP on the African continent was a significant endorsement of the same position. Therefore, a litmus test of African states' commitment and drive is the assessment of whether their harmonisation efforts carry forward that vision to attain fine-tuned IP systems.

To conduct a meaningful assessment or to make cogent arguments, conceptualisations of the public interest have to be nuanced by national contexts and IP right.

DOI: 10.4324/9781003310198-8

Therefore, chapter one focused on TRIPS flexibilities, patents and access to medicines. Chapter two illustrated how national IP policies seek to achieve nuanced IP approaches and chapter three found that significant progress has been made by EAC, ECOWAS and SADC towards giving policy direction to their member states on how to domesticate TRIPS health-related patent flexibilities. However, in many instances African states' existing patent legislation does not adequately serve the public interest by incorporating flexibilities that would enable more effective access to pharmaceuticals. Rectifying this will require legislative amendments, which have taken an unduly long time in most states.

Another important step towards legislative reform is policy realignment. If the policy framework is crafted appropriately, the legislative endeavour is considerably aided by clear policy goals, strategies and timelines. The policy then serves as a blueprint for law-makers. IP is inherently cross-cutting and many state and non-state actors are involved in its development and implementation. IP policies therefore also ensure coherence across different sectors and in relevant government departments. Hence chapter two's focus on IP policies in Africa. This chapter maps IP policy design initiatives across the continent and comments briefly on existing policies. It finds that there has been a flurry of IP policy-related activity, with 14 states having already adopted IP policies. Eight have IPDPs and two of these also have IP policies, with at least 11 others currently formulating policies. However, there is a dearth of information; in some cases adopted policies are not publicly available, or there is limited or no information at all about the policy formulation process in other instances, so this is an approximation based on available information.

In most cases, policies have been formulated, or are being formulated, with technical assistance from WIPO. Chapter two accordingly discusses the import of technical assistance, making the point that it has a significant impact on the content and quality of the resulting national IP policy. Therefore, it is important that the technical assistance be infused with public interest considerations and that it equips states to craft appropriate policies. Unsurprisingly, technical assistance is one of the focal areas of the WIPO DA. The chapter outlines a WIPO DA IP policy project, namely Project DA_10_05, which resulted in the creation and publication of an IP policy formulation toolkit. This project was piloted in six countries, three of which are in Africa. . As shown in chapter two, national IP policy formulation processes instigated by this project are still ongoing in Tanzania and Algeria. The chapter also considered the WIPO Framework for Developing National IP Strategies for Innovation project which is located outside WIPO DA projects. The work of both projects has since been mainstreamed into WIPO activities

In tandem with these WIPO interventions, RECs have also turned their attention to including IP on their agenda. For instance, as mentioned earlier, EAC and ECOWAS have adopted TRIPS policies that seek to guide their member states in their domestication of TRIPS flexibilities. COMESA has a general IP policy that is not limited to TRIPS flexibilities. Indeed, it does not engage with them in a meaningful way. On the other hand, SADC's recently adopted IP Framework and Guidelines give detailed guidance on health-related flexibilities. Further, it extends its guidance to other important aspects, such as access to copyright-protected works for persons with disabilities. It was hoped that the COMESA, EAC and SADC policies would eventually cross-pollinate through the T-FTA and the AfCFTA. However, the first eventuality seems highly unlikely and it is the second that has come to fruition.

Chapter three considered the IP-related legal instruments that have been adopted by COMESA, EAC, ECOWAS and SADC. All of these RECs expressly include IP as part of their integration agenda in their constitutive treaties or protocols. However, only the EAC has attempted to enact an IP-specific instrument, namely the Anti-Counterfeit Bill of 2010, which ultimately did not eventuate. This bill was prefaced with a draft policy on Anti-Counterfeiting, Anti-Piracy and other Intellectual Property Rights Violations (2009). Both the policy and bill fell short of public interest expectations primarily because they were TRIPS-plus. Elements of the policy and bill that made it into Kenyan legislation were declared unconstitutional by a High Court on account of their negative impact on the availability of generics in the country which would compromise the constitutional rights to life, dignity and health.

ARIPO and OAPI have to date focused on securing their member states' technical TRIPS compliance, rather than pursuing the attainment of public interest goals through domesticating flexibilities. Indeed, OAPI led its LDC members to the early adoption of TRIPS standards during the subsistence of relevant transition periods. As discussed in chapter one, this was a very unfortunate route to take. ARIPO has not unified IP law in the same way that OAPI has, so its member states still have national policy and legislative space within which to calibrate their IP systems. However, even in ARIPO's limited and largely administrative function, the first edition of this book argued that it could do more to assist its member states to adjust their IP laws in a way that allows them to pursue public interest goals. For instance, it suggested that the Harare Protocol could be amended in order to provide for pre- and post-grant patent opposition proceedings. As explained in chapter four, the 2022 amendments of this protocol introduced observation by third parties during the application process which enables them to make representations regarding the patentability of the invention.

Another sore point is that both ARIPO and OAPI have chosen to adopt the UPOV 91 model of protection of plant varieties and eschewed the more context-sensitive approach of the AU's African Model Legislation for the Protection of the Rights of Local Communities, Farmers and Breeders, and for the Regulation of Access to Biological Resources of 2000. The latter approach would have been more suitable for the continent. On the other hand, ARIPO has done well to take the lead on providing for the *sui generis* protection of traditional knowledge through its Swakopmund Protocol, which came into force on 11 May 2015.

8.3 Continental Instruments and Institutions

The creation of PAIPO raised concerns about draining the continent's resources to replicate already fulfilled functions or to create a structure for policy debate when informal means seem to be serving the continent well. The need to articulate

African positions on important IP policy matters is indisputable. What is questionable is the need to create a new organisation when the African Group is already effectively mobilising and winning significant victories on global platforms. However, as the decision to create the organisation has been made by the AU, it is important to engage with its future work. Further, as shown in chapter six, the functions and structures of PAIPO have been set out to lead on policy together with other aspects.

PAIPO's future role was scrutinised regarding its promotion, or otherwise, of individual states' ability to further their public interest goals. In this regard the initial failure of the Draft PAIPO Statute to refer to TRIPS flexibilities, the WTO Doha Declaration on the TRIPS Agreement and Public Health, and other important decisions such as the Global Strategy and Plan of Action on Public Health, Innovation and IP was of great concern. It signalled a lack of appreciation of the gains that had been made on the global level to create policy space for states to fine-tune their IP systems. The final statute refers to some, but not all, of these decisions and documents. It could very well be that in practice, PAIPO's work will be infused with public interest considerations due to its interaction with RECs and leading thinkers amongst the African group, but that remains to be seen. In addition to policy concerns, several organisational aspects pertaining to co-operation and overlapping mandates between PAIPO, ARIPO and OAPI also need to be addressed.

Chapter seven's discussion of the IP Protocol's IP standards provisions argues that they demonstrate the required nuancing of IPRs and appropriately centre development imperatives, human rights considerations and the public interest generally. For instance, they address TK and TCEs which are currently unevenly addressed; public interest mechanisms like exceptions and limitations, in accordance with the African Group's 2022 proposal at the WIPO SCCR, for educational and research purposes, online cross-border contexts, multi-country research collaborations and cultural heritage preservation. The patent provisions in Article 15 appropriately refer to flexibilities and centre the need to ensure "access to medicines, vaccines, diagnostics, therapeutics and other healthcare essential tools." They are supported by Article 21 which is specifically on public health emergencies. Forward-looking, light-touch provisions on emerging technologies are also welcome. The institutional arrangements relating to the AfCFTA IP Office have not yet been determined.

Once operationalised, the continental IP institutions, PAIPO and the AfCFTA IP Office will turn to providing policy direction and to leading IP harmonisation efforts of AU member states. There are various models that could be employed, which have been canvassed in chapter six. It is suggested that the most appropriate approach would be to first seek IP co-operation following the ASEAN, APEC or BRICS model. This model is decidedly light on normative content and focuses on practical or administrative co-operation that seeks to boost IP office capacity and efficiency. Currently the RECs, ARIPO and OAPI are working to achieve this on the sub-regional level and the continental IP institutions' role would be to extend the reach of these efforts to continental level. Once this level of co-operation is achieved, perhaps normative or substantive harmonisation may be sought, following either the incremental EU or MERCUSOR approach. This would entail employing a variety of hard and soft law approaches as appropriate. The AU has already engaged in IP harmonisation through soft law by its Model Law on the Protection of the Rights of Local Communities, Farmers and Breeders, and for the Regulation of Access to Biological Resources of 2000. The AfCFTA IP Protocol has ventured into a hard-law approach by setting out binding IP standards in those areas where there is some substantive consensus. This will be achieved through a combination of its Part II and the annexes to the protocol, as listed in chapter seven.

Much of the detail will be in the annexes and the approach will vary by IPR. For example, as has been the experience of the EU, trademark law would be easier to harmonise than patent law. Indeed, as shown in chapter five, there have been recommendations for the establishment of a continental trade mark system. Due to the well articulated African Group position on copyright at WIPO SCCR and patents and public health at WHO, WIPO and WTO, copyright and patent annexes should be easy to negotiate and conclude. Similarly, GIs and plant varieties could be areas where consensus is relatively easy to build, in view of the continent's natural endowments in these areas. Another strong area of convergence would be in relation to the protection of TK and TCEs. ARIPO has chosen the *sui generis* approach via its Swakopmund Protocol, but OAPI is yet to regulate this area. Whatever sequencing of the negotiation of annexes is adopted, all the annexes must be drafted, negotiated and adopted to retain policy space to enable national calibration. Just as there is no global "one size fits all," there is no African "one size fits all." A last consideration to bear in mind is that although the IP Protocol has been adopted by the Assembly of the Heads of State, its rate of ratification and entry into force remains prospective.

Index